TOUCHSTONE

OTHER BOOKS BY THE AUTHOR

First Ladies: The Saga of the Presidents' Wives and Their Power, 1789–1990

America's Most Influential First Ladies

As We Remember Her: Jacqueline Kennedy Onassis in the Words of Her Friends and Family

Florence Harding: The First Lady, the Jazz Age, and the Death of America's Most Scandalous President

America's First Families

An Inside View of 200 Years of Private Life in the White House

C A R L   S F E R R A Z Z A   A N T H O N Y

A Lisa Drew Book / A Touchstone Book
Published by Simon & Schuster
New York   London   Toronto   Sydney   Singapore

TOUCHSTONE
Rockefeller Center
1230 Avenue of the Americas
New York, NY 10020

TOUCHSTONE and colophon are registered trademarks
of Simon & Schuster, Inc.

DESIGNED BY DIANE HOBBING OF SNAP-HAUS GRAPHICS

Manufactured in the United States of America

10   9   8   7   6   5   4   3   2

Library of Congress Cataloging-in-Publication Data is available.

ISBN 0-7432-0303-8 (hc)
     0-684-86442-8 (pbk)

You need no introduction to this house; it is your house and I am but the tenant for a time.
　　　　　　　　　　—President Franklin Pierce

I may be President of the United States, Madame, but my private life is nobody's damned business.
　　　　　　　　　　—President Chester Alan Arthur

For Betty Ford and Hillary Clinton,
who opened their hearts and their homes;
and for Liz Carpenter,
one of the most interesting human beings on the planet

Contents

Contents

America's First Families

The first presidential family, George and Martha Washington, and her grandchildren, Nelly and George "Little Wash" Custis.

Introduction

Plain and Fancy

The President and his family take precedence every-
where in public or private.
          —President Thomas Jefferson

We are plain people from the mountains of Tennessee.
I trust too much will not be expected of us.
          —Martha Johnson Patterson,
          daughter of Andrew Johnson

*I*n the weeks preceding the April 30, 1789, inauguration of the first president, George Washington, in the temporary capital city of New York, there was much public debate on how he should interact with the public, and how they should treat him.

Washington himself rejected the title of king, but soon after he was joined by his wife, Martha, and their two "children," ten-year-old Nelly Custis and eight-year-old George "Little Wash" Custis (who were, in fact, Martha's grandchildren by a first marriage), their behavior seemed rather regal. Washington bowed to guests; he did not touch. Martha wore the starched "queen's cap" and stood on a raised platform to greet her guests at her weekly Friday night "levees," a grand name for a people-watching party. The Washingtons did not repeat witticisms or exchange conversation beyond pleasantries. No guests saw their private quarters. Instead of warmly ushering her guests out, the so-titled Lady Washington tartly told one of them, "The General always retires at nine o'clock, and I usually precede him." They behaved this way to earn respect for the new nation from representatives of the European monarchies, but it provoked debate in public about just how royal a president's family should be.

It was not long before the political opposition seized on this behavior and attacked the president and his family in newspapers, journals, and literary magazines. In the process, they began to describe the family's life in detail. When the president became ill and the street in front of the presidential mansion was chained off, when Mrs. Washington accidentally ate a dollop of cream turned sour, or when Nelly and Little Wash went to Rickett's circus, it was chronicled for the ages by observers in New York and in the second capital city, Philadelphia. Thus, also from the beginning there has been a public fascination with how a presidential family lives.

At a time when celebrities were individual military figures, authors, artists, an occasional doctor-scientist, the appeal of this entire family—husband, wife, children, and often extended family members—took immediate hold. Here was America's most famous family. The head of it was also the leader of the nation. Thrust upon them immediately were the responsibilities of social exemplars and political symbols. They were the foremost, the best—it was assumed— the *first* family. Despite their wealth and privilege, they weren't bred to think themselves royal. Little Wash did not believe in primogeniture, that he would lead his country after his grandpappa's death. Martha would not expect a retinue of ladies to handle her correspondence. Nellie had no notions of marrying a man who would someday become a political leader. Under democracy, this family was expected somehow to be just like "the people," to somehow be familiar.

The idea planted, the reality of these expectations immediately took root. It is a false modern concept that somehow First Families were not considered public property until photography, or radio, or television, the antics of "Princess" Alice Roosevelt, the sudden death of Calvin Coolidge Jr., or the dawn of Jackie Kennedy. Consider the rather stern rebuke to President Buchanan's objections to press coverage of his family that was published on May 8, 1858, in the popular national magazine *Harper's Weekly:*

> *For the time that he is President, Mr. Buchanan ceases to exist as a private individual. He becomes an institution—the Executive—and has no more claim to privacy. . . . Just so with his surroundings. The White House is not a private residence. It is a public building, in the fullest sense of the term; and every person therein . . . is a public functionary for the time being, and has no more claim to exemption from the inseparable inconvenience of publicity.*

Thus, conflicting ideas for First Families arose in the imagination of the people they were expected to serve: be appropriate but not snobbish; remember that you will be considered public figures yet in reality are private citizens who shouldn't seek special treatment; be plain and fancy at the same time. Certain timeless truisms developed for members of a president's family:

- If you live in the White House a greater sense of public expectation will be placed upon you, and your private life—how you eat, sleep, work, celebrate, relax—

will be considered a subject of public domain and inevitably part of the public record.

• If you say or do anything unusual it will be publicly disclosed and you will be made into a celebrity, remembered largely for a single act.

• You are always vulnerable to exploitation by either the public relations of the White House or by the press and political opposition, used in either case as a political tool or symbol.

• Any semblance of a normal life will be confined within the hothouse environment of two stories of private rooms in the White House—the second floor and the converted attic.

• Your relationships with the president—be he husband, father, grandfather, son, brother, or uncle—may often be secondary to his priorities as chief executive, yet oftentimes, simultaneously, a crucial factor in his emotional well-being and efficiency as a leader.

• Your own sense of self will inevitably be affected by your relation to the president, his popularity or unpopularity, his policies, and the manner in which he enters and leaves office.

• The American people will examine even mundane aspects of a relative's life and often turn them into national models of behavior worth emulating—or not emulating—or, at the least, search for similarities to project their own failings and insecurities, aspirations, and values.

The Washingtons never lived in the White House. Its first occupant, a wearied, brilliant patriot who had sacrificed much of his adult life to establish the new nation, moved in on November 1, 1800. A day after his assessment that the two-story mansion, with plaster still wet, "is in a state to be habitable," second president John Adams wrote his wife about their new home, telling her he "wish[ed] for your company." It would take weeks before Abigail Adams would arrive with their granddaughter Suzannah and Abigail's niece, Louisa Smith, who functioned as a daughter. She would happily find her nephew William Shaw residing there too, working as Adams's private secretary. The family circle would be rounded out by an adult son, Thomas.

Emotions were running high. Mrs. Adams arrived seething: in four short months, she might very well have to pack right up and turn around for home. Thomas Jefferson, once a close family friend, had challenged Adams for the presidency and possession of the house. She was also overcome with unspeakable grief. On her way to the new capital city of Washington, D.C., Mrs. Adams had stopped in New York to visit her alcoholic son, Charles, on his deathbed, knowing she would never see him alive again.

Perhaps in an effort to avoid dwelling on the grimness of being removed from his life's work by Jefferson of all people, the president turned philosophical. Although not usually as articulate as the mellifluous Jefferson, Adams was capable of seeing the big picture. On his first night in what he called simply the President's House, Adams spoke for the ages. At the end of his letter of description of the family's new home, he penned what became a sacred reminder to both future First Families and the nation they represented, the unofficial presidential prayer: "I pray Heaven to bestow the best of blessings on this house, and on all that shall hereafter inhabit it. May none but honest and wise men ever rule under this roof!"

Wise *men?* For nearly three decades, Abigail had been responding to John's musings on the formation of this new concept of democracy with exhortations bold and subtle to, as she once wrote famously, "remember the ladies." As the president's lady she had most recently declared, "I shall never consent to have our sex considered in an inferior point of light." Perhaps Abigail Adams would have added "women" to her husband's words for the ages, for although the head of a First Family would always be the president, it was often his wife, mother, daughter, or sister who was the backbone of it. *All* that shall hereafter inhabit it? If Adams could look two hundred years into the future, he might have amended the benediction to include parents, siblings, children, grandchildren, nieces, nephews, and, maybe, even a poor cousin now and then.

Part I
Entrances

If you are as happy, my dear sir, on entering this house as I am in leaving it and returning home, you are the happiest man in the country.

—Outgoing president James Buchanan
to incoming president Abraham Lincoln

*Abigail Adams, in this unfinished portrait by Gilbert
Stuart, pictured the same year she moved into the White
House for her four-month stay. 1800.*
MASSACHUSETTS HISTORICAL SOCIETY

*President John Adams, the first to live in the White
House. Drawn from life by Julien Fevret de Saint
Memin with a "physiognotrace," which precisely mea-
sured the presidential facial features.*
FRICK ART REFERENCE LIBRARY

21 feet and the length of some of them are 30 feet, one room which is unfinished is 20 feet. The window curtains of two of the rooms are white, with a narrow cornice of gilt. The fringe has colours intermixed with the white. The walls being also white displays an elegance that exceeds anything I have seen before. The drawing room is an oval on the second floor. The window curtains, 3 sofas, and 3 dozen of chairs are of crimson damask. The situation is one of the best in the city near half a mile from the river which space is to be laid out with trees and pleasure walks.

Others began taking notes. The same day that Mrs. Adams had arrived in the capital city so too had Margaret Bayard Smith. Wife of the editor of the *National Intelligencer,* a national newspaper based in Washington, Mrs. Smith chronicled the first generations of First Families, recording incidents public and private. A Jefferson comrade, she had a natural bias against the Federalist party of Adams. In Washington, everything social soon became political. The formal Adamses' receptions were easy political targets for Jeffersonian Democrats, who preached antimonarchical egalitarianism. Since Mrs. Adams hosted such events, and was rabidly anti-Jefferson, she became fair game for anti-Federalists, even after the fact. Eighteen years later, when she read accusations of her partisan entertaining in the *Niles' Register,* she rebuked the editor in a letter published January 20, 1818:

Upon taking up your register the other day a communication respecting drawing rooms attracted my attention. Your correspondent must have been misinformed when he states that there was any distinction of party made at the drawing rooms while I had the honor to preside there. Any gentleman or lady, of either party, who chose to visit there were received with equal civility. And from your correspondent I have now for the first time learned that any person withdrew from political motives. The gentlemen of both houses of Congress received and accepted the invitations of the President to dine with him, and but one of the whole number ever so far forgot the character of a gentleman as to send an incivil refusal.

The editor responded with sarcasm: "I could not believe that the public was in any way interested in the domestic arrangements of the president's wife."

Mrs. Adams's entertaining was not the only arena in which actions that would be considered private in any other home were to be publicly questioned. The London marriage of her son, diplomat John Quincy Adams, to a French-educated, British-born woman dubbed the "Princess Royal" in the royal court at Berlin, occasioned a public debate. Anti-Federalists had earlier accused Adams of secretly trying to marry his sons off to the daughters of England's King George III and establish an Anglo-American pseudo royal family. Now Boston's *Independent Chronicle* maliciously sniped, "Young John Adams's negotiations have terminated in a marriage treaty with an English lady. . . . It is a happy circumstance that he had made no other Treaty."

Not only did the bride of the president's son become useful for political attack, but his diplomatic position and his salary did as well. The young man had first been appointed by President Washington, but President Adams retained him in government service, and it smacked of nepotism. This the anti-Federalists had been harping on for nearly four years. Unrelenting was Benjamin Bache of the *Aurora:* "George Washington had never appointed to any station in government, even the most distant of his relations." Bache made untrue claims that between father and son the family was pulling $100,000 annually from the federal budget. Other newspapers added fuel to the fire, including the *Independent Chronicle,* the Boston *Columbian Centinel,* and John Fenno's *National Gazette.* It was not long before the House of Representatives looked into the charge. Naturally the wife and mother of the two accused was furious. "An abused and insulted public cannot tolerate them much longer," Mrs. Adams wrote of the accusations and investigation.

John Quincy Adams would not return from Europe in time to visit his parents in the President's House, but they were not entirely lacking in familial comfort. For five years a nephew of Mrs. Adams, William Cranch, the son of her sister Mary, had been living in the federal city with his wife. On his last night as president, John Adams would appoint Billy Cranch, a failed land speculator, as assistant judge in the District of Columbia.

Tragically, however, it was alcoholism that cobbled together the first White House family. Save for her husband, father, and one son, the men in Abigail Adams's family suffered from alcoholism, and she assumed the burden of it. Not only her brother, William Smith, but her sister's husband, John Shaw, and her own son Charles died as alcoholics. Abigail essentially adopted as her own three of their respective children, Louisa Smith, Billy Shaw, and Suzannah Adams, and they became the children of the First Family in Washington, along with the Adamses' son Thomas, who was also showing a proclivity toward drinking.

At family dinners in the President's House, Louisa Smith often carved the meats at the table. By the time Abigail Adams had assumed her social duties as the vice president's wife in 1789, twelve-year-old Louisa Smith had become her fast companion. Ten years before that, William Smith had found himself financially unable to support his family, and his daughter Louisa came to live with her aunt for life (save for the years the Adamses were on diplomatic service in Europe), satisfied to be the unmarried aunt to her own sister's children and the Adamses' grandchildren. In her will, Mrs. Adams declared that $1,200, which John Quincy had borrowed, should be repaid as part of Louisa Smith's inheritance. Abigail called her "the faithful Louisa."

Already in residence at the President's House with President Adams was twenty-two-year-old Billy Shaw, the son of Mrs. Adams's sister Elizabeth. An indispensable presidential secretary, a year earlier he had personally carried by horseback, from Philadelphia to Virginia, the government's condolence letter to Martha Washington upon her husband's death. His was a bittersweet story. Billy's father had drunk himself to death. Although his intellectual capacity amazed even his erudite relatives, Billy was hapless, damaged physically and emotionally. At

Thomas Adams, the good-natured son of President John Adams and Abigail Adams, who bought his little niece Suzannah toys in Georgetown shortly after their arrival.

LAST APPEARED IN *Children in the White House, 1967*

eight, he absentmindedly walked into a clothesline, tangled his neck in the rope, nearly suffocated, and permanently damaged his spine. He was in a coma for half a day. Six years later, he walked into a hole and damaged his ankle, leaving him with a permanent limp. Two years later, his penniless father's death prompted Abigail to have Billy employed as secretary to her husband, then vice president.

Mrs. Adams thought that being among her sons "rubbed off so many of his peculiarities," but soon Billy became alcoholic. He later grew so obsessed with books that he became socially dysfunctional, his mother lament-ing that he was "a confirmed old batchelor in the most extensive sense of the word." His pas-sion nevertheless led him to create the Boston Athenaeum.

The president's son in residence at the President's House, Thomas Adams, would also develop a ruinous taste for drink, although there is no evidence that he and cousin Billy indulged to excess while living there. The year before, taking his place as part of the First Family alongside his sister "Nabby" and her daugh-ter Caroline, Thomas had returned in 1799 from his work as his brother John Quincy's private secretary in Europe to come live in the Philadelphia President's House and to practice law in that city. That autumn was a happy one for the First Family, not the least because Thomas Adams hosted the first dance for young people in the mansion. As a dinner for two and a half dozen friends was ending, Thomas spontaneously sought and gained the permission of his otherwise disap-proving mother to have the small orchestra strike up some dance airs, and the young couples weaved and circled to the rigidly formal dance steps that prevented the sexes from touching anything but each others' hands. Thomas was an

William "Billy" Shaw, Abigail Adams's eccentric but brilliant nephew, who served as President Adams's private secretary and lived in the White House with them. 1826.

COLLECTION OF THE BOSTON ATHENAEUM

easy-tempered contrast to the harsh eldest child, John Quincy. More impetuous was the Adams daughter, Nabby. She left the Philadelphia President's House and returned to New York by early 1800, opening her house there to her brother Charles and his family. They literally had no home in which he could die with some dignity.

Charles was married to Sally Smith. She was the sister of William Smith, Nabby's husband, so Charles's and Sally's two daughters, Suzannah and Abby, were double cousins to Nabby's and William's three children, Will, Caroline, and Johnny. William Smith's errant personality and get-rich-quick schemes prevented him from ever consistently earning a decent salary. Charles had the same problem, but his situation worsened with his propensity for drinking.

In the spring of 1800, as Mrs. Adams had headed from Philadelphia to Quincy for the summer, she stopped in New York to visit Charles. He was struggling to survive. "When I behold misery and distress, disgrace and poverty brought upon a family by intemperance my heart bleeds at every pore," she wrote to her sister. On this stop, Mrs. Adams also closely observed the behavior of Charles's eldest daughter: "Suzannah is very forward and intelligent for three years, and would stand all day to hear you read stories, which she will catch at a few times repeating, and has all the Goody Goose stories by heart . . . She tells me her letters and would read in a month if she had a good school." When Abigail headed south in the fall for Washington, she stopped again in New York to see "my poor unhappy son . . . laid upon a bed of sickness, destitute of a home . . . soon [to] terminate a life which might have been valuable to himself and others." Assessing the dismal situation, Abigail essentially adopted Suzannah, taking her along to Washington. In Philadelphia, her spirit brightened upon seeing Thomas, who had continued to live there, and she persuaded him to join her entourage for their "unknown and unseen abode."

John Quincy wanted out of public service, Nabby was married to a ne'er-do-well, Charles was dying of alcoholism, and Thomas was on that same road. "Blind, stupid, thoughtless boys and girl!" the bitter president wrote in his last days in the President's House. In more reflective moments, his pain at Charles's death became apparent: "Oh! that I had died for him if that would have relieved him from his faults as well as his disease." Thomas, wanting to make everything all right again, to end his family's pain, pleaded, "Let silence reign forever over his tomb."

John and Abigail held their sons to the highest standards as children of a famous statesman. Was Charles's fall perhaps inevitable under this pressure? When she learned that he died fourteen days after she arrived at the President's House, Abigail softened: "Weep with me over the Grave of a poor unhappy child . . . He was no man's enemy but his own—he was beloved, in spite of his errors." Still, even when Mrs. Adams permitted Suzannah to blow soap bubbles from the president's pipe, she made a grim lesson of it. Only strict adherence to moral values endured, grandmother lectured granddaughter, and "all the rest is balloon and bubble from the cradle to the grave."

Artist Lisa Biganzoli's portrayal of President Adams working in his office on the last night of his residency.
NATIONAL GEOGRAPHIC SOCIETY

Suzannah was a bright but troubled brat, a "four-year-old mite in a black dress," as one account described her presence in the President's House. When the First Grandchild invited her little pal Ann Black to the mansion to play with a china set her uncle Thomas bought for her in Georgetown, the friend purposefully smashed a plate. Suzannah recalled knowing it was done from envy. She remained calm. When invited to Ann Black's house, however, Suzannah picked up Ann's doll, dug her molars into the wax neck, ripped off its head, and returned to the President's House. "How would you manage one," Abigail asked her sister about the problem child, "upon whom you could not impress any subordination—any true deference to age or relation or rank in life?" Suzannah remained just as hot-tempered as she matured, Adams once reprimanding her for provoking "family bickerings."

Beyond any emotional problems emerging in the child who had been taken from her father's deathbed were the routine sicknesses of childhood. In the President's House, Grandma Adams had to nurse Suzannah, the former recalling, "I was waked in the night by a strange noise. She sleeps in a little chamber next to mine. I went in, and found her laboring with a dreadful hoarse cough, a sound which indicated medical aid. We sent for the physician nearest us, who gave her calomil [*sic*], put her feet in warm water, and steamed her with vinegar. She puked and that seemed to relieve her. She has coughed all day, but not with so much hoarseness."

In 1801, before Mrs. Adams, Thomas Adams, Louisa Smith, and Suzannah Adams left Washington for good on February 13, Jefferson came to pay a courtesy call on the family. Despite the long weeks of uncertainty about the victor (due to the final vote being Congress's responsibility), by March 4, Jefferson's Inauguration Day, Adams had had several months to anticipate his public loss of the election and come to terms with the personal loss of Charles. Still, he remained resentful. In such a state, he decided to leave in the early morning. Making himself unavailable to receive Jefferson, however, Adams was too smart to permit himself to be portrayed as a sore loser. Instead, he claimed that he left the President's House early because he was upset by "the funeral of a son, who was once the delight of my eyes, and a darling of my heart, cut off in the flower of his days." It was a lame excuse, considering that Charles had been buried three months earlier. Adams hadn't attended the burial, but he had appeared at numerous public events since then. He hardly seemed to be in deep mourning. It was the first example of a White House family event being used for political purposes by the machinery of the presidency. The second such use occurred when Mrs. Adams attacked Jefferson's private life, focusing on his personal religious beliefs. She predicted the nation would suffer because the Deist Jefferson was "an infidel." President Adams slipped out of the President's House early in the morning of March 4 with Billy Shaw, and the last of the first First Family was gone.

It had been a black winter of four months for the Adamses. "The consequence to us personally is that we retire from public life," a bruised Abigail Adams wrote. "My residence in this city has not served to endear the world to me . . . I am sick, sick, sick of public life."

As for her son John Quincy Adams, Abigail Adams declared that she would prefer to have him "thrown as a log on the fire than see him President of the United States."

2

The Family's First Day

I was now eager to roam around the house, to
familiarise myself with the mysteries of my new
home and to plan the assignment of rooms among
various members of the family.
    —*First Lady Helen "Nellie" Herron Taft*

Only a First Family seemingly has an entire nation scrutinizing them the same day they move into their new home. If that isn't difficult enough, there is a full series of ceremonial traditions on that first day which they are expected to go through, before they can sleep. It is that day, Inauguration Day—coronation and democratic celebration—when the world is fully introduced to all the principal family members and even the extended family.

The procession to the U.S. Capitol

James Garfield takes the oath of office as president. On the far right is incoming vice president Chester Arthur; outgoing president Rutherford Hayes sits behind Garfield. The young girl in the white hat on the left is Fanny Hayes, and beside her, Mollie Garfield. Eliza Garfield, the first woman to witness her son's inauguration, sits in front of them. 1881.

PRIVATE COLLECTION

Second-Term Inaugurals

George Washington, March 4, 1793
Thomas Jefferson, March 4, 1805
James Madison, March 4, 1813
James Monroe, March 5, 1821*
Andrew Jackson, March 4, 1833
Abraham Lincoln, March 4, 1865
Ulysses S. Grant, March 4, 1873
Grover Cleveland, March 4, 1893
William McKinley, March 4, 1901
Woodrow Wilson, March 5, 1917*
Franklin D. Roosevelt, January 20, 1937†
Dwight D. Eisenhower, January 21, 1957‡
Richard Nixon, January 20, 1973
Ronald Reagan, January 21, 1985‡
William Jefferson Clinton, January 20, 1997

*Inauguration Day fell on a Sunday and the swearing in was delayed to the next day.
†Inauguration Day was changed from March 4 to January 20; Roosevelt also became the only president to have a third and fourth inaugural, January 20, 1941, and January 20, 1945.
‡Inauguration Day fell on a Sunday, and a private ceremony was held that day in the White House, the public ceremony delayed to the next day.

Building, where the incoming president is to be sworn in for his term of office, has evolved since March 4, 1809, when Thomas Jefferson simply left his tavern and walked to the Capitol for the ceremony. Beginning in 1837, outgoing president Andrew Jackson rode in an open carriage with his vice president and hand-picked successor, Martin Van Buren, for Van Buren's swearing-in ceremony, thus commencing that tradition. Presidents' wives began to mimic their husbands in 1921, when two formidable women, outgoing Edith Wilson and incoming Florence Harding, paired up in a car and rode right behind their Woodrow and Warren. The family comes into focus on the inaugural stand in preparation for the oath-taking. Moments before Woodrow Wilson appeared to take his oath, his first wife, Ellen, and their daughters, Eleanor, Jessie, and Margaret, all ran up to the front of the podium in wonderment at the masses of people—and when the crowd recognized them, suddenly retreated.

Nellie Grant literally thrust herself into the limelight when, as her father completed his 1869 inaugural speech, she ran from her seat up to him and clasped his hand. The crowd roared for both the new president and his daughter. The moment James Garfield finished the oath, he kissed his mother, Eliza Ballou Garfield, the first presidential parent to witness her son's installation. Eisenhower was the first to kiss his wife. In 1965, Lady Bird Johnson began the custom of a First Lady's holding the Bible for her husband as he took the oath. By 1993, Chelsea Clinton was invited to stand with her parents as her father repeated his oath.

The procession from the Capitol down Pennsylvania Avenue to the White House provides tens of thousands of cheering citizens lining the streets their first close-up glimpse of the new

First Family. Nellie Taft set an historic precedent as she drove in an open carriage with her husband back to the White House in 1909. Live television coverage may have helped to revert inaugurals to a more Jeffersonian model, as the Bushes and the Clintons walked part of the way back, a custom begun by the Carters in 1977—though abandoned by the Reagans in 1981. Spectators first thought there was something wrong with the car as President Carter, his wife, their three sons and daughters-in-law, led by the nine-year-old First Daughter Amy, got out of the cars and started walking. "I began to realize," Carter recalled, "the symbolism . . . I felt a simple walk would be a tangible indication of some reduction of the imperial status of the president and his family."

Although she did not move in right on Inauguration Day, Dolley Madison was to influence life in the mansion for generations. As the secretary of state's wife, she had already served eight years as widower Jefferson's hostess. VIRGINIA HISTORICAL SOCIETY

Public receptions immediately following were intermittently hosted by the new presidents in the White House, but this began to phase out with Buchanan in 1857. On his Inauguration Day, barely recovered from a serious bout of food poisoning, he was served his first meal in two days by his reliable Pennyslvania cook, alone. Julia Grant held a private luncheon for the incoming Hayes family. The Garfields began the tradition of holding a private reception for old friends—in their case, the new president's graduating class from Williams College—followed by a dinner with the outgoing Hayes family. This set a brief tradition: the outgoing Arthur family shared the incoming Clevelands' luncheon. The Tafts, Wilsons, and Hardings had family lunches, then receptions for friends. The Franklin Roosevelts had a thousand guests. One of them, Eleanor Roosevelt's nemesis, her first cousin Alice Longworth—the daughter of former president Theodore Roosevelt—condescendingly assured the new First Lady that she would stay after lunch to show "how things were done here." At the large lunch for numerous branches of her and her husband's families, Jackie Kennedy was so overwhelmed by the thought of being besieged by relatives, she never came downstairs to see them. Instead, she asked that her favorite cousin, Michel Bouvier, come up to talk to her.

Luncheon is followed by the family's appearance on the inaugural parade reviewing stand. Grant had a parade stand built so the public could see the new family—in front of the White House. At Benjamin Harrison's parade the rain was so bad that his son, Russell, and son-in-

Cut just days before their brief one-month residency, these silhouettes represent (left to right) John Scott Harrison, Benjamin Harrison, Anna Harrison Taylor, President William Henry Harrison, and Jane Irwin Harrison. 1841.
INDIANA HISTORICAL SOCIETY C4653

law, Bob McKee, abandoned him for the dry mansion. Whether it is Joe Kennedy, father of JFK, standing proudly on the stand after hiding during the campaign and questions of his influence on it, or LBJ placing one of his beagles in a seat to watch, or George Bush's toddler grandson distracting himself with some Lego toys, there is intense focus on the family in the stand: television interviews, newspaper photographs, and running commentary on their actions and reactions.

The First Family makes a brief appearance at all the evening's inaugural balls, the president usually swirling his wife for part of a dance number onstage and repeating some quips, then they all proceed to the next ball. It was not until Lyndon and Lady Bird Johnson that a presidential couple danced. Their predecessors considered it undignified to join in. When Sarah Polk entered Carusi's assembly rooms for the first of two balls in 1845, all music and dancing stopped because she disapproved of it.

The first recorded presidential children in attendance were the four Van Buren sons, who came with their father to his inaugural balls in 1837. At the "unofficial" 1933 inaugural ball, a fund-raiser for the March of Dimes, all five of FDR's children attended with their mother—but the president didn't. Zachary Taylor's daughter Betty Bliss, promenading on his arm, upstaged socialites by wearing a single white flower in her hair and flirtatiously flattering many of the old lions of the Senate. Amy Carter came along with a novel to ward off bore-

dom. The Bushes permitted their four eldest grand-children to come along. As the members of the Bush family who were to attend the balls finished dressing, they went into the Queen's Suite to display themselves for the president's elderly mother, Dorothy Bush. Twelve-year-old Chelsea Clinton brought several friends to keep her company, all of them dressing with excitement in the rooms of her new home, after having conducted a scavenger hunt to locate historic items throughout the old mansion. Although she dressed in a ballgown for the family portrait, taken just prior to the family departure for the balls, the media speculated correctly that the absence of Reagan's daughter Patti Davis at the 1981 balls was due to political differences with her father.

After the ball, the new First Family is finally alone in their new home. Those first minutes and hours in the historic mansion have made permanent impressions on those who left records of them—even when they were rather mundane. Many nineteenth-century families did not move in on the night of the inaugural. The John Quincy Adamses moved in on April 20, 1825, a long delay because of outgoing Mrs. Monroe's health. They found a series of messy rooms filled with worn rugs, tattered curtains, and beaten, broken furniture. "I believe it would be difficult to find such an assortment of rags and rubbish even in an Alms House," wrote Louisa Adams. Although "[s]ome think I did wrong," she even invited people in to see how shabby the presidential living quarters were. Like Jefferson, Jackson returned to his hotel room instead of to his new home on inaugural night, and he likewise stayed past his successor's inaugural, delaying Van Buren's residency.

Van Buren graciously began the custom of vacating the mansion before his successor's inaugural, making the house available on inaugural night. Thus, the William Henry Harrison family became the first to take residency on Inauguration Day. It was a large and fractured family at that, probably sixteen in all—grandsons, granddaughters, nieces, nephews, great-nieces and great-nephews, daughter, daughter-in-law, and relatives of the daughter-in-law. Moving sixteen people in on that night must have created great confusion, and thus it did not become a precedent for some years. Taking occupancy on Inauguration Day was not always pleasant: Franklin Pierce had to find candles, climb the dark stairs without help from servants,

James Buchanan and his niece Harriet Lane arrive at their new home. 1857.

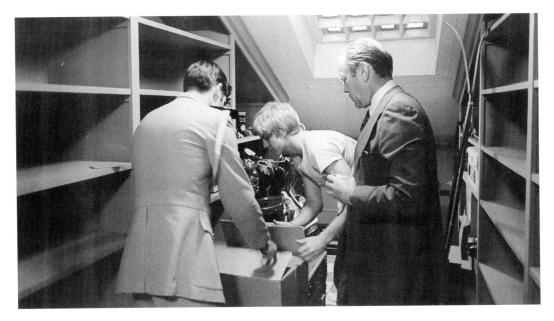

A military aide helps Steve Ford move his items into the attic of the White House, as President Ford watches. 1974.

and locate a mattress to sleep on. Remembering this, Pierce moved out a day early for his successor, James Buchanan. It could not have been too soon. Buchanan and his nephew, Elliott Lane, were deathly ill from bacteria carried by rats in the water system of the hotel where they had been staying and dining. Not everyone has been eager to make the move. Loving her Washington home, Julia Grant delayed moving in by two weeks, taking a perfunctory look at the rooms the day after the inaugural for refurbishing measurements. It took the president's forcing of a breach of contract to sell their home without her signatory permission to get her into the White House.

When a family arrives on the heels of a death or resignation, it naturally takes more time for them to move in. The outgoing family must suddenly pack all their things and arrange for moving, as must the new family. Theodore Roosevelt moved into the White House on September 23, nine days after the death of President McKinley. Two days later, his wife, son Kermit, and daughter Ethel came. Mrs. Roosevelt had the windows opened wide to let the cool air of Indian summer in, ordered fresh flowers from the government greenhouses, and requisitioned rooms for her six children and four servants, placing two of them in rooms she had created in the attic. "Edie says its like living over the store," Roosevelt wrote. Entirely responsible for the move, she got no guidance from the household staff and collapsed in exhaustion for two days after the transition.

Edith Roosevelt brought order to family life during the 1902 White House renovation, which finally moved the presidential office out of the second floor and into the newly built West Wing, giving the family exclusive use of the space. When it was time for her to leave, she initiated the custom of inviting the incoming family to tour the rooms so there was ample time for them to make all the necessary arrangements to take occupancy on inaugural night. Thus, from the 1909 Taft inaugural until the 1933 FDR inaugural, First Families (except the Coolidges, who came in after the sudden death of Harding) all moved in on March 4. Starting with the 1953 Eisenhower inaugural, the families have moved in on January 20, the new Inauguration Day as of 1937.

The first moments a family enters their new home oftentimes foretell the tone of the incoming administration. An exhausted William Henry Harrison quickly lay down on a bed for thirty minutes while his forehead was rubbed with alcohol, in an attempt to soothe his nervous headache. He would be dead within thirty days. William Howard Taft sighed, "Let's go upstairs, my dears, and sit down!" His wife stared at the Great Seal of the President. He would be passively ineffective; she would be highly political. Eleanor Wilson, overwhelmed with fear of what this new life would do to her parents, sobbed, and the president's cousin took a fall, gashing herself; the Wilson administration would be overcast by death and illness. Florence Harding snapped to a maid who was pulling down curtains to shut off the view from the public, "Let 'em look in! It's their White House!" The Harding years had a breezy accessibility for the common folk.

Chief Usher (a role akin to total house manager) Ike Hoover recalled the moments before a new family took occupancy, in this case the Wilsons: "The cleaners and maids were giving the last touch to a bare household. The place was so bereft of any bric-a-brac or ornamental furnishing that it was hard to know just what to do to make the best appearance." By the mid–twentieth century, new First Families and their personal possessions were put in place with seeming magic. At high noon on Inauguration Day, the household staff begins a drill of militaristic precision, loading trucks of objects to go, unloading trucks for the new family, and placing items in designated rooms. Still, rules are made to be broken. Jackie Kennedy managed to get her infant son's crib kept in the basement to be certain it would be ready the first day. Lady Bird Johnson carried a prized portrait into the house in her own hands. This may be wise: despite the fact that the Wilsons were the first to benefit from studying floor plans of the family rooms, the new president's luggage was misplaced, and on his first night he had to sleep in his underwear, his pajamas having become lost.

Depending on the arduousness of Inauguration Day, taking possession of the mansion can bring exhilaration or relief. Jackie Kennedy, recovering from cesarean surgery performed eight weeks earlier, collapsed in physical exhaustion after attending two balls. Rushed off to her new home, she was put to bed. Her husband, however, celebrated until the wee hours of the morning, coming home long after she was asleep. The Nixon daughters giddily raided the refrigerator to consume Dr Pepper soda and butter brickle ice cream left by the Johnson daughters, while their father sat at the piano and played "Rustle of Spring" for his wife. The Carter clan relaxed in front of roaring fires while sipping spiced tea, awed but contented.

Frances Cleveland and her baby daughter, Ruth, were the only family members to take occupancy before tradition dictated. With members of the outgoing Harrison clan still drifting about, Mrs. Cleveland took the elevator to the family quarters, looked around the empty rooms, set Ruth up in one, then headed out to her husband's inaugural. She knew the house better than anyone, having lived there during her husband's first term. Four years before, to the day, as she was clearing out for the Harrisons, Frances had warned a staff member, "Now I want you to take care of everything—the furnishings, the china, the crystal, the silver. I want to see everything just as it is now when my husband and I move back in here precisely four years from today."

Moving into the White House is a moment of renewed faith in the democratic system. As Ronald Reagan eloquently recalled: "We walked through the front door . . . and . . . took an elevator to the second floor, to the rooms where we would be living . . . When I was a kid in Dixon, I'd imagined what the private part of the White House must be like; but I had never imagined myself actually living there. . . . If I

Sudden Inaugurals

John Tyler, sworn in at Washington, D.C., Indian Queen Hotel, April 6, 1841, following the April 4 death of President William Henry Harrison

Millard Fillmore, sworn in at Washington, D.C., Hall of Representatives, U.S. Capitol Building, July 10, 1850, following the July 9 death of President Zachary Taylor

Andrew Johnson, sworn in at Washington, D.C., Kirkwood House Hotel, April 15, 1865, following the death of President Abraham Lincoln that same day

Chester Alan Arthur, sworn in at New York City, Arthur home, 123 Lexington Avenue, September 20, 1881, following the death of President James A. Garfield, September 19

Theodore Roosevelt, sworn in at Buffalo, New York, the Wilcox family home, September 14, 1901, following the death of President William McKinley that same day

Calvin Coolidge, sworn in at Plymouth Notch, Vermont, Coolidge homestead, August 3, 1923, following the death of President Warren G. Harding, August 2

Harry S. Truman, sworn in at Washington, D.C., the White House, April 12, 1945, following the death of President Franklin D. Roosevelt that same day

Lyndon Baines Johnson, sworn in at Dallas, Texas, onboard Air Force One, November 22, 1963, following the death of President John F. Kennedy that same day

Gerald R. Ford, sworn in at Washington, D.C., the White House, August 9, 1974, following the resignation of Richard M. Nixon that same day

could do this, I thought, then truly any child in America had an opportunity to do it."

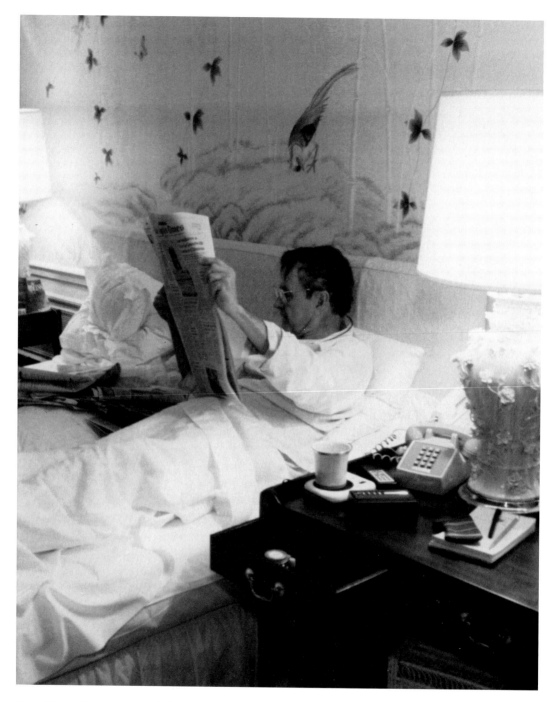

George Bush reads the newspaper in bed, in the Presidential Bedroom. The hand-painted Chinese wallpaper was put in for Nancy Reagan. 1993.

3

A Home Within a Symbol

There is but little privacy here, the house belongs to the Government and everyone feels at home and they sometimes stalk into our bedroom and say they are looking at the house.

—Joanna Rucker, niece of First Lady Sarah Polk

I love these beautiful big rooms with their high ceilings, their wide spaces, their polished mahogany furniture, carved deep with memories of Lincoln and the Madisons. . . . I thrill to the thought I am sitting in a chair where they once sat, eating from a plate which graced the place of McKinley or Grant.

—First Lady Florence Harding

The four standing walls of the White House in the year 2000 are the very same that greeted the John Adams family two hundred years before, and though the suite of family rooms on the second floor has been reconfigured, rebuilt, renovated, and redecorated since then, it has consistently remained the home of First Families. The building's interior was burned in 1814, renovated in 1902, and entirely rebuilt between 1948 and 1952. From 1801 until 1902 office workers and strangers were bustling about daily on the other side of a door from the family's rooms. Despite the challenges of living there, it survives as the permanent residence of the president. The White House is among the nation's most potent symbols. But it hasn't been easy making a real life inside a symbol.

It is not certain how some of the earliest families used the rooms of the family quarters on the second floor, although there were so many relatives living with Jefferson, the Madisons,

Harry and Bess Truman reading on the balcony bearing his name.
HARRY S. TRUMAN PRESIDENTIAL LIBRARY

Sharon Bush, the president's daughter-in-law, and two other grandchildren look on at granddaughter Ashley Bush, who lies on the Lincoln bed on the day of her White House christening. 1989.
GEORGE BUSH PRESIDENTIAL LIBRARY

and the Monroes that some of the rooms were presumably finished and being used. One visitor noted that Jefferson used only part of the available space and left "the rest to a state of uncleanly desolation." The first description of the rooms came under Monroe, with the mention of a bed being crowned with satin and lace curtains.

Since John and Abigail Adams used it, however, the presidential suite—a bedroom, sitting room, and later large walk-in closets and two bathrooms—has always been in the southwest corner of the second floor. This room was often a place of peaceful isolation. Margaret "Peggy" Taylor decorated it with cherished family possessions that had been with her through years of traveling from army post to post. "I always found the most pleasant part of my visit to the White House to be passed in Mrs. Taylor's bright pretty room," recalled visitor Varina Davis, "where the invalid, full of interest in the passing show in which she had not the strength to take her part, talked most agreeably and kindly to the many friends admitted to her presence." Rarely venturing outside, or downstairs to any public events, Mrs. Taylor made the room the center of her life, where friends and family gathered for socializing, and where her young daughters often danced informally with each other under her watchful eye. Just three years later, in the same suite, Jane Pierce, in deep mourning for her recently killed eleven-year-old son, closed the doors and remained sequestered for nearly a year.

The first non-family member permitted to see and describe the presidential bedroom was Austine Stead, who wrote a newspaper column under the pen name Miss Grundy. She was guided through by President Hayes himself. For the first time this inner sanctum was depicted for the curious citizenry. The furniture was crafted from imitation bamboo, and the walls were painted a light blue with pink and gray panels. Here Lucretia Garfield nearly died of malaria in April 1881. Three months later her husband was initially put here after being shot, and the nation saw its first image of the room in newspaper illustrations of the president in bed, surrounded by doctors.

Since the 1902 renovation, the southwest suite has remained fixed as the president's bedroom. The Theodore Roosevelts slept in the Lincoln bed; the Tafts put it in storage and used twin mahogany beds. The twin beds were used by Woodrow and Ellen Wilson, who painted the room blue and white; Ellen Wilson died in this room. Wilson's second wife, Edith, brought the Lincoln bed back here for their use. The Hardings banished it and brought in Nellie Taft's twin beds. Here Florence Harding also had a special closet made for her large collection of shoes. The Coolidges returned the Lincoln bed for their use—and the Hoovers put it in another room and didn't use it. The Franklin Roosevelts designated this room as the "First Lady's bedroom," but Mrs. Roosevelt and then Bess Truman used it as a sitting room, the former hanging hundreds of framed pictures, the latter painting the walls lavender and gray. Mamie Eisenhower used it as her bedroom, in multiple shades of pink with an enormous pink bed and pink pin-cushioned headboard. Jackie Kennedy redecorated it in powder blue and white, placing a pastel portrait of her daughter on the wall, with a favorite terracotta bust of a child on the mantelpiece. This bust so represented her White House tenure to her that it figures in her White House portrait. She had double beds pushed together as one, draped by a powder blue tapestry. Since the Fords the room has been shared by the spouses. The Reagans covered the walls in hand-painted Chinese paper with a design of small birds; the Clintons chose similarly patterned floral paper.

Connected to this room, in the very corner, is the narrow dressing room. It has served a multitude of purposes—bedroom, small dining room, office, dressing room, tearoom. Nancy Reagan placed a portrait of herself with her baby daughter here, with its perfect view of the south and west from which many a First Lady has watched the lights of the Oval Office burn late.

Directly across the hall from the president's bedroom suite is the northwest suite, today used as a kitchen and dining room. Prior to 1961, the larger of the two rooms was a prime bedroom suite. For some unknown reason, President William Henry Harrison took this room; perhaps his death here led his successors to return to the original plan of using the bedroom across the hall. When the Prince of Wales came to stay with the Buchanan family, he slept in the suite, and it was christened the "Prince of Wales Room." Here in 1861 Mary Lincoln placed an ornately carved rosewood bed and matching marble-topped table from the Philadelphia firm of William Carryl. She had the bed, which would forever after be known as the Lincoln bed, crowned with a gold American shield, from which gilt lace, overlaid by rich purple satin curtains fringed in gold, flowed to the floor, covering the bed's perimeter. The bedspread was also purple and gold. Lizzie Grimsley, the First Lady's cousin, called the room "the best in the family suite." Just months after the room's completion, eleven-year-old Willie Lincoln died in the Lincoln bed. Three years later, the remains of his father would be embalmed in this room. This was the McKinleys' bedroom, decorated rather simply in crisp whites, with double brass-knobbed beds; a painting of their daughter, who had died two decades earlier, hung on the wall. Cleveland had the room painted yellow for them, but Ida McKinley demanded that it be changed to pale pink. Here she spent most of her White House life, and it was photographed for the American people for the first time in 1897.

Dining here with the Nixon family some seventy years after she lived in the White House, Alice Roosevelt Longworth looked around the room and realized this was her old bedroom—where her appendix had been removed. In 1961, Jackie Kennedy had made the room the "President's Dining Room," hung with mid-nineteenth-century wallpaper showing battle scenes. Betty Ford found the paper unappetizing and had the room painted yellow. Rosalynn Carter returned the wallpaper, and it remained in place, although in 1997 it was covered—but not harmed—with a more soothing pale green silk fabric.

The small dressing room connected to the "Prince of Wales room," in the far northwest corner, was used frequently by presidential daughters—just across the hall from their parents. Margaret Truman slept here; she said it was so cold that many mornings she hopped out of bed just long enough to build a fire in the fireplace, then went back to sleep—until her father woke her for school. Jackie Kennedy converted it into a kitchen. Here, Ford sometimes made his own breakfast, and the Clintons, who found its informality relaxing, often cooked and ate their meals here.

Moving northeast from the dining room along the north wall are now two mid-size rooms and one small one. There are no floor plans indicating exact location of rooms before the Pierce years, and walls and spaces changed with some frequency before that. These spaces were used as bedrooms—Johnson Hellen, nephew of Louisa Adams, lived in one. A small half-room area, connected by a door to the present-day dining room, with windows facing Pennsylvania Avenue, was a bathing area under Lincoln but has been a grooming room since the Nixon years. Hillary Clinton even put a humorous poster here, poking fun at her various changing hairstyles, and Barbara Bush's dog Millie gave birth here. Through a south door from this half-

Following the Lincoln Bed

1860s Purchased by Mary Todd Lincoln and placed in the northwest bedroom suite, or "Prince of Wales" bedroom; no evidence or even suggestion President Lincoln ever slept in it

1869 Moved by Julia Grant to the small bedroom west, in the shadow of the North Portico

1877 Rutherford and Lucy Hayes moved the Lincoln bed into the newly designated "State Bedroom" in the room currently known as the President's Study, next to the President's Bedroom

1901 Moved one room east, to the southwest bedroom suite, and used by Theodore and Edith Roosevelt

1909 Moved to storage by Nellie Taft

1915 Moved back into the southwest bedroom suite, "the President's Bedroom," and used by Woodrow Wilson and his second wife, Edith

1921 Moved to the northwest suite by Florence Harding, with some Lincoln memorabilia or era items

1923 Moved a third time into the southwest suite, the President's Bedroom, and used by Calvin and Grace Coolidge

1929 Moved by the Herbert Hoovers back into the northwest suite, officially called the Lincoln Bedroom

1933 Moved briefly into the small bedroom west under Franklin Roosevelt for use by his aide Louis Howe and his wife, Grace, but soon returned to the northwest suite, where it was later used by Anna Roosevelt Boettiger, her husband, John, and son Johnny.

1945 Placed by the Trumans in the southeast suite or "Blue Suite," renamed the Lincoln Suite, where it has remained since then

Some Uses of the Family Rooms
(shaded area indicates semi-public rooms)

1. Yellow Oval Room
Ladies' toilette room under Jackson, probably also under Van Buren, Harrison, Tyler. Library under Fillmore. President's private study and family room from Lincoln to Truman. Study/family room under Lincoln, Taft, Wilson, Harding, Coolidge, Hoover. Formal, private entertaining room since Eisenhower.

2. "Living Room"
"Extra" bedroom for presidential couples from Madison to Pierce. Bedroom for Abraham Lincoln, Mary Johnson Stover and her three children, May and Jessie McElroy (Arthur nieces), Russell and Mamie Harrison and their children, Quentin and Archie Roosevelt, Woodrow and Edith Wilson, Warren Harding, Franklin Roosevelt, Harry Truman, Dwight Eisenhower, John F. Kennedy, Lyndon Johnson, Richard Nixon. Living room and study since the Fords.

3. "Master Bedroom"
Bedroom to the John Adamses, Jefferson, the Madisons, the Monroes (assumed), J. Quincy Adams, Jackson, Van Buren (assumed), the John Tylers (assumed), the Polks (assumed), the Taylors, the Fillmores (assumed), the Pierces, Buchanan, Mary Lincoln, the David Patterson [Johnson] family, the Grants, the Hayeses, the Garfields, Mary McElroy, the Cleveland daughters, the B. Harrisons, the T. Roosevelts, the Tafts, the Wilsons, the Hardings, the Coolidges, the Hoovers, Mamie Eisenhower, Jacqueline Kennedy, Lady Bird Johnson, Pat Nixon, the Fords, the Carters, the Reagans, the Bushes, the Clintons; sitting room for Eleanor Roosevelt, Bess Truman.

4. "Sitting Room"
Bedroom to Suzannah Adams and Louisa Smith, Tad Lincoln, Robert Johnson, nursemaid to children of Grover Cleveland, Eleanor Roosevelt, Bess Truman. Private study to Rutherford Hayes, Lou Hoover. Dressing room to Julia Grant, William Howard Taft, Grace Coolidge. Tearoom–private receiving room to Mary Arthur McElroy. Private dining room to Woodrow and Edith Wilson. Clothes storage room for Florence Harding. Dressing–sitting room–office to: Mamie Eisenhower, Jacqueline Kennedy, Lady Bird Johnson, Pat Nixon, Betty Ford, Rosalynn Carter, Nancy Reagan, Barbara Bush, Hillary Clinton.

5. "The Kitchen"
Bedroom to Eliza Johnson, Frances Cleveland, Lorena Hickok (friend of Eleanor Roosevelt), Margaret Truman. Sitting room to Minnie Doud. Nursery–bedroom to Benjamin Harrison grandchildren. Family kitchen since the Kennedys.

6. "The Dining Room"
Bedroom of William Henry Harrison; Willie Lincoln; Grover Cleveland, then shared with Frances Cleveland, then Cleveland alone; Robert and Mary Harrison McKee; McKinleys; Alice Roosevelt, then Ethel Roosevelt; Helen Taft; Eleanor Wilson; Calvin Coolidge Jr.; Louis Howe (FDR advisor) and his wife, Grace; Minnie Doud. Likely bedroom of Nellie Grant, Fanny Hayes, Molly Garfield, Nell Arthur. As a bedroom suite (together with present-day kitchen room), bedroom to Louisa Adams and niece Mary Hellen; Jack and Emily Donelson and their four children; Robert and Priscilla Tyler and their daughter Mary. Living room for Andrew Johnson family. Dining room since the Kennedys.

7. "Cosmetology Room"
Offices of Eleanor Roosevelt and Bess Truman. Painting room of Dwight Eisenhower. Nursery room for John F. Kennedy Jr. Study of Luci Johnson. Makeup, hairdressing, and barber room since the Nixons.

8. Bedroom A (west)
Bedroom for Willie Lincoln, Andrew Johnson and son Andrew Jr., Robert and Charlie Taft, Joseph Lash (friend of Eleanor Roosevelt), Reathel Odum (secretary to Bess Truman), John F. Kennedy Jr., Chuck and Lynda Johnson Robb and their daughter. Playroom for Amy Carter. Gymnasium for Reagans.

9. Hall Room
Room where Lincoln made public speeches from window. Schoolroom for Scott and Fanny Hayes. Bedroom for two Theodore Roosevelt family maids, then Maude Shaw, nurse to Kennedy children. Storage room for dresses of Lady Bird Johnson, Nancy Reagan.

10. Bedroom B (east)
Bedroom for Frederick Dent (father of Julia Grant); Chester Arthur; Mary Dimmick (niece of Caroline Harrison) and John Scott (father of Caroline Harrison); Kermit Roosevelt; Madge Wallace (mother of Bess Truman); Caroline Kennedy; Pat Nugent and Luci Johnson Nugent and their son; Tricia Nixon; Susan Ford; Amy Carter; Chelsea Clinton. Office of Nancy Reagan. Either bedroom A or B was used by Scott, Birch, the sons of Hayes, Garfield, and Taft.

11. The Queen's Bedroom
Formerly called the Rose, or Pink, Bedroom, this is a guest room, once the bedroom of Anna Roosevelt, for example. Before the 1902 renovation it was the usual bedroom for presidential private secretaries, which meant many male relatives, including sons of presidents.

12. The Queen's Sitting Room
An office for the secretary prior to 1902; Ruddy Hayes used it for his botany experiments, and Jim and Harry Garfield studied here.

13. Lincoln Sitting Room
Was used as a small bedroom and office space; it was Florence Harding's social office, for example.

14. Lincoln Bedroom
Once Lincoln's Cabinet Room, it was then the "Blue Suite" bedroom where, for example, Margaret Wilson lived. It became "the Lincoln Bedroom" under Truman.

15. Treaty Room
Was Cabinet Room in the Victorian age, became a study after the 1902 renovation, and was made into the "Monroe Room" by Lou Hoover, then "Treaty Room" under Kennedy. President's private study under Bush and Clinton.

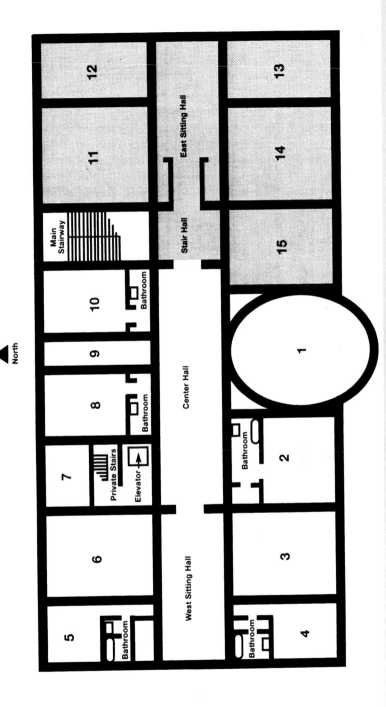

White House floor plan of private family rooms, second floor.

Nancé Hacskaylo

Jacqueline Kennedy carries birthday cake of her daughter, Caroline (who sits in front of her), in the President's Dining Room, which she created; it had been a bedroom. Her mother, Janet Lee Auchincloss, stands watching, at far left. 1962.

JOHN F. KENNEDY PRESIDENTIAL LIBRARY

In the West Sitting Hall, Bess Truman, far left, in what her daughter called "a hot game of canasta," with her two sisters-in-law Natalie and Beuf, and her brother, Frank. c. 1945–1948.
HARRY S. TRUMAN PRESIDENTIAL LIBRARY

room is one of two famous "secret" back stairs, a stairwell that winds down from the top floor to the bottom. (There is another back stairs next to the family kitchen.) Right next to this half-room and the stairwell is the elevator. An elevator had been planned for the use of James Garfield's elderly mother, but his successor Chester Arthur installed the first one. It was replaced with a more efficient model by Theodore Roosevelt (whose son Quentin and his friend Charlie Taft, son of the next president, used to ride—*on top of it*), and then another was installed by Truman.

Farther east along the north wall, there had been a formal guest or "state bedroom," created by Monroe and decorated in yellow by Jackson. By the Pierce years, this room was divided into two bedrooms, the large area now split down the center by a newly created narrow corridor with its window directly over the front door. The two bedrooms still flank this thin space of a room, mostly used for storage. Here, Lincoln often came to give speeches from the window, and a small schoolroom was later established for Scott and Fanny Hayes. The bedroom on the west side of the hall room was used once by a president—Andrew Johnson—and the bedroom on the east side was used once by another, Chester Arthur, who ordered a regally carved headboard, canopied in blue and complete with double mattresses for himself. In the west bedroom, Mary Lincoln lay in shock following her husband's assassination, refusing to enter their own suite. Later it became the Reagans' gym.

During the White House's first century, a large staircase was located in the west hall of the family quarters, right outside the presidential bedroom. It was an odd space: Fanny Hayes played with her dollhouse here; with Garfield's illness, it resembled a hospital waiting room; the McKinleys made it a dining area. The Benjamin Harrisons tried to create a homey feeling

Jessie Wilson's wedding party in front of the West Sitting Hall semicircular window. Jessie Wilson sits at center, her sister Eleanor to her left, her sister Margaret to her right, the President behind Margaret, the First Lady behind Jessie, and the groom, Francis Sayre, next to the First Lady. 1914.
LIBRARY OF CONGRESS

The West Sitting Hall, long a gathering place for First Families. Benjamin Harrison can be spied in the far left corner. The stairwell led to the state floor and family dining room. c. 1889.
LIBRARY OF CONGRESS

Ronald Reagan has breakfast in the West Sitting Hall. c. 1981.
RONALD REAGAN
PRESIDENTIAL LIBRARY

beneath the dramatic semicircular window at the end of the hall, incorporating items like a chair made of elk antlers here. Any sense of its being a private area, however, was broken by the protruding stairwell. The Roosevelt children took trays from the kitchen and slid down the stairs here.

By 1902 the stairs were gone and the hall became a gathering place for families at day's end. Nellie Taft worked with her secretary here during the day and played her piano in the evening. Her dark green burlap wallpaper was replaced with beige grass cloth by Ellen Wilson. Lou Hoover installed palm trees, ferns, wicker furniture, straw matting on the floor, and caged birds, giving it the feel of her California home. This is where she placed her desk, working in the center of this airy, dramatic space. Under FDR, it was the center of frenetic activity. Beneath the window, on solid old furniture including red leather chairs and sofas from the presidential yacht, Eleanor Roosevelt held court, talking to political leaders and social reformers, along with visiting relatives or friends, scrambling eggs in her chafing dish on Sunday nights, or making café au lait while carrying on with debates and conversations. The Eisenhowers put overstuffed chintz-covered chairs here, bowls of pink carnations scattered about. Silver-framed pictures of the Bouviers, Mrs. Kennedy's father's desk, a small bar and hi-fi set, and shelves bulging with family photo albums marked the Kennedy look. The Nixons had yellow walls with pieces of cobalt-colored furniture; the Reagans had peach walls with predominantly red furniture. All the entrances that open into the hall can be closed, giving it the feel of a squarish room.

Across the Center Hall from the two north bedrooms is what became the Yellow Oval Room, decorated in green as a ladies' parlor by Andrew Jackson's niece, Emily Donelson. William Henry Harrison's family clustered here as he lay dying and officials predominated in

his bedroom. It remained, however, largely a gathering place for women guests until Sarah Polk outfitted a downstairs room for the same purposes, thus making the family rooms finally off-limits to mere guests. It was the Fillmores who gave purpose to the room when, in 1850, Congress made a special appropriation of $4,000 to purchase the first multiple volumes of books. This became the first permanent White House library, and here their daughter, Mary Abigail, played her harp for guests. After a long day of telegraphing messages on Union troop movements during the Civil War, Lincoln would join his wife here. Presidents from Hayes to Theodore Roosevelt used it for private meetings. Chester Arthur put his lounge chair here, but Frances Cleveland formalized it with Louis XIII furniture. Nellie Taft dramatically altered the room's look with tapestries and other items she had purchased in Asia.

Despite Prohibition, Harding served alcoholic drinks to his cronies as they played poker in the Oval Room. Draped in "Harding blue," it housed clipping books, a pink doll that shook and winked, and the First Lady's collection of miniature elephants on shelves. The Hoovers created an oddly glamorous look with Chippendale couches upholstered in gold-and-black brocade and green curtains. Under FDR the oval study took on a nautical look, displaying the president's collection of naval prints and ship models. Truman met nightly with his wife in closed-door sessions here, during which they reviewed his speeches and political agenda. Eisenhower's military decorations and awards were displayed in cases here, and it was called the "Trophy Room." Jackie Kennedy created a sitting room, reminiscent of the Jefferson-Madison era, with bright yellow furniture. Since 1961, it has been the most formal room on the family floor, where world leaders are brought before a state dinner, for the exchange of official gifts.

To the west along the south wall is the square room sandwiched between the Yellow Oval Room and the master suite in the southwest corner (the bedroom traditionally used by presi-

Franklin D. Roosevelt in the Oval Study at his desk with his dog Fala. Note the cocktail glasses, sugar, and liquor bottles; FDR enjoyed mixing cocktails for himself and guests here. c. 1940.

dential couples). This had always been the "extra room" of the southwest suite, and some couples used it as a separate bedroom. The Hayeses designated it the "State Bedroom"; Garfield's doctors conferred and rested here, and after its initial use as two of her sons' bedroom, Edith Roosevelt took it over for her office and sitting room. Ellen Wilson, a supporter of Appalachian crafts, brought some of them here, calling it the "Blue Mountain Room." Under Harding it was dubbed the "West Parlor," and he slept here when his wife was ill. Because of Franklin Roosevelt's confinement to a wheelchair, and the difficulties he had in dressing, he took this room as his own, sleeping in a narrow white metal frame bed. Thus, beginning with FDR this room was designated the President's Bedroom. It was blue-green under Truman, green under Eisenhower, blue-white under Kennedy. Presidents from Roosevelt to Nixon maintained a bed for themselves here.

After exchanging LBJ's canopied four-poster bed for the simpler one used by Truman and Eisenhower, Nixon cracked that "politics had literally bred strange bedfellows." Pat Nixon decided to maintain the tradition of a separate room because, as she told the chief usher, "Nobody could sleep with Dick. He wakes up during the night, switches on the lights, speaks

Other "White Houses"

1789–1800: The Washingtons live in rented homes in the capital cities New York and Philadelphia; the Adamses begin their term in the same Philadelphia mansion left by the Washingtons.

1814–1817: With the White House burned in August 1814 during the War of 1812, James and Dolley Madison lived first at the Octagon House, on nearby New York Avenue, and then the end town house on a row of houses at 19th Street and Pennsylvania Avenue.

1817: After the March 1817 inauguration, James and Elizabeth Monroe continue to live in their private home, the present-day Washington Arts Club, on I Street, between 20th and 21st, until the rebuilt White House is ready for occupancy in October 1817.

1881: Upon the death of James Garfield, the new president, Chester Arthur, continued living at the private home of Senator John Jones on Capitol Hill until December 7, when the mansion's refurbishment was completed.

1886–1889, 1893–1897: The Grover Cleveland family, finding the White House family rooms too public, move to two successive private homes, Oak View and Red Top, in a suburban neighborhood, and take occupancy there for long stays. The area is named Cleveland Park.

1901: Theodore Roosevelt stayed at the 1734 N Street home of his sister Bamie Cowles upon the assassination of William McKinley. He moved into the White House on September 22, soon joined by his family.

1902: Theodore Roosevelt lived in the Townsend House at 736 Lafayette Square, on Jackson Place, while the White House was being renovated. His family went directly to their New York home in the last days of June, and he moved in during the first days of July; all returned on November 4.

1923: Upon the death of Warren Harding, the Calvin Coolidge family continued to live in their Willard Hotel suite on Pennsylvania Avenue until August 21.

1927: With the White House roof and attic under reconstruction, Calvin and Grace Coolidge moved into the Patterson Mansion at 15 Dupont Circle—now the Washington Club—where they lived from March 2 until September 11.

1945: Upon the April 12 death of FDR, the Harry Truman family continued living at their private apartment at 4701 Connecticut Avenue. They moved into the White House on May 7.

1948–1952: The Harry Truman family moved out of the White House by Thanksgiving while it underwent its most major renovation and rebuilding. They lived across the street in the government-owned Blair House and returned on May 27, 1952.

1963: Upon the November 22 murder of John Kennedy, the Lyndon Johnson family continued to live in their private home, "The Elms," at 4040 52nd Street. They moved in on December 7.

1974: Upon the August 8 resignation of Richard Nixon, the Gerald Ford family continued to live in their private home in suburban Alexandria, Virginia, at 514 Crown View Drive. They moved into the White House on August 19.

John Tyler, Millard Fillmore, and Andrew Johnson as vice presidents were living in hotel suites without their families when each became president.

into his tape recorder or takes notes—it's impossible." In fact, Nixon's taping of his thoughts—a daily habit also practiced by Lady Bird Johnson—involved a single recorder, considerably simpler than the tangle of wires LBJ had kept under his bed for various electronic gadgets including two clacking wire service printers, a three-television-set console, and a telephone taping system. When the Fords' furniture from their suburban Virginia home was delivered by movers, a press photograph showed their large bed headboard being moved in, and a reporter asked Betty Ford how often they would sleep together. "As often as possible," she quipped. Both the President and Mrs. Ford used the southwest bedroom to sleep in, and the square room formerly known as "The President's Bedroom" became the true family living room. The Reagans often ate dinner from TV trays here, watching television as they sat in matching red-and-white chintz chairs. Here Mrs. Bush placed a large needlepoint rug that she had made. Removing the many television sets around the private quarters, the Clintons placed their one set here.

Before the 1902 renovation, the executive offices were located at the east end of the second floor. With the creation of the West Wing, they were moved out and the entire floor became the private preserve of the family. Still, the five rooms in the east end have a semi-public history.

The bedroom suite now called the Queen's Suite, because several European queens stayed here, was called the Rose Suite after the 1902 renovation, and was often used by visiting relatives: Edith Roosevelt's sister Emily Carow; William Howard Taft's sister and brother-in-law, Frances and William Edwards; Coolidge's cousin's daughter Marion Pollard; Anna Roosevelt,

Betty Ford hugs her son Steve in the First Lady's dressing room. This room is in the southwest corner of the second floor. 1975.
GERALD R. FORD PRESIDENTIAL LIBRARY

FDR's daughter; and most "First Mothers," from Martha Truman to Virginia Clinton Kelley. While the Kennedys' bedroom was being decorated their first weeks in the house, they lived here. Jackie Kennedy's redecoration of the connecting sitting room in blue and white has remained intact for nearly forty years. Lady Bird Johnson sometimes repaired here to work in complete privacy. It was also used for a Catholic mass on the first birthday of Luci Johnson Nugent's son Lyn, and served as a holding room for groom Chuck Robb before his White House wedding to Lynda Bird Johnson.

During the months when First Lady Nellie Taft was recuperating from a stroke, her visiting sisters Eleanor Moore, Jennie Anderson, and Maria Herron lived in the "Blue Suite" across the hall from the Rose Suite. Intermittently during the Wilson tenure, this was the home of Margaret Wilson, the daughter who remained unmarried. When Herbert Hoover decided to move his private office here, the "Blue Suite" became the "Lincoln Study." It was again a bedroom under FDR—where adviser Harry Hopkins and his wartime bride Louise lived—but the Lincoln bed was not yet in place. Finally, in 1945, under Harry Truman's direction the Lincoln bed and accompanying furniture were moved in, and the "Lincoln Study" became the Lincoln Bedroom. The connecting sitting room was Florence Harding's busy office. Jackie Kennedy decorated it as the "Lincoln Sitting Room," in Victoriana to match the bedroom, and it became Nixon's favorite spot in the house. He so liked to work beside its roaring fireplace that in the summer he had the air-conditioning turned on to mitigate the heat

Jimmy Carter's grandsons, Jason (left) and James II, "Digger," watch television in the West Sitting Hall. Note the videotape machine, the first in the White House. c. 1978.
JIMMY CARTER
PRESIDENTIAL LIBRARY

from the fire. He listened to his favorite music, the score of *Victory at Sea*, as he worked in his favorite brown easy chair, and also handed his letter of resignation to his secretary of state here. In 1993, Hillary Clinton redecorated it in vibrant patterns appropriate to the era.

The President's Study, used continuously by Presidents Andrew Johnson through William McKinley, took on a personal look following the 1902 renovation. Theodore Roosevelt and W. H. Taft both displayed personal memorabilia going back to their college days. Today it is called the Treaty Room, because the treaty ending the Spanish-American War had been signed here by McKinley. During World War I, after dinner, Woodrow and Edith Wilson repaired to his desk here, retrieved from it classified dispatches transmitted earlier, and decoded them. Under Coolidge, floor-to-ceiling bookcases were built along the walls. Hoover tore them out. His wife gathered original and copied Monroe furniture in this room and called it the Monroe Room. Eleanor Roosevelt replaced some of it with sturdier pieces from the furniture factory she helped found, and briefly held her press conferences for women reporters here. Jackie Kennedy restored it to a Victorian Treaty Room with a Grant-era East Room chandelier, and used it as her work space. The Bushes made it into a blue presidential study. Hillary Clinton restored the Victoriana, with dark wood and burgundy walls, for use by her husband as his home office.

Across the hall from this room is the Grand Staircase, which goes only between the second floor and the State Floor. Two other smaller staircases at the west end of the second floor, however, go to the next upper floor. Formerly the attic, the third floor is now a fully working suite of rooms used by the families. The attic had long been used for storage along with about

Bill and Hillary Clinton in the Oval Study—called the Yellow Oval Room since 1961—with their nephews Tyler Clinton (near president) and Zachary Rodham. 1996.

THE WHITE HOUSE

eight small sloped-ceiling bedrooms for servants. The 1902 renovation expanded the space for some ironing rooms, linen closets, clothing storage, and guest rooms. One room was dubbed the "Bachelor's Suite" for young men who courted the Wilson daughters, and in another well-lit area painter Ellen Wilson worked on her canvases. When the roof was raised in 1927, the floor became more livable. Lou Hoover's secretaries worked here. FDR's personal secretary and companion, Missy LeHand, lived here, and later so did little Diana Hopkins, daughter of FDR's live-in adviser Harry Hopkins. After enduring the intolerable food supervised by a housekeeper who ignored his wishes, FDR had a small kitchen created on the third floor, and there his meals were made. Dwight Eisenhower cooked his own soups and stews here.

There are various-sized suites and rooms on the third floor. Jackie Kennedy first decorated them with antiques, her most famous being the "Empire Guest Room," with a bed used by John Adams. The Carter family had one of the rooms sentimentally lined with wood panels from an old family barn in Georgia. Julie Nixon and her husband, David Eisenhower, the visiting Reagan and Bush children and grandchildren, and relatives of the Clintons all stayed here, and while in residence the Ford and Carter sons lived in rooms on this floor. Hillary Clinton created her own Eleanor Roosevelt room where she kept memorabilia of her predecessor that had been sent to her as gifts. For her husband's birthday one year, she also had the room at the far east end made into a soundproof music room, where he practiced his saxophone—it had been Jack Ford's old bedroom. Under the Reagans, and then again the Clintons, the bedroom suites were beautifully decorated with items from the White House collection. The Clintons installed an exercise room here. There is also a billiards room.

The most famous and popular room on this floor was created by Grace Coolidge, directly above the Yellow Oval Room. She called it her sky parlor because it offered an open view looking out to the sky from walls of glass. The Trumans installed a linoleum floor and artificial bamboo furniture, and the space was Mamie Eisenhower's bridge party room, Caroline Kennedy's kindergarten, the teenage Johnson daughters' hangout—complete with soda machine. It was the one quiet retreat where Nixon son-in-law Ed Cox could come to study for his law bar exams, and Rosalynn Carter could focus on Spanish lessons with her in-residence daughters-in-law Caron and Annette. Ronald Reagan recuperated in the bright room in the weeks following the assassination attempt. There is a small wet bar here. It was the favorite room of the Clintons, whether for meetings or board games or family dinners. Here they displayed collections of humorous stacking Russian dolls depicting them and other political figures. Just outside the Solarium and around the roof's perimeter is a promenade, hidden from public view, where Mrs. Clinton raised cherry tomato plants. This is where Eisenhower turned his steaks and burgers on a fifties barbecue grill, and Susan Ford brought her cat Shan out to play. In the evenings, the Carter sons used a telescope to identify stars, while during the day, the family suntanned here. A century earlier Jesse Grant had used a smaller roof nook for his telescope. When Theodore Roosevelt prohibited his daughter Alice from smoking her cigarettes "under this roof," this is where she climbed to obey him—to smoke *on* the roof.

No First Family has ever had to function without servants. They have all had staff to cook, serve, clean, sew, wash, manage their pets, place their telephone calls, wind their clocks, fix the plumbing and electricity, and repair anything for them. A succession of stewards, housekeepers, and chief ushers have managed the household staff, answering directly to the First Couple. While no First Lady was reported pushing her vacuum cleaner every week, several found housekeeping to provide some normalcy in the house: on maids' days off, Bess Truman was known to clean and cook, Jackie Kennedy often lugged and moved furniture herself as she rearranged rooms, Hillary Clinton enjoyed cooking for her family.

In the nineteenth century, many servants, particularly those who had come with the family, were housed in the basement. When, amid the growing sectional tensions over abolition, Zachary Taylor brought slaves to serve his family in the White House, they were hidden from public view, living in the cramped attic space. Nellie Taft's housekeeper, Elizabeth Jaffray—who continued to serve under Wilson, Harding, and Coolidge—was actually given a room in

Presidents Who Owned Slaves During Their Administrations

George Washington
Thomas Jefferson
James Madison
James Monroe
Andrew Jackson
John Tyler
James Polk
Zachary Taylor

the family quarters. Before Taft, families paid many of their servants' wages. Thus, it was often not long before some servants found themselves on the federal payroll, with some creative title changes.

Whether paid by the family or the government, notable personalities among some of the servants mark history: Madison's household manager Jean Sioussant, who was with Dolley in the harrowing minutes before she fled the mansion as the British army advanced to burn it; the long-suffering Guistas, who worked for Quincy Adams but quit under the mercurial Jackson; Mary Lincoln's empathetic seamstress, Elizabeth Keckley; Grant's coachman Albert, who ate and talked with the horses; the Hayes's cook Winnie Monroe, who so loved Washington that she returned there later, leaving the family; Arthur's snobbish valet, Alec Powell, who sniped at reporters in defense of his boss; the Theodore Roosevelt family cook, Annie O'Rourke, whose sugar wafers were renowned in Washington; Florence Harding's suspicious maid, Katherine Wynn, who indulged in her lady's penchant for intrigue; the Kennedy valets Providencia Parades and George Thomas, whose families celebrated holidays with the First Family; the Nixons' loyal house managers, husband and wife team Manuelo and Fina Sanchez; Amy Carter's nanny Mary Fitzpatrick, employed on work release from a Georgia prison. When Nancy Reagan's maid Anita Costello made headlines for being wrongly accused of dealing in arms, it was the first time a servant was thrust into public controversy since John Watt, the gardener under Lincoln, was investigated by Congress for passing on to a reporter an advance copy of the president's State of the Union address.

Mansion maintenance necessitates a full professional staff. In the early days the rooms were simply heated by coal or wood fires. The Madisons installed a heating system in the State Dining Room, the heat rising through grates from coal stoves in the basement. Van Buren extended this to other rooms. Under Pierce came a furnace and duct heating system, and Fillmore had its reach extended into smaller service rooms. Before another decade passed, central heating was improved to a rudimentary steam-heat system. Radiators began appearing in rooms with the 1902 renovation, and electric heat came after 1952. Limited air-conditioning came in 1933, central air-conditioning with the Truman renovation in 1952. In the family rooms, candles and oil lamps were used for lighting until gaslight wall brackets were installed under Taylor. In 1889, electricity was installed for the Harrisons, who feared electrocution: servants shut the lights off.

Jefferson had a "water closet," essentially a chamber pot that could be washed with water pumped up through a wooden pipe from outside. It was located in the space occupied by the present-day powder room for First Ladies, off a small entry hall to the southwest corner sitting room. There is a record of Monroe's using a tin bathtub, and certainly his predecessors had used the same, with water being carried up by jug. Under Jackson in 1834, running water was piped in from a spring and pumped up into the east terrace in metal tubes. These ran through the walls and protruded into the rooms, controlled by spigots. Initially, the water was for washing items, but soon the first bathing rooms were created, in the ground-level east colonnade. Van Buren had shower baths installed here,

Grover and Frances Cleveland in their private railroad car on their western tour. c. 1886.
LIBRARY OF CONGRESS

and under Pierce, running hot baths and showers came to the family floor, as well as another rest room, likely with a wood-stalled commode and porcelain sink. Located in the president's suite, it had faux wood wallpapering and faux tile cloth flooring. By Lincoln's time, running water for washing came in from the Potomac River. With the 1902 renovation, modern bathrooms with silver faucets and handles and white porcelain were created in the four corner suites and tucked in elsewhere. The largest bathtub was installed for 300-plus-pound Taft after he got stuck in a regular-size one; four average-size men could fit in it. LBJ had a powerful shower installed with hard-streaming jets and shower heads from every direction. Nixon said it "nearly flung me out of the stall," and replaced it. Andrew Johnson installed the first barber chair, and Truman put in a drinking fountain and even a dental office.

White House life is isolating, but communications have never been a problem. Since the early days families used servants as hand messengers. Andrew Johnson had a telegraph office installed down the hall, in the executive offices, and Hayes acquired the first telephone after watching a demonstration of the wonder by Alexander Graham Bell himself.

The Presidential Bedroom showing bed used by Rutherford and Lucy Hayes. c. 1877.
HAYES PRESIDENTIAL CENTER

Prior to 1902, there were extensive stables, housing horses and coaches, located on the grounds of the present-day Oval Office, Cabinet Room, and Rose Garden. Servants included drivers and coachmen, but going about stylishly was costly; thus many families accepted princely coaches from various public groups. One of the most regal of these was presented to Abigail Fillmore by wealthy New York supporters of her husband, complete with horses and silver harnesses. Fillmore later came under attack for selling it all and pocketing the profit. Arthur had a monogrammed landau, painted green with red detailing, green silk monogrammed lap robes, lace curtains, and silver mountings. "The entire 'turn-out,'" said one observer, "is a model of quiet magnificence and good taste." Grant's children daily went to school in a yellow wicker pony cart, while Grant himself was arrested for speeding—though he praised the officer for "doing his duty."

Taft was the first to travel officially by automobile, and a full fleet of cars was provided for his and his family's use—the first time congressional funds were appropriated for presidential travel. Some members of First Families continued driving themselves. Lou Hoover and Eleanor Roosevelt managed to do so, but Bess Truman found she attracted too much atten-

Frances Cleveland in her private sitting room, the northwest corner room, now the family kitchen. 1886–1889.
LAST APPEARED IN *Grover Cleveland*, 1910

President and Mrs. Clinton celebrate their daughter's birthday with dinner in the Family Kitchen—formerly Mrs. Cleveland's sitting room, and Margaret Truman's bedroom, among other uses. 1995.
THE WHITE HOUSE

Gerald Ford watching morning news in the family room; under presidents from FDR to Nixon, this room was designated as the president's bedroom, apart from the First Lady's room.
1974.
GERALD R. FORD
PRESIDENTIAL LIBRARY

Steve Ford talking on the phone in his third-floor bedroom. The wallpaper was put in by Jacqueline Kennedy.
1975.
GERALD R. FORD
PRESIDENTIAL LIBRARY

Luci Baines Johnson and friend in her second-floor bedroom, facing Pennsylvania Avenue. 1966.
LYNDON B. JOHNSON PRESIDENTIAL LIBRARY

tion, making for potential traffic accidents, and gave it up reluctantly. Only once did President Kennedy drive in his white Cadillac convertible with red leather interior, carrying his wife and friends from his docked yacht back to his family's Hyannis Port compound, a very short distance. LBJ more frequently insisted on the freedom of driving his convertible in Texas. When a policeman pulled him over for speeding, recognized him, and gasped, "Oh, my God," LBJ quipped, "And don't you forget it." With security ever tighter, presidential couples can rarely drive. President Clinton was permitted to drive his classic Thunderbird convertible, for example, only a few hundred feet at an exhibition of old cars. Hillary Clinton had to keep hers in storage for years. Even when Patti [Reagan] Davis drove her car at home in California, she was trailed by the Secret Service.

Presidential train and sea travel gave way to air travel. Although various well-appointed railroad parlor, sleeping, and dining cars were loaned or appropriated by the government for lengthy presidential travel, there was never any official presidential train. Van Buren was the first incumbent president to travel by rail, and it was a regular form of travel for presidents until Eisenhower, overlapping with the jet age. In 1902 Theodore Roosevelt commissioned the first official presidential yacht, *The Mayflower*, ushering in regular voyages by First Families. Before Roosevelt, private or naval vessels were used. Jimmy Carter had the presidential vessel *Sequoia* decommissioned as a relic of the imperial presidency, and there were no more yachts.

Air travel for incumbent presidents commenced in January 1943, when FDR used a PanAm plane, contracted by the navy, to go from Florida to Casablanca. By the fall of that year, in the midst of war, a C-54 cargo plane was converted into *The Sacred Cow* for Roosevelt, the first official Air Force One. Truman and Eisenhower both loved flying, and the former had a plane commissioned with an eagle painted onto its nose. Although both men's wives disliked flying, they made short trips by air, thus beginning the private use of the government planes by family members (Eleanor Roosevelt flew commercial). Eisenhower even had a small twin-engine fly him between Washington and his Gettysburg farm, and was the first to use a helicopter directly from the lawn to Andrews Air Force Base, where the planes are kept. When an aide once pointed out to LBJ "his" helicopter, the president quipped, "Son, they're all my helicopters."

Various improved aircraft have served as Air Force One since the Kennedy presidency (the name applies to any craft carrying the president, not the plane itself). Beige china chosen by Jackie Kennedy is still used, and besides a kitchen, there are an office, a conference room, a press section, and bedrooms onboard. If family members use presidential craft for personal use, they must pay an exorbitant fee. When Jackie Kennedy flew to Italy to vacation with her sister, she had to pay her fare. When the duo went to India and Pakistan, however, it was a semiofficial trip with speeches and appearances deemed to be of political value to the administration—and her tab was paid by the government.

Sometimes the first floor augmented the family rooms. The Tylers, for example, liked to gather in the Green Room; they hung their family portraits and placed busts of their daughters here. The extensive Benjamin Harrison clan tried to close off the smaller parlors and use them as family sitting rooms. The Lincoln family sometimes gathered after dinner in the Red Room to read newspapers and talk. Private dinner parties, weddings, funerals, and other large family events are usually held in the state rooms. Established by the Madisons, the first floor's smaller dining room, the "Family Dining Room" in the northwest corner, was strictly for family meals, and here they were eaten until 1961, when Jackie Kennedy created a dining room upstairs. Some families eschewed the "Family Dining Room," however—the Jackson clan ate on small tables in their rooms as if in a hotel, and the Eisenhowers dined on TV trays in the west hall, simultaneously watching two "porthole" television sets. A dumbwaiter pulley has long brought food up from the big kitchens on the ground floor.

The South Lawn was essentially open to the public, a notion encouraged by the Tylers in their initiating of public Saturday band concerts. By the Pierce administration so much professional care had gone into the gardens (John Quincy Adams appointed the first gardener, John Ousley, in 1825) that they were popular for promenading and—with the gates open from eight in the morning until sunset—gawking at First Families. Julia Grant had the

grounds closed partway into her tenure, when some tourists followed her and her children on a walk. By the 1890s there was an abruptly permanent closing following a disturbing incident: from the family rooms, Frances Cleveland watched in horror as tourists overcame her baby daughters' nursemaid and began picking up the two toddlers for their own amusement.

From Buchanan to Theodore Roosevelt, First Families relished the private world of perfumed flowers and exotic plants in large greenhouses, on the site of the present-day West Wing. "We have the most beautiful flowers and grounds imaginable," Mary Lincoln wrote a friend. It was an especial preserve for those Victorian wives who worshipped flowers: orchid expert Caroline Harrison raised special varieties here, while Frances Cleveland plucked one of her favorite pansies to be painted. Ida McKinley was calmest in her velvet chair amid the cloying fragrance of roses. Little Esther Cleveland's only White House recollection was of the scent of roses, like those at the shore, which wafted up to the family rooms from the greenhouses.

With the south grounds no longer an open public park, First Families made additions to it for personal enjoyment. Edith Roosevelt created a "Colonial garden" of multicolored varieties, Ellen Wilson a formal rose garden with statuary. The grounds were briefly reopened as a public park when Florence Harding fulfilled her campaign pledge to keep the black gates open to the public. They had been closed by lock and chain during the war years and Wilson's illness. Jackie Kennedy made part of the lawn a playground for her children, placing a trampoline, sandbox, treehouse, and swing set there—all obscured from public view by bushes because, she said, she was "tired of starring in everyone's home movies!" Yet it was her husband who asked her to oversee the creation of the modern-day Rose Garden as a setting for public ceremonies.

Eleanor Roosevelt talks to a friend; her new Plymouth car is behind her on the South Lawn. 1933.
FRANKLIN D. ROOSEVELT PRESIDENTIAL LIBRARY

The South Lawn, which is larger than the North Lawn, is mostly exposed to the public, with a clear view of the house. Still, families created refuges there. Tennis courts have been in place since the Theodore Roosevelt years, and here everyone from the Wilson daughters, Coolidge sons, Ford, and Bush has played. Florence Harding hosted the first women's tennis exhibition, and Nancy Reagan held a fund-raiser tournament here. Lady Bird Johnson created a sanctuary in a heavily wooded part of the lawn, with goldfish pond and slate walkway, christened the "Children's Garden." She had her grandchildren's footprints marked in cement, a custom followed by later presidential grandchildren. First Truman, then Bush installed horseshoe pits. Ford built an outdoor pool, and his son Jack immediately took scuba diving lessons in it. Amy Carter practiced her diving technique here. Barbara Bush was one of the pool's most frequent users—despite once having discovered a rat sharing the water. Amy Carter also played in her hidden treehouse on the lawn, sometimes with her young nephew Jason.

Despite its symbolism of open democracy, the mansion was always first a home, and it as well as its occupants soon enough had protection. Jefferson had a stone wall put in on the south border of the property. Under Monroe came a stone wall and iron fencing on the north side, a night watchman, and armed—though not uniformed—guards. By Van Buren's time, the guards were at the outside gates and door on reception days. Tyler successfully petitioned Congress for the first permanent security corps—deceptively called doormen. Pierce had the first federally salaried bodyguard. Lincoln used the back stairs, enabling him to move through, and out of, the house without public notice, and was guarded by some members of the Washington Metropolitan Police detailed to the White House. Still, protection was haphazard. When James Garfield walked into the local train station and was shot, he had no security detail. Following the third assassination of a president, McKinley in 1901, every president has been protected by the Secret Service. The Taft children were the first offspring, and Florence Harding the first spouse, to be given official security protection. In their quarters, or when visiting a secured private home, there are no guards—but they are just outside the doors. Family members not in residence and over the age of sixteen can request no agents: as a singer, Margaret Truman had none during her national concert tour; Chelsea Clinton, a Stanford University student, kept her detail, however, even when those children living outside the White House request no bodyguard their movements are always tracked by the Secret Service.

With succeeding generations of harmful threats against the families, public access to the mansion became limited. By World War II, it was illegal for someone to come onto the property without security clearance. All four streets around the complex are now closed. All of this barricades "the people's house," but it affords First Families necessary safety. Inevitably, it also becomes part of the larger political debate about how the president and his family live. Apart from public judgments on how they conduct their private lives, the taxpayers' burden for the families' comforts becomes a legitimate concern. What they know to be decisions affecting their personal lives are nevertheless always potential political controversies, stirred by other issues of the day: Jackie Kennedy's European vacation was protested at a time of balance of payment problems in America; criticism of Nancy Reagan's acceptance of money from oil tycoons to

Lyndon Johnson rides up to family quarters in the presidential elevator with president-elect Richard Nixon. 1968.
LYNDON BAINES JOHNSON
PRESIDENTIAL LIBRARY

decorate the family rooms occurred during an economic recession; Hillary Clinton's replacement of an usher came just as a controversial restructuring of the travel office staff was being enfolded into an independent counsel investigation. Of course, the press at the time did not know of the exorbitant costs of the Nixons' reconfiguration of a new Air Force One after the chief of staff imperiously botched an earlier design, or of LBJ's demands to keep replacing shower heads until one powerful enough for him was created. Instead, when tales of LBJ's shutting off electric lights proliferated in the press, he was seen as saving taxpayer money—however nominal the real amount.

This was less a problem in the nineteenth century and early twentieth, when the press had little idea of what a First Family's life was really like, yet the paranoia about monarchical First Families always posed a political threat. When John Adams used government funds to purchase coaches and horses with silver mountings, he was roundly criticized by anti-Federalists. Adams made sure to write his successor that this was all government property—and now his to use. The savvy Jefferson permitted Congress to sell the wares that smacked of regalness. The 1814 destruction of the White House by the British was humiliating enough, but that the president and his wife were portrayed as abandoning it was made into hay by the opposition press. Editorials suggested that the cost of the Madisons' cowardice was the loss of an important American symbol and chided that perhaps now their costly entertaining would cease. The Madisons made no demands for a new or speedily rebuilt presidential mansion. Largely for his sons' "exercise and amusement," John Quincy Adams personally bought a secondhand billiards table and its accoutrements. As his father's secretary, John unthinkingly included the billiards room contents in an inventory of items purchased with the $14,000 congressional appropriation for refurbishing. The president wrote Congress that this was "entirely erroneous; and that no part of the public appropriation had been, or should be applied to any such purpose." It was too late. The anti-Adams *United Telegram* vilified him not only for buying these immoral items "out of the public purse" but for setting a bad example for young men, who would surely fall into the billiards room habits of smoking and drinking, and offer as an excuse, "Why, the President plays billiards!" The pro-Adams *National Gazette* worsened the situation by saying a billiards table was "a common appendage in the houses of the rich and great of Europe." The paranoia of royal posturing set in. Cast against Andrew Jackson—whose supporters built his image as the idealized common man of the West—Adams was defeated for reelection in 1828.

In the most famous case of a president's political fortune being ruined by his lifestyle, Van Buren, who served during a depression, was crucified in a congressional speech by William Ogle of Pennsylvania for a perceived White House of regal state bedrooms, luxurious gardens, gold spoons, and French food. In fact, Van Buren's son and daughter-in-law Abraham and Angelica had taken on some royal airs after a honeymoon that included presentation at the British and French royal courts, and they were alluded to in Ogle's speech. The attack on Van

Buren was so exaggerated, however, that he felt no need to defend himself against it. In 1840, he was defeated by William Henry Harrison, who was billed as a log cabin frontiersman when in fact he was born and raised on a regal Virginia plantation. A further irony was that Adams's successor and Van Buren's predecessor, Andrew Jackson, had lived more lavishly and conducted more extensive redecorating than either of them. Since 1826, after Monroe's furniture purchases included some items once owned by French nobility, Congress built an anti-royal caveat into its appropriation: purchases had to be "of American manufacture."

By 1844 royal fever meant political death. Surely John Tyler would not have permitted his wife, Julia, to ride in a carriage with six matching white Arabian steeds, and receive guests seated in a thronelike chair on a raised platform, surrounded by young ladies-in-waiting, if he had been running for reelection that year. If the opposition press had already exploited a president's family, the manipulation of family life by the president himself had begun. Although James and Sarah Polk were wealthy landowners, he won the 1844 election as "Young Hickory," in the tradition of his populist mentor, Jackson. Sarah Polk consciously set a moral

Ulysses Grant drives a carriage with his son Buck. Grant was once arrested for speeding and commended the policeman for doing his duty.

Library of Congress

tone—no hard liquor, no dancing—and consequently won praise from the conservative religious press, escaping censure for her regal Parisian gowns. There was a successful formula in the Polks: New Hampshirite Franklin Pierce was billed in the 1852 election as "Young Hickory of the Granite State," suggesting he was a populist—despite the fact that he was not—and Rutherford and Lucy Hayes also banned hard liquor, morally counteracting the taint of his allegedly stolen election in 1876.

By the Civil War, First Families were acutely sensitive to the repercussions of public criticism of their lifestyles. When Mary Lincoln overspent in her decorating, Abraham hit the ceiling: "It would stink in the nostrils of the American people to have it said that the President approved a bill over-running an appropriation of $20,000 for flub dubs for this damned old house, when the soldiers cannot have blankets." Although there was an attempt to make a campaign issue out of Mrs. Lincoln's purchase of a personal set of purple china, luckily for the Lincolns the press never discovered the overspending—or the use of other household accounts to compensate for it.

Soon, the idea not only of living royally but of profitably exploiting their positions threatened public rebuke of First Families. The Clevelands made a great profit by selling the private home they had used during his White House tenure, and Edith Roosevelt managed to take a favorite White House sofa home with her when she left: both incidents ignited the press. In contrast, if the profit somehow seemed to offset taxpayer expenses, personal benefit might be permissible: unchallenged in the press was Nellie Taft's 1909 contracting with the White Company to get a government discount on a fleet of cars in exchange for their shameless advertisement of the fact. When that gift was offered by an influential citizen, however, favoritism was often the charge. Not long after the Benjamin Harrisons accepted the outright gift of a Cape May summer house in 1889 from wealthy businessmen, the family was criticized and ridiculed, and Harrison felt pressured enough to pay for the house. Andrew Johnson, in announcing that no government workers were ever to accept gifts from those who might have business dealings with the federal government, decided to set a very public example in refusing an 1865 offer of a beautiful coach and team of horses from a group of New York businessmen.

Conversely, when hardship is mirrored by the First Family, they are praised for setting an example. Thus, though the Wilsons lived a life remote from wartime Washington, their saving gas by using the horse and old victoria, or not serving meat or wheat on certain days, connected them to the daily realities of most Americans. Often criticized for keeping a shabby house—even in the midst of the Great Depression—Eleanor Roosevelt was praised during World War II when she kept the White House to a rigorous food rationing system under government guidelines, making sacrifices for the First Family as all American families themselves were doing.

Finally, although the rooms of the family quarters are intended solely for the private use of the First Families, it is still technically "public housing," as Ronald Reagan called it. As such, the American people feel a certain proprietorship about even these decidedly unpublic rooms. Of all those in the family quarters, the Lincoln Suite is the most symbolically potent. There is a reverence for it akin to a shrine. This explains the angry editorials and press attacks on Nancy Reagan when it was mistakenly reported that she intended to tear down a wall there, or on President Clinton when it was learned that friends—some of whom naturally would be contributors to his 1996 reelection campaign—were overnight guests in the famous bed. That other First Ladies had walls altered, or that all presidents invite friends to sleep in the Lincoln bed, seemed moot. That anyone even appeared to desecrate the sacrosanct room is political ammunition—even though Lincoln never slept in the bed, or even in the room.

Part II
Relationships

Don't mind what he [the president] says. Upstairs here he is just like anyone of us, and we pay no attention to him.

—First Lady Edith Wilson

Richard and Pat Nixon in Key Biscayne, Florida.

LAST APPEARED IN THE NIXON 1968 YEARBOOK

4

The Spouse

If I had to bear the responsibilities of a president without her it would be much more difficult for me.
—*President Jimmy Carter*

The one thing that happens to a president is that his ties with the outside world are cut. And the people you really have are each other. . . . I should think that if people weren't happily married, the White House would really finish it.
—*First Lady Jacqueline Kennedy*

In the White House, the most intimate of family relationships—that between spouses—is under constant surveillance for political significance and is thus often of global interest. Presidential couples often manipulate their marriage for public consumption and political gain, but it is their real interdependence that most impacts an administration.

The forty-one men who have been presidents have largely hesitated to offer up their personal lives for public discourse. For all of the nineteenth century, they sought to prevent public discussion of their wives and children even when these were a potential campaign asset. Not until 1920, in fact, did a presidential candidate publicly discuss how large a contribution his wife made to his political success. That year Warren G. Harding credited his wife as being a "good scout who knows all my faults yet has stuck with me" in his nomination acceptance speech.

If commanders in chief tended publicly to keep their emotions in check, the impact of the love between presidents and their wives can end up affecting a nation. Factors such as separate schedules or the secrets that must be kept for the sake of national security may prevent a

Although often exasperated by her blunt assessments of his cabinet and generals, Abraham Lincoln never asked his wife, Mary Todd, to desist from her quiet inquiries into their characters and motives, and he relied in part on her savvy.

National Archives [Lincoln]; Library of Congress [Mary Lincoln]

president from sharing his burden entirely with his spouse, but presidents have usually drawn on them for advice, support, and emotional strength. While a wife may not always be visible in bad times, she inevitably has contributed to keeping her husband steady, strengthening her marriage and, through it, often, the nation.

In the case of the first White House couple, John and Abigail Adams, the strains were exacerbated by their constant separation. "My dearest Partner," he wrote to her for political advice, "my best, worthiest, wisest friend in this world...I think you shine as a Stateswoman." Through his presidency, sickness and financial difficulties kept Abigail at home in Massachusetts; as Lady Adams she was in the capital cities of Philadelphia and Washington for only eighteen months total. Nevertheless, it still became common knowledge how much Adams depended upon his wife's advice, and the opposition press soon parodied them as "The Happy Old Couple." When the press mentioned that Adams appointed an anti-Federalist diplomat, they made specific notice of the staunch Federalist Mrs. Adams's absence at the time of the appointment.

During his bleak reelection effort in 1932, when Herbert Hoover was futilely struggling to stem the Great Depression, it was his wife who provided emotional comfort to him. At one point on his dismal campaign train, he turned to her and said, "I can't go on." She simply rubbed his back and he found the energy to continue with his day of speeches. Jacqueline Kennedy played a similar role in the weeks following the disastrous Bay of Pigs crisis, which her husband considered his worst failure as president. In inviting guests to dine with them, she made certain first that they would not discuss how the crisis might otherwise have been resolved.

During the endless years of the Vietnam War, Lyndon Johnson often went without eating or sleeping. Had it not been for the purposeful intervention of his wife—sometimes during his military meetings—Johnson would have been on the brink of physical breakdown. LBJ considered passage of a congressional bill for highway beautification she was fostering to be a "matter of personal honor." He told his staff and cabinet, "I love that woman and she wants that Highway Beautification Act . . . By God, we're going to get it for her." It passed. When he was first considering running for president in 1964, having assumed the presidency on Kennedy's death, she wrote him an emotionally honest memo: "Beloved, you are as brave a man as Harry Truman—or FDR—or Lincoln. You can go on to find some peace, some achievement amidst all the pain. You have been strong, patient, determined . . . I honor you for it. So does most of the country. To step out now would be wrong for the country." Four years later, she wrote an equally emotional letter gently urging him to step down. He did so. "We were better together than we were apart," she later said. "He made me grow, he flattered me, shoved me, ridiculed me, loved me into doing things I never thought I was big enough to do."

The presidency makes First Families the targets of all sorts of public attacks, motivated by the social, political, and economic context of the times. Some of the presidents' toughest defenders have been their wives. Abigail Adams wanted newspaper critics of her husband's foreign policy imprisoned for sedition. Sarah Polk articulated a simple defense, with religious

The Lyndon Johnsons in their bedroom at the LBJ Ranch, watching the riots at the 1968 Chicago Democratic National Convention on television. Daughters Luci (left) and Lynda (right) look on. LYNDON BAINES JOHNSON PRESIDENTIAL LIBRARY

allusions, of her husband's controversial Mexican War. Ida McKinley, infirm with phlebitis, epilepsy, and arthritis, minced no words in praising her husband's economic measures and conduct of the Spanish-American War, often embarrassing others with her stridently loving defense of him. Throughout George Bush's presidency, his wife was his most aggressive defender against personal attacks claiming he was weak, as well as attacks on his policies, ranging from the Persian Gulf War to economic trade with Japan.

Usually criticism aimed at First Ladies is intended to damage the president, and in nearly every instance of this, husbands have risen to defend their wives' actions. When Elizabeth Monroe instituted European-style protocol, it provoked harsh reaction in Washington from American congressional leaders who considered it royalist. Monroe understood that she was trying to raise the status of the new nation and earn respect by treating powerful European representatives with the same protocol to which they were accustomed. He defended her. When the situation became critical enough for a cabinet meeting, Monroe refused to ask his wife to change her position. In time, the Monroe etiquette was incorporated into U.S. diplomatic protocol.

From the beginning of their marriage, it was evident that Mary Lincoln was not only highly intelligent and interested in politics, but a woman of high ideals. "My husband placed great confidence in my knowledge of human nature," she later admitted. Had she become First Lady at any time other than the Civil War, Mary Todd may very well have been ranked as one of history's most successful, but with her southern background—yet abolitionist stance—extravagant tastes, and interest in politics, she was the target of a wide variety of attacks. The most serious charge, of course, was that she was a Confederate sympathizer and thus undermining the Union cause. In truth, Mary was passionately pro-Union. According to legend, Lincoln finally appeared before the Senate members of the Committee on the Conduct of War, and declared, "It is untrue that any of my family hold treasonable relations with the enemy."

The Reagans' uniquely interdependent relationship enabled them to weather public crises together. When he was made to appear as if he favored nuclear war with the Soviet Union, or she was portrayed as insensitively spending money during economic hardships, the first to defend one was the other. As he explained, "In some ways, Nancy and I are like one human being: when one of us has a problem, it automatically becomes a problem for the other; an attack on one of us is an attack on the other. When one suffers, so does the other. . . . As in any good marriage, I value her opinion and we talk over everything . . . I'm not sure a man could be a good president without a wife who is willing to express her opinions with frankness. . . . There aren't any

Lou Hoover taking home movies at the presidential retreat, "Camp Rapidan," she planned for her husband's relief from work. 1932.
HERBERT HOOVER PRESIDENTIAL LIBRARY

secrets between us. . . . I just assume she's been cleared for top-secret." Nancy echoed this: "We have a genuine, sharing marriage. I go to his aid. He comes to mine. I have opinions. He has opinions. We don't always agree. But neither marriage nor politics denies a spouse the right to hold an opinion or the right to express it. It's silly to suggest my opinion should not carry some weight with a man I'd been married to for years."

The Reagans' partnership was spawned by their mutual profession as film actors. Few people begin courting with the notion that marriage will lead to the White House. In looking at what drew together some of these marriages, however, there is great evidence of shared pursuits. As early as John and Abigail Adams, with their mutual studies of government and philosophy, and as recently as the Clintons, who met while both were students at Yale Law

School, numerous presidential couples' commitment solidified by sharing such interests: the Hardings in newspaper publishing and music, the Hoovers in mining, the Carters in the agricultural business. This sort of bond has often had a sustaining power during otherwise stormy relationships and can even result in political achievments. Both John and Jackie Kennedy were drawn to the writing profession, and both even worked briefly as reporters. When he was recovering from back surgery, she helped draft his book *Profiles in Courage.* She taught him about French history, and how to paint in oils, and often provided historical and literary material for his speeches. The impact of this symbiosis was in ideas she initiated and he—now more fully appreciating their value—put forth in the administration's promotion of art and history: Pennsylvania Avenue redevelopment, the first presidential arts adviser and council, and preserving Lafayette Square.

At the core of public fascination with the balance of power between presidential spouses is the fear that the spouse may exercise unaccountable control. Certainly among the most passionate relationships, there is some indication of this strength. "You can have but little idea of the influence you have over me," Ulysses Grant wrote his wife from the war front; "absent or present I am more or less governed by what I think is your will." Julia Grant occasionally used this influence in politics, urging him to name a friend to the Supreme Court and to veto a finance bill. Knowing this power, Grant refused to share with her his decision not to run for a third term. Only after his declaration had been publicly released did he tell her. Jimmy Carter, while dependent on his wife's devotion to his well-being, also relied on her blunt assessment of political decisions.

Mamie Eisenhower lets out her trademark husky laugh at Ike's seventieth birthday party. He called her "my invaluable, my indispensable, but publicly inarticulate lifelong partner."
DWIGHT D. EISENHOWER PRESIDENTIAL LIBRARY

Woodrow Wilson was utterly dependent upon the affection and approval of both of his wives, but with the latter, it had global consequences. After his 1919 stroke, Edith Wilson assumed what she called stewardship of the American presidency, deciding which policy issues were important enough to disturb her recuperating husband. Wilson's blind adoration gave her carte blanche to conduct herself in this manner, making her possibly the most powerful—and destructive—First Lady in history. Through a petty personal vendetta, she refused to have the new British ambassador received, he having been sent specifically to help negotiate for Wilson's dream, U.S. entry into a League of Nations.

James and Lucretia Garfield, with their mutual devotion to the classics as the basis for their early years together, grew to become extraordinarily close lovers in their brief months in the White House. In the early part of their marriage, however, Garfield had strayed into adultery with one Lucia Calhoun, and rumors circulated in the 1880 campaign that the Garfields would divorce after election day. In fact, there had been such a turnaround that Lucretia felt compelled to write herself a sort of prayer: "My husband! In his changed, purified cherishing affection I abide content. Thank God it is past now that long arctic night amid the frozen ice-flows of estrangement . . . at last the clear 'Open Sea' of married love and trust . . ."

Oftentimes, White House marital troubles had primarily to do with the pressures that came with the position. "The loving relationship between Ike and Mamie," said their son, John, "was rarely smooth." When he asked her to take on some of his public appearances, she snapped, "Don't push me, Ike!" Yet if she was running late just a few moments, his famous temper flared. She, said John, "could more than hold her own with him in private." Behind the scenes she fought for herself. "It wasn't that I didn't have my own ideas, but in my own era, the man was the head of the household," she explained. "I did all the things that ladies did then when they want their little way. I cried, and I argued—finally got my way." Each

A life study sketch by Edward Williams Clay of President Jackson, 1831, and a Washington B. Cooper portrait of his late wife, Rachel. NATIONAL PORTRAIT GALLERY [JACKSON]; AND TENNESSEE STATE MUSEUM COLLECTION [RACHEL JACKSON]

morning in the White House Ike sentimentally brought her a pink carnation, and every Valentine's Day he surprised her by wearing his "love bug" boxer shorts embroidered with red hearts. Mamie enjoyed sharing their bed because she could "reach over and pat Ike on his old bald head."

It was immediately apparent that John Quincy Adams and his wife, Louisa, were ill suited in temperament, his aloofness offending her, a self-described "romantic animal" who felt neglected. "Family is and must ever be secondary consideration to a zealous Patriot," she wrote. "I was not patriotic enough to endure such heavy personal trials for the political welfare of the Nation, whose honor was dearly bought at the expense of all domestic happiness." She enthusiastically supported his 1824 run for the presidency, but advised that he actively campaign—which he abhorred and equated with begging. "Do for once gratify," she asked with sarcastic exasperation. In the White House, the Adamses even became estranged one summer, vacationing separately and signing their letters to each other formally. When Adams was attacked in the press during his reelection campaign, however, Louisa wrote a defending magazine account of their marriage.

When a strain was obvious between a presidential couple, rumors of divorce were inevitable. Such rumors briefly circulated about the Coolidges. Despite the fact that they had a highly sensitive and tender love for each other, Calvin and Grace Coolidge were a seemingly disparate couple. He often put her down publicly, and while this was intended as humor, outsiders saw condescension in it. The reality was that he desperately leaned upon her ease with strangers to pull him through a lifelong crippling shyness that seemed to border on social

Gerald Ford's "Definition of a Successful Marriage"

A successful marriage cannot thrive on simply a mutuality of interests, important as that ingredient is over the years for compatibility. There must be understanding, compassion and emotion which fits under the umbrella of love.

A marriage that has these attributes can weather the storm clouds that are inevitable in an intimate relationship. They can strongly bond a man and wife who are challenged by temporary disagreements, financial problems, individual illnesses, children disappointments [*sic*] and career opportunities and failures. There must be a belief on the part of both that there is nothing of a higher priority than the sanctity and continuation of the relationship.

Gerald and Betty Ford eat dinner from trays in their bedroom.

phobia. Politically, this played out positively. Grace was popular among the voters, as well as with officials who had to deal with the president. She offset his peculiarly cranky tendencies. Privately, there was a sad poignancy to the dynamic. "I hoped to teach him to enjoy life," Grace admitted. "He was not very easy to instruct in that way."

Bess Truman had deeply resented her husband's accepting the 1944 nomination as vice president when FDR was visibly in failing health. When Truman succeeded to the presidency, she reacted with passive anger to the expectation he now placed on her as First Lady. During his first Christmas as president, when Truman returned to Washington from celebrating the holiday with Bess in Missouri, he wrote her—obviously after a tiff:

> *Well I'm here in the White House, the great white sepulcher of ambitions and reputations. . . . You can never appreciate what it means to come home as I did the other evening after doing at least one hundred things I didn't want to do and have the only person in the world whose approval and good opinion I value look at me like I'm something the cat dragged in and tell me I've come in at last because I couldn't find any reason to stay away. . . . you . . . must give me help and assistance: because no one ever needed help and assistance as I do now. If I can get . . . a little help from those I have on a pedestal at home, the job will be done.*

Despite this, the Trumans, both in their sixties, enjoyed a healthy intimacy. One morning a rather demure First Lady told the chief usher, "[W]e have a little problem. . . . It's the president's bed. Do you think you can get it fixed today? Two of the slats broke down during the night."

If the presidency can isolate a president from real life, sometimes a crisis can isolate him from his wife. Although before and after his presidency there is ample evidence of Richard Nixon's surprisingly passionate love for his wife, Pat, during the worst days of the Watergate crisis he cut himself off even from her.

"And when the winds blow and the rains fall and the sun shines through the clouds (as it is now)," Nixon had written to her of himself as they courted, "he still resolves as he did then, that nothing so fine ever happened to him or anyone else as falling in love with Thee—my dearest heart." A month before their wedding, he predicted:

> *From the first days, I knew you were destined to be a great lady— You have always had that extra something . . . I want to work with you toward the destiny you are bound to fulfill. As I have told you many times—living together will make us both grow—and by reason of it we shall realize our dreams. You are a great inspiration to me, and though you don't believe it yet, I someday shall return some of the benefit you have conferred on me. It is our job to go forth together and accomplish great ends and we shall do it too. Whatever happens, I shall always be with you—loving you more every hour and attempting to let you feel that love in your heart and life.*

Throughout Nixon's career, Pat's absolute faith in him proved crucial. Moments before giving his famous "Checkers" speech defending himself against charges of using a slush fund, he panicked. Pat forcefully urged him on and steadied him. "Without her," he admitted, "I could not have done what I did." Still, she came to despise politics for disrupting her family life. Knowing this, as the Watergate scandal ensued he withdrew from her, depending on devious aides and their bad judgment. She had advised him to burn his taped conversations before they were subpoenaed as evidence. His ignoring of her advice changed history.

In the twentieth century, several presidential wives endured the anguish of adultery. There was no worse situation than that experienced by Florence Harding. In reaction to Warren Harding's series of outside relationships, his wife developed the courage to confront him. When he returned late one night from being out with two Palm Beach society women, the First Lady berated him in front of friends, "Where have you been? Out with a lot of hussies, I think!" Alice Roosevelt Longworth, often at private parties of the Hardings', later confirmed the wild tale of the First Lady's breaking up an office assignation, and one night, as Harding was slipping out of the house, she yelled down the hall, within earshot of the servants, that she knew "all about that girl of yours!" Even on his fatal western trip, during a stop in Yellowstone National Park, as the president flirted with several waitresses, the First Lady bawled him out in front of the press corps: "Warren, I watched you while those girls were here! It took you just as long to say goodbye to those girls as it did for you to run through three thousand tourists yesterday at Old Faithful!" Despite all of this, the Hardings were devoted—if not intimately, then with an emotional loyalty to each other.

> ## Presidents Without Wives in the White House
>
> Thomas Jefferson, widowed
> Andrew Jackson, widowed
> Martin Van Buren, widowed
> William Henry Harrison; wife didn't come to Washington
> James Buchanan, bachelor
> Chester Arthur, widowed

Oddly, although FDR's earlier love affair with his wife's secretary halted further intimacy between the Roosevelts, it forged an effective partnership between them. It was only after the marital rupture that Eleanor developed her truly independent voice and consistent political activism, which dovetailed with her husband's New Deal agenda. FDR did sometimes resent the White House residency of Eleanor's companion Lorena Hickok, and her continuing closeness to New York state trooper Earl Miller. He however made no attempt to hide his affectionate relationship with his in-residence secretary, Missy LeHand, who thought nothing at all of visiting his room in her nightclothes, or sitting on his lap. Still, the Roosevelts' genuine abiding respect, love, and understanding of each other—as reflected in their deeds for, and letters to, each other—helped the nation, and then the world, in some very dark hours when they led together as a united front.

Like Harding and FDR, John F. Kennedy had outside relationships that were unknown to the general public during his presidency, although there is indication that his wife was aware of them. Both the media and the White House disseminated an image of the attractive young couple as blissfully happy—and indeed they did share a full intimacy. When both were in residence they lunched together and then, with strict orders for uninterrupted privacy, closed themselves in their bedroom alone for an hour with each other. Only a handful of household staff knew about this ritual. Ironically, although it would have countered some of the impact when news of his assignations later did break publicly, Jackie Kennedy, determined to preserve the privacy of her marriage, asked historian and Kennedy biographer Arthur M. Schlesinger Jr. not to write about their post-lunch hour in the bedroom. In her own oblique way, however, she acknowledged this intimacy: before leaving the White House, she placed a plaque on the bedroom mantel stating that she and her husband "lived" in that room.

More recently, when President Clinton, pressured by mounting scandal, had to take the unprecedented act of disclosing an outside relationship, his marriage sustained intense global scrutiny. In large part, this was due to their poised adherence to a "zone of privacy," which Mrs. Clinton valued highly. Thus, any marital strain was resolved discreetly between the couple. In the tense days following his confession in August 1998, the First Lady released a single public statement of her personal commitment to her husband. It was speculated that had she not done so in the midst of the crisis, the president would not have had enough public or congressional support to stay in office.

Even those women publicly removed from their husbands' work affected it. "My wife was as much a soldier as I was," admitted President Taylor in reflecting on Margaret "Peggy" Taylor's life in army camps and forts with him. Though she rarely appeared at public events with him, upstairs in their private rooms she "took every opportunity to drop a good word in company that might help her husband," recalled a friend. Eliza Johnson was broken with tuberculosis, yet during her husband's impeachment trial she convinced him that he'd be acquitted, and she had the ability to calm his rage against political enemies just by patting his shoulders. During the trial, she read to him each morning from praiseful editorials and other articles in his favor.

Four presidents—Jefferson, Jackson, Van Buren, and Arthur—entered the presidency as widowers. Except for Van Buren, these losses affected aspects of their presidencies.

Jefferson's publicly controversial relationship with his slave Sally Hemings may have been based in part on association to his late wife, Martha: Martha Jefferson and Sally Hemings were half-sisters. Hemings, who was three-quarters white, probably had a physical resemblance to Mrs. Jefferson.

Rachel Jackson had unwittingly committed bigamy when she married Andrew Jackson; the divorce from her first husband was not yet secured. For the rest of Jackson's political career, his enemies made insinuations that she was a loose woman. She died weeks before his inauguration. When the personal character of the navy secretary's wife, Peggy Eaton, was attacked by several other cabinet wives, President Jackson fired their husbands, considering theirs an act of disloyalty aimed at his late wife. He even fired the Librarian of Congress for gossiping about her.

Haunted by the memory of his late wife, Ellen, Chester Arthur donated a stained-glass window in her memory to St. John's Church, across the park from the White House. At night he often glanced at it, illuminated by candles inside the church, from his bedroom on the north side of the mansion. He kept her silver-framed oval photograph at his bedside and ordered that fresh flowers be placed before it each morning. Beneath the glitter of his Gilded Age lifestyle, Arthur was a broken man because of his wife's death. "Honors to me," he said of his loss, "are not what they once were."

Chelsea Clinton in her White House bedroom, talking on the phone to her father as she prepares for the 1997 inaugural festivities. His taped inaugural speech appears on television.

THE WHITE HOUSE

5

The Children

One of the worst things in the world is being the child of a President! It's a terrible life they lead!
—President Franklin D. Roosevelt

I scarcely know my own children, or they me.
—President Zachary Taylor

When the general public and press feel they have the right to analyze how "successful" children of presidents are, the pressure on those children can sometimes prove daunting. Both young and adult children who are members of First Families can maintain more routine lives than their parents, but how they live—and are raised—remains potent fodder for the media and the opposition party as well as for internal presidential public relations.

Thomas Jefferson was acutely aware of this. In devising *The Canons of Etiquette to Be Observed by the Executive,* he created rule twelve, which said First Families "take precedence everywhere in public or private." It was a hypocritical ruling for a self-professed egalitarian who had otherwise claimed his private life and behavior to be unconnected to his public life. As it turned out, there was little chance for his rule to be tested, since his daughter Martha Randolph made only two White House visits in eight years, and her sister, Maria, only one. He had meted out

Martha Randolph, Jefferson's daughter, drawn from life by Julien Fevret de Saint Memin. 1801–1804.
LAST APPEARED IN NOW OUT-OF-PRINT
JEFFERSON BIOGRAPHY, 1920S

Mary Todd Lincoln and her sons Willie, left, and Tad, right. 1861.

strict ideas to his daughters on how women should please men in everything from grammar to appearance to needlework, using a mixture of guilt and ego to motivate: "Keep my letters and read them at times, that you may always have present in your mind those things which will endear you to me. . . . The acquirements which I hope you will make . . . will render you more worthy of my love."

Rather than rebel, the daughters drew devotedly closer to their father than to their husbands, and became so psychologically wrapped up in him that they seemingly served the emotional role of wives. During his presidency, he constantly turned to Martha especially to quell his insecurities. Even by mail, she was probably the crucial personal factor stabilizing him during his presidency.

The same approach, applied by another president to his *sons*, backfired. As he was raised, John Quincy Adams harshly barked orders or sent sharp letters to his three sons, instructing them on how to behave, but it was their mother who connected with them emotionally and contended with their weaknesses—John, an alcoholic; George, who used opium to sleep and fathered a child by a maid; and Charles, who kept a working-class mistress. When Louisa Adams found one of their books of "disgusting pictures of nature" she warned that it would destroy their "relish for moderate and virtuous enjoyment." Still, she was particularly close to the sensitive George, and they often exchanged poetry. When, under pressure from his father, George collapsed in depression, he seemed unable to carry out his appointed task to oversee the moving of his family's possessions into their post–White House home. Onboard the steamer bound for Washington, the twenty-eight-year-old likely committed suicide: he went overboard and drowned.

In contrast was the parenting of the Lincolns. As one associate of the president observed, "He worshipped his children." Of the two youngest, Willie (ten years old when he came to the White House) and Thomas, or "Tad" (so nicknamed by Lincoln because he looked "like a little tadpole"), eight, once kept up an uproar of mischief on a train. One passenger noticed that Lincoln, "instead of spanking the brats, looked pleased as Punch, aided and abetted the older one in his mischief." Mary Lincoln explained, "It's my pleasure that my children are free, happy and unrestrained by parental tyranny. Love is the chain whereby to bind a child to its parent." White House secretary Noah Brooks discerned that Lincoln's unusually open expression of love toward them helped him cope. "Let him romp," the president said of wild Tad, in comparison to the remote eldest, Robert,

who was at Harvard during the presidency. "Bobby used to be just like him, but look at him now." In getting through the horrifying trials of civil war and his own bouts of depression, Lincoln's day was brightened when Tad came running into his office and with a total lack of self-consciousness hugged and kissed his father.

In stark contrast to the Lincoln leniency was the tough love of the Hayeses, who entered the White House with a young daughter and son, Fanny and Scott, nine and six respectively. Although privately tutored, Scott had many difficulties in learning. His father gently, patiently encouraged him to keep studying. When he later went to boarding school, Hayes told Scott, "First of all, keep your conscience at the helm. . . . Do not be uneasy for salary or promotion. . . . Watch workmen, learn all facts, be practical as well as a man of theories." He gave similar instruction to the eldest of his three older sons, Birch, a Harvard law student: "I want you to resolve always to do what you know is right. No matter what you lose by it, no matter what danger there is, always do right. . . . Be kind to your brothers . . . and above all your mother." Within the close-knit family each child was respected as an individual—and the president had no parental problems to distract him.

Theodore Roosevelt's children had a mother who counterbalanced his exuberant encouragement of their antics. The Roosevelts were the largest family of younger children to live in the house: Alice, seventeen; Ted, fourteen; Kermit, twelve; Ethel, ten; Archie, seven; and Quentin, three. TR did consider a degree of harshness necessary to make each son into the idealized stalwart man—though he didn't necessarily want to employ it himself. When the president received a letter from Quentin's teacher recommending that Roosevelt discipline the boy for dancing in class and doodling instead of working on math, he responded: "Don't you think it would be well to subject him to stricter discipline—that is, to punish him yourself. . . . Mrs. Roosevelt and I have no scruples against corporal punishment. We will stand behind you entirely in doing whatever you decide is necessary. . . . If you find him defying your authority or committing any serious misdeed, then let me know and I will whip him; but it hardly seems wise to me to start in whipping him for everyday offenses which in point of seriousness look as if they could be met by discipline in school and not by extreme measures taken at home." Whipping his son was not so much a distraction from Roosevelt's duties as it was an unpleasant task for what he considered just boyish mischief.

As is true in any family, only children of presidents are often especially close to their parents. Despite both of their demanding schedules, for example, the Clintons limited the length of their official overseas trips while their daughter, Chelsea, was still in high school and living with them in the mansion—or always tried to schedule trips during vacation periods when she could come along. They also avoided going to Camp David in the first term because Chelsea wanted to spend weekends in Washington with many of her friends, and her parents did not want to leave her home alone. Mamie Eisenhower readily admitted that she had "smother loved" her son, John. Determined to keep away from publicity, John Eisenhower returned daily to his family of four children and his wife in their suburban Virginia rambler house during his stint at the Pentagon, instead of having them all live in the nearby White House. He admitted that his family connection caused a "decided conflict of loyalties" at work, given the inevitable friction between the Pentagon and the White House. When Ike was elected president, John had been removed from the front lines of the Korean War. During the campaign, Ike had told him, "If you're captured, I would just drop out of the presidential race."

> ### Presidents and First Ladies Who Had No Living Birth Children Together at Time of Presidency
>
> George and Martha Washington
> James and Dolley Madison
> Andrew Jackson
> James and Sarah Polk
> Franklin and Jane Pierce (children deceased)
> James Buchanan (unmarried)
> Grover and Frances Cleveland (first term only)
> William and Ida McKinley (children deceased)
> Woodrow and Edith Wilson
> Warren and Florence Harding

In October 1958, when John came to work for his father as assistant staff secretary, Ike shared confidential information with him, relying on family loyalty. "Working in the White House is pretty heady stuff, being so close to the throne and not having to go through twelve great minds to get your boss your ideas," John recalled. Still, he was not treated as special. If he came into the Oval Office in the morning, Ike often snapped at him, "What the hell do you want?" John recalled of this unique work-family arrangement, "In person I always called him 'Dad,' ... speaking of him in the third person, I would use the common term 'the Boss.' ... I became conscious one day that I was getting more than my share of the bad news to take in [to him from other staff] ... I found it amusing but quickly decided it was inevitable. The only problem was with the Boss himself. He was a man who . . . chose to leave his worries at the office. From the White House days to the end, I think he unconsciously associated me with work—and bad news at that!"

Certainly one of the closest of parent-child relationships existed in the Nixon family. Despite the anti–Vietnam War protests fueled by contemporaries of his daughters, Tricia and Julie, and even through the emotional wall he created during Watergate, the girls stood loyally by him. "It was hard for young people to grow up and lead useful lives during the spiritual turmoil of the 1960s and 1970s, and particularly so for children of celebrities who are always in the spotlight," recalled Richard Nixon in old age. "With their father subject to massive political and personal attack, it is a miracle that Tricia and Julie came through as they did. They have survived it all with the strength and serenity of their mother." In the darkest last days of his administration, as others began abandoning him, Nixon's daughters had such an unconditional love for him that they accepted his explanation of his role in the cover-up of the scandal and bucked him up emotionally—as much as he would permit—insisting that he not resign.

Like Pat Nixon, Lady Bird Johnson was often torn by the constant separation from her daughters that political life required. When First Ladies have to choose between a perceived duty to either husband or children, they often choose the former on the premise that it is, after all, the "family business." Before she ran off to some event—across town or the world— Lady Bird would tell her daughters, "Remember—you are loved." Seemingly cavalierly, but actually speaking with pride, her father quipped, "Lynda is so smart she always can take care of herself. Luci's so feminine some man will always want to make a living for her." Luci admitted, "I get along best with Daddy," and it was to her that Lyndon Johnson turned for momentary solace during the Vietnam War. Late at night, in the middle of one crisis, he asked her, a Catholic convert, to take him to a local church, where he knelt with her in prayer for strength, and sought guidance from local monks who knew Luci.

Similarly, Franklin D. Roosevelt grew to depend on the companionship and bright personality of his daughter, Anna, during World War II. She served as his hostess, confidante, and traveling companion to even such a top-secret meeting as the 1944 Yalta Conference with Churchill and Stalin. Her company, said brother Jimmy, provided their father with "that touch of triviality he needed to lighten his burden." FDR took each one of his children as his official companion on various public trips. Nevertheless, FDR's closeness to them was limited to superficial jovialities. "Father had great difficulty in talking about anything purely personal or private," said Franklin Jr., "especially if it involved anything unpleasant. He left that to Mother."

Indeed, whatever shortcomings she felt she had as a young mother, Eleanor tried to address them as First Lady. As Chief Usher J. B. West recalled, "Whenever one of them was sick, she was right at their side, even if it was clear across the country." Yet both parents were careful never to censor their children—even when the latter publicly criticized their parents' views. "I am not good at giving advice," the First Lady told reporters who asked what motherly advice she gave her recently married son John. "I believe in letting them work out their own plans." When her son Elliott divorced and remarried quickly, she said it forced her to accept any change her children made in their own lives, "without making them feel guilty about it."

Still, with both Roosevelts reluctant to control their children, the parents had to face not only the repercussions of their actions, but potentially negative publicity. "Will you speak seriously & firmly to F. Jr. & John about drinking and fast driving?" Eleanor penned her husband. Only when pressed by her did the father softly scold one son—putting it all off on the mother: "Your Mother tells me I must ask you to give me your license until you have learned your lesson." On the other hand, when a policeman who stopped Franklin Jr. for speeding discovered his identity, he took the president's son home for dinner. Mrs. Roosevelt concluded that her children were "five individualists who were given too many privileges on the one hand and too much criticism on the other." When the Roosevelt boys needed to see their father, they had to make an appointment; their mother was virtually on call to them. In retrospect, Jimmy Roosevelt confessed that his father "should have been a lot tougher with all of us. . . . he should have counseled us more instead of leaving us free to steer our own courses." Ironically, however, considering all the trials in the personal lives and public criticism of his children, FDR's remoteness toward them permitted him to keep family matters from distracting him during the Depression and World War II.

The difficulties faced by a child having to adjust to a new parent through remarriage were no different for First Families. Following his wife's lead, James Madison indulged Payne, her son by a first marriage. Lacking any discipline, he became the bane of Madison's life. Twelve years old when he became the presidential stepson, the vain, snobbish, and soon-to-be alcoholic boy was dubbed the American Prince by the press when he was finally shipped off to Europe as an attaché during the War of 1812 peace negotiations. Across the Continent he fell in love with a Russian princess, who was said to be abducted and "never seen again," then gallivanted with a forty-eight-year-old German "authoress." Madison became alarmed when instead of letters home, he received Payne's gambling debts—for which the youth would later be repeatedly imprisoned. When he failed to appear one Christmas Eve, even Dolley Madison grew angry over "how long my only child has been absent from the home of his mother." She still made excuses for his behavior. "My poor son," she wrote. "Forgive him his eccentricities. His heart is good and he means no harm."

Although her stepmother, Edith Roosevelt, was the only mother that Alice Roosevelt Longworth ever knew, stories of friction between the two were legion. While it was true that Alice often created scandalous publicity by doing such things as dancing on motorcars and jumping into pools fully clothed, it was less known that Edith did not always make Alice feel welcome in the home of her father. When she finally married, and officially left the house, Alice turned to hug her stepmother. Mrs. Roosevelt snapped, "I want you to know that I'm glad to see you leave. You have never been anything but trouble." With her later-alcoholic son

Portraits by unknown artists of Robert and Lizzie Tyler, a son and a daughter of President John Tyler.
LAST APPEARED IN *Priscilla Tyler*, 1955, AND *White House Brides*, 1966

Kermit, Edith could be far more lenient: "I know he's a naughty boy, but I just love him."

There was not even the illusion of civility between Letty Tyler Semple and her father's young second wife. Although the three other daughters of the first Mrs. Tyler—Lizzie, Mary, and Alice—eventually came to accept the shocking news that a twenty-four-year-old New York debutante named Julia Gardiner was to be their new stepmother, Letty never would. She refused to stand in the presence of, or in any other way respect, Julia—particularly if her father was not around. Even Letty's husband found her spiteful. "Your remarks relative to Mrs. T are not worthy of a daughter of John Tyler," the estranged James Semple later wrote her.

No fight between a parent in the White House and a stepchild garnered more international attention than that which occurred in 1984 between Nancy and Michael Reagan, the son of the president's first marriage. Although there had been tension between the two of them stemming from earlier unresolved problems, it was the fact that they happened to be a First Family which actuated the circumstances of their feud. Michael had been wrongly accused by Secret Service agents of stealing small items (no charges had ever been filed and the matter was later dropped). When this was reported to the Reagans, they believed it and contact with Michael was limited. Although he joined the family to be photographed for publicity during the 1984 convention, weeks after Reagan had been reelected Michael angrily told reporters that his stepmother was the reason they weren't invited to share Thanksgiving. This in turn prompted Nancy Reagan to tell the press that there was, that fall, an "estrangement."

Presidents Who Adopted Children, or Had Stepchildren or Legal Wards

George Washington, adopted wife's grandson and granddaughter from a previous marriage
James Madison, adopted wife's son from previous marriage
Andrew Jackson, adopted wife's nephew
James Polk, legal guardian of orphaned nephew
James Buchanan, legal guardian of orphaned niece and nephew
William McKinley, legal guardian of orphaned niece and nephew
Warren Harding, adopted wife's son from previous marriage (deceased by time of presidency)
Ronald Reagan, adopted son with first wife

*the term "adopted" is used loosely to indicate either legal or informal parenthood

Reagan's children spoke publicly about a gulf between them and their father. Once when daughter Patti raised the subject of their not being close, he simply showed her pictures of them standing close together as proof that they were. Yet it wasn't that Reagan didn't feel emotional love for them—in fact, he kept a framed childhood poem of Patti's on his desk in the Oval Office. Rather, she observed, he refused to engage them in depth because he hated confrontation, a habit stemming from his need to create even artificial happiness since his childhood with an alcoholic father. Only into his second term, when his daughter Maureen was frequently in town, did any children visit him regularly: his bond and reliance were never with them but with his wife—a point even more dramatically illustrated during his presidency.

Calvin Coolidge more consciously distanced himself from his son. Shortly after the death of his younger son, he ordered the older boy, John, away, to return to his summer job. Only through the intercession of Mrs. Coolidge—to whom the teenager was extremely close—was John able to stay with his grieving mother for a longer time.

Through nearly all of his only son Dick's life, Zachary Taylor had been a controlling yet distant father. At ten Dick was sent away from fort life in the wilderness to a private school in Louisville. In the next eleven years, he saw his father only once, briefly, before being shuttled off to Boston prep school. "In consequence of having been separated from him," Taylor admitted, "I am not sufficiently acquainted with the progress he has made." When he entered Yale, handsome, natty, hot-tempered Dick did not write his parents for a year and a half—and Taylor seemed not to care.

convention, weeks after Reagan had been reelected Michael angrily told reporters that his stepmother was the reason they weren't invited to share Thanksgiving. This in turn prompted Nancy Reagan to tell the press that there was, that fall, an "estrangement."

Presidents Who Adopted Children, or Had Stepchildren or Legal Wards

George Washington, adopted wife's grandson and granddaughter from a previous marriage

James Madison, adopted wife's son from previous marriage

Andrew Jackson, adopted wife's nephew

James Polk, legal guardian of orphaned nephew

James Buchanan, legal guardian of orphaned niece and nephew

William McKinley, legal guardian of orphaned niece and nephew

Warren Harding, adopted wife's son from previous marriage (deceased by time of presidency)

Ronald Reagan, adopted son with first wife

*the term "adopted" is used loosely to indicate either legal or informal parenthood

Reagan's children spoke publicly about a gulf between them and their father. Once when daughter Patti raised the subject of their not being close, he simply showed her pictures of them standing close together as proof that they were. Yet it wasn't that Reagan didn't feel emotional love for them—in fact, he kept a framed childhood poem of Patti's on his desk in the Oval Office. Rather, she observed, he refused to engage them in depth because he hated confrontation, a habit stemming from his need to create even artificial happiness since his childhood with an alcoholic father. Only into his second term, when his daughter Maureen was frequently in town, did any children visit him regularly: his bond and reliance were never with them but with his wife—a point even more dramatically illustrated during his presidency.

Calvin Coolidge more consciously distanced himself from his son. Shortly after the death of his younger son, he ordered the older boy, John, away, to return to his summer job. Only through the intercession of Mrs. Coolidge—to whom the teenager was extremely close—was John able to stay with his grieving mother for a longer time.

Through nearly all of his only son Dick's life, Zachary Taylor had been a controlling yet distant father. At ten Dick was sent away from fort life in the wilderness to a private school in Louisville. In the next eleven years, he saw his father only once, briefly, before being shuttled off to Boston prep school. "In consequence of having been separated from him," Taylor admitted, "I am not sufficiently acquainted with the progress he has made." When he entered Yale, handsome, natty, hot-tempered Dick did not write his parents for a year and a half— and Taylor seemed not to care.

Portraits by unknown artists of Robert and Lizzie Tyler, a son and a daughter of President John Tyler.
LAST APPEARED IN *Priscilla Tyler*, 1955, AND *White House Brides*, 1966

Kermit, Edith could be far more lenient: "I know he's a naughty boy, but I just love him."

There was not even the illusion of civility between Letty Tyler Semple and her father's young second wife. Although the three other daughters of the first Mrs. Tyler—Lizzie, Mary, and Alice—eventually came to accept the shocking news that a twenty-four-year-old New York debutante named Julia Gardiner was to be their new stepmother, Letty never would. She refused to stand in the presence of, or in any other way respect, Julia—particularly if her father was not around. Even Letty's husband found her spiteful. "Your remarks relative to Mrs. T are not worthy of a daughter of John Tyler," the estranged James Semple later wrote her.

No fight between a parent in the White House and a stepchild garnered more international attention than that which occurred in 1984 between Nancy and Michael Reagan, the son of the president's first marriage. Although there had been tension between the two of them stemming from earlier unresolved problems, it was the fact that they happened to be a First Family which actuated the circumstances of their feud. Michael had been wrongly accused by Secret Service agents of stealing small items (no charges had ever been filed and the matter was later dropped). When this was reported to the Reagans, they believed it and contact with Michael was limited. Although he joined the family to be photographed for publicity during the 1984

When he was home with his mother, however, Dick was given instructions on how to spend his time in letters from his father, who attempted to keep him clear of any idleness. When they finally saw each other after six years, Taylor's reaction was, "if he has learned nothing else he has learned to chew, to use tobacco. . . . I have not as yet made up my mind as to the occupation in life it would be best for him to adopt or pursue." A strained, passive-aggressive relationship had set in; Dick often became ill when stress arose; his father was frequently exasperated with him. Taylor concluded that it was "better to make no very great calculations as regards the prominent positions our children are to occupy . . . they are but rarely realized." When Taylor became president, however, he made certain Dick did not become a celebrated First Son; he insisted that the young man run the family's Mississippi plantation. "I do not want him to locate at or near Washington," Taylor wrote his son-in-law, "or to fill any office." Not invited to his father's inaugural, Dick simply turned up in person one day at the White House, ostensibly to report on a devastating flood that wrecked their property. He was soon sent home. He never saw his father again, missing his death and funeral in Washington.

Richard Taylor, whose father said he and his son hardly knew each other.
HISTORIC NEW ORLEANS RESEARCH CENTER

Described by a reporter as having "eyes as soft as dewdrops," Andrew Jackson Jr., the president's adopted son and namesake, was also sent by his father to manage the family plantation, the Hermitage, in Nashville, Tennessee. At nineteen, however, Andy Jr. was so preoccupied with girls that he stopped in Virginia to pursue one he had recently met. Shocked at his forwardness, the girl spurned him. It required an apology from the president, explaining his son's lack of courting experience, to soothe her family. Andy Jackson was no better at farm management, running up huge bills and putting the president into debt. Jackson encouraged Andy to return to live in the White House, prompted perhaps not only by the president's desire to spend time with his new daughter-in-law, Sarah; it also kept his son's spending in check.

Examples abound, however, of presidents who kept their children close to home, even as adults. James Monroe's daughter Eliza Hay was not only the social manager of the mansion but—with an abrasiveness that deterred poking into the president's life—became a public voice for him. Questioned on the whereabouts of her husband, George, the president's primary adviser, Eliza finally snapped, "He is dead. And I'll hear nothing more of it." She never

Although Maureen Reagan was a step-daughter to Nancy Reagan, they became close during the White House years. 1984.
RONALD REAGAN
PRESIDENTIAL LIBRARY

For her son Ron's birthday, Nancy Reagan took him and his wife, Doria, for a blimp ride over Washington. 1981.
RONALD REAGAN
PRESIDENTIAL LIBRARY

did say where he was. Millard Fillmore turned to his son, Powers, fresh out of law school, as a sounding board, and put him to work as the official presidential secretary. Earlier, John Tyler had done the same thing with his namesake—but more to keep the reckless young man close at hand. Estranged from his wife, alcoholic John Tyler Jr. once was found by his father to be soliciting the Pottsville, Pennsylvania, postmaster to place an order for seventy-five copies of the president's biography. In contrast, James Garfield was so attached to his boys that he frequently joined in their pillow fights, and he convinced the eldest two, Harry and Jim, to live at home in the White House instead of going away to school as planned. Woodrow Wilson was emotionally dependent on his three daughters, Margaret, Nell, and Jessie, not only for loyal support but their laughter at his limericks, dialect singing, and mimickry. In a similar vein, Taft was much closer to his three children, Helen, Robert, and Charlie, than they were to their mother. As the formidable Mrs. Taft admitted, the four of them always found humor in situations she distinctly did not. During his 1976 election campaign, Gerald Ford prevailed upon his middle son, Jack, to return home and help manage the campaign.

The delight that Jack Kennedy found in his two young children was widely known through media accounts of his daughter, Caroline, interrupting a press conference wearing her mother's high heels, and photos of his son, John, famously crawling under the cavity of his Oval Office desk. Yet it was in the early morning when the trio spent their quality time together. As Kennedy was having his breakfast, the children rushed in and turned on the TV set to watch cartoons as they ate with him. When he went in for his bath, they followed, playing with their floating animal toys in the tub. By the time he dressed, the TV was featuring an exercise program, and Kennedy got a kick out of watching the children tumble around the floor, mimicking the host, as their mother began to wake up. Finally, he usually took one or the other by the hand and walked with them, as he headed from the mansion to his office in the West Wing.

Widower Martin Van Buren made his four adult sons his closest friends, companions, and advisers. All lived in the White House with him. Shy and scholarly Martin organized his father's papers with the intention of someday helping him write a book. Abraham worked as his father's private secretary and military aide. As for law student Smith, Van Buren instructed him on study as any father would—in any age, on any subject: "The only way to acquire fondness for law is to read constantly. A month's study is made completely unprofitable by a moment's abstinence . . . To resolve yourself to it you must keep at it. Keeping at it, you will grow half fond of it."

If a President and First Lady never lose their responsibilities as parents, conversely they also can learn from their children. Jimmy Carter frequently gathered his daughter, Amy, sons Chip and Jeff, and their wives, Caron and Annette, together to discuss "our individual roles and our common responsibilities." They were not only his "strongest supporters" but "most severe critics," and Carter drew on their everyday observations and experiences: Chip worked for the

Democratic National Committee, Jeff was a college student, and Amy was an inner-city public school student. Often, there were routine discussions as there would be around any family table, but as Carter reflected in his memoirs, "[W]e were in a unique position to act on the ideas generated within our small group. There is no doubt that the members of my family helped me to be a better President."

Gerald Ford hugs his son Steve and sees him off as he leaves home. 1975.
GERALD R. FORD LIBRARY

Ford the Father

In preparation for his published memoirs, Gerald Ford drafted several introspective personal reflections. He had three sons, Michael, Jack, and Steve, the last two living in the White House for a time.

Advice to a Young Man Going
Off on His Own

Look upon "going off on your own" as a new challenge with optimism and opportunity. The right mental attitude is crucial. You must believe in yourself and you must have conviction that "out there" there is a "pot of gold" at the end of the rainbow. It matters not that our goals are different. Eventually they cover the spectrum of life.

You must recognize along the path of life there will be disappointments and the best way to avoid another is to plan better and work harder. Remember—the harder you work the luckier you are.

You must set a goal realizing that it will be different for each individual. Satisfaction and happiness are the best targets. For one the target is material wealth. For another it means public recognition. To another it is achieved by unlocking the mysteries of science. Others might prefer a quiet life.

Whatever your objective get up everyday pledging to yourself "I am going to make progress" and remember one fundamental—one must learn to walk before trying to run.

Lyn Nugent watches his grandfather LBJ howl with favorite dog, Yuki. 1968.
LYNDON BAINES JOHNSON PRESIDENTIAL LIBRARY

6

The Grandchildren

[My grandson is] a jolly boy, not a bit spoiled, and he and I had some famous times.
—Benjamin Harrison

Every moment I spend with my grandchildren is the best moment of my life.
—Mamie Eisenhower

Grandchildren have almost universally served as a welcome distraction for presidents—and have proven to be more appealing to the public than any other members of the First Family.

"Happy is the man whose quiver is full of them," Jefferson somewhat ribaldly told one son-in-law, Tom Randolph, about the capacity for multiple fatherhood. "I consider a woman who brings a child every two years as more profitable than the best man of the farm," he told the other, Jack Eppes. Jefferson's Randolph grandchildren (he had a total of twelve: one had died, one was born at Monticello

When President Jefferson's grandson "Jeff" Randolph (in a portrait by Charles Willson Peale) visited the White House, he had the task of passing the decanters of French wine to guests at the dinner table. 1816.
THOMAS JEFFERSON MEMORIAL FOUNDATION

nine months before his presidency ended, three were born after his presidency) were a source of much interest to those who glimpsed them during their mother's second lengthy stay at the White House. There were five Randolph granddaughters at the White House—Anne, born in 1791; Ellen, born in 1796; Cornelia, born in 1799; Virginia, born in 1801; and Mary, born in 1803—and one grandson, Thomas Jefferson "Jeff," born in 1792. Jeff was special to the president for the simple fact that he was the only male in that generation of Randolphs.

The president thought Jeff a "heavy-seeming boy," and took personal direction of the serious teenager's preparation for boarding school in Philadelphia while he stayed in the White House just prior to his departure. Jefferson examined the boy's wardrobe and possessions, then personally went shopping for accoutrements he considered appropriate for the president's grandson. Once Jeff was in school, Jefferson advised the boy to "keep aloof" from politicians, "as you would from the infected subjects of yellow fever . . . the patients of Bedlam, needing medical more than moral counsel. . . . Get by them . . . as you would an angry bull. . . . You will be more exposed than others to have these animals shaking their horns at you because of the relation in which you stand with me. . . . Never, therefore, consider these puppies in politics as requiring any notice from you, and always show that you are not afraid to leave my character to the umpirage of public opinion."

Jefferson, however, had exacting expectations. When Jeff didn't pursue further education or a professional career, the president hung the young man's portrait not on the first tier on his salon wall of pictures, but on the second, explaining that "had you been educated you would have been entitled to a place on the first. You will always occupy the second." He also passed on a sense of racial superiority. When they were out riding one day, a slave bowed to the young man, but he did not return the bow. His grandfather angrily chastised him, "Do you permit a negro to be more of a gentleman than yourself?" In later life, Jeff, who declared African-Americans "an inferior race," acknowledged that the nearly white children of Jefferson's slave Sally Hemings were blood kin. It was prompted when he found a newspaper article claiming that his grandfather fathered Hemings's children. He confronted the president's nephews Samuel and Peter Carr, lounging under a tree at Monticello, who burst into tears and claimed that they were responsible. Jeff believed them and publicly declared his grandfather was as "immaculate a man as God ever created."

Among what he dubbed "the sisterhood" of his granddaughters, Jefferson encouraged the intelligent Ellen's ability in a way that he had never done with his daughters. Stunned by her ability not only to read but to write well by the age of five, he sent her adult reading and bought her her first Bible, a book of Shakespeare, and a writing table. He predicted, "If you continue to learn as fast, you will become a learned lady and publish books yourself." He trusted her judgment enough later to send her as an emissary with Jeff to visit his momentary nemesis but longtime friend John Adams—quite an extension of trust for a man like

Jefferson, who never approved of women's entry into public life. "I loved and honored him above all earthly beings," Ellen admitted.

During the second White House visit of Martha Randolph, in 1806, Jefferson friend and chronicler Margaret Bayard Smith noted that the First Daughter was "seated by him [Jefferson] on a sopha and all her lovely children playing around them. . . . I sat looking at him playing with all these infants, one standing on the sopha with its arms round his neck, the other two youngest on his knees, playing with him." At a ball, the squinting Mrs. Randolph asked Anna Cutts (Dolley Madison's sister), "Who is that beautiful girl?" about a young woman across the room. Snapped Mrs. Cutts, "Are you so unnatural a mother as not to recognize your own daughter?" It was the fifteen-year-old Anne—the eldest Jefferson grandchild—a belle in a gown. Just weeks before, Martha Randolph had given birth, on January 17, to her son James Madison. Although no details are known about his White House infancy, he was the first child born in the mansion. Jefferson named the child after his great friend the secretary of state, following family tradition; he insisted on choosing the names for all of his grandchildren.

Little is known about the 1822 White House birth or life of James Gouverneur, named for his grandfather, President Monroe, except the fact that the family was shattered when it later became apparent that he was unable to hear or speak. The prominent grandchild during the administration was Hortensia Hay, the daughter of the elder Monroe daughter, Eliza. Age seven at the time she came to live in the White House, Hortensia was named by her pretentious mother to honor her regal friend and Parisian schoolmate Hortense de Beauharnais, the Queen of Holland. When the Monroes entertained, there were often descriptions of the beautiful clothes of the three generations of women, Mrs. Monroe, Mrs. Hay, and little Hortensia; at one formal evening dinner, the child was done up in a plaid gown. Hortensia was also the only presidential grandchild to undertake any official role. In 1825, in the last weeks of his presidency, James Monroe petitioned Congress to be reimbursed for expenditures made during his French and British diplomatic career. Hortensia worked as his assistant, copying the detailed financial accounts to make a strong case.

"Looly" Adams unconsciously aided her grandfather. In November 1828, John Quincy Adams was severely depressed after losing a reelection campaign in which his entire family was

Andrew Johnson's grandchildren Andrew, Sarah, and Lillie Stover, who, with their cousins Andrew and Belle Patterson, were the core of a close-knit family. They played instruments and took dancing lessons at the prestigious Marini Studios. c. 1865.
ANDREW JOHNSON NATIONAL HISTORIC SITE

attacked. On December 2, however, his first grandchild, Mary Louisa, nicknamed Looly, was born in the White House. The next morning he recorded his "tranquility of mind" in his diary. Almost instantly his own "little rosebud" opened his heart in a way that neither his marriage nor fatherhood ever had. It so lightened his dour mood that political enemies feared his "assumed gaiety" on being thrown out of office was a fraudulent front, and that he had some other plot up his sleeve.

Mid-nineteenth-century presidents seemed to delight in publicly showing off their grandchildren. Infant Julia Grant had perhaps the first public exposure of a presidential grandchild. The First Lady arranged for her namesake to be brought down to "receive" at the 1877 annual New Year's Day reception as thousands of political figures, diplomats, and the general public streamed by, peeking at the baby, held by her nursemaid and dressed in antique lace. Cabinet members sometimes encountered John Tyler outside the executive offices wheeling his granddaughter Mary Fairlee in her carriage, taking a break from his work. Responding gleefully to any sound of music, she was also a pet of the Marine Band. The child sat so poised despite being a center of curiosity for the public that the Russian minister declared her "The Empress of a Baby."

When his five grandchildren arrived at the White House in August 1865, Andrew Johnson excitedly left his office and ran outside, squatting down to hug Belle, nearly six, and Andrew, five, children of Martha Johnson Patterson; and Lillie, ten, Sarah, seven, and Andrew, eight, children of the widowed Mary Johnson Stover. During the intense impeachment hearings in the House and trial in the Senate, President Johnson found no escape except in his grandchildren. During the week, Johnson would easily put aside his work to go out to the South Lawn and watch the children run races, roll, and turn somersaults. Some days they unceremoniously barged into his office, and a thrilled president expected those at his meetings to share his enthusiasm. At night, they scrambled into his lap as he worked alone there, to have him tell them stories. As the impeachment trial proceeded, he took them for frequent picnics in Rock Creek Park, strolling the woods, picking wildflowers, wading barefoot, skipping stones, and catching frogs. Colonel William Crook of the executive office staff left a particularly intimate characterization of the power the grandchildren had on the president: "Although his life of fighting for principles had developed him into a stern, forbidding, uncompromising man . . . [w]hen he was with his . . . grandchildren he relaxed and relapsed into what must have been his endowment by nature—a genial, happy man for the hour—until official duties called him away from his family circle."

Other presidents found respite from their work by making a special grandchild their favored companion. Although Andrew and Rachel Jackson never had any natural children between them, Mrs. Jackson had nearly two dozen nieces and nephews from her ten siblings. In 1829, one nephew and niece—married first cousins, Jack and Emily Donelson—came to the White House with their three-year-old son, Andrew "AJ" Donelson. For much of the long coach journey from their Tennessee home to Washington for the inaugural, the president-elect held his squirming namesake on his lap. Later, political figures hoping to curry favor with the president in a ride alongside him found that the honor was frequently reserved for the growing AJ, on his pony. When AJ was later put in boarding school in nearby Virginia, he made the White House his home base, and the president wrote frequent admonitions to the boy on how to conduct himself. Most unusual for the era, President Jackson openly showered affection on AJ, as he did even more noticeably with his two favored little children, a great-niece and an adoptive granddaughter, Mary Donelson and Rachel Jackson, respectively.

Emily Donelson gave birth in the mansion to three more children: Mary in 1829, John Samuel in 1832, and Rachel in 1834. Jackson thought nothing of stopping his work to join their games. After the nearly successful assassination attempt on the president in 1835, the vice president, hurrying to check on Jackson, found him relaxing with his two grand-nieces and grand-nephew on his lap. "They are the only friends I have," said the president, "who never pester me with their advice." He dubbed the eldest of the three White House–born children, Mary, his own "Sunshine of the White House," and placed a lock of her hair in mementos cemented into the cornerstone of the Treasury Building. As one observer wrote, "She only could woo the great man from his widowed melancholy, or banish his characteristic irascible moods."

By 1834, Jackson's adoptive son Andrew Jackson II, daughter-in-law Sarah and their children Rachel, born in 1832, and Andrew III, born two years later, came to live in the White House. It was "my dear little Rachel" (not to be confused with his great-niece Rachel Donelson) that the president seemed to idolize above all others. Jackson said his adoptive granddaughter was "sprightly as a little fairy," and alternated between calling her "my sweet little babe" and "my dear little pet." At the child's birth he wrote Sarah, "[I]t will be a great pleasure to watch over and rear up the sweet little Rachel, and make her a fair emblem of her for whom she is called." It was not uncommon for the usually cranky Jackson to permit a half-disrobed little Rachel to run into and delay a cabinet meeting.

In the unsettling final months of his term, Lyndon Johnson's first grandchild, Patrick Lyndon Nugent, born on June 21, 1967, seemed the only antidote to the president's stress. Known as Lyn, the boy lived in the White House with his mother, when his father went to serve in Vietnam. Vignettes illustrating the importance of the child's presence to the beleaguered LBJ are many. On one occasion, LBJ insisted that his daughter and grandchild suddenly change plans and stay with him. In the Family Dining Room, the child was fed the only immediately available meal—breast of pheasant being served simultaneously at a state dinner in the adjoining room. Lyn's mere presence was therapy for LBJ, his doctor stating that when he "could play with the baby," the president could "lose himself." In the midst of a difficult meeting on April 3, 1967, following a decision to halt bombing in North Vietnam, and Senate attacks on his war policy, LBJ admitted that he was in a "bad mood" as he prepared for an Oval Office meeting with his military advisers, "but I cheered up when my grandson Lyn came in. I always felt better when I saw him, and this morning I needed to feel better." As a press aide said once when Lyn was going back to Austin with his parents for a period, "Oh, we sure are going to miss that boy—that little Lyn. He was a good story every day with all the riots and the war—he was a big help."

In the last weeks of his presidency, LBJ put renewed focus on a new grandchild—Lucinda Robb, who lived briefly in the mansion as an infant, her father also serving in Vietnam. As Lynda Robb went into labor, her father reminisced to her about the day she was born. At Lucinda's birth, he briefed the waiting press and handed out cigars. Two months later, at a

"Baby" McKee, the famous Benjamin Harrison grandson and namesake, runs down the White House driveway with his sister Mary; photo snapped by their mother. c. 1891.

BENJAMIN HARRISON PRESIDENTIAL HOME

Christmas Eve party, dressed in a Dior dress with white fox fur, Lucinda was wheeled in her carriage through the state rooms, giving guests what her mother called "an impassive Buddha stare."

Little Lyn, however, still held court among the LBJs, and his grandfather delighted in his public exposure—such as letting him run to the fountain and flowers on the South Lawn for the delight of camera-clicking tourists at the fence. His most famous public appearance was at the last nationally televised State of the Union address by LBJ—who insisted on his presence. "I would as soon have taken a sack full of lighted firecrackers," Mrs. Johnson wrote. "He had been exposed a bit too much to cameras and crowds and newspaper stories and was inclined to wind up inappropriately on center stage." Indeed Lyn was crawling over laps, waving a booklet, reaching for the railing, twenty feet below which sat the august Senate, and banging and swinging his full bottle of milk. Before the full array of reporters, Congress, and television cameras, the usually controlled First Lady began crying with laughter. As the administration—and Lyn's Secret Service protection detail—ended, his mother said the eighteen-month-old boy "just lost twenty-one of his best friends."

No grandchild got more newspaper coverage in his day or was more a president's daily companion than Benjamin Harrison McKee, the namesake of Benjamin Harrison. Son of First Daughter Mary Harrison McKee, the child was only eighteen months old when he came to live in the mansion with his parents. His famous sobriquet, "Baby" McKee, preceded his White House occupancy when curious crowds at the family home spied the child and, not knowing his name, shouted for Baby. "The phrase was at once taken up by newspaper correspondents," recalled Colonel Crook of the executive staff, "and within forty-eight hours 'Baby McKee' became famous. . . . Columns were written about him and his appearance, and what he ate or didn't eat, and what he wore, and how he was taken care of. For some reason the American people seem dearly to love unimportant details concerning prominent persons, and they certainly were furnished with enough of them in this instance."

Harrison kissed and teased his two granddaughters, Mary McKee and Marthena Harrison,

President Taylor's favorite grandchild, Bob Wood. After the president got this grandson into West Point, he wrote the boy's father, his son-in-law, "There is nothing more important to ensure a young man a high standing either in the army or navy than literary attainments and a taste for study . . . a source of amusement as well as education."

HISTORIC NEW ORLEANS RESEARCH CENTER

when the noisy girls quietly visited the executive offices, but Baby McKee could do no wrong in the eyes of his grandfather. Many government officials and diplomats often found his wet hand wrapping around their legs under a table during meetings in the president's study. On one occasion he climbed atop the president's desk and banged the call bells, sending all of the attendants rushing into the room to see what was wrong. Another time the boy took some important papers from the office and was found churning—and staining—them in a spittoon. Regularly bathed in a porcelain tub painted with pink magnolia blossoms by his grandmother, Baby McKee habitually leaned over it to kiss the flowers and flood the carpet, which he found to be "fine sport." It was soon joked that the politically obstinate president crawled on the floor to only one official in Washington—Baby McKee.

Harrison's friend Indiana congressman W. S. Holman confessed that, "As for the general public, Harrison's dignified reserve has not aroused any great warmth or enthusiasm." Thus, it was only natural to mete out to the press corps warm stories of the president's loving relationship with his grandson. For the first time the public feasted on intimate photographs of presidential family life. There was Baby leading the Marine Band with a baton, Baby presiding over a miniature teatime, Baby mimicking the president's public speaking posture, Baby and his sister and cousin in the private nursery with their mothers, or on the lawn with their goat cart. Finally, the president's secretary E. W. Halford put a sudden halt to it all, "lest the people of this country should come to believe the tales about this child's having more influence than members of the Cabinet."

The exploitation soon enough backfired, with critical satire picturing an easily persuaded president removed from his duties and an imperious little brat who got everything he wanted from government servants. Baby was lampooned as a fictional figure in a real scandal involving his grandfather's acceptance of a cottage. One ditty, playing on the fact that Vice President Morton owned a hotel with a famous bar and that Postmaster General Wanamaker taught

A rare public event for Peggy (second from left) and Peter Hoover, accepting a holiday card from the city of Washington. 1930.

HERBERT HOOVER PRESIDENTIAL LIBRARY

Sunday school, ran, "The baby runs the White House,/Levi runs the bar,/Wanny runs the Sunday school,/And, damn it, here we are." With her grandson now a national joke, the First Lady's propriety was bruised. "Oh, what have we done! . . . That we should be held up to such ridicule by newspapers . . . and even . . . little, helpless grandchildren be made fun of, for the country to laugh at!"

Benjamin Harrison was himself the grandson of a president, but he never knew his grandfather, William Henry Harrison. President Benjamin Harrison's first cousins, James Harrison, sixteen, and William Harrison, fourteen (sons of the late William Jr.) and Montgomery Pike Harrison, twelve (son of John Cleves Harrison) did, however, call the White House home during their grandfather's thirty-day presidency. Since the president's daughter Anna Taylor also lived there, another grandson and a granddaughter mentioned in some sources as also being there were almost certainly hers—three-year-old William Taylor and either Lucy Taylor, age two, or Anna Taylor, one. All that is known of the grandchildren's brief stay there is that the two older boys went to the open-air food market with their grandfather. Among First Families, Harrison's is the only one to extend into four generations at the time of his inaugural: he had two great-grandchildren, Gabriella and Symmes.

There is almost an equal dearth of documentation on Zachary Taylor's four grandchildren, who made frequent and lengthy stays at the White House, traveling from their home in nearby Baltimore with their mother, Ann Taylor Wood, and father Robert Wood. John, eighteen when his grandfather was elected president, was enrolled at the Naval School at Annapolis, having served on the *Brandywine* during the Mexican War. The third and fourth children, Blandina ("Nina"), fourteen, and Sarah ("Dumple"), nine, grew particularly close to their aunt Betty Bliss, who was to have no children. The Woods' second child, Robert ("Bob") sixteen, was the favorite of his grandparents and the center of their concerns. He had lived with them in Baton Rouge, and his grandfather president got him into West Point. At the 1849 New Year's Day reception, Taylor's four grandchildren publicly received the children of various officials.

Sistie and Buzzie Dall, with their mother Anna and grandparents Eleanor and Franklin D. Roosevelt. The man at right is unknown. c. 1936.

Taylor showed a sensitivity to the expectations placed on his grandchildren, advising his son-in-law: "It is perhaps as well if not better not to make too favorable calculations in favor of our children in early life for should they fail to meet or come up to them the disappointment will be felt with double the effect it would under different circumstances."

A century of media sophistication, however, did not necessarily make presidential grandchildren more accessible. Rarely did Herbert Hoover's appear in the press. In 1930, with their father seeking tuberculosis treatment in a sanitarium, and their mother often with him, Peggy Ann, four, Herbert ("Peter"), three, and Joan Leslie, age one, moved into a third-floor nursery. Peggy had the self-appointed task of ordering the overworked president to lunch: "I said luncheon was ready! Come you lazy man!" In the midst of the Depression, with all of the nation's ills being attributed to Hoover, his advisers desperately sought ways publicly to humanize him, but he steadfastly refused to permit any stories of his unspoiled and personable grandchildren to be released. Save for their posing on the North Portico to receive a Christmas card from the children of Washington, and Peggy's acceptance of a dress made of "doodle cloth" fabric printed with Hoover's drawings on it, the grandchildren remained off-limits—as far as could be controlled. One afternoon, having escaped his nurse, Peter stood in a windowsill wearing a hat, but otherwise naked as a jaybird, waving to shocked pedestrians on Pennsylvania Avenue.

In contrast were Eleanor "Sistie," six years old, and Curtis "Buzzie" Dall, three, the grandchildren of Franklin Roosevelt by his daughter Anna, all of whom lived in the White House from the fall of 1933 until the summer of 1935. Although her husband, Curtis Dall, attended the 1933 inaugural, Anna Roosevelt was in the process of divorcing him at the time her father became president. In August 1934, there was an extortion plot to harm Sistie and Buzzie unless a ransom of $168,000 was paid. Although the threat never materialized, the duo became the first presidential grandchildren to receive Secret Service protection. Having worked in journalism, Anna Roosevelt was perhaps the first member of a First Family to ponder the long-term psychological harm of exposing children of political families to the press and public. Whenever her children were publicly applauded, she emphasized to them that the acclaim was not for them personally. To entertain her children and give them an appreciation of where they were now living, Anna wrote two children's books—*Scamper, the Bunny Who Went to the White House,* and *Scamper's Christmas, More About the White House Bunny.* Many times, at parties for the children, the First Lady gathered some of their smaller friends on her lap and read from the books. Later published at $1.85 apiece, they became best-sellers, although one citizen wrote the White House that "the quicker the Roosevelts scamper out of the White House, the better it will be for the country." Nevertheless, the books' main character sustained such popularity that stuffed dolls of the White House bunny were mass-manufactured. Clearly based on Sistie and Buzzie, the books' characters were called Babs and David.

Anna Roosevelt took Sistie and Buzzie to hear their grandfather deliver his 1934 State of the Union Address, and like Lyn Nugent, three-year-old Buzzie fidgeted throughout the speech, at one point loudly complaining that his trousers were too tight. He successfully horrified his pompous great-grandmother Sara one day in the White House by pulling up his shirt, pointing to his stomach, and chanting, "Belly button, belly button!"

Eleanor Roosevelt was an indulgent grandmother. There were frequent parties and gatherings for the duo, sometimes to see a new Walt Disney cartoon movie. For her granddaughter's sixth birthday—described by a guest as a "gala affair that included the president"—the First Lady had a jungle gym, sandbox with awning, and rope swing installed on the South Lawn. Not only did the children enjoy it but one night the First Lady and First Daughter "pumped up" the swing rope—to the shock of the intruding chief usher. The playground was in addition to the nursery on the third floor and an open-air playroom on the roof.

In 1939, after Anna had married John Boettiger and moved to Seattle, the First Lady was in the delivery room holding her daughter's hand when she gave birth to her third child, Johnny—as she had been when the first two were born. Anna wrote her father, "Ma was such a comfort before the event, during and after." At Christmas, the Boettigers came to celebrate in the White House and on the last day of the year, baby Johnny was christened there. In 1944, during World War II, when John Roosevelt prepared to serve in the navy, his children Haven, three, and Anne "Nina," eighteen months, came to live temporarily in the White House with their mother. James Roosevelt's daughters by his first marriage, Kate and Sara, briefly lived there too, in the winter of 1944–45. On one

Mamie Eisenhower made sure she gave a special theme party for each grandchild, in the long corridor of the ground floor. David Eisenhower had a cowboy theme one year and a Roy Rogers movie. When he and his pals emerged from the theater the real Roy Rogers was there. Left to right: Roy Rogers, Mamie Eisenhower, Barbara Eisenhower, John Eisenhower, Minnie Doud (Mamie's mother), President Eisenhower, and Dale Evans. 1956.
DWIGHT D. EISENHOWER PRESIDENTIAL LIBRARY

of the rare days she had free time, the First Lady took them all to the National Gallery of Art. "It is years since I've had to see children go to bed," the First Lady wrote, "& I love it & am having a good time."

With the postwar advent of television, political advertisers exploited the wholesome Eisenhowers in the 1952 presidential campaign, including the first use of a candidate's grandchildren. This medium introduced the twentieth century's most famous presidential grandchild, David Eisenhower, age five. He was the eldest of four—the others were Barbara Anne (always called Anne), four, Susan Elaine, one, and Mary Jean, born in 1955. During weekends, vacations, and other intermittent stays, they lived in bedrooms and played in a toy room on the third floor. They drove electric-powered mini Thunderbirds outside on the circular drive of the South Lawn, and swam in the pool, using water wings, inflated ducks, and tire tubes. David lined the long hall of the second floor with his extensive baseball card collection, while Susan displayed her doll collection in the linen room. Ike even let them rummage through his Oval Office desk. Although she let them do likewise with her bedside table, and knit their carriage covers and afghans, Mamie Eisenhower was stricter than Ike. "No running up and down corridors, no sliding down banisters, no greasy fingers on the woodwork, no getting down from the table before the meal was over," Susan recalled of her grandmother's rules.

The foursome kept an important perspective for President Eisenhower: "[T]he toys strewn across the path to the office, the children's extreme audibility . . . somehow helped to remind me that the country would not go to the dogs nor the world collapse in ruins. Perhaps they suggested, too, that it must not."

Ike particularly indulged David. Although he named a presidential yacht *Barbara Anne,* he famously rechristened the official presidential retreat established by FDR as "Camp David." A White House electrician observed that Ike was "happiest when his grandson came to visit." Merriman Smith, dean of the White House press corps, said that Ike "naturally put the spotlight on David when they're in public, and Mrs. Eisenhower and daughter-in-law Barbara, if they sense it fast enough, will heap affection and attention at the same time on the two cute blonde girls [Anne and Susan]."

There seemed at times to be a subtle battle between the proud but naive grandparents who enjoyed publicly showing off their grands, and the more sober parents who were highly conscious of the effect of public exposure on their children. Even baby Mary Jean picked up enough Secret Service code words to spout over the agents' car radio: "Man-man Sunflower with Grand 124 en route to Barracuda" (translation: "We're leaving the Eisenhower house with all the children, on the way to church"). Their mother donated to charity the hundreds of toys sent daily to them from strangers. One Easter, vacationing at the presidential retreat in Augusta, Georgia, David's mother forbade him to fire his cap gun. When she briefly left and photographers surrounded him and Ike, the president goaded the boy to take out his gun, and hundreds of cameras went off for the photo op, as the president praised his fast draw and kept clapping for him to continue. His horrified mother flew out of the door, grabbed her son, and took him into the house. Ike turned away, embarrassed.

With the grandchildren so effectively used by the White House as the idealized fifties family, it was inevitable that they would be exploited for political purpose by outsiders as well. When David and Anne were transferred to a private school from a public one in the Washington suburbs at a time when the president promised that local schools would be used "to demonstrate to the world how easily and effectively integration would work," it touched off a political firestorm. Mississippi Senator James O. Eastland declared, "Eisenhower's own grandchildren have been removed from a system that permits integrated schools and placed in a private segregated school. Ike's like all the interracial politicians. He wants it for the other fellow." Eastland conveniently ignored the fact that the youngest child was in an integrated kindergarten and all three of the president's grandchildren attended an integrated Sunday

Ronald and Nancy Reagan, Michael Reagan and his wife, Colleen, and Cameron, all celebrate Ashley Marie's fourth birthday at Rancho del Cielo, the family ranch. 1987.

school. It prompted a livid response from the White House press office: "When you try to get the President's grandchildren into politics, you are reaching a new low."

Despite this incident, the president found his grandchildren useful as he conducted diplomacy. When British prime minister Harold Macmillan became agitated in meetings with Ike, he visibly relaxed in subsequent talks after watching David shoot basketball hoops. Even icy French premier Charles de Gaulle had to laugh when four-year-old Mary Jean yanked his eyeglasses, put them on, and chanted, "Poor me, poor me!" When, in the depths of the cold war, Soviet premier Nikita Khrushchev visited the United States, he "assumed the role of the beneficent grandfather," recalled the president's son, when he met the little ones. After wowing them with Russian translations of their names, the wily Khrushchev invited them to the Soviet Union. The President, First Lady, and their grandchildren were all excited at the prospect, but it was followed by widespread press coverage of David's innocent quip to a fellow sixth-grader: "I'd be a Communist because Khrushchev was such a nice guy." When David proudly wore the red star pin Khrushchev gave to him and his sisters, his father, John, angrily told him that "[i]f Khrushchev could take us over, guess what family would be the first to be shot." John recalled, "To my mind, our battle to avoid spoiling the children by excessive publicity and attention was difficult enough without this exercise. When I told Dad a couple of days later that the children were not available, he showed his irritation." As he broke up an

unsuccessful May 1960 summit meeting with Americans, Khrushchev abruptly rescinded his invitation. "Mimi"—as the First Lady had her grandchildren call her instead of the old-sounding "grandma"—insisted that he did so because of John's "unreasonable stand." Despite the family tiff and world drama, David still loved the spotlight. Just before his grandfather left the White House, he tucked little notes of paper behind furniture and under rugs with one message: "I will return." And he would.

When Jimmy Carter was elected president he had a two-year-old grandson, Jason, the son of his eldest child, Jack. Since the family lived in Georgia, however, the president's grandson was in the mansion only on lengthy visits. Jason still made a permanent impression on the household staff there, who doted on him as a little friend. One servant even taught him to speak Spanish. Four weeks after the inaugural, a second grandson, James Earl Carter IV, the son of Chip Carter, was born in Washington, at Bethesda Naval Hospital. His first home was the White House, where both of his parents lived until their separation in November 1978, and the First Lady and President often baby-sat for the child. Once, as they played tennis on the South Lawn court, "Digger" (as James was nicknamed, after his Secret Service code name) watched from his carriage, parked alongside the court. A third grandchild, Sarah Rose Mary—Jason's sister—was born in December 1978, and celebrated her first birthday party in the Solarium.

The Reagans were rarely with their grandchildren. In 1983, *People* magazine asked five-year-old Cameron Reagan if he ever saw his grandfather. "Sure—on TV," he replied. His mother added about both Ronald and Nancy Reagan, "Sometimes I think they should spend more time with Cameron and Ashley [their granddaughter] than with the foster grandparent program." As often as the Reagans were in Los Angeles, the press soon learned, a visit to their grandchildren was never scheduled. They did not see Ashley until twenty months after her birth. It became a hot story for the political opposition—especially in 1984 as Reagan championed "family values" in his reelection campaign—and part of a schism within the family. Months later, when Michael Reagan brought them to meet the president, the press office exploited the rapprochement by announcing that Reagan and his grandson would "build" a snowman. In fact, aides made everything but the snowman's head. Reporters and photographers came, while Michael reflected "how sad it was" that something "private" was manipulated for a "media event." He wondered, "[W]as the cost worth the price?"

Although none of George Bush's grandchildren resided in the mansion, Marshall and Walker Bush, ages three and newborn in 1989, and Sam and Ellie LeBlond, ages four and two in 1989, lived nearby and visited often. When Mrs. Bush placed the star atop the national Christmas tree, she often took several of her grandchildren with her to participate. All one dozen of the grandchildren were used by the 1988 Bush campaign's public relations machinery. In television commercials, photographic posters, and a convention biography film, the numerous boys and girls were omnipresent, effectively humanizing Bush's image. This emphasis brought negative attention when the press overheard him remark during the convention to a departing President Reagan that the "little brown ones" were his grandchildren, a reference to the children of his son Jeb and Mexican daughter-in-law Columba. Despite his description, Bush was devoted to his grandchildren and especially sensitive to their Latino blood and any bigotry they experienced because of it. Once, when the eldest—"George P." as the family dubbed him—had been playing ball, another child yelled a racial epithet at him; when the president learned about it, tears came to his eyes.

During the 1992 reelection campaign, the grandchildren were utilized even more. One reporter posed questions to the president on sensitive social concerns by asking how he would react if his grandchildren hypothetically had to face them. Bush himself exemplified his opposition to terminating pregnancy by mentioning that one of his granddaughters was adopted and that she would not have been with them had her birth mother decided against carrying her to full term. At the 1992 convention, which renominated Bush, he was surrounded at the podium by his twelve grandchildren, "as primed by the handlers," the First Lady noted. Unprecedented was the August 19 convention speech by George P., who extolled his grandfather to millions of Americans watching on television, explaining, "Despite the enormous pressures of his job, he always has time for his twelve grandkids . . . I just wish people who see George Bush on TV or read about him in newspapers could know him as I do." The speech was the farthest a presidential grandchild had ever come into the political arena, but not the first time that the Bush grandchildren had campaigned: not only had George P. and his sister, Noella, done so in 1988, but their cousins, the twins Barbara and Jenna, six, were on the campaign trail in Indiana with their grandfather and parents. The most public role ever undertaken by a presidential grandchild was also played by George P. some weeks before the 1989 inaugural, when he and his father led a goodwill mission to earthquake-devastated Armenia. Afterward, "Gampy" wrote him:

> *Men are not supposed to cry, says convention; but we do and we should and we should not worry when we do. I cry when I'm happy and I cry when I'm sad, but when I saw you and your wonderful dad in that church in Armenia on Christmas Day I cried because I was both happy and sad. Don't ever forget what you saw there. Don't ever forget what you participated in. In less than two weeks I will be President of the United States. I know I will not forget what that little trip of yours meant to people all over the world.*

Months later, when George P. came to stay briefly at the White House, his grandmother was sensitive to the fact that he seemed to have shut down and had "lost all his energy, and I worried about his attitude." It was a fear allayed when his enthusiastic personality burst open again at a baseball game, and Mrs. Bush realized that "thirteen-year-old boys live a life of their own."

The intensity with which Bush valued his grandchildren was an aspect of his personality that the general public never quite realized. Never perceived as an expressive man, he was extraordinarily emotional in a series of letters he wrote his grandchildren when each of them was born. To granddaughter Lauren, he concluded, "We want to see you smile, to hold you, to love you. It's a funny thing—when you get older, even if you have an exciting life surrounded by interesting people and having the chance to meet all the world leaders—even with all that—what counts is family and love."

Beyond the political expediency serving White House public relations, the universal experience of grandparenting has greatly served the emotional health of a president. "How different the house is when Lyn is here," Lady Bird Johnson wrote of her grandson in 1968. "Passing by the Treaty Room, I saw by that august door the engine of a little toy train . . . in one of those lovely Hepplewhite chairs there was a little pink teddy bear. Well, it will be that way again, as it has been in the past. That's one of the wonderful things I love about this house."

Grandchildren Born During Presidents' Terms

Abigail Louisa Smith Adams, granddaughter of John Adams, 1798

Virginia Randolph, Thomas Jefferson granddaughter, 1801

Mary Randolph, Thomas Jefferson granddaughter, 1803

*James Madison Randolph, Thomas Jefferson grandson, 1806

Benjamin Franklin Randolph, Thomas Jefferson grandson, 1808

*Samuel Lawrence Gouverneur, James Monroe grandson, 1820

Elizabeth Kortright Gouverneur, James Monroe granddaughter, sometime between 1821 and 1825

*James Monroe Gouverneur, James Monroe grandson, sometime between 1822 and 1825

*Mary Louisa "Looly" Adams, John Quincy Adams granddaughter, 1828

Rachel Jackson, Andrew Jackson's adoptive granddaughter, 1832

Andrew Jackson III, Andrew Jackson's adoptive grandson, 1834

Thomas Jefferson Jackson, Andrew Jackson's adoptive grandson, 1836

*Rebecca Singleton Van Buren, Martin Van Buren granddaughter, 1840

*Singleton Van Buren, Martin Van Buren grandson, 1840

*Robert Tyler Jones, John Tyler grandson, 1843

*Letitia Christian Tyler, John Tyler granddaughter, 1842

John Tyler IV, John Tyler grandson, 1844

William Griffin Waller, John Tyler grandson, born sometime between 1842 and 1845

Letitia Christian Tyler (second so named), John Tyler granddaughter, 1844

*Julia Grant, Ulysses S. Grant granddaughter, 1876

Grant Greville Edward Sartoris, Ulysses S. Grant grandson, 1875

*Francis B. Sayre, Woodrow Wilson grandson, 1915

Eleanor Axson Sayre, Woodrow Wilson granddaughter, 1916

Woodrow Wilson Sayre, Woodrow Wilson grandson, 1919

Ellen Wilson McAdoo, Woodrow Wilson granddaughter, 1915

Joan Leslie Hoover, Herbert Hoover granddaughter, 1930

John Roosevelt Boettiger, Franklin D. Roosevelt grandson, 1939

Kate Roosevelt, Franklin D. Roosevelt granddaughter, 1936

Ruth Chandler Roosevelt, Franklin D. Roosevelt granddaughter, 1934

Elliott Roosevelt Jr., Franklin D. Roosevelt grandson, 1936

David Boynton Roosevelt, Franklin D. Roosevelt grandson, 1942

born in White House

Franklin D. Roosevelt III, Franklin D. Roosevelt grandson, 1939
Christopher Dupont Roosevelt, Franklin D. Roosevelt grandson, 1940
Haven Clark Roosevelt, Franklin D. Roosevelt grandson, 1940
Anne Sturgis Roosevelt, Franklin D. Roosevelt granddaughter, 1942
Mary Jean Eisenhower, Dwight Eisenhower granddaughter, 1955
Patrick Lyndon Nugent, Lyndon B. Johnson grandson, 1967
Lucinda Desha Robb, Lyndon B. Johnson granddaughter, 1968
James Earl Carter III, Jimmy Carter grandson, 1977
Sarah Rose Mary Carter, Jimmy Carter granddaughter, 1978
Ashley Marie Reagan, Ronald Reagan adoptive granddaughter, 1982
Ashley Walker Bush, George Bush granddaughter, 1989
Charles Walker Bush, George Bush grandson, 1989

Despite the debilitating stroke he suffered in 1963, Joseph Kennedy remained his clan's patriarch. They gather here in his Hyannis Port home with funny hats and toasts for his birthday. His wife, Rose, stands behind Jackie, and Robert Kennedy, and his sister Loretta is seated next to Edward Kennedy (foreground). 1962. His daughter Jean applauds him (facing page).

7

The Parents

I don't believe I raised the boy to be President. . . .
The first thing I knew, my son turned around and
began to raise me to be mother of a President.
—*Nancy McKinley*

[My presidency] was the culmination of the lifelong
desire of a father for the success of his son.
—*Calvin Coolidge*

There is an old legend that all American mothers raise their sons with the hope that they will someday become president. If that is true, in two centuries only one dozen of such women ever saw their dream achieved—and only half as many fathers. A larger pool of elderly adults has been presidential parents-in-law. Many a senior First Family member dominated a presidency and reveled in the public attention received, eager to offer unsolicited advice and criticism to all.

So controversial was brash multimillionaire businessman and former U.S. ambassador to England Joseph Patrick Kennedy that his profile threatened to shadow his son John. The irony was that during his son's campaign he kept out of public view, and

Parents of Presidents and First Ladies Alive at the Time of the Inaugurals

Mary Ball Washington, George Washington's mother
Susanna Boylston Adams, John Adams's mother
Eleanor Conway Madison, James Madison's mother
John Adams, John Quincy Adams's father
Julianna McLachlan Gardiner, Julia Tyler's mother
Jane Knox Polk, James Polk's mother
Nathaniel Fillmore, Millard Fillmore's father
Sarah Bush Lincoln, Abraham Lincoln's stepmother
*Jesse Grant, Ulysses Grant's father
Hannah Simpson Grant, Ulysses Grant's mother
*Frederick Dent, Julia Grant's father
*Eliza Ballou Garfield, James Garfield's mother
Zebulon Rudolph, Lucretia Garfield's father
*Emma Folsom Perrin, Frances Cleveland's mother
*John Scott, Caroline Harrison's father
*Nancy Allison McKinley, William McKinley's mother
John Herron, Helen Taft's father
*Sally White Bolling, Edith Wilson's mother
*George Tryon Harding, Warren Harding's father
Alice Severn Harding, Warren Harding's stepmother
Caroline Denman Kling, Florence Harding's step-
mother
*John Coolidge, Calvin Coolidge's father
*Lemira Barrett Goodhue, Grace Coolidge's mother
*Sara Delano Roosevelt, Franklin Roosevelt's mother
Martha Ellen Truman, Harry Truman's mother

*witnessed swearing-in ceremony

eleven months into his son's presidency, was robbed of free movement and speech by a devastating stroke. The family made no secret of the fact that the Ambassador, as they called him, bred competition among the clan. Nor was he modest about his influence: "I got Jack into politics. I was the one. . . . He didn't want to. He felt he didn't have the ability," Joe firmly bragged. The president admitted as much: "My father wanted his eldest son in politics. 'Wanted' isn't the right word. He demanded it."

Although Joe Kennedy used both his personal expertise in advertising and his media contacts to help his son's 1960 presidential campaign, he was too controversial a figure to appear at the convention in light of his past friendship with the late, discredited senator Joe McCarthy and allegations that in the late 1930s Joe had initially appeased Hitler. When he retorted that the attacks came because of his Catholicism, former president Truman piped up, "I am not against the Pope. I'm against the Pop." When both Democrats and Republicans claimed that Joe had rigged the election by buying votes, the candidate quipped: "I got a wire from my father." He said, reading from a piece of paper, "'Dear Jack: Don't buy one more vote than necessary. I'll be damned if I'll pay for a landslide.'"

Worth an estimated $250 million, seventy-two-year-old Joe Kennedy was at loose ends after the win. "Hell, I don't know how it feels to be the father of a president," he snapped at a reporter. "Jack doesn't belong any more to just one family. He belongs to the country. That's probably the saddest thing about all this. The family can be there for him. But there is not much they can do sometimes for the president." Father and son wrote letters to each other and often spoke several times a day. "I want to help," Joe said, "but I don't want to be a nui-

* Madge Gates Wallace, Bess Truman's mother
* Elvira "Minnie" Carlson Doud, Mamie Eisenhower's mother
* Joseph Patrick Kennedy, John F. Kennedy's father
* Rose Fitzgerald Kennedy, John F. Kennedy's mother
* Janet Lee Bouvier Auchincloss, Jacqueline Kennedy's mother
* Hugh Dudley Auchincloss, Jacqueline Kennedy's stepfather
* Lillian Gordy Carter, Jimmy Carter's mother
* Allie Murray Smith, Rosalynn Carter's mother
* Loyal Davis, Nancy Reagan's stepfather
* Edith Lucket Davis, Nancy Reagan's mother
* Dorothy Walker Bush, George Bush's mother
* Willa Martin Pierce, Barbara Bush's stepmother
* Virginia Cassidy Clinton Kelley, Bill Clinton's mother
* Richard Kelley, Bill Clinton's stepfather
* Hugh Rodham, Hillary Clinton's father
* Dorothy Howell Rodham, Hillary Clinton's mother

*witnessed swearing-in ceremony

sance." He successfully urged the reappointments of J. Edgar Hoover as FBI head and Allen Dulles as head of the CIA, and the naming of his second son as attorney general, explaining, "I want Bobby there. It's the only thing I'm asking for and I want it." However, he publicly embarrassed the president by pushing for the appointment of his crony Frank X. Morrissey to a federal district court judgeship, and the dismissal of a tax problem of another friend, James Landis. JFK refused both requests. After President Kennedy's famous showdown with U.S. Steel resulted in a stock market drop, Joe cracked, "To think I voted for that son-of-a-bitch."

Indeed, both men recognized their polar differences—Joe had become a reactionary conservative on nearly all issues—JFK rhetorically telling a friend, "Do you always agree with your father? No. But you love him." Joe thoughtfully bought a golf cart for the president to get around their compound at Hyannis Port, because of his bad back, but could still knock him down a notch in public. "When he comes over to use my [New York] apartment," Joe told a *Time* magazine writer, "he still takes my socks if I happen to have some new ones around."

Joe and Rose Kennedy were the first presidential parents to have Secret Service agents. At seventy-one Rose Kennedy fully participated in official life. As there was no formal ranking of a president's mother, she was given the protocol status of a former ambassador's wife. Shopping in Paris at the time her son made his triumphant visit there in 1961, she was incorporated into the official entourage. Although there was a slight strain between Jackie and her mother-in-law ("You want Caroline to be like you," she bluntly told Rose, "and I want her to be like me"), the First Lady occasionally asked her to substitute as official hostess. Rose stayed in the Lincoln Suite while visiting the White House, where her daily nap kept the historic room closed to private tours, even those led by the president.

In public, Rose always addressed her son as "Mr. President," and though she did sometimes walk onto the lawn and peek into the Oval Office as he worked, she generally kept her distance: "I never want to intrude on his time . . . I wouldn't think of going to talk to Jack. I think if he had something particular to say he'd come to me . . . [I never] expected to see him at lunch or dinner, no I never expected that." Mrs. Kennedy publicly spoke about the mental retardation of the president's sister Rosemary because, she said, "I want people to know it should be talked about. Not hidden." With her daughter Eunice, she successfully urged the president to sign the first federal mental health legislation, providing $329 million for community mental health centers. Having instilled in him a love of history and current events, she kept herself fully abreast of his work, the president calling her "a natural politician." Indeed after hearing his speeches, Rose often called up his speechwriter to discuss his word choices. Having been one of his most visible campaigners during the 1960 election, and standing with him at the convention podium after he won the nomination, Rose Kennedy continued to deliver countless speeches and hold press conferences about how she raised a president and the rest of her family. When he arrived late for a speech where she was introducing him, he asked, "How do I look?" She quipped, "You would have looked better two hours ago."

Much like Joe Kennedy's efforts to groom his son for the presidency was the influence of John Quincy Adams's father—President John Adams. By the time John Quincy became president, however, the older man, retired in Quincy, Massachusetts, had mellowed. "Poor human nature," John reflected on problems that his son faced, similar to those he himself encountered a quarter of a century earlier, "disputes in religion and dissensions in politics without end." The old man kept abreast of White House life through letters from his daughter-in-law Louisa, who had the "love and duty of a daughter," and his beloved grandson George.

No presidential parent had a more dramatic role in his son's inauguration than John Coolidge. On August 3, 1923, he—a notary public—swore in his son Calvin as president in their Vermont farmhouse upon hearing of the sudden death of President Harding. A sophisticated man who served in state and local office, the First Father was nevertheless cast by the popular press of the twenties as a grouchy Yankee farmer, progenitor of his twangy-voiced son's laconic humor. On one occasion, John Coolidge turned down an invitation to a prestigious dinner of potential campaign contributors by telegram: "Gentlemen: Can't come. Thank you." When a friend asked how he felt after prostate surgery, "the Colonel" cracked that he guessed he would "have to read the papers to find out."

Coolidge maintained an extraordinarily tender relationship with his father, drawn to him all the more by the early deaths of both the president's mother and his only sibling. "My father had qualities that were greater than any I possess . . . untiring industry and great tenacity of purpose . . . unerring judgment," the president later recalled. "He would be classed as decidedly a man of character." The father felt equally emotional about the son: "I think of him just as a good and honest boy, who will do his best with any job given him. He always has been that way and I guess he always will be. A trusty kind of boy who always attended to whatever he had in hand." They kissed each other in public—once even kissing a second time for photographers.

Although he visited the White House, Colonel Coolidge refused to move in, even after he knew he was terminally ill. Via a direct telephone line hookup, the president called him daily. "I think only two or three fathers have seen their sons chosen to be president," he said in one note. "I am sure I came to it largely by your bringing up and your example. If that was what you wanted, you have much to be thankful for that you have lived to so great an age to see it."

In 1850, Nathaniel Fillmore became the first father to visit his son as president in the White House. He made the trip to see his beloved granddaughter, as he had promised, but when he received guests with his son and daughter-in-law at one of their weekly public receptions, he was a figure of wonder. The Washington elite flocked to meet this specimen of pioneer living and wonder of elderly health, tall, ramrod straight, and ruddy-complexioned with a thick full mane of white hair. For different reasons, Dr. George Tryon Harding was also a center of attention when he visited his son Warren in the White House. A recognizable and sought-after personality for the press and political supporters, he had already played the most important public role any president's parent had up to that time in an election. Persistent rumors that he had partial African ancestry threatened his son's presidential campaign. Democratic operatives distributed both darkened pictures of Dr. Harding as mute proof, and flyers claiming he had negroid features. While the Republican National Committee decided against distributing the dubious family tree he provided as refutation (tracing the family to the Doomsday book and scattering about it illustrious but imagined relatives like Jefferson

Jesse Grant sought to exploit his son's fame by advertising his business endeavors using the president's name. To his wife, Ulysses S. Grant confided, "I feel myself worse used by my own family than by strangers . . . although I do not think Father, of his own accord, would do me injustice." Jesse blamed Julia for spending his son's money and the resulting hostility kept him from being a White House guest. c. 1869.

Davis), George confronted those who spread the story and nearly beat up one young man for doing so.

As First Father, George made the most of his celebrity, accepting free train tickets and hotel suites, headlining veterans' conventions, and, after being lavishly entertained by Des Moines Democrats, endorsing that party's U.S. Senate candidate—against his son's support of the Republican. He stunned the nation—and his son—by eloping with a third wife (he took ten years off his age and put ten extra on his young wife's on the marriage license). In 1922, when the president came home to Marion, Ohio, for its centennial, he invited his father to parade through town in a caravan of open limousines with celebrities like General Pershing, and stayed with his proud father in his simple wood-frame house. A year later, in that same house, the president lay in his coffin as thousands of mourners filed through the narrow parlor to pay their final respects.

Unlike Coolidge's and Harding's fathers, Jesse Grant tried to control his son's career. When Grant initially resigned from the army early in his military career, Jesse, feeling that he knew best, audaciously wrote the secretary of war requesting that Ulysses be given only a leave of absence. The request was denied. The father was shameless in trying to use his son's prominence for his own benefit. When, years later, Grant became general of the Union Army, Jesse pressured him to use his influence to obtain the lucrative postmastership of his town, Covington, Kentucky. Grant did refuse to give a job to the son of one of Jesse's friends in exchange for a favor from his friend—as Jesse had requested. Jesse Grant also may have prompted the greatest taint on his son's reputation. The "greedy" and "nasty" father (so dubbed by Grant's campaign biographer) asked his son to buy military supplies from a friend—who happened to be Jewish—so Jesse could reap a commission. Overwhelmed by requests from suppliers whose identities he could not possibly know, but intent to cut short his father's scheme, Grant issued a blanket order banning anyone who was Jewish from using trains going south, or even making a contract with the War Department. This forever labeled him as anti-Semitic.

It was then, perhaps, understandable why Mr. Grant was not encouraged to attend his son's

Despite the fact that President Grant offered his father-in-law Fred Dent free shelter and privileges in the White House, the old man never hid his rude contempt for his "no-account son-in-law." He is seen here with his daughter Julia and grandchildren Nellie and Jesse. 1864.
LIBRARY OF CONGRESS

inauguration. Pathetically, he wrote to Julia Grant's brother, who was charged with the inaugural arrangements, asking for rooms in a private home for himself and the president-elect's mother. No effort was made to comply, but he came. Hannah Grant did not—nor did she ever visit the White House.

Hannah Grant, who was in perfectly good health and who often visited a daughter in New Jersey, responded to a reporter's question about her attending her son's inaugural with a dead, silent stare. Modest to the point of leaving the room when she heard compliments for her son, she had, thought one observer, an emotional disorder. Her reaction, however, may have stemmed from the time she had once been pushed to the platform of a Cincinnati Independence Day rally as the great general's mother. It was, explained Jesse, "enough to frighten an old woman. Since that she can't be got out to any public place. She says she don't want to make a show of herself." He added that she nevertheless "interests herself a good deal about politics." Hannah did defend her son against the political scandals caused by underlings, declaring that "every one of the people Ulysses has appointed were highly recommended to him by people who ought to know better. After all, he has given the country a good administration."

During his frequent trips to see his son, it is not certain that Jesse Grant ever stayed, or was even invited to stay, in the White House. Instead, stooped and walking with a crutch, he came over from his cheap hotel room to meet his son for lunches, walks, and carriage rides. One reason he may have been unwelcome was the presence there of the First Lady's father, Frederick Dent. An unabashed racist Confederate, the former Missouri slaveholder enjoyed

Edith Bolling Galt (right) warned her fiancé, President Wilson, of her mother's "peculiar suppression of all emotions" and not to "discuss intimate things with her, for she simply can't do it." Though living nearby in a shabby hotel, Sally Bolling (left) soon relished being part of presidential events—like the baseball season's opening day. 1915.
LIBRARY OF CONGRESS

arguing with the abolitionist president's father, to the delight of their young grandson Jesse. Julia Grant always deferred to her father, who had an opinion on everything in the White House, including the "coarse" china (Julia had to buy a set just for him). When she received, he sat in a chair behind her in the Blue Room. Guests were advised to pay their respects to him first. Most mornings, he offered unsolicited advice to political and business figures who waited in an anteroom before a scheduled conference with the president.

In contrast was Caroline Harrison's eighty-nine-year-old father. John Scott, a founder of Oxford Female Institute, a Miami University math and science professor, a Presbyterian minister, and, most recently, a pension office clerk, remained in the White House the quiet and religious man he had always been. Zeb Rudolph and John Herron, the fathers of Lucretia Garfield and Nellie Taft, respectively, were too frail to visit the White House. Nancy Reagan's adoptive father, neurosurgeon Loyal Davis, made two brief visits there with her mother, once for the inaugural and then, weeks later, for a ceremony inducting him into Ireland's College of Surgeons. At age fourteen Nancy had sought to become his legally adopted daughter, her natural father having divorced her mother. Davis strongly influenced Nancy's sense of decorum, and Reagan, many assert, absorbed his conservative view against government intrusion on the medical industry. Famous for her bawdy mischief and salty language, stage and radio actress Edie Davis was the opposite of her husband—even defiantly remaining a Democrat after her marriage to him. President Reagan was particularly close to her, swapping jokes and sending her flowers on Nancy's birthday. By the mid-1980s, however, Edie's memory had failed and she was confined to a wheelchair in a small apartment with nursing care.

Another Chicago Republican father of a First Lady—who did *not* influence his son-in-law's politics—was the feisty businessman Hugh Rodham. Democrat Bill Clinton was not even certain Rodham would permit him into their home, but by Clinton's first run for office, Rodham was manning the campaign telephones. "Lord, how they loved to argue," Clinton recalled of his wife and her father. "Each one tried to rewrite history to put the proper spin on it. It was wonderful

Nancy Reagan called her frail mother, Edie Davis, every day at her Phoenix home. She and husband and their daughter Patti visit her here. 1982.

RONALD REAGAN PRESIDENTIAL LIBRARY

preparation for politics." The Rodhams gave Hillary what she called "drop-dead stability," balancing tough expectations with unconditional support. "I may not always like what you do," Rodham told her, "but I will always love you." Dorothy Rodham instilled her daughter's trademark compassion for the less fortunate. Said the First Lady, her mother had "a great spirit of resilience and caring about people." She also found that by seeing her father do some cooking and her mother enjoying sports, she could make choices that were not confined to stereotypes. Mrs. Rodham continued to be a strong presence in the White House life of her daughter's family, and her Little Rock home served as the official residence of the president when he visited there. She accompanied the Clintons on an Asian state visit, vacationed in Hawaii with Hillary, and went with the president and her granddaughter on a state visit to Australia.

With all his power, President Woodrow Wilson was still frightened of meeting the mother of his fiancée, Edith Bolling Galt, telling his intended, "I shall try hard to make her love me and to overlook my faults." Eventually he won her over and she was frequently at the White House—to celebrate her birthday or the Armistice, or just to consult the Ouija board with her daughter. So intimidating was heiress Julianna Gardiner that despite the fact that she was actually younger than her prospective son-in-law, John Tyler timidly wrote her for permission to marry her daughter Julia, reminding her of his "position in Society"—President of the United States. She would "acquiesce" only if he could provide "necessary comforts and elegancies of life." Tyler was not nearly as wealthy as the Gardiners, but the marriage (an elopement) took place. Mrs. Gardiner said that it hit her at breakfast that her new "son" was president— a job she had fancied for her own sons. Despite her frequent migraines, Julianna often visited the White House, paying for its thorough cleaning and decoration ("You know how I detest a dirty house") while dismissing Washington as "vastly inferior to New York in point of wealth." Snobbish, obsessive, hypochondriacal, explosive, absolutist, she was not easily ignored. "Let your husband work during business hours," she told Julia. "Business should take the precedence of caressing—reserve your caressing for private leisure and be sure you let no one see it unless you wish to be laughed at. . . . You must not believe all the President says about the honeymoon lasting always—he has found out that you in common with the rest of Eve's daughters are fond of flattery." On running the country, Julianna admonished Julia to "be a politician" and "look deep into the affairs of state." Her warning about the press struck a modern tone: "You must not mind any objections made of you in the newspapers. You will not escape censure. Do your best."

Many a mother-in-law has directed her maternalism toward the president. Perhaps the feistiest was Emma Folsom, mother of Mrs. Grover Cleveland. When she was discovered by reporters in Paris—buying clothes for her second marriage, to a John Perrin—the yellow press printed rumors that Cleveland "pummeled his mother-in-law" and "exiled her to Europe." Emma pummeled back: "All this is beneath notice, and is a matter best treated with contemptuous silence. It is all a foolish campaign ploy without a shadow of foundation." An equally close loyalty existed between Eisenhower and his mother-in-law, Elvira Doud, whom he nicknamed Minnie, or Min, after the Andy Gump cartoon strip character. She and the president, her grandson John Eisenhower said, "constituted a mutual admiration society, and each took the other's part whenever a family disagreement would arise."

Min practically adopted Ike. During the president's annual summer sojourn to Denver, her house became his official residence and it was then that Min's sassiness emerged and was reported by the national press. Reporters were confounded to see a red carpet rolled out from the front steps of the relatively modest home to the sidewalk: remembering how daughter Mamie always complained about having to sit on the cold concrete steps, Min had humorously, literally, rolled out the red carpet. When the president received a gift of a large cheese from friends, Min whacked her carving knife into it and gleefully handed out hunks to neigh-

Emma Folsom was a longtime friend of Grover Cleveland, her late husband's law partner. Before her twenty-one-year-old daughter Frances surprised the nation by marrying the bachelor president in 1886, it was widely believed that Emma was his secret fiancée. 1886.

LIBRARY OF CONGRESS

bors along the street. It was also in Mrs. Doud's home, however, that the president suffered his heart attack in 1955.

Min delighted in belying the image of an old granny. Living in the White House during the winters, she lingered in bed after waking—as did Mamie in her room—and the two got on the phone with each other. "This is a long-distance call from Mother!" Mamie chirped to a staffer one morning, waving her cigarette to indicate Min in the suite across the hall. Adopted as mascot of the Air Force One flight crew, she often popped up at the air force base to take practice flights with them. She also unabashedly enjoyed the limelight. On Mother's Day, for example, she endlessly posed for the press with her two daughters kissing each side of her face. In presidential motorcades, she rode in the front seat of the limousine right behind the president's so she could watch the crowd reaction to him. Always available for a colorful quote at the Denver dog races, which she frequented, she made headlines—and irritated Ike—by declaring, "Mamie can't stand another four years in the White House." Her statement was taken by political analysts as a sign that Eisenhower wouldn't seek a second term, and put him under pressure to declare his candidacy.

Min could also whip up a little controversy. Annoyed by the noise of congressmen and other officials who talked to reporters as they left meetings with the president in the West Wing, right below her bedroom window, she successfully requested that the conferences be banned from the area—until news of her edict made the news. An electrician recalled coming in to fix Mrs. Doud's color television as she snapped about the darkened figures on the screen using a racial epithet—leaving the president in stunned silence. Mrs. Doud, recalled her grandson, was "an odd mixture of Victorian propriety and outgoing friendliness." Her death in September 1960 was a hard loss for both Mamie and Ike.

One mother-in-law never won over was Lemira Goodhue. She had futilely tried all she could to prevent her daughter Grace's marriage to Calvin Coolidge. Even after he became president, she sniped that he would never have risen to anything had he not married her daughter. No presidential mother-in-law, however, was more disrespectful of her son-in-law than was Truman's, Madge Wallace. The haughty crone called him a "dirt farmer" and often said in his presence, "My daughter could have married someone from her own background!" Though she lived in the White House, her attacks on him continued unabated. She found

Former First Lady Mamie Eisenhower was the grandmother of David Eisenhower, who married Nixon daughter Julie. She was considered part of the Nixon family and spent much time with them in the White House, always staying in the Queen's Bedroom. She is seen here with Tricia Nixon, and Pat Nixon, who relaxes on the floor. 1972. NIXON PRESIDENTIAL MATERIALS, NATIONAL ARCHIVES

Madge Wallace is separated at the breakfast table from her son-in-law Harry Truman by her daughter-in-law Natalie. c. 1945–1948.

everything from his bow tie to his table manners to be undignified. During his 1948 campaign, Mrs. Wallace remarked that he was delusional in thinking he could defeat "that nice man" Thomas E. Dewey, adding, "I know dozens of men better qualified to be in Mr. Truman's place in the White House."

With Madge's emotional hold over her daughter, Bess Truman was often forced to choose loyalties between her parent and spouse. When Mrs. Wallace wanted her daughter she simply refused to eat until Bess dropped what she was doing—official or otherwise—and came to her. Every day, Bess read her the newspaper, and when a friend offered to substitute, Madge yelled at her to get out of her room. When the president tried to help, she turned her back on him, not even acknowledging his presence. Finally, after Truman fired General Douglas MacArthur and Madge sniped, "Why did your husband have to fire that nice man?" Bess shot back, "My husband, Mother, happens to be commander in chief! My husband does what he believes is best for the country!" Truman managed a subtle revenge through his campaign jokes, such as he did in Helper, Utah, where he cracked that Congress was like a "big-mouthed mother-in-law."

Some mothers-in-law do come around. Kennedy's became his rabid supporter after initial resistance during the planning of her daughter Jackie's wedding to him. Janet Lee Bouvier Auchincloss played the grande dame—even so far as to declare that she was a descendant of Virginia's aristocratic Lee family, when in fact she was the granddaughter of an Irish immigrant from New York's East Side tenements. Wanting a private society wedding at her Newport summer home, Hammersmith Farm, she clashed with the Kennedys, who saw it as a chance to promote the political career of groom Senator Kennedy. They won. Soon enough, however, it was Republican Janet who was pushing friends to make large contributions to Kennedy's presidential campaign—and refused to permit anyone to criticize him even mildly in her presence. Making her permanent home only about twenty minutes' drive from the White House, when she heard about plans for commercially developing the wooded area nearby, she convinced JFK to have the land federally protected. Janet and Jack enjoyed indulging each other in mock horror at Jackie's decorating in shades of beige, her "rather wild" windswept hairdo, and her clothes—"which not *everyone* approved of," her mother pointedly informed admirers of the First Lady's casual style.

One president directly credited his mother-in-law for his rising to his position. "If Mother Allie hadn't brought up Rosalynn the way she did, I would probably not be president," Jimmy Carter admitted. When she had become suddenly widowed at thirty-four, Allie Smith had raised her four children by working as a seamstress, relying on Rosalynn, the eldest. After being forced to retire at age seventy as postmistress of her town, Plains, Georgia, Mrs. Smith determined to continue working, and despite her son-in-law's position, managed to keep busy, employed part-time in a local flower shop. She taught her daughter tremendous self-reliance and discipline. "I take after my mother," said the First Lady, "because she worked all her life, was active, and didn't depend on anyone." Although her sudden fame prevented Allie from keeping her door unlocked or her phone number listed, she had no Secret Service protection, a rather remarkable feat by the late 1970s. She visited the White House often.

Several mothers never visited their sons in the White House. John Adams's lived only forty-five days into his presidency. Madison's never came to Washington from her relatively close Virginia home. Polk's mother abhorred the idea of her son in the ungodly capital; her life focused instead on "the Bible, the Confession of Faith, the Psalms and Watts' Hymns." The first First Mother who called the White House home did so for only four months, but Eliza Garfield enjoyed every moment of it, starting with the Inaugural Ball, when she dressed in a black silk robe. "This is a happy day," she said, "when a mother can see her son inaugurated President of the United States. I am a proud mother."

The public already knew much about "Mother Garfield" from the previous summer's campaign news stories and illustrated drawings of her benign countenance. During the transition she was in fact the recipient of an avalanche of grasping requests for public office, the supplicants appealing to her assumed motherly benevolence. The story of how the scrappy widow went against conventional wisdom to keep up her late husband's farm, and "by the sterling force of character and high resolve" to keep her family together all became part of Garfield's lore. There were further lessons for American mothers in the churned-out tales of how she planted trees, hoed potatoes, husked corn, hauled manure, plowed fields, repaired wares, did carpentry, split rails, sewed clothes, and made candles. Recalling her counsel to "remember God and study books," Garfield admitted, "At almost every turning point in my life, she has been the molding agent."

On Christmas, the Carter family traditionally went for breakfast to the home of the president's mother, Lillian, seen here with the president and her other son, Billy, who carries a can of the beer manufactured with his name. Afterward, the family went to the home of Allie Smith, the First Lady's mother (at right in lower photograph). 1978.

JIMMY CARTER PRESIDENTIAL LIBRARY

That dear Mother Garfield had also remarried and then divorced was not published. Nor were the stories of how she demanded to be escorted into dinner on the president's arm and sit at his right hand at the table, and to be given the choicest accommodations. When James and his wife seemed too interested in their duties as hosts, Mother Garfield railed against "vicious and ungodly company." If others seemed to preoccupy the president, she reminded him that she might die at any moment and he must devote himself to prayer for her.

In the mansion, the eighty-year-old woman gleefully reported to her little red diary on everything from the "parties every night" to the president's tooth ailments. Initially, she seemed neglected: "I am alone a good deal and have time for meditation—my prayer is that this administration may prove a success. I am piecing a quilt. I must have something to do. I can't sit and fold my hands." By early April, however, she began appearing at public events such as the unveiling of Admiral Farragut's statue, and went to inspect the nearby accommodations at the anticipated summer White House. Keeping abreast of any press criticism of the president, she gloated when praise came. "I guess they have found that he has got some Back bone yet," she scribbled. Idealized as a Victorian model of motherhood ("hers is a heroic soul . . . from no common mould. . . . In her veins runs the blood of the Puritans, and all the energy, intelligence and perseverance of that grand old race. . . . such a mother is a fit woman to raise a President"), she managed her own public image by editing her studio photographs for public release.

It seemed that Ohio Republicans knew a good thing when they had it, for sixteen years later Nancy McKinley was pictured on posters and souvenirs with her son William during his presidential campaign from the front porch of his Canton home. As the candidate spoke, "Mother McKinley" often sat rocking in her chair on the porch before the eyes of voter delegations and reporters as a live tableau of American domesticity. Appearing at a Methodist rally where her son was being endorsed, Mrs. McKinley's well-known religiosity was a political asset. "In honoring your mother," one political group wrote the candidate about his escorting his mother to church each Sunday, "you have honored womankind." On election night, when the *Chicago Times-Herald* editor phoned, he was told the president-elect and his mother were kneeling in prayer as she chanted, "Oh, God, keep him humble." The second woman to witness a son's inauguration, she was rather unimpressed. "Mother, this is better than a bishopric," her son Abner repeated to her through that day. Although Nancy McKinley made no further trips to Washington, the president established his summer White House in 1897 in her home—her famous fruit pies being one of the nightly perks.

The political culture of the twentieth century saw so many examples of a tough and forthright First Mother that she now seems almost a requisite figure among First Families. Sara Roosevelt, Martha Truman, Rose Kennedy, Lillian Carter, Dorothy Bush, and Virginia Clinton Kelley were radically different, but each was indomitable.

With a strong emotional grip on her only child, Franklin, Sara Delano Roosevelt tried to extend control over his own family. When Franklin Jr. wrecked a car, for example, his parents refused to buy him a new one—so Grandmother Sara indulged him. If the First Lady seemed to ruffle the president with political questions, Sara simply nodded for the butler to bring FDR's wheelchair, and she helped wheel him out and away from his wife. When, during one of her frequent stints in the mansion, she said it was improper for the presidential mansion to have African-American servants, Eleanor Roosevelt finally confronted the grande dame. "Mother," the First Lady told her, "I have never told you this before, but I must tell you now. You run your house, and I'll run mine."

The First Mother sarcastically complained about the First Lady's social reformer associates and working-class friends, particularly former New York state trooper Earl Miller. "First it was Private Miller. Then it was Sergeant Miller. Then it was Commander Miller. Now it's Earl dear," she said, mimicking the First Lady's voice. Her son's associates fared just as poorly. She refused to permit his adoring secretary Missy LeHand to stay in the main family house—which she still owned—at Hyde Park, New York, when he visited. She disapprovingly called his political ally, former New York governor Al Smith, "that man"—loud enough for him to hear—and witheringly referred to Labor Secretary Frances Perkins and Assistant Treasury Secretary Jo Roche as "these women!"

Sara relished her public status. She presided over the New York March of Dimes Ball, one of several regional fund-raisers held annually on FDR's birthday, staying well past midnight, "grand old war-horse that she is," said a niece. She became the first First Mother to write a book—*My Boy Franklin*—a precedent followed by Kennedy's and Clinton's mothers, and she greedily expected all sorts of gifts and privileges, for despite her great wealth she was notoriously tightfisted. Whenever the president came to Hyde Park, Sara demanded and was granted the official status of his hostess. When she pushed for similar standing at the White House, FDR finally stood up to her and said he could not overrule protocol. "Am I proud of being an historic mother? Indeed I am," she boasted to reporters.

In contrast was the earthy, peppery Martha Ellen Truman. When she emerged from her first airplane flight—for her first visit to the White House—into a thicket of photographers and reporters, she snapped, "If I'd known there was going to be all this fuss, I wouldn't have come." An unreconstructed Confederate, she balked at the idea of sleeping in the Lincoln Bedroom, saying she'd sleep on the floor instead. Put up in the Queen's Bedroom, she moved into its more modest sitting room. Despite the strangers and reporters who pestered her, she initially refused to have a fence built around her Missouri home, and often invited people in. Reporters found her sharp answers to their questions refreshing. Of course she was proud of Harry, she said, "but I've got another son I am just as proud of, and I have a daughter that I am just as proud of." Asked later that year if she had voted, the old woman cracked, "I certainly did. And I'm thinking of voting again on my way home."

If his inheritance of that directness proved a political asset for Truman, Martha's plain elo-

Harry Truman's mother, Martha Truman, is joined by her daughter Mary Jane in a visit to the White House.

HARRY S. TRUMAN PRESIDENTIAL LIBRARY

quence helped calm a nation still at war and having doubts about his ability. "I cannot really be glad my son is President because I am sorry that President Roosevelt is dead. If he had been voted in, I would be out waving a flag," she said. "Harry will get along. . . . Everyone who heard him talk this morning will know he is sincere and will do what is best." In fact, said his daughter, it was to his mother that Truman "turned again and again for the emotional support he needed to maintain his balance in the presidency." Frequently the president wrote her daily, even confiding to her his top-secret Potsdam Conference talks with Winston Churchill and Joseph Stalin. She read the *Congressional Record* and debated with her son when she disagreed with his decisions. "Harry," she asked him bluntly in the spring of 1947 about the next year's presidential election, "are you going to run?" He said he didn't know. "Don't you think it's about time you made up your mind?"

Reminiscent of Martha Truman was the witty Lillian Carter, a former nurse, college fraternity housemother, and Peace Corps volunteer. The first presidential mother to serve as her son's official representative overseas, she attended the funerals of Pope Paul VI, Golda Meir, and Marshal Tito, and led an African fact-finding mission to regions overcome by drought. In the United States, she campaigned for Democratic candidates, and was even in demand on the college campus lecture circuit. "Miss Lillian" kept her permanent base in Plains (where she always hosted the family's Christmas morning gathering, while Rosalynn's mother gave the dinner), but she frequently stayed at the White House, in the Queen's Room—"Where I belong," she cracked. No one escaped her blunt quips. When Morocco's Prince Hassan came for a state visit, the president took him upstairs to see his mother. Recalling her recent trip to his country, she remarked on the multitude of perfumes she had found in her suite. He offered to send her some. "You damn foreigners are all alike," she retorted.

Seemingly game for any repartee, instantly recognizable in her snow-white pixie haircut, Miss Lillian was an eager celebrity of the late 1970s—whether cheering heartily at the World Series, playing poker on the way back from the pope's funeral, or sounding off on everything from the Equal Rights Amendment ("Don't ask me, I've been liberated all my life") to her son's judgment ("Jimmy's always right . . . the greatest man on earth"). Certainly her most controversial remark came during the crisis when the leader of Iran held Americans hostage. "If I had a million dollars," said Miss Lillian, "I would hire someone to shoot the ayatollah!" The statement made world headlines.

In contrasting style, but with a similar influence on her son was George Bush's mother, Dorothy. A former champion tennis and golf player, the fiercely competitive Dorothy Bush instilled a strict value system of compassion toward the less fortunate and enforced a code of modesty in her son, attempting to keep him from becoming spoiled by his wealthy background. A former U.S. senator's wife, she was also well informed on politics, and during her son's vice presidency her disagreement with his tie-breaking vote in the Senate to resume nerve gas production became public knowledge—President Reagan even phoned to try to convince her that it was a necessity. During her son's 1989 inaugural (for which she was transported by ambulance plane from her Florida home), Dorothy Bush stayed in the Queen's Room and greeted tourists from the window, and then on the driveway in her wheelchair. The next day, she sat beside her son on his first workday in the Oval Office. Her frail condition, however, prevented further trips. Instead, she was a quiet presence at the summer White House at her home in Maine, matriarch of four generations and relishing her family's gathering there during her July birthday celebration. Her bungalow was even used as the official guest house for visiting French president François Mitterrand. Most evenings, Mrs. Bush would silently hold her son's hand as they watched the news on television. Time often faded her memory, but she surprised everyone with sudden quips. When Bush asked at her eighty-eighth birthday which one had been her best, she piped up, "Well, of course, today, George. I am sitting here holding the hand of my son, the President of the United States."

Virginia Kelley, widowed three times, had to leave her son Bill Clinton with her parents in order to earn a nursing degree as an adult. The turbulence of her life served as a lesson to Clinton in his presidential bid: "During those really tough days in the campaign I would think about how so many of Mother's difficulties had gone on for years and years. In my case, the voters would simply make up their minds and everything would be resolved with the election." Mrs. Kelley became a nationally recognized figure during the 1992 campaign with not only what she called her "weird hair, my heavy makeup, my loud colors, and my penchant for playing the horses," but the fact that her State Department passport file had been searched by a Bush White House official for any damaging information on her son. Along with her husband Dick Kelley, Virginia attended the inaugural and made several White House visits. Using the Queen's Bedroom, she found her first night there unbelievable. "Even for an old girl who's pretty much seen everything that goes on after dark," she said, "sleeping in the White House for the first time is quite a feeling." The next morning, Clinton took her to the exact spot in the Rose Garden where as a teenager he had shaken the hand of President Kennedy. During other visits through 1993, she stayed at Camp David, traveling there by Marine One, the presidential helicopter, and conferred with Clinton privately in the Oval Office.

If parental instincts endure regardless of a child's age, being a parent to a President or First Lady must convey a mixture of personal pride and a remote sense of loss. "Sometimes when I watch him," said Virginia Kelley, "I can separate the man from my son. In those moments I see him as the world leader he is, the eloquent speaker and erudite thinker and earnest consensus builder. Other times, especially when he's hurting, he's just a big old gray-haired version of my little boy."

8

Extended Family

*Public policy clearly indicates the propriety and
desirability of the President's private secretary being,
if possible, a blood relation, upon the ground that the
honor and interests of the President and his high
office can be most safely entrusted to one having an
interest in his good name and fame, and therefore
more guarded against temptation of any kind. I
therefore do not consider the selection of myself, or
my cousin Mr. James Buchanan who followed me,
as any exception to what I have stated.*

—James B. Henry, *nephew of James Buchanan*

They are usually the embarrassing ones—the kin to be investigated, exploiting their connection—yet among extended family members have been the most loyal and protective, willing to halt their lives to aid their famous relatives: siblings, nieces, nephews, aunts, uncles, and assorted in-laws.

White House life before the Civil War was often dominated by extended family. With travel to Washington by stagecoach and steamer sometimes taking weeks, relatives would often stay for a month or longer during the social and holiday season, November to March. Also, before 1857 presidents were not provided with funds for a clerical staff, and relatives were pressed into service. This was the case from the beginning—John Adams used his wife's nephew Billy Shaw, and James Madison used his wife's cousin Ned Coles as their private secretaries. It also meant that presidents often had not only to provide kin with food and lodging but sometimes a salary, paid out of their own pockets.

Occasionally, it was worth it for damage control. James Monroe's hotheaded brother Joseph, long a financial burden, was finally reined in by living in the White House with his son James and third wife, Elizabeth, and sharing the work of presidential private secretary with Monroe's son-in-law George Hay. It was surely tense. Some years earlier, Joseph had bitterly feuded with Eliza Hay, the president's imperious daughter, over her apparent resentment of his debts and marriage to a less than socially prestigious woman. Joseph left abruptly, expecting his daughters to be supported by Monroe—who refused to do so. "Situated as I am in public life with a painful recollection of many distressing circumstances . . . which have attended my connection with your father through life," he wrote one of the nieces, "I cannot undertake to invite you into my family, but will always be your friend."

Three years later, Joseph created a potentially damaging political situation. Jefferson's unpredictable nephew, Peter Carr, stirred rumors that his uncle wouldn't support Monroe for president. Monroe asked George Hay to quash the tale, but Joseph suddenly threatened to publish a pamphlet blasting Carr and other Jefferson loyalists for their ingratitude to Monroe. Monroe managed to quell his brother, now living with him again. James Madison proposed getting rid of his friend Monroe's troublesome sibling by giving him an official post in Mississippi Territory, but the assignment never came through. Three years into Monroe's presidency, Joseph finally left for Missouri.

Joseph may have resented his brother's reliance on the wily lawyer Hay. The government attorney who successfully prosecuted Aaron Burr for treason, Hay was an excellent campaign manager and confidant to Monroe. He was twenty years his wife's senior, and sparks apparently flew between the couple, but Hay remained indispensable to the family, sometimes serving as their central point of correspondence when members were apart, and a skillful editor of his father-in-law's speeches and public statements. Monroe's successor, John Quincy Adams, named Hay to a federal judgeship and Monroe's other son-in-law, Samuel Gouverneur, as New York postmaster.

Having relatives in an official capacity provoked no public debate under Monroe and Madison since they weren't on the federal payroll. Until federal law preventing nepotism was enacted (after Kennedy appointed his brother Robert attorney general), it was rampant. Still, it was a matter of honor with certain presidents to be free of any nepotism charges. Jefferson explained to his cousin George, for example, that: "The public will never be made to believe that an appointment of a relative is made on the grounds of merit alone, uninfluenced by family views; nor can they ever see with approbation offices, the disposal of which they intrust to their Presidents for public purposes, divided out as family property. Mr. Adams degraded himself infinitely by his conduct on this subject, as General Washington had done himself the greatest honor. With two such examples to proceed by, I should be doubly inexcusable to err. It is true that this places the relations of the President in a worse situation than if he were a stranger, but the public good, which can not be effected if its confidence be lost, requires this sacrifice."

Jefferson's swipe at Adams was in reference to his appointing his son-in-law William Smith to numerous federal posts, reappointing his son John Quincy as minister to Portugal and then

Prussia, naming his wife's brother as Quincy, Massachusetts, postmaster, and making John Quincy's father-in-law Joshua Johnson superintendent of stamps in Washington, D.C. Andrew Jackson figured a way to make nepotism benefit himself. He had his nephew Jack Donelson hired onto the government payroll as general land office clerk, then requisitioned him to work in the White House. Van Buren followed suit, placing his son Martin in Donelson's old job and his son Abraham in that of second auditor of the Treasury department, using both sons as his secretaries. John Tyler used the land office trick to have his son Robert work as presidential secretary, and Fillmore did so also, with his son Powers. Henry Harrison worked as his great-uncle William's aide, but it is not certain by whom he was paid. Polk found this unprincipled and personally paid his nephew James Knox Walker, twenty-six, to fill the post, while Walker's wife, Augusta, aided the First Lady. The Walkers and four of their eventual nine children received free room and board in the White House and lived richly on his salary—too richly for the man paying it. "In truth, he is too fond of spending his time in fashionable & light society," Polk noted of his nephew, "and does not give that close attention to business which is necessary. This I have observed for some months with great regret."

Joseph Taylor, confidant and Mexican War comrade of his older brother, Zachary, was asked by him to serve as a presidential aide. Joe, his wife, Evelyn, and daughter Becky stayed in the White House when Congress was in session, but lived in nearby Baltimore. Similar in appearance and manner to the president, Joe was courted by senators such as Salmon Chase and William Seward to get the president's ear. He shared his duties with Taylor's son-in-law William W. Bliss, nicknamed "Perfect Bliss," for his gallant demeanor in the eye of administrative flurries. Well-spoken and literary, thirty-three-year-old Bliss was indispensable as private secretary but was frequently criticized by the *Washington Union* for having what the newspaper perceived to be too much power. Taylor kept Bliss and Joe Taylor on active military duty, thus providing them with salaries besides the free housing.

Buchanan took full advantage of the 1857 congressional appropriation that finally provided a federal salary of $2,500 for the president's private secretary. He put his ward and orphaned nephew, James Buchanan Henry, on the dole, watching the Princeton graduate like a hawk. From eight to five, the twenty-three-year-old "Buck," as he was called, would pay the steward—who was also now federally salaried—requisition coal and oil, manage Buchanan's finances, maintain incoming and outgoing correspondence, and deliver documents to the cabinet and Congress. "No father could have bestowed a more faithful and judicious care," Buck recalled of his uncle, "than this somewhat stern but devoted bachelor." The president had forced Buck to eat vegetables and told him that unless he achieved academic honors "your presence will afford me no pleasure," but forbidding the young attorney to grow a mustache was the last straw. Buck quit, then married without his uncle's approval. Another nephew, James Buchanan II, took the job.

Examples of presidential nepotism abound. Despite the fact that Polk paid out of pocket

William Bliss with his arm around his father-in-law, President Zachary Taylor, to whom he was indispensable. 1848.
NATIONAL PORTRAIT GALLERY

for his nephew to work as his secretary, he had no qualms about appointing his younger brother William as chargé d'affaires to Naples. William Polk had initially entrenched himself and his wife, Belinda, in the White House for a lengthy stay. He was constantly in debt and, as Polk correctly predicted, "abandoned to other vices," so William's being sent to Italy was probably worth the risk of criticism compared to the drain on the president.

Many a First Lady pulled strings for kin as well. Abigail Fillmore's brother David Powers was made postmaster of Sanderly City, New York. Living in the White House, Edith Wilson's brother Randolph Bolling was presidential secretary in the last four months of the Wilson administration. Certainly no family was more indulged with patronage than that of Julia Dent Grant. Despite his having crushed Dixie as a Union general, Grant's southern in-laws got so many favors from him that the White House was derisively known as "Dents' Retreat." As inaugural chairman, Julia's brother Fred arranged for a "private" ball so black Republican leaders would not have to be invited, and was federally salaried as a Grant aide. Her brother John was given an interest in an Indian post tradership—and later discovered to be profiteering illegally from it. Her sister Emma's husband, James Casey, was named collector of the Port of New Orleans and implicated in corruption on the job. Her sister Nellie's husband was made marshal of the District of Columbia, and the couple was omnipresent at the White House, Nellie even substituting for her sister at some events. Only brother Louis, a white supremacist who ran for governor of Mississippi, got no help from the Grants. A constant source of political ammunition, the Dents were even criticized in 1872 on the Senate floor by Charles Sumner: "A dozen members of the family billeted upon the country!" The June 1872 issue of the *National Quarterly Review* cracked that the nation's worst criminal mob was "the Dent family ring."

Grant's family created their own trouble. His brother Orvil avariciously used his fame for business deals and was also involved in the Indian trading post scandal, admitting to having had a partial interest in two posts. Sister Virginia was married to one Abel Corbin, who

Carolyn Votaw (far left), her father, Dr. George Tryon Harding, brother Warren Harding, and their sister Miss Daisy, the local high school principal. 1920.

SCHERMER COLLECTION

schemed with financiers Jay Gould and James Fisk to corner the gold market and manipulate the president to go along with it in fiscal policy. The rather entangled scheme resulted in the president's sister—and possibly the president's wife—speculating in gold at the urging of Corbin. Learning of this, Grant released Treasury gold and told his wife to tell his sister to stop her transactions, but not before a monumental crash of gold prices ruined thousands in a scandal known as Black Friday. Democrats pressed to have Grant's sister and wife interrogated in Congress—a move squashed by Republicans.

Warren Harding's sister Carolyn Votaw did find herself before congressional investigators, implicated in scandal—but she had taken action immediately to report malfeasance when she first learned of it. She and her husband, Heber, were Seventh Day Adventist missionaries who had also worked in health and education professions. Harding named Heber as superintendent of prisons, but his cover-up of a large narcotics ring in an Atlanta penitentiary prompted

[1 4 5]

Ronald Reagan shares a joke with his brother Neil "Moon" Reagan and sister-in-law Bess, in the presidential suite of the Century Plaza Hotel, which was the president's Los Angeles headquarters. 1984.

RONALD REAGAN PRESIDENTIAL LIBRARY

With his brother the president and mother Virginia Kelley, just days before her death to cancer, is Roger Clinton. In 1999, he led an unprecedented goodwill trip of musicians to North Korea. 1993.

THE WHITE HOUSE

a federal investigation. Carolyn was an intelligent, articulate, and dynamic woman with progressive ideas about health. Harding made her director of the industrial hygiene service of the U.S. Public Health Service, and she persuaded him to support the long-term concept of a department of health and welfare. Determined to create an experimental model of healthy working conditions in the veterans bureau, she came under the wing of its director, Charlie Forbes, a poker-playing crony of the president's. On trips to scout sites for hospitals, she realized that Forbes was taking kickbacks and reported this to Florence Harding, then testified against him in congressional hearings. Carolyn was more innocently used by a young hometown friend. When Nan Britton came to Washington with her daughter Elizabeth Ann, Carolyn brought them to the White House to see Harding—who turned out to be busy. Unknown to Votaw, Britton was a mistress of the president's who claimed that he was also the father of her daughter.

Presidents' brothers have most often been the source of *potential* embarrassment: Roger Clinton, who had once been imprisoned for illicit substance use; Prescott Bush, investigated by the Securities and Exchange Commission for alleged business ties to Japanese mobsters; Neil Reagan, revealed—during the Reagan presidency—to have been an FBI informant on suspected communist sympathizers; Billy Carter, famous for marketing "Billy Beer," who accepted a $220,000 payment to lobby for Libya; Donald Nixon, who had his phone tapped for trying to peddle influence with his brother; the self-described "drinking and wenching" Sam Houston Johnson, who admitted that his brother, LBJ, put him under Secret Service surveillance to curb his behavior; Senate candidate Teddy Kennedy, who during his brother's presidency confessed to cheating on law school exams. Even a century ago, Abner McKinley tried to exploit his famous name—selling worthless railroad bonds, printing telegraph stock, and trying to market "artificial rubber." All he got out of the president were some free railroad passes.

Brothers-in-law also posed problems. Alcoholic brothers of Florence Harding, Eleanor Roosevelt, and Bess Truman were unpredictable. Florence's brother Vetallis—who married a Catholic and scandalized their small town—was not even invited to the inaugural. In the case of Mrs. Truman's brother, the fear of public discovery created an ongoing undercurrent of family tension. The murder of Ida McKinley's brother during her husband's presidency—and the ensuing trial in which his mistress was exonerated for pulling the trigger—was ignored by the White House. Madison sent away his drunken brother-in-law John Payne—to Tripoli as the American consul's secretary. On the other hand, men like Nancy Reagan's brother Richard Davis, Jackie Kennedy's stepbrother Yusha Auchincloss, Ellen Wilson's brother Stockton Axson, and Florence Harding's brother Cliff rushed to the mansion to offer support in times of crisis.

Women relatives have tended to be more helpful. Julia Tyler's witty sister Margaret Gardiner volunteered as social secretary, and their cousins Phoebe and Mary Gardiner came

When Sarah Yorke (right), a Quaker from Philadelphia, married President Andrew Jackson's son and namesake (left), she helped calm the young man's impetuousness and grew extraordinarily close to her father-in-law.

Ladies Hermitage Association

Harriet Lane, James Buchanan's niece, managed to sneak letters back and forth with a friend—who had become a political enemy of her uncle—by putting them in dairy kettles that came full to the White House and went back empty to a dairy near her friend's home. c. 1857

Wheatlands, home of James Buchanan

to serve in Julia's "court," dressed alike in white as "vestal virgins" who sat, six on each side of Julia, on a raised dais in the Blue Room. The eighteen-year-old—dubbed "Phoebe the Coquette" by the president's son Robert—received marriage proposals from a Virginia state senator and the governor of Washington Territory within a half-hour of each other, but she was smitten with the already betrothed brother of president-elect Polk. Meanwhile, Mary pined for her absent lover, Eben Horsford, whom she later married. After Mary's death, Phoebe married him too.

Caroline Harrison's sister Lizzie Lord served as social secretary until her health deteriorated, and then Lizzie's widowed daughter Mary Dimmick filled the post. A strong emotional—some suggest romantic—relationship developed between niece Mary and the president to the point that the First Lady considered returning to Indianapolis. After her aunt died, Mary married her uncle.

In other cases, a First Lady's poor health required that a relative assume some of the entertaining duties. After Nellie Taft's stroke, her sisters Eleanor Moore, Maria Herron, and Jennie Anderson took turns as hostess and living in the mansion. Hester Gouverneur of New York did the same for her rheumatic and perhaps epileptic sister, Elizabeth Monroe. Four nieces who came to aid invalid Ida McKinley became press favorites: vaudeville singer Mabel McKinley, who had hits like "Nona from Arizona" and "Honey, You Stay in Your Own Backyard"; Mount Holyoke graduate Grace McKinley; athletic Sarah Duncan, a Chicago kindergarten teacher; and the First Lady's niece, Smith College student Mary Barber—who detested waiting upon her aunt but enjoyed the attention.

Abby Kent Means initially substituted as hostess for Jane Pierce. The wealthy widow of Jane's maternal uncle, Robert Means, Abby was able to cope with Jane's severe neurosis and endless illnesses, and was something of a progressive in her abolitionism and intolerance of anti-Catholicism (she called a table of congressmen "very stupid" because they were bigoted Know-Nothing Party members).

The president and Mrs. Pierce had no children, all three sons having died young; the last one, Bennie, died just weeks before the inaugural in a train crash in which he was killed before their eyes. They are an interesting case study of the importance of an extended presidential family. To the outside world, there appeared to be a lonely White House of two grieving parents. Yet in the private quarters, the rooms were filled with a wide and dependable group of relatives. Particularly in his closing days, the president depended heavily upon the presence and advice of his brother, Henry, who had earlier helped manage Pierce's political rise. "You ought to come on every account," Pierce beseeched Henry, "but I desire to see you especially to converse about plans for life when my labors here shall come to a close." His nephews Frank and Kirk also visited.

A circle of Mrs. Pierce's kin kept her spirits up, and at least one was always with her: sister Mary Aiken, her husband, John, and their children Jenny, Mary Elizabeth, John, and

Relatives Who Worked Officially and Unofficially in the White House

Bartholemew Dandridge, nephew of Martha Washington, secretary-accountant to
  George Washington
William Shaw, nephew of Abigail Adams, private secretary to John Adams
Martha Randolph, daughter of Thomas Jefferson, hostess
Edward Coles, cousin of Dolley Madison, private secretary to James Madison
Joseph Monroe, brother of James Monroe, private secretary to him
Samuel Gouverneur, son-in-law of James Monroe, private secretary to him
George Hay, son-in-law of James Monroe, private secretary and adviser to him
Eliza Hay, daughter of James Monroe, aide to mother
Charles Adams, son of John Quincy Adams, private secretary to him
John Adams II, son of John Quincy Adams, private secretary to him
Andrew Donelson, nephew of Andrew Jackson, private secretary to him
Emily Donelson, niece of Andrew Jackson, hostess
Sarah Jackson, adoptive daughter-in-law of Andrew Jackson, hostess
Smith Van Buren, son of Martin Van Buren, private secretary to him
Martin Van Buren Jr., son of Martin Van Buren, private secretary to him
Abraham Van Buren, son of Martin Van Buren, military aide
Angelica Van Buren, daughter-in-law of Martin Van Buren, hostess
David O. Coupeland, nephew of William Henry Harrison, private secretary to him
Henry Harrison, great-nephew of William Henry Harrison, private aide to him
Jane Harrison, daughter-in-law to William Henry Harrison, hostess
John Tyler Jr., son of John Tyler, private secretary to him
Robert Tyler, son of John Tyler, private secretary to him
Priscilla Tyler, daughter-in-law of John Tyler, hostess
Lizzy Tyler, daughter of John Tyler, assistant hostess
Letty Semple, daughter of John Tyler, hostess
Margaret Gardiner, sister of Julia Tyler, social secretary
Knox Walker, nephew of James Polk, private secretary to him
John Hayes, brother-in-law of James Polk, presidential physician
William Bliss, son-in-law of Zachary Taylor, private secretary to him
Betty Bliss, daughter of Zachary Taylor, hostess
Joseph P. Taylor, brother of Zachary Taylor, private secretary to him
Robert Wood, son-in-law of Zachary Taylor, presidential physician
Powers Fillmore, son of Millard Fillmore, private secretary to him

Mary Abigail "Abbie" Fillmore, daughter of Millard Fillmore, assistant hostess

Abby Kent Means, aunt-by-marriage to Jane Pierce, hostess

James Buchanan "Buck" Henry, nephew of James Buchanan, private secretary to him

James "Jim" Buchanan II, nephew of James Buchanan, private secretary to him

Harriet Lane, niece to James Buchanan, hostess

Robert Johnson, son of Andrew Johnson, private secretary to him

Martha Patterson, daughter of Andrew Johnson, hostess

Mary Stover, daughter of Andrew Johnson, hostess

Ulysses "Buck" Grant Jr., son of Ulysses S. Grant, private aide to him

Fred Dent, brother-in-law of Ulysses S. Grant, secretary to him

Webb Hayes, son of Rutherford Hayes, private aide to him

Emily Platt, niece of Rutherford Hayes, social secretary

Molly McElroy, sister of Chester Arthur, hostess

Rose Cleveland, sister of Grover Cleveland, hostess

Mary Hoyt, sister of Grover Cleveland, social assistant

Mary McKee, daughter of Benjamin Harrison, assistant hostess

Robert McKee, son-in-law of Benjamin Harrison, sometime aide to him

Mary Barber, niece of Ida McKinley, sometime social aide to aunt

Jennie Anderson, sister of Nellie Taft, substitute hostess

Maria Herron, sister of Nellie Taft, substitute hostess

Helen Taft, daughter of William Howard Taft, social assistant to mother

Helen Bones, cousin of Woodrow Wilson, personal secretary to Ellen Wilson

James Roosevelt, son of Franklin D. Roosevelt, private aide to him

Anna Dall Boettiger, daughter of Franklin D. Roosevelt, private aide to him

John Eisenhower, son of Dwight Eisenhower, administrative aide to him

Barbara Eisenhower, daughter-in-law of Dwight Eisenhower, state trip representative

Julie Nixon Eisenhower, daughter of Richard Nixon, assistant to mother

Susan Ford, daughter of Gerald Ford, substitute hostess at state dinner

Jack Ford, son of Gerald Ford, campaign aide to him

Chip Carter, son of Jimmy Carter, aide to him

William; sister Elizabeth Packard, her husband, Alpheus, and their children Charles and Fanny; her mother's sister, aunt Mary Mason, her husband, Jeremiah, and their children Jane and Robert; and her mother's other sister, aunt Nancy Lawrence, her husband, Amos, and their children Amos—later the famous Kansas abolitionist—and William. In one letter, Charles Packard wrote his mother: "I . . . am impelled to raise my voice in favor of the renewed proposition to Aunt Jane, that the girls Mary [Elizabeth] and Fanny make her a visit. It seems to me that the present or a few weeks hence would be the most propitious and pleasing time. . . . Aunt Abby [Means] is there, whose advice and counsel would be of great service . . . Had she [Fanny] gone with Father, she might have found her visit a little wearisome. . . . Jane herself, suffered from very indifferent health whereas now she writes Father that she is quite well for her, which is a considerable and encouraging admission for her."

One gets a sense that sixteen-year-old niece Mary Elizabeth was not always thrilled to be with her sickly aunt Jane. Mary Aiken wrote to her daughter in the White House, "I am sorry to hear that your Aunt Jane's cold still holds on. I do think dear Mary that you may and will be a comfort to her." In another note she admonishes her daughter to be a solace among too many caretakers, "do what you can for your Aunt Jane's comfort, while they have so many of their relatives." Soon it was the First Lady who—despite a "violent cold which has deprived her of her voice"—was nursing her niece, who was hit with a fever. As Mary Elizabeth wrote her mother, "I am getting to love her very much though she isn't as fit like you." Nor was the First Lady unappreciative. Cousin Anne Hall reported to Mary Aiken that Jane's constant loving remarks about Mary "made me realise anew how blessed a treasure is a sister." As her nephew William Aiken was traveling west, the First Lady wrote and sent on a letter to be held for him in Milwaukee, so he would arrive with a sense of family welcome in the new territory.

Numerous women put their own family lives on hold to help their brothers. For her widowed brother Chester Arthur, Mary McElroy—or Molly, as the family called her—ran the mansion during the fall, winter, and spring, living there with her two daughters, May and Jessie, while her husband, John, remained in Albany, New York, with their sons William and Charles. Mary Hoyt had acted as her bachelor brother Grover Cleveland's housekeeper and hostess when he was governor of New York in Albany, and she briefly did so in the first months of his presidency. Cleveland was closest to Mary among his siblings, but when she had to go back to her husband and children in Albany, the arch and erudite Rose Elizabeth Cleveland, "Libbie," took over as hostess for her brother. After he married, she and her lifelong woman companion, Evangeline Marrs Simpson, moved to Chicago, and then Bagni di Luccain Tuscany, Italy, and lived discreetly. The couple is buried together.

On Inauguration Day, Woodrow and Ellen Wilson had nearly a hundred cousins, aunts, and uncles at receptions in the house, and the open door never seemed closed to them. They had an endless stream of women relatives as long-term guests—Florence Hoyt, Lucy Marshall Smith, Mary Randolph Smith, Annie Wilson Howe, Alice Wilson, Lucy Maury—

but the president's cousin Helen Bones moved in permanently, living on the third floor. Bones handled the First Lady's correspondence and family finances, the "greatest possible help and comfort to mother," recalled the president's daughter Nell. "Her room was always a sort of rendezvous; the door was open all day long, and we drifted in and out, sometimes ending the day with an impromptu tea around her fire—mother, relaxed in the corner of a big sofa; father, teacup in hand, standing before the fire; my sisters and I telling the day's adventures."

Perhaps the most magnetic presidential relative was Tyler's daughter-in-law, Priscilla—the first White House resident to have made a career in acting. As a stage actress Priscilla had often lived in poverty with her father, tragedian Thomas Cooper, but after Robert Tyler fell in love with her as Desdemona in Shakespeare's *Othello*, they married. When Robert's father became president, his disabled mother, Letitia, turned over the hostess role to Priscilla, and to it she brought the serio-comedic sensibilities of her theatrical training. Caring for her toddler daughter and pregnant with another child, she organized and presided over receptions, dinners, and open houses so well that the rich and powerful immediately befriended her, yet her singular lack of materialism (she felt it was better to go through life with "light field equipment") provided a healthy distance from pretense. In her diary, she called it as she saw it: Charles Dickens wore "too much jewelry," the British minister was a "perfect bat," the Russian minister "unusually hideous," and his wife "of the milkmaid order of beauty," which nevertheless got her a "fine house, fine carriage, and fine clothes—and a fine husband too."

So taken with Priscilla was the president that he permitted her impoverished sister, Louisa Cooper, to live briefly in the mansion; he commissioned and salaried her father as an infantry captain; and, in his absence, Tyler asked her to officially welcome the Grand Marshal of Napoleon's court. "It is so easy to entertain," she cracked, "at other people's expense." As she made an official eastern tour with the president and Robert, the *New York Sun* gave unprecedented coverage to a First Daughter-in-Law: "She has sound judgment . . . a keen perception of the true and the false . . . without being affected by false flattery . . . She understands human nature perfectly."

The importance of other women relatives in First Families was not so much the public role

A congressman's wife, Anna Cutts lived for a time with her husband and their children in the White House with her sister Dolley Madison. 1813.
VIRGINIA HISTORICAL SOCIETY

they served as the companionate one. Certainly, Jackie Kennedy's sister Lee Radziwill, dubbed Princess by the press because she was married to a deposed Polish noble, added a glamorous public element to the Kennedy administration. Although she lived in London, Lee frequently came to stay in the White House, occasionally secreting in Givenchy gowns from Paris for Jackie—who had vowed to wear only American-made clothes. Once the guest of honor at a private dinner where everyone danced "the Twist," Lee, and her family, also spent each Christmas with the Kennedys in Palm Beach. It was as the First Lady's confidante and traveling companion, however, that Lee became indispensible to her sister: they went together twice to Greece, and also to Pakistan, India, Turkey, and Morocco.

A resident of Washington, D.C., Frances "Mike" Moore and her sister Mamie Eisenhower played cards, shopped, and attended the theater together. Mike and her family spent holidays at the White House, and she was often in attendance at state dinners. Lou Hoover's sister Jean Large made frequent White House visits, but she was usually seen only in the morning with the First Lady as they headed out on horses for Potomac Park or the bridle paths of Rock Creek Park.

Dolley Madison and her sisters Anna Cutts and Lucy Washington were dubbed "the Merry Wives of Windsor" by Washington Irving: at one point all three lived in the White House together. A Maine

Emilie Helm, widow of a Confederate soldier, who came to live briefly with her sister Mary Lincoln in the White House.
THE LINCOLN MUSEUM, FORT WAYNE, INDIANA, #3767

Only eighteen, President McKinley's nephew Jim volunteered for the Spanish-American War. James McKinley was the president's ward. 1900.
STARK COUNTY HISTORICAL SOCIETY

congressman's wife, Anna was inseparable from her sister and was mentioned in many contemporary accounts. One of the more indelicate ones was a Federalist newspaper's slander that Madison and Cutts had made their wives available to President Jefferson and other men who could potentially aid Madison's presidential bid. Cutts threatened a duel with the editor. When the Cuttses left Washington during the War of 1812, the two sisters kept in close correspondence, Dolley apprising Anna of many political decisions and naval maneuvers—issues of importance to the Cutts family, who had heavy investments in mercantile shipping. Even in her legendary role as hostess, Dolley eagerly shared the spotlight with Anna.

Mary Lincoln's sisters were political liabilities during the Civil War. The First Lady's four brothers and three brothers-in-law fought for the Confederacy—though she hoped they would all be killed because "they would kill my husband if they could and destroy our government." Her sister Martha White, a rabid Rebel, seemed consciously intent on humiliating the First Lady. White came to the White House demanding to see Mary—who refused—but Lincoln issued her a return pass south. One newspaper alleged that Martha's real mission was obtaining a pass to transport Union medical supplies to Dixie—suggesting that the First Lady was a Confederate sympathizer, or worse, a spy.

It was the brief White House residency in the spring of 1864 of Mary's "Little Sister," Emilie Helm, and her children, which provoked the most controversy. Emilie was the widow of a Confederate soldier. When Lincoln had learned that she refused to take an oath of allegiance at the border as she tried to come north, he ordered, "Send her to me." The sisters were thankful to see each other. "This frightful war comes between us like a barrier of granite closing our lips but not our hearts," Emilie wrote in her diary, "for though our tongues are tied, we weep over our dead together and express through clasped hands the sympathy we feel for each other." There was political liability in having a Rebel in residence, however. One night, New York senator Harris confronted Emilie about her allegiance, and she blurted back, "If I had twenty sons, they should all be fighting yours." Feeling uncomfortable there, Emilie turned down Lincoln's pleas to stay through the summer.

During the Spanish-American War, President McKinley, a Civil War veteran, took personal pride in the fact that his nephew and ward Jim McKinley fought as a lieutenant. During Jim's time in the White House, in June 1898, he calmly announced his intentions to his uncle, asking only that he and his friend, Ida's nephew John Barber, be placed together in the Eighth Ohio Volunteers. Making the recommendation, McKinley wrote, "He is a good boy. I am very fond of him and have the deepest interest in him. He is only 18 years old, and possibly rather young for a soldier, still I cannot but admire his patriotism." As Jim and John were sent right into the heart of the action at Santiago Bay, the former received letters from "Uncle who loves you as dearly as though you were his own son." In one note, he admonished, "I want you to make a good soldier. Be attentive to your duties. Do everything the best you know how and if you are in doubt ask some superior officer. . . . See that your words are spelled correctly. Better have a little pocket dictionary with you. It mars an official paper or letter to have a word misspelled."

As the anti–Vietnam War movement gained momentum in the last years of LBJ's presidency, the fact that his sons-in-law Patrick Nugent and Marine captain Charles Robb were at the front was a dramatic statement that the First Family received no privileges. On March 31, 1968, Lynda Robb returned from the West Coast, having seen her husband off to fight; he had volunteered for duty. Later the same day Johnson announced that he would not run for reelection. On April 11, Nugent embraced his wife and son in their White House room, signed his will, then also headed to Vietnam. The family was as frightened as any other about their safety. On Christmas, the two men joined each other near Da Nang and took their holiday call from the White House together. LBJ read the letters and listened to the tape recordings Robb sent Lynda—often to her chagrin: "I would get angry—'They're my letters!'—[but] my father found them more revealing of the real situation than all his Generals' briefings." At one point, she asked her father bluntly, "Dad, why do they have to go to Vietnam?" She recalled, "I was a big pregnant reminder [to him] that it was his policy that was separating husbands from wives, children from parents."

After World War II, presidents openly used relatives for public purposes. JFK's sister Jean Smith and her husband went as his personal representatives on a state visit to Saigon. Tony Taylor, Lady Bird Johnson's brother, was sent by LBJ as his representative on a Middle East mission. Bush's brother Bucky represented the United States at the Independence Day celebration of Malta, and after his report on the island nation, the president decided to hold a summit with Soviet president Gorbachev there. Bush subsequently sent his sister Nancy Ellis to represent the United States at ceremonies marking 2,500 years of democracy in Greece.

Numerous relatives have had political advisory roles. Certainly few had as great an impact on policy and procedure as Milton Eisenhower, Ike's brother. Respected in business and academia, and by leaders of both political parties, Milton was not only often in Oval Office conferences during the day but, along with his children, and another brother, Edgar, was a frequent guest for dinners and holidays. Hillary Clinton's brothers Hugh and Tony Rodham also proved important to her family, both in terms of political and personal support. Hugh

mounted a campaign for the Senate from Florida. Though he lost, he had family in the Senate—Tony was married to Nicole Boxer, daughter of the U.S. senator from California. The Rodhams also encountered criticism. Public interest advocate Ralph Nader protested attorney Hugh's presence at a White House meeting on tobacco industry settlements, although he represented clients who had a claim. Both had to cease a legitimate exporting endeavor in the former Soviet satellite of Georgia when leaders of that country assumed they represented the White House. Hugh and Tony were often at the White House—particularly during the crisis leading to the 1998 Clinton impeachment trial.

Theodore Roosevelt was often in conference with, and quite openly depended on the sage political advice of, his sisters Anna Cowles and Corinne Robinson, the latter of whom lived just a few blocks from the White House—to the jealousy of his wife. Corinne later served as one of the first National Republican Party's Women's Committee chairs, and became the first sister of a president to write her memoirs. Certainly, William Howard Taft could not have become president without the financing, connections, and advice of his half-brother Charles, the powerful editor of the *Cincinnati Times-Star* and a former congressman. Using the White House as their Capitol base, Alex and David Gardiner, Julia Tyler's brothers, served as liaisons between the New York Democratic machine at Tammany Hall and President Tyler in his quest for Texas annexation.

Having a relative on hand for political advice or to act as a liaison can provide a president with absolute loyalty. LBJ insisted that his younger brother, attorney Sam Houston Johnson, live in the White House, immediately after the family moved there in December 1963. Sam was leery: he had been a confidant and political adviser throughout LBJ's career, but he also knew his wrath. Sam Johnson eventually did move into a third-floor suite, a shadowy but important figure, with his distinctive limp and known fondness for a drink. Almost the only thing the public learned about him was that Sam kept the lights on—which made LBJ explode at the waste of electricity. Upstairs, he hosted small dinners in the "penitentiary" for friends.

In 1968, Sam went on the payroll of the Democratic National Committee as a White House liaison, but some officials thought him "a sort of spy or hatchet man," as he clipped and collected items for LBJ's future presidential library. LBJ wanted Sam in on every important DNC meeting, but Sam insisted that keeping a low profile was more effective. "Lyndon realized that in me he had someone who had no reason to hide anything from him," he wrote. "My concern was . . . to relay, if possible, any feelings—good or bad—other people had on their minds. He knew I was a disinterested party, that I was his brother, had his best interests in mind; that I had no special axe to grind and that he couldn't really fire me. You can't fire your own kin. . . . I had this peculiar role and it was soon apparent to people in the political structure that I was a sounding board placed close to the President. I might be able to get their views directly to the President."

When Jane Pierce's seventy-two-year-old aunt Nancy Lawrence came to stay in the mansion during the bloody fighting between pro- and antislavery forces following the Kansas-Nebraska Act, she made her abolitionism clear, but she never told Jane that she felt Pierce was "too small for the job." The president said he valued Mrs. Lawrence's views "more than that of all the politicians," and did give in to pressure from Jane and Nancy to release some imprisoned abolitionists in Kansas. Through Jane's relatives, Pierce further tried to stem some of the harsh sentiment against him from Whigs in his native New England, but when her cousin, U.S. Senator Charles Atherton, died suddenly, Pierce lost his most vital link in Congress. Another of her cousins, the famous abolition advocate Amos A. Lawrence, even volunteered to make a case for Pierce with abolitionists in Congress. Despite this, and efforts by yet another cousin of the First Lady, William Appleton, a U.S. Representative from Boston, Pierce was reviled in the North.

Jack Kennedy had more family members who made news on their own than any other president. Brother Bobby, the attorney general, was his closest confidant. Brother Teddy was elected to the U.S. Senate during his presidency. Kennedy named brother-in-law Sargent Shriver to head the Peace Corps. Brother-in-law Peter Lawford, a film actor, was the White House connection to Hollywood. Sisters Eunice Shriver and Jean Smith served as his official hostesses in October 1963 when his wife was away, and they had both joined him four months earlier on a trip to Ireland, where they also met with cousins who still lived there.

Eunice Shriver made headlines when she publicly disclosed that their sister Rosemary, who lived in a Wisconsin home, was mentally retarded. Mrs. Shriver's action helped begin a process by which the public began to understand more compassionately the issue of mental retarda-

President Kennedy's sisters Eunice Shriver (far left) and Jean Smith (third from left) on his official state visit to Ireland, visiting with two of their cousins who still lived in County Wexford. 1963.

tion and to face it without embarrassment in their own families. The latter was an interesting counterpoint to an earlier First Family. Thomas Jefferson's sister Elizabeth had also been mentally retarded, but in her day, Jefferson never dared directly address her condition. When she died he could only bring himself to clip a poem for his scrapbooks called "Elegy on the Death of an Idiot Girl."

As a group, the dozen and a half or so Kennedy nieces and nephews were also part of the political landscape. Even they could serve political purposes of the White House. In 1961, JFK used the christening of his baby niece Christina Radziwill as his ostensible reason for a trip to London: it also let him meet informally with Prime Minister Harold Macmillan, without an official agenda or expectations. When Maria Shriver sold lemonade and postcards of her uncle to Hyannis Port tourists, or a Lawford son fell off a golf cart overloaded with little ones, or the president took the crew to the candy store, or the parents of David, Joe, and Robert withdrew their applications to a school that they learned discriminated on race, it made the news. One night, as Jack and Jackie watched local television news, a nine-year-old

Franklin Roosevelt depended on advice from his uncle Fred Delano, on federal architecture. (Delano is immediately behind FDR.)
1936.

boy appeared on screen mugging for the camera. "My God," the president yelped, "that's Bobby Shriver!" Amused, he called the Shrivers about it. "He's the biggest publicity hound we've got around here!"

Kennedy was the only president who had a grandparent—his mother's mother, Josephine Fitzgerald—alive during his incumbency. He visited her in Boston when he went up to vote on election day 1962, but she was too frail ever to come to the White House. (Neither did Jackie's staunchly Republican grandfather Jim Lee visit.) Other presidents' elderly relatives were frequent visitors. FDR's uncle and aunts, Frederick A. Delano, Kassie Collier, and Dora Forbes, were as regal as their sister Sara. Dora, a tall, slender woman who paraded about with an ebony walking stick, lived in Paris, and at the outbreak of World War II, the president's mother vainly demanded that FDR send a navy vessel to fetch her sister in Europe. For FDR, Washingtonian "Uncle Fred" was a wise and comforting presence. As a National Capitol Planning Commission member, he often reviewed architecture plans for the city with his nephew.

Numerous other aunts and uncles gave a grounding and sense of continuity to the lives of presidents. Taft lovingly turned to his late mother's elderly sister, the well-educated and strong-willed Aunt Delia, for advice and approval and saw to it that a family member always

escorted her down to White House family events. She never hesitated to provide him with her sound logic—or the press with a colorful quote. A suffragette, she was nevertheless proudest of her nephew when he made the trip to Provincetown, Massachusetts, to dedicate the Pilgrim Monument—because her ancestors had immigrated on the *Mayflower.* Mamie Eisenhower remained close to her uncle Joel Carlson; he always came from Iowa for White House family gatherings. LBJ's seventy-eight-year-old paternal aunt Jessie was unintimidated by his position. "You're doing all right so far," she told him during his first weeks in office. "But don't let your britches ride too high, Lyndon. Don't let those people brag on you too much and make you go forgetting you're just plain folks like the rest of us."

No families had more concentrated political power under one roof than Jefferson's and Madison's. During the early Madison presidency, the First Lady's brothers-in-law Richard Cutts, Anna's husband, and John G. Jackson, husband of her late sister Mary, served in Congress and lived in the mansion. There was considerable tension when Cutts later opposed Madison's naval war with England; it damaged his shipping fortune.

Jackson—a much closer presidential confidant—vigorously defended Madison. "My blood boils," he wrote Madison about those like Cutts who did not want to retaliate against the British pirating of American ships. "Blows, blows, blows, alone will make them substitute war for words," railed Jackson. Luckily, the two men did not live in the White House simultaneously.

In contrast, living with Jefferson in the White House at the same time were his two sons-in-law, Thomas Mann Randolph and John Eppes, both Virginia congressmen. Insecure Randolph, feeling inadequate compared to his imagined rival brother-in-law, at one point moved out and into an anti-Jefferson boarding house, prompting rumors that he had had a political break with the president. Every slight change in family relations was observed through a political lens. Thus, perhaps in part to prove there was no political break, Randolph returned to dine at the White House when some Indian chiefs were being feted. Still, the belief that the president controlled two puppet seats in Congress lingered. Frustrated, Jefferson finally defended himself:

I am aware that in parts of the Union and even with persons to whom Mr. Eppes and Mr. Randolph are unknown, and myself little known, it will be presumed, from their connection, that what comes from them comes from me. No men on earth are more independent in their sentiments than they are, nor any one less disposed than I am to influence the opinions of others. We rarely speak of politics, or of the proceedings of the House, but merely historically, and I carefully avoid expressing an opinion on them in their presence, that we may all be at our ease.

Quite expectedly, President Andrew Johnson used his power with Unionists in the Tennessee legislature to secure their votes for his son-in-law Judge David T. Patterson's election to the U.S. Senate. When the Senate was passing the resolution to again include Tennessee's delegation, Johnson's hated enemy Massachusetts senator Charles Sumner questioned Patterson's loyalty, noting that he had once taken a Confederate oath of allegiance. An investigating committee, however, made clear Patterson did so as a matter of life and death, and Senator Daniel Clarke called him "a Union man as would put some of us to shame." Patterson was sworn in, but Republicans continued to denigrate him as a way of attacking his father-in-law. Kansas senator Pomeroy spread a story that he had seen both men and the president's son Robert drunk in the White House. The gossip spread as far west as St. Louis before Pomeroy confessed that only Robert had been inebriated. Living in the White House, Patterson began his day conferring with Johnson, for whom the alliance was particularly important. Not only could he count on Patterson's legislative support, but during the Senate impeachment trial of Johnson, Patterson became his father-in-law's eyes and ears.

Not all family members who stayed or lived at the White House were liabilities, symbols, or confidants. Most were average people who enjoyed the once-in-a-lifetime experience.

Perhaps the most refreshing example was Marion Pollard, the red-haired daughter of Calvin Coolidge's first cousin. The only reason the wide-eyed young woman never made news, however, was simply by the grace of her decorous cousin.

Neither Coolidge had any siblings. The president's late mother's sister, Sarah Pollard, however, had two sons, Frank and Park, and they were the closest Coolidge had to brothers. Frank's daughter Marion, who said she was "poor as a church mouse," came from rural Vermont to live briefly with the Coolidges in 1923 and 1924. When she arrived, Coolidge warned her, "Now, Marion, don't talk to any newspaper people nor have your picture taken. I object to publicity." At a luncheon, she dutifully told inquiring Senate wives, "I can't tell you anything. Cousin Calvin forbade me to talk to anyone." As she was leaving, pleased at her success, someone yelled her name. She turned around and was photographed. Mortified, she quickly told Coolidge. The next day she couldn't find her picture in the papers. He had forbidden all picture services to release Marion's image and, as a reporter of the era noted, "a request from the White House being equivalent to a command, Marion's picture was never used."

Indeed, sometimes it is the cautiousness of the president that prevents his kin from creating any stir. Not that Marion, had she spoken to the press, would have had much fodder to embarrass the president with. When she returned home, Marion could recall for her grandmother nothing important, exciting, or revealing he had said to her. "It's no wonder," responded Coolidge's beloved aunt. "No one in the family ever did have much to say."

Part III
Life in the White House

*I am living here with my wife and children just
exactly as you are at your home.*
—Theodore Roosevelt

9

Celebration and Ceremony

It's been my desire all my life to be able to give a
Christmas gift to everybody who works for me.
—First Lady Mamie Eisenhower

That I was a White House debutante hardly made
up to me for not having a cotillion!
—First Daughter Alice Roosevelt Longworth

When Herbert and Lou Hoover woke up early on the first day of 1930, they were shocked at the news that a long line of people had been standing in the bitter cold winter night for hours, just for the chance to shake hands with the president and his wife. "Not to keep the people waiting, Mrs. Hoover suggested we begin at once. Before the day was over," he recalled, "I had shaken hands with over 9,000 people." It was the death knell for the 140-year-old New Year's Day Reception. The next year, the Hoovers left town over the New Year's holiday.

The Nixons would spend their New Year's Eves watching band leader Guy Lombardo's telecast from the Waldorf-Astoria Hotel, and the Kennedys with both of their extended families in Palm Beach. At the turn of the twenty-first century, the Clintons hosted a massive White House party, forgoing their tradition of attending the Hilton Head "Renaissance Weekend" of lectures and seminars. The Reagans were always with their California friends at the Palm Springs estate of Walter Annenberg. No family ever revived the New Year's Day Reception.

Hillary and Bill Clinton with their daughter Chelsea at her high school graduation. 1997.
THE WHITE HOUSE

[1 6 7]

New Year's Eve: The Eisenhowers welcome in 1958 with friends in Augusta, Georgia; the Johnsons toast 1969 with their friends in Austin, Texas; the Clintons welcome 2000 at the Lincoln Memorial before hosting their millennium party, which included dance tents in the Kennedy and Rose gardens and was perhaps the largest party in White House history.

THE DWIGHT D. EISENHOWER PRESIDENTIAL LIBRARY; THE LYNDON BAINES JOHNSON PRESIDENTIAL LIBRARY;

THE WHITE HOUSE

Jackie Kennedy paints Easter eggs with her son and daughter, and two friends, in the family's Palm Beach, Florida, kitchen. 1963.
THE JOHN F. KENNEDY PRESIDENTIAL LIBRARY

Nevertheless, what others consider to be a family celebration or ceremony continues to interest the public when that family is the president's. Despite the predictable fare for Thanksgiving, for example, news stories about how First Families celebrated the day always list the invariable menu served that year. Knowing how well stories of family togetherness play, the White House has often conceded to this curiosity, releasing some photographs or revealing what gifts were exchanged. There has also been a history of "sharing" the holiday with the public. Even on St. Patrick's Day, there is a ceremony at which a president is given an Irish crystal or silver bowl of shamrocks from a representative of Ireland.

Easter has been marked by the famous egg-rolling contest for children on the South Lawn. Although the Hayeses are credited with hosting the first "official" egg roll, presidential families evidently held smaller such events for their friends. Tad Lincoln was recorded as sharing

The Benjamin Harrison family watches the Easter Egg Roll from the South Portico. c. 1889–1892.

his eggs with a disabled child, returning throughout the event to the boy, "watching over him with tact and sympathy." William Crook of the executive staff recalled how tubercular Eliza Johnson "would come downstairs and sit in the portico, sheltered from the winds, where she could see all the fun and hear the shouts of laughter; and I am sure that nobody enjoyed the egg-rolling more than she. After it was over she would return to her room and her rocking chair." The anticipated presence of First Families presiding at the event was part of what began to draw not only children but adults. Cleveland began an East Room reception for the children; Harrison had a stand built so the Marine Band could be heard. Edith Roosevelt disapproved of the event, saying, "It seems such needless destruction of the lovely grass."

Woodrow Wilson canceled the event in 1918, with America's involvement in World War I. Florence Harding revived it, delighting the kiddies with the presence of her Airedale, Laddie Boy. Grace Coolidge brought her raccoon, Rebecca; the Hoovers, their police dog, Weegie.

Halloween

In the 1950s, as Halloween evolved into a more commercialized holiday, it was recognized for the first time in the White House, by Mamie Eisenhower at an October 1953 luncheon. She decorated the State Dining Room tables with paper witches on brooms; lined the hallway with pumpkins, papier-mache ghosts, black cats, gnomes and goblins, and Indian cornstalks; and had orange lightbulbs placed in the chandeliers, which were hung with paper skeletons.

In subsequent years, the families dressed in costume. Seen here (clockwise from top left) are Jackie Kennedy, her sister-in-law Jean Smith, daughter Caroline, and nephew Stephen Smith on their way to surprise the president in the Oval Office; Tricia Nixon hosting a Halloween party for underprivileged children; Jimmy, Rosalynn, Amy, and "Digger" Carter at pumpkin mouth entrance on North Portico; Bill and Hillary Clinton as Thomas Jefferson and Dolley Madison, at one of the First Lady's annual birthday costume parties, her birthdate being October 26; Marvin Bush in Barbara Bush mask—with his mother; Luci Johnson (fifth from left) and Lady Bird Johnson (third from left) with face masks at a party.

Eleanor Roosevelt, her daughter, and grandchildren, along with Scottie dog Fala, loved the egg roll. Eleanor often appeared in her riding habit and headscarf, and despite her constant travels, she never missed the event. Each year she also bought large painted tin eggs, filling them with gifts for each of her grandchildren. Though it was canceled during the Truman renovation, the Eisenhowers revived the egg roll contest in 1953. Some 50,000 people attended, so many rushing and grabbing eggs from little David that he was left in tears. "Don't you worry," his grandfather told him. "There's plenty more."

As some traditions have fallen by the wayside, new ones recognizing other holidays have developed. Independence Day was once celebrated, as were Easter Monday and New Year's Day at the White House, shared by First Families and the public. Jefferson hosted the first of these in 1801. Two years later, an eighteen-gun salute, parade, and oration preceded his open house of wine, cakes, handshaking, and the Marine Band's rendition of "Hail Columbia!" Quincy Adams and his son John first went to the Capitol for a reading of the Declaration of Independence, followed by a parade in which new states of the union were represented by boys in Native American dress and facepaint, and then held an open house reception with a military review and band music. Although Van Buren held the last such event, the day was still important enough by 1850 to interest Peggy Taylor in making a rare public appearance in the state rooms, welcoming the Sunday School Union, a children's group.

In the Reagan years, a lawn party was held for the staff to watch fireworks, and one year the couple—usually in California celebrating the First Lady's July 5 birthday—surprised everyone by waving from the Truman balcony. Their most famous July Fourth appearance was in 1986, at the New York centennial celebration of the Statue of Liberty. After ceremonies in the harbor, the First Lady climbed to the top of the statue's crown, waving for photographers in helicopters.

The evolution of Thanksgiving as a national holiday is intertwined with how First Families viewed the meaning of the day. "Forefathers' Day" on December 22—the date the Pilgrims had landed at Plymouth—had been celebrated in New England since the seventeenth century, as well as in Dutch New Amsterdam, with pigs roasting on spits in the street. George Washington issued a proclamation of national thanksgiving for November 26, 1789. Adams celebrated Forefather's Day in December but issued no proclamation for the nation to do so. Jefferson considered the issuance of such official edicts for national reflection to be "a monarchical practice," while Jackson said it violated "the constitutional separation of church and state." Madison issued a November day of thanksgiving—but to mark the end of the War of 1812. New Hampshirite Sarah Josepha Hale, editor of the widely circulated monthly magazine *Godey's Ladies Book,* was appalled, and each autumn fired off pleas to presidents to acknowledge Forefathers' Day. Apparently the Polks agreed, for they hosted the first White House Thanksgiving dinner for friends and visiting family in 1845. "This new idea of Thanksgiving in Washington," a Washington paper said, "was well observed and gave such

The Reagans celebrate Thanksgiving at their California ranch with Maureen Reagan.
RONALD REAGAN PRESIDENTIAL LIBRARY

general satisfaction as to lead to the deduction that it will be an annual custom hereafter."

Thanksgiving stuck after Lincoln's 1864 declaration of "national Thanksgiving Day" to be celebrated on the last Thursday of November. The Grants set the pace by releasing a public statement that they would be celebrating with a dinner. The Hayeses celebrated in 1877 with three turkeys ("one a monster," Hayes noted) and a roast pig. Soon wives' recipes were being requested. Mamie Eisenhower released hers for pumpkin chiffon pie, a fifties concoction with gelatin. Caroline Harrison's peculiar recipe for forcing a walnut and slug of sherry into a turkey three times daily before its demise prompted a torrent of protest from temperance women. TR was the first president presented by the turkey farmers' association with a live bird, but when his sons Quentin and Archie chased the escaped bird with swinging hatchets, papers criticized them for cruelty.

Late-twentieth-century families rarely spent the four-day holiday weekend in the White House; most were at their permanent homes or at Camp David. The Carters were the first to spend it overseas—traveling in Nigeria—and the Bushes shared an army mess meal with American troops in the Persian Gulf. Perhaps the most interesting dinners were those celebrated by the Nixons. In 1969, they invited several hundred elderly residents of nursing homes to dinner in the mansion, one member of the Nixon or Eisenhower clan each sitting at a table with the guests. The next year, it was wounded Vietnam veterans dining with the

Christmas among First Families (clockwise from top left): Herbert Hoover, his son Allan (left), daughter-in-law Margaret, and son Herbert Jr. (right) shop for a doll for his granddaughter Peggy, 1931; Luci Johnson shows off a present given her by fiancé Pat Nugent (at right), 1965; Jackie Kennedy tries to organize a Christmas pageant as her sister Lee Radziwill looks on; the Fords open presents in Vail, Colorado; Franklin D. Roosevelt holds grandsons in front of a Christmas tree. Granddaughter Sistie holds Johnny Boettiger in her lap, while grandson Buzzie stands behind FDR's chair.

First Family. In 1970, Pat Nixon became the only First Lady to issue her own Thanksgiving message, recalling that as in her era, the Pilgrims "experienced their own times of hardship yet were able to find hope amidst their fears."

There are scant accounts of what the earliest families did on Christmas. John Adams allegedly hosted a reception for some congressmen. Jefferson purchased geese at the open-air market on Christmas morning, 1803, presumably for dinner that night, while his daughter Martha and Dolley Madison took five of his granddaughters out for a carriage ride to Georgetown.

In 1811, the Madisons had a three o'clock meal with her sisters Lucy and Anna, brother-in-law Richard Cutts, cousin Sally Coles, and numerous friends, including Monroe and his wife, followed by games—probably the card game loo. Guests left at ten. Three years later Dolley's son Payne, Lucy, and her brother John never arrived as expected, compounding a depressing wartime holiday. In 1815, although in a temporary residence following the burning of the White House, they had the navy secretary and his wife over for Christmas dinner, while Dolley permitted her green parrot to fly free through the rooms.

On December 19, 1835, Jackson hosted the first White House party exclusively for children, the highlight being a "snowball" fight of cotton puffs in the East Room. Mary Donelson recalled how Vice President Van Buren stood on one leg, sang a ditty, and ran across the room as a turkey. The first evidence of Christmas decorating of the White House was by Julia Tyler's sister Margaret Gardiner in 1844; she decked the state floor with evergreen wreaths, and even the stately portrait of George Washington was framed in greenery. "We commenced the day with Egg Nog," she wrote, "and concluded with Apple Toddy." Benjamin Harrison had the first genuine Christmas tree set up in the house. Not only did he help decorate it, but the white-bearded president also dressed as Santa Claus for his grandchildren. In 1918, Woodrow and Edith Wilson became the first First couple to spend Christmas overseas, in France for the peace conference after World War I.

Much of Christmas centers around children, and this has been true in the White House. In 1902, the Theodore Roosevelts stuffed stockings with fruit, nuts, and small toys, then hung them over the mantel in their bedroom. On Christmas morning the children began pounding on the door, and when let in they jumped onto the bed with them and spilled out their stockings. Archie came in with his own little tree from which he pulled his gifts for his family. Quentin immediately set up his gift of an electric train.

During his first two Christmas seasons, bachelor Grover Cleveland's White House swelled with his five sisters and his brother, their spouses, and twenty nephews and nieces. When he himself had three little daughters, during his second term, in 1895, the first tree with electric lights was set up. The young Hayes children Scott and Fanny were showered with gifts in the Red Room in 1880; three years earlier Fanny had been given a massive dollhouse. Sometimes children have even performed at holiday events. In 1977, Amy Carter played the violin with her music class for guests at the annual congressional Christmas party. In 1916, Margaret Wilson was the headline soloist at a pageant of caroling on the Treasury Building steps.

Caroline Kennedy assured her father that she *would* get everything she wanted, but she wished she could confirm this with Santa. Later that day, the president phoned Caroline and put her through to one of the switchboard operators. Caroline listened briefly, then excitedly reeled off her list. She burst with joy down the hall. "I've just talked to *Mrs.* Santa Claus. I left a whole list of presents for me and John!"

Children have also been taught to share the holiday with the less fortunate. Jackson took the little children of his family to distribute gifts at an orphanage, reminding them that as a child he too had neither gifts nor living parents. Nell Arthur helped serve a hot dinner to some two thousand local children. Recipient of dozens of gifts from the public, Tad Lincoln carried a stack of books into his father's office, impulsively deciding to donate them to Union soldiers. "Yes, my son, send a big box," said Lincoln. "Ask mother for plenty of warm things, and tell Daniel to pack in all the good eatables he can, and let him mark the box, 'From Tad Lincoln.'" First Ladies have also led holiday charity efforts. Frances Cleveland, an official of the Christmas Club of Washington, gave out toys, candy, and gifts, and took in the post-dinner Punch-and-Judy puppet show. Grace Coolidge, Lou Hoover, and Eleanor Roosevelt did likewise on Christmas Eve, before dinner. Mamie Eisenhower sent toys and other items given to her grandchildren by the public to those parents who had written her saying they could not afford to buy gifts for their children.

Since Edith Rooosevelt and her children hosted the first one, there have been large, formal holiday parties for friends of all ages. Eleanor Roosevelt held one for her grandchildren, boys in the Family Dining Room, girls in the State Dining Room. Sixty friends of the Coolidge sons came to a party hosted by their mother, who did a turn on the dance floor with each boy around the spruce tree in the Blue Room. Lou Hoover combined children and adults in one Christmas Eve party. After listening to caroling, children took adults by the hand, led by Hoover and his granddaughter, his wife and their grandson, into dinner. Afterward, the women rang bells and the men carried candles as they made their way up the staircase to the surprise finale—a moving picture show.

Presents for First Families can be rather unusual. Harding let his wife decide which federal prisoners would get holiday paroles. Ida McKinley liked diamonds: after her husband gave her bracelets and combs two years in a row, he had a picture frame especially created (in which to place a portrait of their long-dead daughter, who had been born on Christmas), the entire piece set with diamonds. Barbara Eisenhower, the president's daughter-in-law, recalled that the most unusual gift she and her children were given for the season were glass ornaments from Soviet premier Nikita Khrushchev, for their family tree. "Here was a Communist acknowledging a Christian holiday," she said. "But there were space rocket designs on them . . . 'Merry Christmas, but we're still ahead of you on the space program.'"

Nancy Reagan celebrates her July 5 birthday on Independence Day. 1981.

RONALD REAGAN PRESIDENTIAL LIBRARY

Christmas is also a time when adults enjoy themselves as much as children. For Mamie Eisenhower the delight was being able to give presents to the entire staff. Eleanor Roosevelt did this as well, also handing out gifts to each of their spouses and children—and a fruitcake for each family. Shopping all year, she stored gifts in marked bins for individuals; then, days before Christmas she sat down to wrap and address each. Taft loved going into the shopping district to buy gifts on Christmas Eve. Initially unrecognized, he laughed with the clerks, asking them, "Do you know who I am? Do you know where I live? Is my credit good?"

Other residents have had their own traditions. Pat Nixon joined the electrical and household staff, climbing ladders and unpacking boxes, as she and her daughter Julie helped decorate, recalling the story behind each family ornament as it was handled. FDR read *A Christmas Carol* to his family, then went with them to midnight church services. Clinton read "The Night Before Christmas" annually in the White House to local schoolchildren.

Christmas for presidents' families is celebrated largely as it is with most families, filled with relatives, dinner and gifts. On her last White House Christmas Lady Bird Johnson impulsively held a party for old friends, making most of the telephone calls herself. After the friends left,

Fred Grant, who graduated at the bottom of his class at West Point, in his cadet uniform.

SCHERMER COLLECTION

the family gathered to open gifts. Lynda quickly put on a dress from her father since, as the First Lady said, "As soon as he gives you something he can't wait for you to wear it." With a phone call to Vietnam came the sobering reminder that two sons-in-law were at the front. "We had an early bedtime," she wrote, "wrapped in that warming sense of family and Christmas and the hope of better days to come."

In the first year of President George Washington's administration, his birthday was turned into a holiday, in the custom of public celebration of the king of England. By the seventh year, there was a cannon salute and peal of bells at dawn through the capital, Philadelphia, then an open house reception at the presidential mansion, with free punch and cake. That night, a grand ball was held. The final year celebration was unprecedented: a ball and buffet dinner for 12,000, held in Rickett's Amphitheater. "There was danger of being squeezed to death," recalled an attendee.

Washington's deification did not sit well with his successor. As president, John Adams wrote "declined" across his invitation to the 1798 Washington Birthday Ball. The fall of the Roman Empire had been helped along by the overglorification of military heroes, said Abigail, who further asked, "How could the president appear at their ball and assembly but in a secondary character . . . to be held up in that light by all foreign nations?" The rejection touched off a political controversy, anti-Federalist Jefferson recording that, "The late birthnight has certainly sown tears among the executive Federalists."

Jefferson did not recognize Washington's birthday as a holiday, but in 1837 Jackson, a fellow Democrat, did. On that day, the public was invited to vist the frail man who sat in the Blue Room while his daughter-in-law Sarah shook hands, along with president-elect Van Buren. A century later "Jefferson-Jackson Day" was being celebrated as a Democratic Party holiday of sorts. The Republicans matched it with a "Lincoln Day."

As late as the Clevelands, First Families marked the day with a special reception. At Tyler's 1843

Washington Birthday masquerade ball, in passionate pursuit of his future wife, as she came off the dance floor, he asked her to marry him. "I said, 'No, no, no,' and shook my head with each word," Julia Tyler recalled, "which flung the tassel of my Greek cap into his face with every move. It was undignified, but it amused me very much to see his expression as he tried to make love to me and the tassel brushed his face." In 1970, two years after Washington's birthday was made part of a three-day federal holiday, Pat Nixon hosted a February 22 performance of the musical *1776*. The lead character of the show? John Adams.

It is not Washington's birthday but that of each incumbent president which is now regularly celebrated. Since the time when FDR's birthday was used to hold a fund-raising party for polio research, presidential birthdays have been the occasion for gargantuan political fundraisers in theaters, convention centers, and hotel ballrooms. The press corps even participated in Reagan's 1984 birthday, when his wife interrupted his press conference with a surprise cake, encouraging reporters to sing and offering them champagne. This stands in contrast to all those between Washington and FDR: presidents' birthdays were not only publicly ignored but rarely acknowledged by their families.

It was not until he was sitting in church with his nephew Knox Walker on November 2, 1845, listening to a "solemn and forcible" sermon that James Polk realized it was his fiftieth birthday. He grimly reflected that he would soon "be sleeping with the generations which have gone before me. I thought of the vanity of this world's honors, how little they would profit me half a century hence, and that it was time for me to be 'putting my house in order.'"

On his fifty-ninth birthday, July 11, 1826, John Quincy Adams had similar thoughts, in

Julie Nixon at the commencement party her mother held for her and her husband, David Eisenhower. The president is at far left; his friend Bebe Rebozo presents a mock diploma to Julie. 1969.
NIXON PRESIDENTIAL MATERIALS

reaction to his wife Louisa's birthday gift: a copy of *The Death of Socrates* (she gave it, she said, "as a tribute of respect for those superior talents and requirements which all acknowledge and venerate"). "Your affectionate, truly elegant present on my birthday," he wrote her, "will be kept and cherished by me till I join the assembly of my fathers." Adams was alone in a Philadelphia hotel, but the "very merry" gathering of Louisa, nieces Mary and Abby, and son Charles toasted him in absentia at the White House with champagne. Charles supposed the "little fete" would have scandalized "the prudish citizens who make it a business to censure others."

Over time, other presidents began to celebrate with a family dinner, as did Taft and Wilson, and then with small delegations of friends or civic groups, as did Harding and Coolidge. In August 1929 all of Madison County, Virginia, turned out to honor the president on "Hoover Day." The chamber of commerce invited the Hoovers—at their nearby camp—never expecting they'd show up. The governor came in a blimp, the Marine Band drove from Washington to serenade, five hundred chickens and three hundred loaves of bread were ordered. With an anticipated crowd larger than the entire county population, locals went out to shoot squirrels for Brunswick stew and kill pigs for pork spits. Hoover arrived to a twenty-one-gun salute, and at his table sat a fifty-pound ham. The enthusiastic president even served heaping plates of barbecue himself.

Only rarely are the birthdays of other members of First Families publicly celebrated. Pat Nixon's birthday of March 16 was always celebrated on St. Patrick's Day, often marked by some official event. Her birthday was made part of the event—once it was a state dinner for the Irish president. Hillary Clinton's fiftieth birthday in 1997 was celebrated throughout

Chicago, her native city. A park was named in her honor, her hometown street was renamed Rodham Way, and a gala dinner was held, featuring local food specialties. On her first birthday in the White House, in August 1964, Lynda Johnson held a costume party, dressing as the "Spirit of the South"—and taking fiendish delight in being photographed on the bed bought by the Union president's wife, the Lincoln bed. Susan Ford's eighteenth birthday in July 1975 was a barbecue at picnic tables on the South Lawn, with a cake featuring a picture of her and, to the delight of those who recently came of age, kegs of beer. The teetotaling Hayeses celebrated son Webb's twenty-first birthday more sedately by keeping the candles burning on his cake until midnight.

The parties of small children have been memorable. The first known was held for the third birthday of presidential granddaughter Mary Fairlee Tyler, in 1843. Her mother—who enjoyed dressing the child up as a miniature adult—held a costume party. Mary was a woods fairy, with wand, wings, and crown, and her one-year-old sister, Letty, was dressed in a starched white hat, blue dress, and wooden shoes as a Dutch girl. "There is more innocence in that room than ever was there before, or ever will be again," said the doorkeeper, "until we have another children's party." It was a quarter of a century before another such event took place. In 1868, a "Juvenile Soiree" was hosted by young Andrew Johnson Jr., joined by the president's grandchildren Belle Patterson, Andrew Patterson, Sarah Stover, Lillian Stover, and Andrew Stover, in honor of the President's birthday. Some four hundred fellow dance students of the grandchildren joined them in such formal dances as the Promenade, Quadrille Sociable, Esmeralda, Varsovienne, Waltz, Polka Redown, and Galop.

Numerous other children's birthdays have been held since then, including those of the FDR, Eisenhower, Kennedy, LBJ, and Bush families. Each has had its own flavor: Harrison's grandson Benny "Baby" McKee's fourth, in 1891, had eighteen attendees sitting on high chairs chomping on chicken-shaped biscuits; except for the fact that milk was served, Peggy Hoover's birthday table was set like an adult's, with formal china, silver, stemware, and floral arrangements.

Four grandchildren born in the White House were also christened there in the presence of

Maria Monroe, the first presidential daughter married in the White House.
LAST APPEARED IN *The Story of the White House,* 1902

John Adams, the son of John Quincy Adams, the only "First Son" to be married in the White House.
ADAMS NATIONAL HISTORIC SITE

the cabinet and diplomatic corps. The baptism of Mary Louisa Adams, granddaughter of John Quincy, took place in the Green Room with legendary War of 1812 general Stephen Van Rensselaer serving as godfather. At that of Jackson's great-niece Mary Donelson, in the East Room, the secretary of state was her godfather. Jackson declared, "Spare no expense nor pains. Let us make it an event to be remembered. We will do honor to the baby." For the christenings of both Jackson's grandson and Grant's first granddaughter, in the East Room, the cabinet was again present. Because the 1889 Red Room christening of his granddaughter (not born in the White House) followed a cabinet meeting, Benjamin Harrison sent invitations to cabinet members to "see my granddaughter receive the name of Mary Lodge McKee." The ceremony was presided over by her great-grandfather, Reverend John Scott, who used water from the River Jordan. Christenings of the grandchildren of Wilson, FDR, Eisenhower, and Bush, however, have been small family events.

First Families have proudly attended the graduation ceremonies of the younger members of their tribe, but only three had graduation parties at home. Weeks before she earned her degree from George Washington University, Margaret Truman hosted a dinner and showing of the movie *Henry V* for her Pi Beta Phi sorority on April 21, 1945. Susan Ford hosted the first White House prom, held in the East Room for her fellow Holton Arms high school graduates. "We couldn't serve beer because we'd have had to get a slip from each student's parents saying they approved," she recalled. On June 1, 1965, while Luci Johnson had on what her mother called "a sloppy shirt" and shorts, with her hair in curlers under the dryer, her friends were gathering in the Solarium for her surprise graduation party. Since she was going into nursing, they told her she needed a cadaver and carried in a body on a stretcher, under a sheet. Out popped a friend from Minnesota. Earlier that day, at her graduation, LBJ delivered the commencement speech, cracking that he would miss "the small consolation of knowing that no matter how much homework the night held for me, Luci had brought home more from the National Cathedral School."

When a president attends a graduation, the focus is inevitably on him. In June of 1877, for example, when the Hayeses came to their son Ruddy's Harvard graduation, the ceremony was eclipsed by the president's commencement address, on Reconstruction policy. Awarded

Family Christenings in the White House

James Gouverneur, James Monroe's grandson, 1821

Samuel L. Gouverneur Jr., James Monroe's grandson, 1822

Mary Louisa "Looly" Adams, John Quincy Adams's granddaughter, 1829

Mary Donelson, Andrew Jackson's great-niece, 1829

John Samuel Donelson, Andrew Jackson's great-nephew, 1832

Andrew Jackson III, Andrew Jackson's adoptive grandson, 1834

Letitia Christian Tyler, John Tyler's granddaughter, 1842

Robert Tyler Jones, John Tyler's grandson, 1843

Julia Grant, Ulysses Grant's granddaughter, 1876

Scott and Fanny Hayes [young adults], son and daughter of Rutherford Hayes, 1877

Marthena Harrison, Benjamin Harrison's granddaughter, 1889

Francis B. Sayre, Woodrow Wilson's grandson, 1915

Elliott Roosevelt Jr., Franklin D. Roosevelt's grandson, 1937

John Boettiger Jr., Franklin D. Roosevelt's grandson, 1939

Mary Jean Eisenhower, Dwight Eisenhower's granddaughter, 1955

Ashley Bush, George Bush's granddaughter, 1989

Walker Bush, George Bush's grandson, 1989

an honorary Doctor of Laws and given a dinner by the university president that night, Hayes quipped, "God grant during the remainder of the term I may be able to do something to deserve it."

The appearance of President Grant at his son Fred's 1871 West Point graduation was an ugly moment in history. Though James Webster Smith, the first African-American cadet there, excelled in scholarship, both officers and cadets had tried to get him to quit. Junior Fred Grant did all he could to abet the physical and mental harassment, though he denied being "organizer" of the effort. When Smith's sponsor met with Grant on the matter, Fred was there. "[N]o damned nigger will ever graduate from West Point," he declared. Grant wrote his war secretary, "Fred . . . informs me that the cadet is very objectionable there." At the plebes' first ball, prominently attended by the First Lady, Smith and his siblings were heckled with further epithets. Smith was finally arrested for marching with his head down and convicted by a West Point court. The war secretary refused to decide on an appeal that could "spoil the Grant family graduation celebration," though Fred was ranked last of forty-one for discipline. Wrote Smith's sponsor, "Fred Grant, a low miserable scamp has been the cause of much of his trouble."

Societal issues marred the graduations of other students just because they were related to a president. The 1970 graduation ceremonies at Smith College and Amherst College, of Julie Nixon and her husband, David Eisenhower, respectively, took place in the midst of increasingly violent anti–Vietnam War protests on college campuses throughout the nation. Nixon felt that his presence at his daughter's and his son-in-law's graduations could provoke riots and decided that not only he and the other elders but also the graduates should not attend the ceremonies. Pat Nixon's parents had both died before her graduation; she and her daughter had especially anticipated having the family together for this one. Nixon called it a "very painful decision," as Julie fought back tears when he first told her the news. Pat organized a Camp David dinner for the families instead.

More lighthearted was Margaret Truman's 1946 graduation. As she climbed the stairs to receive her diploma, the university president temporarily invested his rights in Truman. "Grinning broadly, my father handed me the hallowed sheepskin," she recalled. Given an honorary L.L.D., the president cracked to the audience, "It took Margaret four years. But it took me only four minutes."

In the years before women sought higher education, finishing school polished their grammar school years, and for the upper classes, reaching eighteen was marked by a coming out party as a debutante. There have been five such events in the White House, the last being in 1960 when Mamie Eisenhower hosted a tea for her sister's daughters, Ellen and Mamie Moore. Before that was the 1937 party Eleanor Roosevelt hosted for her brother's daughter, also named Eleanor. In pink silk, sixteen-year-old Nellie Grant was the first to be honored at such a reception with her friend Anna Barnes, in 1872.

Ethel Roosevelt was also given a debut party, on December 28, 1908. There were two orchestras, so East Room dancing would be continuous. "We served 400 guests at tables with a four-course supper in less than an hour," military aide Archie Butt wrote. "It was the first time that I had ever seen that many people entertained at the White House and yet have plenty of room. The old place never seemed so beautiful." Ethel, who had been a gregarious tomboy—but who also took time to tutor underprivileged African-American children—had blossomed into a strikingly beautiful, poised, and generous young woman. Dressed in white, she received guests with her mother, who wore blue brocade, in the Blue Room. Watching Ethel, Butt thought, "There is nothing snippy about her."

Two years later, Ethel's former Cathedral School classmate Helen Taft had her East Room debut. Having earned a scholarship to Bryn Mawr through her extraordinary intelligence, this advocate for suffrage and better working conditions and rights for women toiling in shirtwaist factories seems to have had the party at her mother's insistence. A December 1, 1910, tea was followed twenty days later with a ball. Dressed in "Helen pink," she received 200 guests and danced until two in the morning, breaking only for the midnight supper. Her mother tried all night to figure out which beau was Helen's best financial prospect. "Don't worry about Helen," Taft told his wife. "She'll be all right because she has a head on her shoulders."

Among the guests at the Taft party were Ethel Roosevelt and her sister, Alice. The New Year's Eve 1902 debut party of "Princess Alice" plunged her into a lifetime of publicity. Although "carloads" of her eastern seaboard society pals attended, to Alice it was a flop. "The crash [a linen covering of the carpet] in the East Room I considered personally humiliating, and the fact that punch was provided instead of champagne was a horrid blow to my pride . . . Other girls had . . . rafts of favors and flowers." Among the guests that night was Alice's distant cousin, Franklin Roosevelt, on whom she was said to have had a slight crush.

After her White House debut came Alice's famous wedding to Congressman Nicolas Longworth. The February 17, 1906, wedding was like a three-ring circus, and fifteen reporters were permitted in to cover it—one had even come from London. Easter lilies and palms crammed the East Room, the windows of which were hung with a gold cloth. A staff of 101 servants, policemen, maids, and butlers scampered about. One woman fainted. Although there were eight ushers, Alice wanted no bridesmaids, so as she arrived at the altar, it was cousin Franklin—now married to cousin Eleanor—who fixed her train. Alice brandished a military sword to slice the wedding cake, and left in what she called a "hideous and unbecoming" going-away dress. From all corners of the world "loot" poured in on her: The king of Italy sent a huge mosaic table; the Cuban government, a diamond and pearl necklace; the empress of China, a white fox coat, an ermine coat, and eight rolls of gold brocade cloth with the Chinese sign for longevity in the designs. From the public came a barrel of popcorn, snakes, and feather dusters. As for the groom, Alice glanced at him at the altar, "thinking how hopelessly Midwestern he did seem."

The White House weddings that drew the most attention were those of daughters. The first was Maria Monroe's on March 9, 1820. A shy poet and horsewoman, at seventeen she fell in love with her cousin Samuel Gouverneur, who had come to live there with his mother, Hester, the First Lady's sister, and work as a presidential secretary. There were four bridal attendants, and a supper was served afterward. The event was marred by her sister Eliza's edict that the wedding was not to be acknowledged by the diplomatic corps. This angered the groom, who declared that her "meddling" would no longer apply to him or his new wife and caused a breach between the two sisters. Louisa Adams said Eliza was "so mean . . . [with] her love of scandal, no reputation is safe in her hands and I never from the first moment of my acquaintance with her have heard her speak well of any human being."

Children Who Married During Their Father's Presidency, but Not in the White House

Andrew Jackson Jr. to Sarah Yorke, 1831, Philadelphia, Pennsylvania

Abraham Van Buren to Angelica Singleton, 1838, Sumter, South Carolina

Fred Grant to Ida Honore, 1874, Chicago, Illinois

Elliott Roosevelt [divorced] to Ruth Googins, second wife, 1933, Burlington, Iowa

Anna Roosevelt Dall [divorced] to John Boettinger, second husband, 1935, New York

Franklin D. Roosevelt Jr. to Ethel DuPont, 1937, Wilmington, Delaware

John Roosevelt to Anne Clarke, 1938, Nahant, Massachusetts

James Roosevelt [divorced] to Romelle Schneider, second wife, 1941, Beverly Hills, California

Elliott Roosevelt [divorced] to Faye Emerson, third wife, 1944, Grand Canyon, Arizona

Luci Johnson to Patrick Nugent, 1966, Immaculate Conception Shrine, Washington, D.C.

Maureen Reagan [divorced] to Dennis Revell, third husband, 1981, Los Angeles, California

Patti [Reagan] Davis to Paul Grilley, 1984, Los Angeles, California

Doro Bush LeBlond [divorced] to Robert Koch, second husband, 1992, Camp David, Maryland

Maria Monroe did not return to the White House for the 1842 wedding of Lizzie Tyler to William Waller, but she did send her a several-verse-long poem, suggesting that President Tyler's daughter would have continued enjoying the "glitter, show and elevation" of the "palace walls," but that her "heart's too pure, your mind too high,/To prize such empty pomp and state." Indeed her sister-in-law Priscilla wondered if Lizzie could really be happy in Williamsburg, after the White House. Lizzie had enjoyed dancing the quadrille with Prince

Groom Chuck Robb polishes his shoes, while bride Lynda Johnson has her hairstyle completed, before their 1967 East Room wedding.
LYNDON BAINES JOHNSON
PRESIDENTIAL LIBRARY

de Joinville of France, and strolling the crowded South Lawn, welcoming the public to the Saturday afternoon band concerts there. At the wedding, however, Daniel Webster assured her, "Love rules the court, the camp, the grove."

Two of Woodrow Wilson's three daughters married in the mansion. A graduate of Goucher College, Jessie had wanted to be a missionary but worked in a Philadelphia settlement house as a compromise to her parents. Blue-eyed and golden-haired, she was strikingly beautiful, with firm but delicate features, "beaming with health and beauty . . . [and] ethereal loveliness," her husband Francis "Frank" Sayre later wrote. The 1913 ceremony took place on a Tuesday—because that was the day of the week the couple had become engaged. Her five bridesmaids wore shades of pink, ranging from pale to dark, and pointed caps wired like Russian Orthodox crowns. Frank, having taken a stroll with his best man, wasn't carrying an invitation, and when he came to the White House just before the ceremony began, he was not permitted to enter. His increasingly vocal protests brought the captain of the police guard, who let him in. At the wedding, her sister Eleanor got the piece of wedding cake with the ring in it, and she caught the bouquet. Earlier that day, she had pulled the millionaire secretary of the Treasury William McAdoo—twenty-six years her senior—into the Blue Room, and flirtatiously taught him how to fox-trot. Five months later they were married there.

The Wilsons were the only family to have two weddings in the house. On August 6, 1966, Luci Johnson, married that day to Patrick Nugent, held her reception on the first floor, in the state rooms. A year later, on December 9, her sister, Lynda, held both her ceremony and reception there. In attendance at both was former White House bride Alice Roosevelt Longworth; at Alice's wedding, another former White House bride, Nellie Grant, had been a guest. Longworth and both LBJ daughters attended the June 12, 1971, wedding of Tricia Nixon to Ed Cox, the first held outdoors, in the Rose Garden. Rain was in the forecast, the lemon cake was said to be collapsing, but the day proved to be the family's happiest of their tenure. The guests were as colorful as the event—the attorney general's wife, Martha Mitchell, with a psychedelic yellow floppy hat and parasol; liberal activist Ralph Nader, for whom the groom had once worked; a poker-faced J. Edgar Hoover, head of the FBI, who jumped when Lynda Robb kissed him; and, of course, Alice Longworth. Asked by live television reporters if the wedding brought back sentiments of her own wedding day there, the eighty-eight-year-old "Princess" snapped back, "It doesn't bring back one goddamn memory."

In 1992, another precedent was broken. That day, Bush's daughter Doro married her second husband, Robert Koch, in the first wedding ceremony to be held at Camp David. On June 26, the Bushes hosted a rehearsal dinner where Doro and her two children, Sam and Ellie, sang a rap song they had written for the groom. The next day, she was escorted down the aisle by her father, who, thinking the event "informal," wore an old pair of white pants with a blue stripe in them. His new son-in-law provided him with a tie. Doro's brother George did a reading in the contemporary chapel with flagstone floor, and the groom's brother stuck Bush

Tricia Nixon in her wedding dress talking to her maid of honor, sister Julie Eisenhower (third from right), two young cousins, Amelia and Elizabeth, who were flower girls, and bridesmaid Maize Cox, the groom's sister (second from right), before they exit the Blue Room for the first Rose Garden wedding. 1971.

reelection campaign stickers on the bottom of the groom's shoes—unknown to him, a former employee of the Democratic House majority leader. (Koch had made good on his offer to resign before becoming part of the Republican clan.)

The first White House wedding, on March 29, 1812, was actually that of a president's sister-in-law, Lucy Payne, sister of Dolley Madison. A widow, she had initially refused the proposal of Supreme Court Justice Thomas Todd, but after he left for his native Kentucky, she bade him return, having changed her mind. Dolley's son, brother John, and cousin Ned Coles were among the six attendants for the Sunday night ceremony.

Four nieces (two of Jackson's and one each of Wilson's and Hayes's) and one brother-in-law (Hillary Clinton's brother) have also married in the White House. The only wedding there of a president's son caused trouble. When Louisa Adams took in her two nephews and niece, she had no idea of the havoc the latter, Mary Catherine Hellen, would wreak on the three presidential sons, George, John, and Charles, with what the last called her "alluring ways."

First Mary was attracted to cousin Charles, but when poet George came briefly to the White House, she fell in love with him. They were engaged in 1823. John—who had been expelled for joining a student riot—came home from school and cousin Mary went to work. Mother Louisa was now "half opposed" to George's still-pending marriage to Mary, the president "tacitly opposed." Charles said he pitied John as "the victim of her arts," but they shocked everyone when, on Monday night, February 25, 1828, she and John married in the Blue Room, hung with flower garlands and ribbons by the four bridesmaids and four grooms-men. Neither George nor Charles attended, and although their mother entreated them to visit and make peace, she reported to the latter, "Madame is cool easy and indifferent as ever and . . . John looks quite sick."

Three presidents married in office—though only Grover Cleveland's wedding to Frances Folsom in 1886 took place in the White House itself. In 1844, after the sudden death of her father, Julia Gardiner capitulated to John Tyler's marriage offer. Although thirty years his junior, she felt that he was "more agreeable in every way than any

Family Weddings in the White House

Lucy Payne Washington Todd, sister of Dolley Madison, to Thomas Todd, 1812

Maria Monroe, daughter of James Monroe, to Samuel L. Gouverneur, 1820

John Adams, son of John Quincy Adams, to Mary Catherine Hellen, 1828

Mary Eastin, great-niece of Andrew Jackson, to Lucius Polk, 1832

Elizabeth Tyler, daughter of John Tyler, to William Waller, 1842

Nellie Grant, daughter of Ulysses Grant, to Algernon Sartoris, 1874

Emily Platt, niece of Rutherford Hayes, to Russell Hastings, 1878

President Grover Cleveland to Frances Folsom, 1886

Alice Roosevelt, daughter of Theodore Roosevelt, to Nicolas Longworth, 1906

Jessie Wilson, daughter of Woodrow Wilson, to Francis Sayre, 1913

Eleanor Wilson, daughter of Woodrow Wilson, to William McAdoo, 1914

Alice Wilson, niece of Woodrow Wilson, to Isaac McElroy, 1918

Luci Baines Johnson, daughter of Lyndon Johnson, to Patrick Nugent, 1966 (reception only)

Lynda Bird Johnson, daughter of Lyndon Johnson, to Charles S. Robb, 1967

Tricia Nixon, daughter of Richard Nixon, to Edward Finch Cox, 1971

Anthony Rodham, brother of Hillary Clinton, to Nicole Boxer, 1994

Ronald Reagan escorts his daughter Patti on her wedding day. 1984.

RONALD REAGAN PRESIDENTIAL LIBRARY

younger man ever was or could be." Eloping on June 26 in New York, they stunned the nation. "Treaty of Immediate Annexation," joked the *New York Herald*, "Ratified without the consent of the Senate." His son John Jr. was best man, and as the party proceeded south, they shared supper in Philadelphia with his son and daughter-in-law, Robert and Priscilla. Tyler's four daughters were another matter. Not told of the plans, they were hurt. "She is all I could wish her to be," Tyler wrote to Mary—who was older than Julia— "the most beautiful woman of the age . . ." Only teenager Alice was at the White House reception days later, but Priscilla begged Tyler to send her some cake—or have a new one baked.

Four months after meeting widowed President Wilson through his cousin Helen Bones, local widow Edith Galt accepted his marriage proposal. Calling Edith "my Queen," he would "dream that her dear, beautiful form is close beside me . . . my kisses on her lips and eyelids." Love quickly intertwined with politics, the possessive Edith admitting, "I feel I am sharing your work and being taken into partnership." Unsuccessful efforts to break it up were made by Wilson advisers including his son-in-law, Treasury secretary William McAdoo, who feared her hold and the political effect of remarriage barely a year after his first wife's death. The result was a permanent alienation between Edith and her stepson-in-law McAdoo, and even to some extent from Wilson's daughters. For weeks preceding the December 1915 wedding, the Secret Service agents had to keep the press at bay when Wilson called at Edith's home, where they married.

On October 11, 2000, the Clintons marked the twenty-fifth anniversary of their wedding, only the fourth couple to do so in the White House. During the Grants' 1872 silver anniversary, they were summering at their beach cottage, but four years later, the Hayeses reenacted their wedding ceremony in the East Room, with family, the minister who married them, and Lucy crammed into her original wedding dress.

The Tafts celebrated their silver wedding anniversary on June 19, 1911, at one of the most spectacular evening lawn parties in White House history. Bands played ragtime beneath strings of thousands of twinkling electric lights, and the couple received under a bow of flowers. Taft saw to it that all members of his family came, including his spry aunt Delia. As he wrote his son Bob, who was ready to leave for Europe, "It would gratify your mother very much if you could be with us. We don't like to have a wedding anniversary without the presence of our three children."

The list of eight thousand guests, a wide cross section of influential religious, civic, industrial, and political leaders, was composed by Nellie with an eye toward Taft's 1912 renomination, but it included former residents Webb Hayes, Buck Grant, Alice Longworth, Molly McElroy, and Andy Jackson III, as well as future residents, the Hardings. The House presented a $1,700 silver service. Nellie put the inundation of silver gifts in cold storage—and had the Taft initials and dates rubbed off many an item by a silversmith, so she could give them away as gifts herself over the years.

Doro Bush LeBlond married Robert Koch in the only Camp David wedding. 1992.
GEORGE BUSH PRESIDENTIAL LIBRARY

Mamie and Dwight Eisenhower exit the East Room after repeating their wedding vows on their anniversary, after which they entertained friends at dinner—but not before dancing "The Anniversary Waltz." 1959.
DWIGHT D. EISENHOWER PRESIDENTIAL LIBRARY

At midnight, Nellie Taft retired with her sisters Jennie and Maria, relieved by news of their ailing father's improvement. Taft circulated among guests who dined on the west terrace and danced until two in the morning. He sat alone for a while on the south balcony and decided to have the same program of music played for the public the next day, at an open house.

The Grants focused not on their wedding anniversary, but on the annual commemoration of their engagement, May 22. On that day in 1875, Julia sent "Ulys" a note asking, "How many years ago today is [it] that we were engaged: Just such a day as this too[,] was it not?" To this, he responded, "Thirty-one years. I was so frightened however that I do not remember whether it was warm or snowing."

10

Well-Being

I have been so ill since the adjournment [of Congress] that I have hardly been able to dispose of the accumulation of business still before me.

—President Chester Arthur

A President has advisors, but no one among all those experts is there to look after him as an individual with human needs. It's legitimate for a First Lady to look after a President's health and well-being. And if that interferes with other plans, so be it.

—First Lady Nancy Reagan

First, because of the swamps which bred disease, and later, because of the confinement required for security, the White House has hardly been the healthiest place to live. At least there has almost always been a doctor in the house.

Since 1897, when McKinley named U.S. Navy physician Newton Bates as his official doctor, there have been federally salaried physicians on hand to serve First Families. Previous families had relied on

Woodrow Wilson, seen here out for a drive with his wife Edith, never fully recovered from his 1919 stroke. c. 1919–1920.
LIBRARY OF CONGRESS

James Garfield lingered in a White House hospital bed for two months after he was shot. He is visited here by his daughter Mollie and wife, Lucretia. His mother, Eliza, attended his Cleveland funeral services. 1881.
LIBRARY OF CONGRESS; PRIVATE COLLECTION

army and navy physicians, but none had been on call. Perhaps because Ida McKinley's health was so precarious, Bates and then his successors—Leonard Wood, George Sternberg, and Preston Rixey—always traveled with the family, establishing a precedent. This has hardly been a comfort, since several of these doctors have sometimes given more concern to the political consequences of presidential illness than to proper treatment.

Woodrow Wilson's friend and physician, the charming Cary Grayson, knew that his patient suffered from blinding headaches, vision trouble, finger numbness, and weakness in his right arm—yet he merely prescribed golf and horseback riding. The family never questioned Grayson's lack of concern. When Wilson suffered his stroke in 1919, Grayson, counseled only by Edith Wilson, refused to suggest the most obvious treatment—that the incapacitated president resign—on the premise that it would depress, perhaps kill him. He even kept the extent of the stroke damage from the patient himself. Luckily, World War I was over and no major crises arose during the illness. Conversely, during the Second World War, Marvin McIntire followed the lead of his patient, Franklin Roosevelt, that it was appropriate to sacrifice the president for the presidency. He brushed off concern over FDR's deterioration, ascribing it

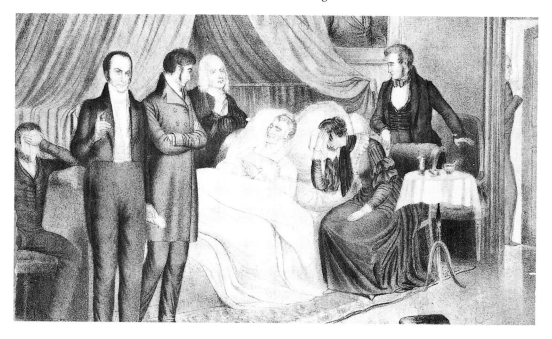

The depiction by Currier engravers of the death of the first president to die in office, William Henry Harrison. 1841.
LIBRARY OF CONGRESS

to the flu and aging and refusing to permit the truth about FDR's hypertension and heart disease to be divulged. Said Anna Roosevelt, "I didn't think McIntire . . . really knew what he was talking about. I felt Father needed more care." FDR reduced his smoking and salt intake but nearly collapsed at his fourth inauguration. He died three months later.

Jack Kennedy, elected on an image of youthful vigor, permitted only an occasional picture of himself in his rocking chair as vague acknowledgment of his severe back pain. The efforts to treat it by the only woman presidential doctor, Janet Travell, were unknowingly undermined by Max Jacobsen, a practitioner who gave amphetamine solutions to the president and his wife for energy boosts—they having been assured it was perfectly safe by friends. Friendship may have sped Harding's demise. Loyal to his hometown physician Charles Sawyer, Harding gave the ambitious but incompetent homeopath a military commission so he could be federally salaried as the president's doctor. Harding did this because "Doc" seemingly miraculously kept the First Lady alive, despite her chronic nephritis. When a naval physician correctly detected Harding's failing heart during a western trip, the possessive "Doc" insisted it was seafood poisoning. Flushing Harding with heavy doses of undisclosed purgatives, he further weakened the cardiac system and may have sent it into arrest. Sawyer had the naive support of the First Lady and this, in combination with her refusal to permit an autopsy, spurred rumors that she had actually poisoned her husband.

Although there is now a medical office to treat routine needs and even emergencies located on the ground floor of the White House, more complex treatment is available at Bethesda Naval Hospital, where there is a presidential suite. Previously, care was provided at the older Walter Reed Army Hospital. Since the mid–twentieth century First Families have relied on the expert staff available at the two hospitals. When reporters asked John Eisenhower if he wanted the historic distinction of having his child born in the White House he quipped, "I would rather have the obstretrical facilities than the distinction."

Earlier families relied on local physicians. Thomas Miller became the unofficial family doctor for the White House, on call from Van Buren through Buchanan. It was ironic given the fact that Miller was accused of "killing" William Henry Harrison with excessive bleeding and "cupping" (an ancient practing of blistering the skin with red-hot cups in the hope of cleansing impurities from the system). Overcome with fever, Harrison had called for Miller after dinner on March 27, 1841. His fever only increased after treatment with other concoctions, and he contracted pneumonia. "Ah, Fanny," he told an attendant, "I am ill, very ill, much more so than they think me." He was right. On Sunday, April 4, he became the first president to die in office. The city fell into deep mourning, storefronts being hung with cotton sheets dyed black, bell-knockers on private homes wreathed or draped

Family Funerals in the White House

William Henry Harrison, 1841
Letitia Tyler, First Lady, 1842
Zachary Taylor, 1850
Willie Lincoln, son, 1862
Abraham Lincoln, 1865
Fred Dent, father of Julia Grant, 1873
James Garfield, 1881
John W. Scott, father of Caroline Harrison, 1892
Caroline Harrison, First Lady, 1892
Ellen Wilson, First Lady, 1914
Warren Harding, 1923
Calvin Coolidge Jr., son, 1924
Franklin D. Roosevelt, 1945
John F. Kennedy, 1963

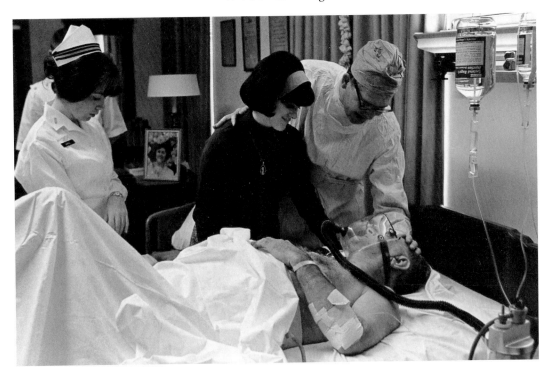

Lyndon Johnson visited by his daughter Luci just before his gallbladder surgery. 1965.

LYNDON BAINES JOHNSON PRESIDENTIAL LIBRARY

in black crepe. On Wednesday, April 7, the first White House funeral for a president took place, and Harrison was laid out in a velvet-lined coffin in the East Room. "The expression was calm and natural," noted one who looked through the glass plate on the coffin, "his white hair lying close to his head, and his features regular and peaceful."

Ultimately, the president must take responsibility for what course of medical treatment he receives. When Dr. Brodie Herndon, the cousin of Chester Arthur's wife, came to live in the White House from May to September 1882, he revealed in his private diary, "The President [is] sick in body and soul." When Arthur was seized with severe pain during a coastal voyage, the press got wind of it. Enraged, the president attacked them as liars for reporting his illness, further solidifying his denial. "I am feeling perfectly well," he told a friend. "I have not been sick at all." Many found it odd that he didn't seek the 1884 election. He died twenty months after leaving the White House. Only to his son had Arthur revealed his terminal kidney ailment.

Eight presidents have died in office. Of those assassinated, Garfield suffered a slow decline in the mansion for two months. His entire family was directly involved. He had been with his sons Jim and Hal [Harry] when he was shot in a Washington train station. "I was frightened

and could do nothing but cry," sixteen-year-old
Jim wrote in his diary. "Hal was very brave and
helped."

Just weeks earlier, it was his wife who nearly
died, of malaria, and the new president wrote,
"My anxiety for her dominates all my
thoughts . . . in comparison with whom all else
fades into insignificance." Through his demise,
Lucretia kept a bedside vigil, even cooking his
meals herself. "Well, my dear, you are not going to
die as I am here to nurse you back to life," she told
him, "so please do not speak again of death." His
teenage daughter Mollie was optimistic too: "You are
going to get well, I know you will." The children were daily
visitors to their bedridden father, sometimes playing with the com-
pressed air machine in the room, otherwise spending the hot summer outdoors and making
day trips.

When the president died in September, Mollie's emotions seemed most poignant: "after
suffering with all the tortures that any human could possibly do, he died . . . Dear little
Mamma bore up with heroic courage and bravery until the very last, and then she was completely broken hearted for about an hour, after which she calmed herself . . . But oh! it is so
hard to lose him; there never was a kinder father, or more devoted and loving husband . . . I
suspect I am wicked but these are my feelings: Guiteau [the assassin] ought to be made to suffer . . . more than Papa did . . ."

As Garfield lay in an open coffin in the Capitol, Mrs. Garfield and Mollie approached to
pray—as hundreds watched them. For the teenage girl, it was too surreal and she went numb,
unable to cry. "Child, have you a heart of stone?" her mother asked. Garfield's mother had
been away with the president's two youngest sons during the shooting, but Hal had wired her:
"Don't be alarmed by sensational rumors; doctor thinks it will not be fatal. Don't think of
coming until you hear further." For ten weeks Eliza waited, encouraged by an August letter
from her son, saying, "I am gaining every day." She next gazed upon him at his Ohio funeral
and moaned that she had no one to depend upon now. Hal told her he was there for her. "I
never knew what a noble brother I had until now," Mollie wrote. Yet, she reflected, there was
"a large vacant something in the family circle, which can never be found again."

Garfield's first cousin Silas Boynton was among the physicians attending the president, but he was not the first relative who was a doctor to First Families. John B. Hayes, the husband of Polk's sister Ophelia, served as the presidential physician, and in the next administration, Dr. Robert Wood fulfilled an even more important role for his father-in-law, Zachary Taylor. A Columbia Medical School graduate and prominent army surgeon, Wood was a sensible man to whom the president often turned for political and personal advice. When Taylor made an 1849 national tour, the forty-seven-year-old doctor was his companion. Wood also attended Taylor in his final illness. Taylor's deathbed scene was pitifully mournful. Peggy Taylor wailed, and fainted, unable to believe her husband would die without saying goodbye to her, while her two daughters and son-in-law William Bliss burst into sobs. She refused to have his remains embalmed, and three times had the ice preserving the remains removed, so she could look at him. Taylor's brother, sons-in-law, and grandsons were the only family members to attend the funeral and ride in the burial procession.

Taylor's successor Millard Fillmore strove to maintain his health. "I never smoked or chewed tobacco," he recalled. "I never knew intoxication. Throughout my public life I maintained the same regularity and systematic habit of living to which I had previously been accustomed. I never allowed my usual hours of sleep to be interrupted." The most important step he took, however, was to move his family into a private summer home on the higher ground in Georgetown, removed from the swamps at the south end of the White House, where until the late nineteenth century mosquitoes carrying malaria made presidential families prime targets.

In the nineteenth century, only John Quincy Adams seemed to value vigorous, daily exercise. He walked four miles a day and, with his sons or nephews, took daily swims in the dangerous Potomac River. As his wife fearfully had predicted, the president nearly drowned one morning.

Exercise for most nineteenth-century presidents was limited to morning rides on horseback. Although his routine was often broken by bouts of bleeding lungs, shortness of breath, failing vision, swollen legs, and an open, often infected gunshot wound, Andrew Jackson still forced himself to ride out alongside grand-nephew AJ on his pony. Taft went riding with his son Charlie and daughter Helen; it did little to reduce his enormous and unhealthy 300-plus-pound weight, but it refreshed his soul as he reconnected daily with the children.

Hardy exercise for health benefits didn't reach widespread practice until the 1970s. This was also true for First Families. Ford kept up an exercise routine from his college days, when he was scouted for professional football. At the White House, he had the outdoor pool built and frequently swam laps, in addition to playing tennis and golf. Carter jogged, and continued to do so even after he became faint during a marathon. Reagan chopped wood and vigorously rode western-style while at his ranch; he worked out with dumbbells and other free weights in the White House. Bush played tennis and swam, but it was during one of his reg-

ular jogging sessions that shortness of breath provoked his doctor to have him rushed to Bethesda Naval Hospital, where a heart fibrillation was detected. After Clinton tore ligaments when he tripped on some steps, he was put on a strict physical therapy routine and had to stop jogging temporarily. Early in his presidency, his morning jogs around the capital were covered by the press, and frequently special guests were asked to join him. When this was determined to be a security risk, a thin jogging track was made around the blacktop driveway of the South Lawn.

Earlier presidents took up more moderate exercise: Taft worked with a professional trainer in doing calisthenics. Coolidge did as well, besides vigorously riding a mechanical horse. Hoover played medicine ball with colleagues on the South Lawn; Truman took brisk daily walks in the early morning; Kennedy and LBJ swam in the White House pool built for the polio-stricken FDR's therapeutic use; Nixon used the White House bowling alley.

Making a clean break with his predecessors, Theodore Roosevelt became the living model of the "strenuous life," as he called it. Roosevelt set the first conspicuous example of presidential fitness and health. Stories and photographs of him hunting, riding, hiking, chopping wood, playing tennis, and swimming were published frequently, and he challenged his children and other relatives to keep up with him. TR installed the first tennis courts at the White House, finally providing an opportunity for exercise within immediate reach of the house. "I always believe in going hard at everything," he told his son Kermit. "My experience is that it pays never to let up or grow slack or fall behind." It was a philosophy borne out by his boxing in the East Room (where one eye was punched so hard he lost sight in it), or riding 100 miles on horseback.

Concerning the growing popularity of golf, however, TR called it "the sissy game." Still it became the most popular of all presidential sports. Taft tried to keep his weight down with it. Wilson used it to ward off his depression. Harding found constant escape from the stress of his office in it, and his obsession with this sport became a running national joke, from cartoons to comic routines. After Harding, Eisenhower was perhaps the president most associated with golf. The National Golf Association even created a putting green for him just outside the Oval Office.

Not until expert horsewoman Edith Roosevelt was there a First Lady who exerted herself for health benefits. Even by 1916, for example, Edith Wilson was so unaccustomed to exercise that she didn't know how to ride a bicycle—which her husband tried to teach her to do, in the long ground-floor hall of the mansion. Eleanor Roosevelt began most mornings as First Lady with a riding jaunt through Rock Creek Park on her favorite mare, Dot, and swam regularly in the White House pool—once shocking the chief usher by appearing in his office in her yellow rubber bathing suit. Grace Coolidge was also an expert swimmer, but more famous for her lengthy hikes around the city or countryside. She played tennis and ice-skated as well. Lou Hoover had been an outdoorswoman since childhood, and hiked, swam, camped, and rode horseback even in mountainous terrain. Since Jackie Kennedy all the First Ladies have had some form of exercise routine. Most identified with foxhunting, Jackie was also an expert swimmer, unafraid even of shark warnings on Cape Cod. She particularly loved waterskiing, telling her sister-in-law Joan that it was "the best way to trim thighs."

Three First Ladies—Letitia Tyler, Caroline Harrison, and Ellen Wilson—died during their residency in the White House. Although Letitia Tyler came there paralyzed from a stroke, and thus never had any public role, the fact that she was married to the president was enough to have her honored by lying in state in the East Room, where her funeral was attended by public officials she had never met. Newspapers like the *Intelligencer* and *Madisonian* revealed startlingly personal details, such as the fact that she had lost the ability to speak—despite the numerous quotations attributed to her during her tenancy!

Less unexpected were the deaths of the elderly. Julia Grant's

Marthena Harrison, the president's granddaughter whose scarlet fever threw the entire White House into quarantine. c. 1889–1893.

Benjamin Harrison Home

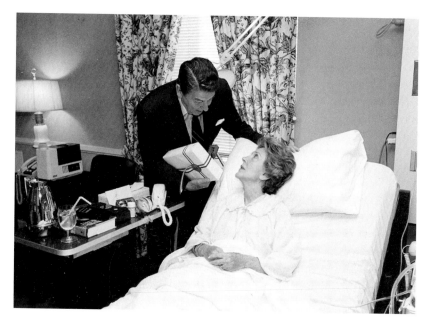

Ronald Reagan visits his wife, Nancy, following her mastectomy. 1987.
RONALD REAGAN
PRESIDENTIAL LIBRARY

father died in the mansion at eighty-nine, in December 1873, "a clear case of life worn out purely by time," wrote Grant, "no disease, care or anxiety hastening dissolution." Fred Dent's funeral was held in the Blue Room. When Caroline Harrison died, her ninety-two-year-old father, John Scott, was reported by the *New York Tribune* to be standing with a "symmetrical and strong frame" at her East Room funeral, but it proved too shocking. He died in the mansion barely five weeks later. The last person to die in the mansion was ninety-year-old Madge Wallace, Bess Truman's mother, in 1952.

Numerous other elderly parents died at home. Former president John Adams was too feeble to visit his son John Quincy in the White House as hoped, for the fiftieth celebration of Independence Day. He died that day at home in Massachusetts, with grandson George and granddaughter Suzannah—the first White House child—beside him. When Grant learned in 1873 that his eighty-year-old father had had a stroke, he rushed to his side but arrived too late. Depite the strain between them, Jesse's proud last words were, "I am the only man who ever lived to see his son twice elected to the presidency." When McKinley's mother began to fail, he sped by special train to be with her when she died. Dorothy Bush died two weeks after her son lost his bid for reelection, while President Clinton lost his mother to cancer just days after she had spent the Christmas holiday season with her family at the White House. On New Year's Day, 1926, Calvin Coolidge wrote to his dying father in snowbound Vermont, "I wish you were here where you could have every care and everything made easy for you, but I know you feel more content at home . . . Great changes have come to us, but I do not think we are any happier, and I am afraid not much better." The old man died two months later, at eighty-one, a symbol, said one newspaper, "which put most of us to shame in a blatant and hysterical age." That he was not with him when he died haunted Coolidge. "When I reached home, he was gone. It costs a great deal to be President."

Certainly modern transportation has made it easier for First Families to be with their elderly parents. Nancy Reagan managed to be at the deathbed of her father in Phoenix in 1982. "I tried to tell him how much he had meant to me," she recalled, "how he had really changed my life." Three weeks after Nancy had breast cancer surgery, her mother died. At Edie Davis's Catholic funeral, Reagan delivered a eulogy, imagining that she was dancing in heaven. Two months into her residency, Hillary Clinton faced the loss of her father—while she was also charged with leading health care reform. The difficult choices faced by Americans in choosing health care hit her personally as she remained at his bedside for the last two weeks of his life in a Little Rock hospital. Medical advances, she observed, made questions about exactly when life ended more difficult to answer. "How do we dare to impinge upon these areas of such delicate, difficult questions?" she asked, as much personally as publicly. "In hospitals and homes and hospices all over this country, people are struggling with those very profound issues."

One of the most intimate moments between Franklin and Eleanor Roosevelt occurred when her sole sibling, her beloved brother, Hall, had died of alcoholism in 1941, this after she spent the last ten days of his life seated beside his bed at Walter Reed Hospital. As their son James recalled, his father, in his wheelchair, "struggled to her side and put his arm around her. 'Sit down,' he said, so tenderly . . . And he sank down beside her and hugged her and

Hillary Clinton welcomes her father, Hugh Rodham, ten days after the inaugural in his only White House visit. He died three months later. Her mother, Dorothy Rodham, stands behind him. 1993.
THE WHITE HOUSE

kissed her and held her head to his chest." This came on the heels of a different—though also emotionally turbulent—loss, the death two weeks earlier of Sara Roosevelt at age eighty-seven. In her newspaper column, the First Lady wrote publicly of the old woman's "jealousy and possessiveness." Privately she was even more blunt. Having looked at the remains of her late mother-in-law, Eleanor wrote, "It is dreadful to have lived so close to someone for 36 years and feel no deep affection or sense of loss." FDR's attachment to Sara had been deep, and he keenly felt her loss. The picture of him signing the declaration of war wearing a mourning armband circulated throughout the world.

Certainly, death is even more difficult when it happens to children. Several have died suddenly in the mansion, or while their father was president. In each case it changed the family permanently. The pain is no less when a newborn is lost, as were six-month-old Rebecca Van Buren, the president's granddaughter, or Patrick Kennedy, the son of the president. Nothing altered President Kennedy more than his premature son's death on August 10, 1963. The loss drew him closer to his wife, whom he told, "[W]e must not create an atmosphere of sadness in the White House because this would not be good for anyone—not for the country." Yet it was he who cried "copious tears" at the infant's funeral, according to Cardinal Cushing, who conducted the funeral. "The president was so overwhelmed with grief that he literally put his arms around that casket as though he were carrying it out." Among his twenty-two nieces and nephews and fifteen grandnephews and -nieces, bachelor James Buchanan depended upon his niece Harriet to serve as his hostess and her brother, Elliott, to serve as a presidential aide. Just before entering the White House, however, Buchanan and Elliott fell deathly ill from tainted water; within their first month of residency, Elliott Lane died. The loss stunned his frivolous sister into a sudden maturity, and she emerged not only as the president's sole confidante and comfort, but as a social reformer.

Jefferson's grief at the death of his daughter Maria Eppes was no less because she was an adult. Except for one brief 1802 White House visit, she stayed away, insecure about the "civilitys and attentions" she would receive there. She believed people noted her beauty because "they cannot praise me for better things," whereas she believed her sister Martha was superior. Underpinning this was the fact that Maria had only one son, Francis, an epileptic. Jefferson assured her that pregnancy was "no more than a jog of the elbow." In 1804, shortly

The chronically depressed Jane Pierce (center), and her sister Mary Aiken and nephew Charles Packard, just two of a circle of relatives who tended to her delicate physical and mental health. c. 1853–1857.

after Maria gave birth to a second child, a daughter, she fell ill. He arrived in time to see her die on April 17 at age twenty-five. Because she was a president's daughter and congressional wife, Maria's death made the national newspapers.

What the nation at large is experiencing at any given moment has also affected the reaction to the death of a child in the White House. In the midst of Civil War, there was little public sympathy for the Lincolns when their eleven-year-old Willie died in February 1862. In contrast was the death of sixteen-year-old Calvin Coolidge Jr. in July 1924, by blood poisoning, contracted from an infected blister he had developed while playing tennis at the White House. The boy had become a young hero for his honest humility. When a comrade quipped that if *his* father was president, he wouldn't be working as a fieldhand on a tobacco farm during the summer, young Cal remarked, "If your father were my father, you would." He furthermore told a friend: "I think you are mistaken in calling me the first boy of the land since I have done nothing. It is my father who is President. Rather, the first boy of the land would be some boy who has distinguished himself through his own actions." All of this was widely reported in the press, and when news of his illness broke, thousands of phone calls and telegrams poured in on the family.

Taken from the White House to Walter Reed Hospital, he died there on July 7. "In his suffering, he was asking me to make him well. I could not," wrote the president; "the power and glory of the presidency went with him." The Democratic Convention, then picking a nominee to run against Coolidge, adjourned in mourning. Said one editorial, "This suggests . . . the nearness of the White House to every American home, and the solicitous regard in which all the people hold their President. . . . his grief is also theirs." The boy's funeral was held in the East Room, and the Coolidges ordered the White House gates opened to the public, so they could feel part of it.

Young Calvin Coolidge Jr., who died at sixteen; his brother John, parents, Grace and Calvin, and grandfather "Colonel" John, in mourning, on White House lawn. 1924.

SCHERMER COLLECTION AND LIBRARY OF CONGRESS

Illness of children has been treated with as much alarm as if the president were sick. With his grandchildren Rachel and Andy Jr. in a nursery adjoining his own room, President Jackson walked the halls in fear when they had measles, and panicked unless "croup sirup" was on hand. When Benjamin Harrison's granddaughter Marthena contracted scarlet fever on Christmas Eve, 1892, the entire mansion was put under quarantine; since the executive offices were adjacent to the family quarters and dozens of people came there daily, the illness could have had serious consequences had it not happened during a holiday. The president's daughter-in-law stayed with her daughter in their bedroom. If she wanted to convey a message, she shouted to a servant posted outside the door, who would run down the hall and yell to another servant—who wouldn't come that close to him. The second servant would carry the message to the First Lady. Everyone was paranoid about getting sick. Before Bob McKee, the president's son-in-law, left for New York, he wanted to inquire whether Russell, the president's son, needed anything in that city. McKee asked the chief usher to "tell one of the doorkeepers to tell the steward to tell Mr. Russell Harrison's man to say to Mr. Harrison that I am going up to the city."

When FDR's granddaughter Sistie Dall came down with the measles, the illness made the wire services, and soon the White House was flooded with letters, postcards, and poems from commiserating citizens. As a solution to the girl's boredom during recovery, one person in Cape Cod offered to send her a letter each day for the charge of thirty cents—at a time when stamps were only two cents apiece. In 1945, her half-brother Johnny Boettiger was hospitalized when it was feared that he might have contracted polio. On April 12, word went out that a death in the family had occurred. Some feared it was Johnny—it was FDR. Johnny's mother, Anna, told him that the president had died, and the boy was ecstatic to be leaving the lonely place at last. He burst into tears when he realized his *grandfather* was gone.

Naturally, families in the mansion have had to rearrange their lives for a disabled relative. For elderly Eliza Garfield, an elevator was planned. Mabel McKinley, the president's beautiful niece who had a spinal deformity, found that there was never a lack of servants ready to aid her, as she had difficulty in walking. Whenever her father-in-law, a stroke victim, came to stay, Jackie Kennedy arranged to have a hospital bed, phonograph, and soft drink setup made to look like a cocktail bar, in the Lincoln Suite, and a lift in the bathroom. She would meet him at the airport, having him ride in the front seat as he liked, and she and the children ate their meals with him. To ease his embarrassment, she made sure to kiss the side of his face and hand that were paralyzed, and allowed her children to ride on his wheelchair with him.

Reagan also used a hospital bed in the Lincoln bedroom during his recovery from his 1981 shooting, but no pictures were taken of it. There has always been an effort to mimimalize a president's illness. In the midst of the War of 1812 both President Madison and his secretary, the First Lady's cousin Ned Coles, were taken deathly ill with fever. Dolley Madison penned a subtle note to keep legislators at bay, without revealing the gravity of the president's condition: "James Madison is sorry that a continuance of his indisposition will not permit him to see the commit-

Immediate Family Deaths During Presidencies

Charles Adams, John Adams's son
Susanna Adams, John Adams's mother
Maria Jefferson Eppes, Thomas Jefferson's
   daughter
unnamed Eppes granddaughter of Thomas
   Jefferson
Emily Donelson, Andrew Jackson's niece
Rebecca Van Buren, Martin Van Buren's
   granddaughter
William Henry Harrison
Letitia Tyler, John Tyler's first wife
Zachary Taylor
Elliott Eskridge Lane, James Buchanan's
   nephew
Willie Lincoln, Abraham Lincoln's son
Abraham Lincoln
Fred Dent, Julia Grant's father
James Garfield
Caroline Harrison
Dr. Scott, Caroline Harrison's father
Lizzie Lord, Caroline Harrison's sister

tee of the Senate today." The emergency surgery on Grover Cleveland's jaw cancer was held for three decades from the public. Speculation that Harding had cardiac trouble appeared in print only as dirty rumors, owing to the old idea that a weak heart was unmanly. Not until Eisenhower's 1955 heart attack was the public fully informed of the details of a president's health crisis.

Although Florence Harding's 1922 near-death experience was publicly exposed, it was an anomaly; not until the post-Watergate era, with Betty Ford's breast cancer, did the public come to *expect* full details about a family member's health. This had its drawbacks. Nancy Reagan's personal decision to have a radical mastectomy for her breast cancer was publicly debated, and after George Bush, his wife, and their dog were all found to be suffering from a thyroid condition, there was speculation—later proved untrue—that the White House water system was tainted.

Presidents naturally become distracted when their wives' health is in jeopardy. During what he called the "lowest and loneliest moment" of his presidency, as his wife was undergoing breast cancer surgery, Gerald Ford was in the Oval Office. "The thought that the woman I loved might be taken away from me was almost too much to endure . . . Although I tried to concentrate all my energies on the job of being President, I was feeling pretty low and I guess it showed."

Ida McKinley suffered from epilepsy and phlebitis, and demanded her husband's constant attention—which he devotedly gave without complaint. Since she was often sensitive to cool breezes, he kept all the windows shut. McKinley changed protocol to be seated next to her at public dinners. At night he often held her until she fell asleep. To the nation, such selflessness made McKinley martyrlike and proved to be a political asset. On the rare occasions when they were separated, he was overcome with anxiety. "I am quite solicitous to know how you are," he wrote her when she was away shopping, "Please send me a line saying how you feel." Seconds after he was shot, he blurted to those who rushed to help him, "My wife, be careful how you tell her!"

In a larger number of cases, it was wives who took charge. Nancy Reagan steadfastly refused to permit her husband to give speeches or appear publicly before he had fully recovered from prostate surgery. She even battled his press secretary when he wanted to release information on the removal of a skin cancer lesion, feeling that it would give a false perception of its seriousness. Following her husband's 1955 heart attack, Mamie Eisenhower limited Ike's business and visitors as he recuperated, and assumed responsibility for much of his correspondence. "Mamie, above all others, never accepted the assumption that I had incurred a disabling illness," he recalled; "she could not reconcile herself to the idea that efforts on behalf of what I believed in had come to an end. . . . she perhaps more than any other retained the conviction that my job as President was not yet finished. . . . [that] idleness would be fatal for one of my temperament." Ike ran, and won again. When he later suffered a slight stroke yet insisted on attending a scheduled state dinner, they had a spirited argument, she insisting that he rest; he relented.

The actual incidence of alcoholism or heavy drinking in nineteenth-century First Families was probably no greater than that of most American households of the time, but numerous presidential sons were affected: George and John Adams (sons of the sixth president), Andrew Jackson Jr., John Van Buren, John Tyler Jr., Charles Adams (the second president's son), Madison's stepson Payne Todd, Robert Johnson, and later in life Kermit Roosevelt. George W. Bush decided to give up drinking altogether when he turned forty, during his father's presidency.

Some presidents intervened. John

William McKinley
George Saxton, Ida McKinley's brother
John Herron, Nellie Taft's father
Ellen Wilson
Warren Harding
Calvin Coolidge Jr., Calvin Coolidge's son
Colonel John Coolidge, Calvin Coolidge's father
Sara Roosevelt, FDR's mother
Hall Roosevelt, Eleanor Roosevelt's brother
Franklin D. Roosevelt
Mary Ellen Truman, Harry Truman's mother
Madge Wallace, Bess Truman's mother
Elvira Doud, Mamie Eisenhower's mother
Patrick Kennedy, John F. Kennedy's son
John F. Kennedy
Loyal Davis, Nancy Reagan's stepfather
Edie Davis, Nancy Reagan's mother
Dorothy Bush, George Bush's mother
Virginia Kelley, Bill Clinton's mother
Hugh Rodham, Hillary Clinton's father

Quincy Adams tried to use guilt and concern to stop son George's Boston drinking sprees, writing him, "I have been horror struck at your danger." Although a political opponent wrote a scurrilous *Secret History of the Tyler Dynasty*, claiming that the president partook of "blasphemy and revelry" in drinking binges with his sons, the reality was quite the opposite. John Tyler did all he could to support his namesake—even paying for his salary as private secretary—but John Jr.'s drinking led to such recklessness that he was actually dismissed by his father. "What you may regard as innocent and harmless indulgence will take you years to overcome in the public estimation," Martin Van Buren warned his son John. "Washington is full of reports . . . that you had been twice carried drunk from the race course."

Thirty-one-year-old former Union colonel Robert Johnson was so dissolute in the White House that there were unsubstantiated rumors about hired women slipping into his room there. Although he was exceedingly professional in his role as the president's private secretary, his problem nevertheless concerned his father enough for him to ask the Navy Secretary to confer with a naval physician about possible cures for alcoholism. It was finally decided to send the problematic president's son on a fact-finding mission to Liberia, but his leave was delayed when Robert disappeared on a drinking binge. His alcoholism was publicized nationally by his father's bitter enemies. On his death four weeks after his father's term ended, the *Nashville Banner* noted, "He had his faults and weaknesses like other men, but he was generous and chivalrous, a true friend."

Franklin Pierce, Andrew Johnson, and Ulysses S. Grant were often said to be alcoholic, but there is no evidence that they drank heavily during their presidencies. Betty Ford, after leaving the White House, disclosed her alcohol and prescription drug dependency and recovery; this, in addition to her candor about her breast cancer, made her a symbol for families who confronted the same crises, and became a watershed in permanently altering the perception of those illnesses. "Because I lost my mother to breast cancer, Betty Ford is a heroine to me," President Clinton said in 1999. "Because my family has been victimized by alcoholism and I know what it's like to see good, fine people stare into the abyss of their own personal despair, I will be forever grateful to Betty Ford."

Alcoholism often masked emotional or mental health problems—which were more feared especially in the nineteenth century. Most individuals were loath to reach for help. John Quincy Adams confessed his intense, disabling bouts of depression only to his diary: "uncontrollable dejection of spirits. . . . a sluggish carelessness of life, an imaginary wish that it were terminated." His wife Louisa found her only outlets in writing sad, sometimes bitter poetry and plays, and binge-eating chocolate. Her depression stemmed directly from her realization that she was "used" only as a "puppet" for political purposes, and was exacerbated by illness caused by the soot that rose from the coal grates in her room. She at one point feared that she was on the verge of insanity. Mary Lincoln's post–White House committal to an insane asylum—predicted by her husband in the White House—forever shadowed her reputation.

Wilson's doctor recognized his impulses for passive death and deep depression following his wife Ellen's death, but not until the 1970s was clinical depression openly discussed. Thus, it is only from a modern context that it might be recognized in John Adams, Abraham Lincoln, the Tafts, the Hardings, Coolidge, or Eleanor Roosevelt.

Some cases present substantial evidence. Jane Pierce was always emotionally fragile. When, weeks before her husband's inaugural, her last remaining child, eleven-year-old Benny, was crushed to death before her eyes in a train accident, she became permanently depressed. Pierce tried to engage "my dear Noble stricken one" in other interests to no avail. She closed herself in her room, penning pathetic pencil notes to her dead son. After a large, convivial dinner and even a vigorous horseback ride with the president's secretary, Sidney Webster, Jane Pierce herself confessed to her sister that such pleasures were "of course, for me, to be endured rather than enjoyed." In the process, she helped debilitate her husband's presidency. "She shrank with extreme sensitiveness from public observation," admitted Pierce. "I cannot help being influenced by that very controlling trait."

Documentation does not mean a definitive diagnosis can be made. Examples of FDR's phobia of fire, Mamie Eisenhower's claustrophobia, the social anxiety of crowds that Jackie Kennedy and Bess Truman experienced, LBJ's mood swings, Nancy Reagan's panic following the attempt on her husband's life, the manic activity of Theodore Roosevelt, Ida McKinley's infantile tantrums, Reagan's emotional disengagement ("I've never been a great one for introspection," he admitted), are all based on limited information. Books attempting to psychoanalyze Jefferson, Wilson, Kennedy, Nixon, and Clinton have been written, yet only in-depth personal disclosure can provide genuine assessments of emotional problems. Ironically, this is provided through family letters in the case of one of the earliest First Family members, Thomas Mann Randolph.

As a student, Randolph had idolized Jefferson, his future father-in-law, who took direction of the young man's education. This dynamic remained after Randolph married Jefferson's daughter Martha. No matter what he did, he never seemed as worthy in her eyes as was her father, whom she assured that no "*new* ties can weaken the first and best of nature." Each of their eleven children was named by Jefferson. He told Randolph, "It is essential to my happiness, our living near together." Martha, recalled their daughter Ellen, "suffered greatly" from his "sullen moods and angry furies," and what Martha called the "agonies of Mr. Randolph's mind," eccentricities like riding straight through rivers and brush. Jefferson felt that Randolph's illnesses were psychosomatic, and advised him "by force of reason" to "counteract . . . this disease on your spirits," and enter politics because the public's "esteem will contribute much to your happiness." For him, however, Randolph said, "The voice of reason is low." He often had to take loans from Jefferson, who also bought indulgences for Martha, making Randolph further feel "something like shame," as a "silly bird . . . in the company of swans." Yet only Jefferson could calm him and keep him from angrily caning the favorite presidential grandson, Jeff.

It is no wonder then that during his residency in the White House, living with his father-in-law and his "golden boy" brother-in-law congressman Jack Eppes, Randolph suffered a nervous collapse. By 1807, he broke under his own sense of inferiority. He fought with Eppes after Jefferson inadvertently invited Eppes to join in some activity but excluded Randolph—who rashly moved out, to a boarding house filled with anti-Jeffersonian congressmen. There he isolated himself, talked of suicide, and kept pistols on his mantel. Jefferson aide William Burwell kept a suicide watch, noting that Randolph was "indifferent to life." Jefferson pleaded with Randolph to return—but with some emotional manipulation, saying that he hoped the end of his political career "may close that of my life also." Jefferson admitted that he had "perceived in you a gloom which gave me uneasiness. I knew there was a difference between Mr. Eppes and yourself, but had no idea it was as deep seated. . . . My affections for you both were warm. . . . What acts of mine can have induced you to suppose that I felt or manifested a preference of him, I cannot conceive."

Randolph responded by getting sick. Jefferson sent an aide to nurse him through the night—and tell him how sick the president himself had now become. Only when Eppes left to visit home did Randolph return. Jefferson assumed what his granddaughter called a "seeming ignorance" of Randolph's odd behavior, but patiently responded with gentle, almost modern sensibility; he felt that "confirmed insanity" was a "recoverable disease." For himself, Jefferson stated, "Hope is so much pleasanter than despair, that I always prefer looking into futurity through her glass."

11

Faith

A s he drew up a treaty with Tripoli, a Moslem state, President George Washington pointed out, "The Government of the United States of America is not, in any sense, founded upon the Christian religion." He may have been right about the legal and constitutional separation of government and religion, but the personal religious beliefs of all of the presidents and their families would be examined and questioned. How First Families practiced their faith could be made into a political liability by the opposition—and used to advantage by the White House.

The private beliefs of the most public family became a political issue from almost the start of the presidency. During the election of 1800, citizens were warned by Federalists to hide their Bibles in tree

Although he was Dutch Reformed, there was no such church in Washington during his presidency; thus, Martin Van Buren attended St. John's Episcopalian Church.

[2 1 7]

James Polk (front row, second from right), photographed here in the State Dining Room with his cabinet, dutifully went with his wife to her Presbyterian church—but attended the Methodist church when he went alone. 1846. JAMES K. POLK HOME, COLUMBIA, TENNESSEE

stumps because if the anti-Federalist "infi-del" Thomas Jefferson won, he would confis-cate all copies of the holy book. Jefferson was actually a student of the history of Jesus, and even drafted his own interpretation of Christ's life, later called "The Jefferson Bible." Public controversy, however, came with his immutable view that clerics were corrupt and his rejection of organized religion. Proud as he was to be a Deist, in the winter of 1802, in the midst of the published charges that he fathered children by his slave Sally Hemings, he suddenly began appearing with his daughters Martha and Maria, and grandchildren Jeff and Ellen, at the Sunday religious services held in the hall of Congress. The *Port Folio* magazine sarcastically called it "one of the most remarkable events of the present time," and a Federalist minister thought that Jefferson's effort at "overturning our religious institutions . . . is now given up."

The Madisons also attended the services in Congress, but during their tenure St. John's Episcopal Church was completed just across the street from the White House. Beginning with the Madisons, every president has attended at least one service there. St John's became the unofficial "court" church, and several of its pastors acted as de facto ministers to the First Families. Reverend William Hawley, for example, presided over Madison, Monroe, Adams, and Tyler weddings; Adams, Jackson, and Tyler christenings; and Harrison and Tyler funerals. The history of St. John's is intertwined with that of the families. The otherwise elusive Peggy Taylor left the mansion every day only to attend services there. William Henry Harrison managed to attend St. John's for two of the four Sundays he was alive as president, and the pneumonia which killed him may, in fact, have been contracted as he walked home from the church in a cold rain. Nell Arthur was active in St. John's Guild of the Holy Child, volunteering to aid indigent local children. Creating a Christmas Club, the nine-year-old oversaw the collec-

A member of the Masons, Andrew Johnson did not belong to any organized religion but frequently attended Catholic mass at old St. Patrick's in Washington.

ANDREW JOHNSON NATIONAL HISTORIC SITE

tion of over 20,000 gifts of clothing and toys. In modern times, the Fords and Bushes regularly attended St. John's.

Some families did not worship together. Taft went to the Unitarian church and his wife and children went to St. John's, just as her predecessor, Edith Roosevelt, had done with her children, while Theodore Roosevelt went to the Dutch Reformed church. Although she had studied the Bible as instructed, Alice Roosevelt refused to attend church in preparation for confirmation—a fact kept from the public during her White House tenancy. With her fervency and fashionably late appearance, Sarah Polk overshadowed her husband when they went to her Presbyterian church. Polk confessed his "predilections are in favor of the Methodist," but he attended that church with his nephew Knox only when Sarah and her niece decided not to go out on Sunday. Polk refused her efforts to get him to join a church. He did so only on his deathbed—as a Methodist.

The Grants chose their church rather differently. On their first Sunday as First Family, they went down the aisle and found that there was no reserved pew for them in the front section in the fashionable Metropolitan Methodist Church. The insulted First Lady led her husband, children, and sisters out, and over to First Presbyterian. The next time they appeared at Metropolitan Methodist, there was no mistaking them as the most prestigious family in the elite church.

In stark contrast was Grant's immediate predecessor. Andrew Johnson—who had no church affiliation—regularly attended the Roman Catholic mass on Sundays held at St. Patrick's Church, drawn to its liturgy and lack of social stratification in the seating of its members. Numerous families had ties to the Catholic church during a time of intolerance toward it. Dolley Madison befriended several Georgetown nuns, and children of Jefferson, Monroe, and Andrew Johnson were educated in Catholic schools. Inquiring of his convent-educated niece Harriet whether she was converting, James Buchanan assured her, "If you should become a good Catholic, I would be satisfied." Andrew Jackson hosted the only Catholic wedding in the White House, for his aide's daughter. When Polk was approached by

Rutherford and Lucy Hayes in their pew at Foundry Methodist Church. This was the same church (although at a different site) where the Clintons later attended. 1877.

HAYES PRESIDENTIAL CENTER

a "fanatic," as he called him, with a "most intolerant attack on the Roman Catholics," who pleaded that priests be expelled as army chaplains, the president was enraged—as he was at a request to stop the Mormons from their westward trek.

Such association impacted campaigns. Taft's friendships with bishops and his daughter's attendance at a Catholic school were personal factors, yet used against him with as much might as his official statement that the church was a "bulwark against socialism and anarchy." Unfounded suspicions were spread that Ida McKinley was Catholic. Fear of the issue led Florence Harding to steer her brother Vetallis—married to a Catholic woman—away from the press. In 1960, the religious Rose Kennedy argued with a Protestant minister over her Catholic son's right to be president. On Inaugural morning, she slipped anonymously into Trinity Church, "bundled-up with a lot of funny-looking scarves," shocked to see him there also: "I hadn't urged him to go. I would have except I thought he was so overwrought with work and with responsibilities. But the fact that he did go on his own, and did think it was important to start his new administration out with mass in the morning, gave me a wonderful happy feeling." When Luci Johnson converted to Catholicism in 1966, debate was not about her new faith but her decision to be re-baptized. One Episcopalian bishop called it "sacrilegious" because it suggested that her previous Protestant baptism was invalid. The Vatican said it was not a requirement for conversion, and called it "regrettable" for the stir it caused. By the time Pat Nixon and later Ronald Reagan were living in the White House, the fact that both of their fathers had been Catholic was moot.

Not all families were tolerant. Rose Cleveland tried unsuccessfully to keep her brother from appointing Catholics, and Fillmore later supported banning them from running for office. "The Catholic Church is in no way suited to this country," Theodore Roosevelt told a Methodist group, "and can never have any great permanent growth except through immigration for its thought is Latin and entirely at variance with the dominant thought of our country and institutions."

Dwight Eisenhower escorts his wife, Mamie, out of church, with his daughter-in-law Barbara (at far left), and his mother-in-law, Minnie Doud (at far right). c. 1953–1956.

DWIGHT D. EISENHOWER PRESIDENTIAL LIBRARY

Perhaps with Christianity being America's predominant creed, other faiths such as Judaism, which had relatively smaller numbers in the total population, seemed less threatening than the growing numbers of those who practiced Catholicism. Although there were politically motivated whispers that FDR's family were originally "Rosenfelds," that Harry Truman rarely used his middle initial because it stood for his secret "Solomon" grandfather, and that the Eisenhowers were actually German Jews, Jewish-American political figures were invited as guests in the mansion without forethought as early as the Madison administration. Despite a pale attempt to attack Harding with the local lore that his wife had Jewish ancestors, they were the first presidential couple who genuinely counted members of that faith as intimate friends. Most notably, Albert and Flora Lasker were frequent house guests and dinner companions at the family table, often taking lengthy junkets with them. Lasker—appointed chairman of the

shipping board—was also a regular at poker and golf with the president. A similar spirit prevailed at the Hoovers' White House table. "The Hoover fireside is a place where tolerance is reality," recalled Assistant Attorney General Mabel Walker Willebrandt. "I have been there with Catholic, Jew and unbeliever."

The only openly hostile anti-Semitic member of a First Family was Madge Wallace, Truman's mother-in-law. Never permitting his Jewish friends to cross the threshold of her Missouri home, where the Trumans lived with her, she criticized his pro-Israel policy. On White House tapes released after his death, Nixon characterized Jewish voters and some individuals in political terms; whether it proved he was genuinely anti-Semitic was debatable.

Even presidents' private beliefs became fodder for public discussion. Taft, for example, was attacked as an atheist since, as part of his Unitarian faith, he stated, "I do not believe in the Divinity of Christ," but he angrily refused to publicly "go into a dogmatic discussion of creed." Although Lincoln studied the Bible and attended Wednesday night prayer circles, the fact that he never joined the Presbyterian faith—in the church where he worshipped—was a contentious issue. His wife had to defend his belief in God's existence, and others strove to prove that, two weeks before his murder, he stated he would soon join the church. When Buchanan heard mistaken rumors that Lincoln had done so, the former president hoped that "the act was done in sincerity." Indeed, Eisenhower and Coolidge risked being accused of politicizing religion when they suddenly joined churches at the start of their presidencies; Jackson, Buchanan, and Polk resisted doing so. When, however, Abigail Adams abruptly switched from the Congregational to the Episcopal church (preferring "liberal good sense, devotion without gri-

George Bush escorts his frail mother, Dorothy Walker Bush, out of church after attending Sunday services. 1989.
GEORGE BUSH PRESIDENTIAL LIBRARY

mace, and religion upon a rational system," she called southern Congregationalism "solemn phiz" and "foaming, loud speaking"), there was no public reaction.

Few presidents had public roles in their churches. Truman and Harding addressed groups in their Washington Baptist churches—a children's and a men's class, respectively. In recent times, Carter spoke from the pulpit and taught a Sunday school class during visits to his Plains, Georgia, Baptist church. Although Disciples of Christ James Garfield's preaching was quite publicized, he refused to have fellow members "use me as the promoter of their views." When one Disciple came to the White House and attempted to lobby for a job, the president reported to his wife, "She was greatly grieved not to have seen 'Sister Garfield,' and still more grieved that 'Brother Garfield' would not give her the P.O. [post office appointment]."

Save for the presence of his elderly mother at Garfield's side, one of the most potentially horrific moments of the presidency was averted during his term. Charles Guiteau, who was ultimately successful in shooting Garfield, stalked the president at church several Sundays in a row. Once he aimed a gun at Garfield through a church window, but the sight of Eliza Garfield stopped him from shooting. There are other risks. In November 1967, when Lyndon and Lady Bird Johnson attended Episcopal services in Williamsburg, Virginia, they sat in stunned silence when the minister denounced LBJ's Vietnam War policy. "Wonderful choir,"

President Clinton sings with the choir at Sunday services in the interdenominational chapel at Camp David. Ronald Reagan initiated the chapel, and George Bush dedicated it. 1994.
THE WHITE HOUSE

the First Lady managed to tell him afterward. "Going to church has become a problem," LBJ admitted.

Access to a presidential family as they went to church was easy in the early days. A political enemy confronted Martin Van Buren as he was entering church one Sunday. The president's nimble son Smith invited him to join them in their pew. Won over, the man recalled that he didn't find his "devotions interfered with, nor my political principles contaminated." By the end of the nineteenth century, however, the prospect of glimpsing the family became a spectator's sport. Cleveland was so disgusted by this that when his coach arrived at the church, he always bolted out and marched up the stairs, leaving his wife to make her own way. McKinley hated having people staring at him while he read Psalms, sang hymns, put money in the collection plate, or took communion. He entered church through a side door held for him only, and left through it before the congregation could get up and talk to him.

By the 1920s, getting a presidential family in and out of church was a production. Secret Service agents had to cordon off a clear path from the curb to the church entrance before the Coolidges arrived. Once there, they were swiftly escorted to their third-row pew; the minister was in place, and the service began immediately. Afterward, crowds of tourists surged to take snapshots of the president. The church presence of a presidential family was a distraction that could no longer be ignored. Tired of hearing about his church only in reference to FDR, who attended it, one congregant complained, "It used to be God's church. Now it's the President's."

The problem became acute in 1981 following the Reagan assassination attempt. Preceded by motorcade sirens and a security phalanx, followed into church by reporters, having congregants pass through metal detectors—and getting terrorist threats—made the Reagans understandably uncomfortable. "We were told that our going to church might result in an assassination attempt that could cause the deaths of many other people there. Very unhappily, we just had to stop going to church altogether," Reagan recalled. It prompted him to break ground for an ecumenical chapel at the secure Camp David, completed under Bush. An earlier alternative proved just as controversial for the Nixons. They hosted large Sunday worship services in the East Room, complete with guest ministers, rabbis, priests, choirs, and organists—even serving sweet rolls and coffee afterward. They were so relentlessly attacked for allegedly breaching the separation of church and state that they phased out the services by their second term.

While the Nixons had the first worship services for guests other than family, they were hardly the first to use the mansion as a place for prayer. Every morning after breakfast, Reverend John Scott led his son-in-law President Benjamin Harrison, daughters, grandchildren, and great-grandchildren in prayer. "We've been trying to be Christians in our home for many years," Harrison explained. "We try to live in the White House just as we did at home as nearly as possible." Mamie Eisenhower placed a plaque with a prayer and a picture of the Virgin Mary on a wall in the White House kitchens—technically a place of employment for government workers—but the staff was flattered rather than perturbed. The Hayeses also held morning prayer service: the Bible was passed around to each family member, who read a verse of a chapter; the session concluded with them on their knees repeating the Lord's Prayer. The Hayeses and then the McKinleys gathered friends for Sunday night hymn singing, the latter couple using the Blue Room. The Pierces began the day with prayers, the servants included. Wilson frequently invited clergy for dinner, and read from a book of devotional exercises to his family at night.

Certainly, presidents used their home for their own spiritual consultations. Practically on call to the White House, the Reverend Billy Graham was the unofficial spiritual adviser for presidents from Truman to Clinton, always available to confer during crises, from war to scandal. Lincoln relied on Methodist bishop Matthew Simpson and Presbyterian minister Phineas Gurley. In the aftermath of his impeachment trial, Clinton sought the counsel of Philip Wogaman, the Methodist minister of the church he attended, and two other ministers. Numerous others turned to a family member. Buchanan's brother, Edward, a highly regarded Episcopalian rector, played no particular role in his brother's presidency, but the sisters of Harding and Carter, Seventh Day Adventist missionary Carolyn Votaw and minister Ruth

Stapleton, respectively, were close to their brothers. Grover Cleveland's brother, the Presbyterian divine William Cleveland, participated in the president's wedding ceremony in the Blue Room, but their eldest sister, a missionary, was ministering in Ceylon at the time, and unable to participate.

As with many families in emotional turmoil, faith sustained those of the presidents. In the days following Clinton's disclosure of marital indiscretion, the Reverend Jesse Jackson called on the president's wife and daughter, philosophically recalling Scripture. Only through her faith was Mollie Garfield able to accept her father's assassination, writing in her diary that, "if any one deserved reward it is Papa Garfield & I think he has got it. I think if he really is happier than he would be if on earth, we ought to try and be comforted." As Florence Harding lay in a coma, Warren prayed outside her room, constantly repeating the 121st Psalm. Surviving the attempt on his life profoundly affected Reagan. "God, for some reason, had seen fit to give me his blessing and allow me to live a while longer," he reflected. This belief infused his sense of purpose in the presidency, according to his diary: "Whatever happens now I will try to serve Him in every way I can." Grace Coolidge was similarly transformed by her teenage son's death. Observed her secretary, "I have never seen a truer submission to the Divine Will." Apparently coming to a peaceful acceptance of death, Grace later permitted the publication of a prayerlike poem she wrote at the time of her experience.

In politics, hypocrisy is a professional hazard. Still, when the private behavior of a president seems inconsistent with his claims of being religious, he is called on it publicly. No matter how often Jackson referred to the Almighty, for example, the fact that he murdered a man and took a married woman as his own wife forever branded him an infidel to his enemies. The depth of any person's genuine convictions are difficult to detect—but it's hopelessly convoluted for an iconic figure like a president. Thus, not only the men themselves but the populace often accepted at face value their public actions—if not their real behavior and feelings. Franklin Roosevelt always had church services held on his Inauguration Days and moments of national crisis, yet had little interest in faith. When he told his wife that their children should be taught religion as he was, she questioned whether he believed what he had learned. "I never really thought about it," he said. "I think it is just as well not to think about things like that." Only when forced to face the truths about Nazi crimes against humanity did he seek answers, finding the teachings of nineteenth-century mystic Kierkegaard helpful in comprehending how the Nazis "are human, yet they behave like demons."

In ironic counterpoint is Harding. Harding's faith was absolute, retaining a view of God, heaven, and angels he had learned as a child. He even asked a friend to "talk to God about me every day by name and ask Him somehow to give me strength." Despite his drinking, smoking, gambling, and adultery, Harding never seemed to indulge without a guilty sense that he violated his own moral ideals. With point-blank honesty the president told his minister he

Religious Affiliations of Presidents and Wives
(Not Necessarily Baptized or Members)

Episcopalian: George and Martha Washington, James Madison, James and Elizabeth Monroe, Louisa Adams, William Henry Harrison, John and Letitia Tyler, Zachary and Margaret Taylor, Chester Arthur, Edith Roosevelt, Nellie Taft, Edith Wilson, Lou Hoover (converted to Quaker), Franklin and Eleanor Roosevelt, Bess Truman, Lady Bird Johnson, Gerald and Betty Ford, George and Barbara Bush

Presbyterian: Andrew Jackson, James and Sarah Polk, James Buchanan, Abraham and Mary Lincoln, Eliza Johnson, Grover and Frances Cleveland, Benjamin and Caroline Harrison, Woodrow and Ellen Wilson, Dwight and Mamie Eisenhower, Ronald and Nancy Reagan

Methodist: Ulysses and Julia Grant, Rutherford and Lucy Hayes, William and Ida McKinley, Florence Harding, Rosalynn Carter (converted to Baptist), Hillary Clinton

Catholic: Julia Tyler (born Presbyterian, attended Episcopal, converted to Catholicism), Andrew Johnson (attended only), John and Jacqueline Kennedy, Pat Nixon (father was Catholic, but she attended all denominations)

Congregationalist: John and Abigail Adams, Franklin and Jane Pierce, Calvin and Grace Coolidge

Quaker: Dolley Madison (converted to Episcopalian), Herbert Hoover, Richard Nixon

Baptist: Warren Harding, Harry Truman, Jimmy Carter, Bill Clinton

Unitarian: John Quincy Adams, Millard and Abigail Fillmore, William Howard Taft

Disciples of Christ: James and Lucretia Garfield, Lyndon Johnson

Dutch Reformed: Martin Van Buren, Theodore Roosevelt

Deist: Thomas Jefferson

couldn't participate in communion Sundays because he was "unworthy."

Had it been widely publicized at the time, Sarah Polk's belief in ordained predestiny would have drawn heated debate from abolitionists. She saw no hypocrisy in the fact that the expensive gowns she wore to church were paid for by slave labor on her cotton plantation. Looking out a window one afternoon, watching slaves work, she told the president that God created the slaves to be "toiling in the hot sun." Franklin and Jane Pierce came to believe in a tortured sense of godliness. Overcome with religious guilt after the death of their three sons, he concluded that the loss was "doubtless needed." He rationalized, "We are commanded to set up no idols in our hearts . . . my prevailing feeling has been that we live for our children. In all my labors, plans and exertions, in them was the center of all my hopes . . . We should have lived for God and have left the dear ones to Him." The Pierces kept a strict sabbath, not even reading mail that day.

Among presidential families, "keeping the Lord's day" presented a curious contrast to traditional expectations: it has been the men, not the women, whose regular church attendance the public observed and judged. Few presidents ignored this—even the not particularly pious ones. For all the unprecedented aspects of Kennedy's being the first Catholic president, for example, he often resisted going off to Sunday mass. Certainly not everyone trotted off to church for the sake of political expediency. Even though Hayes, for example, never sought membership in a church, he always attended on Sunday. "I hope that you will be benefitted by your church-going," he explained to his son Webb. "Where the habit does not christianize, it generally civilizes." On the other hand, despite her zealotry, Jane Pierce rarely made it out to church, although she requested that the government clerks who worked for her husband attend services. After breakfast, over which her husband said grace, then prepared to leave for church, Ida McKinley often begged off for reasons of her health. Yet after McKinley returned, joining her for lunch and a stroll through the greenhouses, she often managed to take in theater matinees. Still, Ida, like women such as Dolley Madison, Letitia Tyler, Lucy Hayes, Eleanor Roosevelt, Rosalynn Carter, Barbara Bush and Hillary Clinton, maintained a strong commitment to local church and community charities.

In grief or fear, many members of First Families relied upon nontraditional beliefs and practices such as astrology, tarot cards, and even spiritualism. After the assassination attempt on her husband, Nancy Reagan—filled with anxiety each time he appeared in any open space—decided to "hedge my bets," through zodiac consultations with San Francisco astrologer Joan Quigley. Quigley outlined the dates that her charts indicated to be "safe" days for the president's appearances, as well as optimum days for important decisions, treaty signings, and other events not held in public. Reagan himself seemed to have a detached but bemused curiosity about it all, once asking his wife about an uncertain day, "What does Joan say?"

The Reagans were hardly the first to consult the stars. Astrologer Jeane Dixon claimed that she provided FDR and Truman with predictions, and in at least one documented instance before his presidency, Dwight and Mamie Eisenhower consulted a Manila fortune-teller. Edith Wilson used seeress Marcia Champrey, as did Florence Harding. The astrologer later became famous for her correct prediction during the 1920 campaign of the "sudden, violent and peculiar death" of President Harding, a fact partially corroborated by Mrs. Harding's public statement at the time that she saw "nothing but tragedy" over her husband, and her

Faith

confirmation that she did indeed consult Marcia. Discreetly slipped into the White House via the service entrance, Marcia did tarot card, crystal ball, and astrology chart readings, as well as clairvoyance sessions for Florence in her bedroom.

Other families sought to contact the spirit world. Garfield and his mother both believed in séances despite their parochial Christianity. Jane Pierce used the famous Fox sisters as mediums, and Mary Lincoln depended on a number of unsavory mediums in the Red Room to contact her "beloved dead." In April 1863, the *Boston Gazette* reported that President Lincoln attended one such séance with his wife. In reaction to the channeling of spirits and their advice, Lincoln said the "celestials . . . sound very much like the talk of my Cabinet."

Several wives believed they had extrasensory perception: Julia Tyler later correctly envisioned her husband's death in a vivid dream; Julia Grant claimed that she heard an inner voice predict her husband's glory. Abraham Lincoln was convinced his dreams were prescient, the most famous and documented instance being his vision of his East Room funeral several weeks before it happened. "I shall meet with some terrible end," he predicted.

"I think of Lincoln, shambling, homely, with his strong, sad, deeply furrowed face all the time," admitted Theodore Roosevelt, somewhat suggesting that he sensed the dead president's presence. "I see him in the different rooms, and in the halls." There have been many claims of White House ghosts from servants and visiting royalty alike. "Sometimes when I worked at my desk late at night I'd get a feeling that someone was standing behind me," Eleanor Roosevelt confessed—as had Grace Coolidge and Dwight Eisenhower about Lincoln's spiritual presence. Jackie Kennedy said that when she went into the present-day Lincoln bedroom—the space where much of his White House life had been spent, his Cabinet room—she felt the sort of peace she experienced only in church. "I used to feel his strength," she admitted; "I'd sort of be talking to him." Margaret Truman, and later Amy Carter, had friends sleep over in the room to see if the ghost would appear. Ronald Reagan, his daughter Maureen, her husband Dennis Revell, and even the president's spaniel dog Rex all sensed the spiritual presence in the Lincoln bedroom.

On two occasions, Rex barked incessantly as if there were a person in the hall. When Reagan investigated and then walked into the Lincoln bedroom, the dog stared unnaturally, refused to enter, and then ran away. Maureen always stayed in the room because the bed was the only one in the house long enough to accommodate her tall husband. Despite the fact that it seemed "weird as all get-out," she claimed that Revell awoke one night to see a shadowy figure in a red coat. Later staying there alone, Maureen also saw a transparent image of a man that matched her husband's description, not certain if it was Lincoln or Jackson. "Then he slowly turned around and stared at me before vanishing into thin air." When she told her father, Reagan cracked, "If you see him again, send him down the hall. I have some questions."

Maureen mused, "It's funny that he wouldn't take his own daughter at her word, or his son-in-law, but he'd begin to believe a barking dog."

12

The Home Office

I have found by experience that the only place I can get things done is the White House. We are so safely (almost annoyingly) guarded here nowadays that we, as a matter of fact, have a great deal of seclusion and privacy.

—*President Woodrow Wilson*

If I feel depressed, I go to work.

—*First Lady Eleanor Roosevelt*

One of the blessings of family life in the White House is the fact that the head of the family works at home. For the first century of the mansion's life, in fact, twenty-four families—the John Adamses through the William McKinleys—needed only to walk down the hall from the family rooms to interrupt their husband, father, grandfather, son, brother, or uncle in his office. With the 1902 renovation and creation of the West Wing during the Theodore Roosevelt tenure, the office was a bit more removed, but not by much—just a walk down the stairs and a stroll through a hall and two colonnades. In fact, from the window in the room that was traditionally the First Lady's sitting room, she could see into the window of her husband's office. Inevitably, with the presidency, the man of the house brought his work home, using a private study in the family quarters—even after the Roosevelt renovation. The space used has been either the Yellow Oval Room or one of the two smaller square rooms flanking

One of the things Jackie Kennedy liked about the presidency was that her husband's office was connected to their home. She often coaxed him out of the Oval Office during the day with the children—or pets—coming to the French windows.

JOHN F. KENNEDY PRESIDENTIAL LIBRARY

[231]

it. Other areas have become favored work spaces for them. Nixon used the Lincoln Sitting Room in the family quarters, and a suite in the Old Executive Office Building. LBJ and George Bush used the Oval Office in the West Wing for larger meetings, but found the small suite off the office better for small meetings. Bush had a small television here to keep up with the news during the Persian Gulf War, and the kitchen there provided him with quick meals prepared by a steward.

Most presidents awoke, dressed, and breakfasted early and then went right to the office. As interaction with the public in ceremonial duties increased, a president's day was broken up between his office and the public rooms. Oftentimes, a president would "come home" for dinner with his family, only to retreat to his study for long hours into the night. There were notable exceptions. At five o'clock, Ronald Reagan left the office, went upstairs and exercised for a half hour, then usually got into his pajamas and ate dinner on TV trays with his wife as they watched the news—which had been previously videotaped for them by the staff. There might be some office paperwork, and Reagan always wrote in his journal a bit. Then he went to bed with a novel and was often asleep by ten. Chester Arthur didn't get to work until ten in the morning, and often left by four P.M. Then he rested, read, or rode horseback until seven-thirty. "President Arthur never did today what he could put off until tomorrow," a clerk recalled. He even had a basket of phony documents in his office, created by the staff to give the appearance that he was hard at work.

Before 1902, relatives such as Ned Coles, Sam Gouverneur, John Adams II, Jack Donelson, Abraham Van Buren, Robert Tyler, Knox Walker, William Bliss, Joseph Taylor, Powers Fillmore, Buck Henry, Jim Buchanan, Robert Johnson, Buck Grant, Webb and Ruddy Hayes, who served as aides, reported to work down the hall from their bedrooms, occupying a small office or partitioned area adjacent to the president's office. Here they filtered out office-seekers, welcomed waiting officials, prepared documents and correspondence for the president's signature or perusal. Several even acted as personal messengers and kept hours as long as the president's. Daughters, sisters, nieces, and other women relatives who aided First Ladies with social duties were confined to work space in the bedroom suites, such as Margaret Gardiner did in assisting her sister Julia Tyler in writing out social invitations. FDR's daughter Anna, who served as a personal but unofficial aide to her father in his last months, reported for work not down in the West Wing but rather beside him in the oval study in the residence, where he preferred to work at the end of his life. Other relatives such as Sam

James Monroe's daughter and son-in-law, Eliza and George Hay, were indispensable to the functioning of the presidency, she as the manager of events and protocol, he as an adviser.

JAMES MONROE MUSEUM AND LIBRARY; FRICK ART REFERENCE LIBRARY

Houston Johnson or Chip Carter, who had jobs with the Democratic National Committee, or Nell Wilson, who volunteered as a nursery school teacher, left the premises to work.

How First Family members worked depended on their habits. Ulysses S. Grant dealt with telegrams and correspondence until ten in the morning, saw officials until noon, and worked on "official business" until three. His successor Rutherford Hayes sometimes met with officials as late as eleven at night. In the days before staff speechwriters, Cleveland would scribble out his own speeches well into the night, chewing tobacco. When Teddy Roosevelt worked too late in the oval study, his wife's trill of "The-o-dore!" promptly got him up and into bed. In the depths of the Great Depression, Herbert Hoover went over dictation as many as three times, and "labored practically all his waking hours," according to the chief usher.

Others integrated a sense of relaxation into their routine. Harry Truman always took a brisk morning constitutional in the vicinity of the White House to clear his head for morning office work ahead. After a morning in the office, John Kennedy liked to take a quick dip in the pool—often meeting and swimming with staff there. Afterward, he headed upstairs to lunch with his wife and their private nap hour, and then, freshly dressed, he worked until evening. Although Harding worked longer hours than any of his predecessors going back thirty years, according to the chief usher, he tried to get in a golf game at the nearby estate of friends Ned and Evalyn McLean. According to Alice Longworth and the wife of Attorney General A. Mitchell Palmer, Harding was also meeting his mistress there, whom both women identified as Nan Britton. Back at the White House, he thought nothing of working until two

John Quincy Adams kept to a strict work schedule.

in the morning. Even if tired, Harding refused to lounge in the morning—"No, it is too much like a woman." Sometimes he napped on the couch in the anteroom to his office—and he was sometimes joined by Britton, according to her.

Harding's successor Calvin Coolidge slept about eleven hours a day. After lunch, without fail, he napped, sometimes for two hours. His bedtime of ten o'clock became so well known that once, while attending a late evening musical, performer Groucho Marx looked up at the presidential box and cracked, "Isn't it past your bedtime, Calvin?" Taft liked to relax and read newspapers in his office. His habit of falling asleep anywhere, anytime, resulted in his wife's prodding him in the side. Taft developed his own system. He balanced his spectacles on the end of his finger. When he dozed, his finger went limp, his glasses fell, and he awoke.

Taft was one of the last presidents who tried to maintain the unwritten code of conducting no work on Sunday, based on the belief that it was the Lord's day for meditation and rest only. Yet even before the Civil War the custom was sometimes broken. "On commencing my presidential career," recalled Fillmore, "I found that the Sabbath had been frequently employed . . . for private interviews with the President. I determined to put an end to this custom, and ordered my doorkeeper to meet all Sunday visitors with indiscriminate refusal." Several other presidents—with particularly pious wives like Sarah Polk and Lucy Hayes—didn't work Sundays. "If it were not for Sunday, I would die," admitted Benjamin Harrison. "I will have my Sundays free. On that day I will not receive a letter, nor have any business brought to me unless there is something immediately urgent from the State Department." As the nation's business became more global with World War I, and technology increased communication, keeping Sunday entirely free became increasingly impossible. The attack on Pearl Harbor came on Sunday, December 7, 1941: when President Roosevelt rushed into meetings that day, the old presidential rule of conducting no public business on Sunday was forever broken. On Sundays in the late twentieth century, Reagan had to respond to attacks on a Marine base in Lebanon, Bush had to conduct the Gulf War, Clinton had to deploy troops to Bosnia.

John Quincy Adams managed to integrate prayer into his every workday, but kept to the grindstone even on Sundays. "I rise at about five, read two chapters of Scott's Bible and Commentary," he wrote in his diary, "then the morning newspapers and public papers from the several Departments; write seldom and not often enough; breakfast, an hour from nine to ten; then have a succession of visitors, upon business in search of a [job] place, solicitors for donations, or for mere curiosity from eleven until between four and five o'clock. The heads of the Departments, of course, occupy much of this time. Between four and six I take a walk of three or four miles. Dine from half-past five until seven, and from dark until about eleven I generally pass the evening in my chamber, signing land-grants or blank patents . . . About eleven I retire."

Certainly, there has been no longer history of "stay-at-home" working wives and mothers than the First Ladies. Besides directing the household through stewards, housekeepers, and chief ushers, presidents' wives have been expected to function as upper-class hostesses—writing thank-you notes, arranging dinners, and drawing up invitation lists. They were the recipients of endless requests for charity or political intervention, but these requests were filtered first by their husbands' staffs, and the women kept only a writing table in their sitting rooms. Sarah Polk was the exception, serving as one of the president's private aides, working from her portable desk, which traveled with her.

As women took a larger civic role after the Civil War, public expectations of the First Lady grew—and so did her need for a staff. The first documentation of a secretary being used by a First Lady is from a letter to Adams Express on behalf of Lucy Hayes, signed by a "Miss Foote." With Frances Cleveland, the first privately salaried secretary, a friend named Minnie Alexander, reported to work in the family quarters. Belle Hagner, the first federally salaried secretary, hired by Edith Roosevelt, also worked for Ellen Wilson, and Edith Helm worked for Edith Wilson, Eleanor Roosevelt, and Bess Truman. In the West Sitting Hall, then in the Solarium, Grace Coolidge worked beside her secretary Mary Randolph, starting the work day with coffee and doughnuts and listening to the radio, handwriting or typing a portion of her own correspondence. During the Depression, Lou Hoover used her suite as an office, and often spread out and filed papers on her bed, attempting, with her four secretaries—who worked in attic rooms—to keep up with pleas for help from the unemployed. In pink bed jacket and hair bow, Mamie Eisenhower worked directly from bed, signing and composing papers on a pink bed tray. If staff came in to confer while she was watching her favorite soap opera, they had to wait until a commercial break.

While most kept a desk in their bedroom, many took a separate room as work space. Florence Harding established a professional office with phones, reference books, and typewriters in the present-day Lincoln Sitting Room. Lady Bird Johnson often used the small

Sarah Polk aided her husband as one of his secretaries, clipping newspaper articles for his attention.

JAMES K. POLK HOME, COLUMBIA, TENNESSEE

Queen's Sitting Room to work in—because, she said, "it only has one door"—and would hang a taped note on the door, MRS. JOHNSON AT WORK. Despite her strict businesslike schedule, she always found time to dictate her diary into her tape recorder. Pat Nixon used her dressing room as her office, spending at least four hours a day signing her own public correspondence, believing everyone deserved a personal response. Eleanor Roosevelt, Bess Truman, and their secretaries used the present-day cosmetology room and were dubbed "The Girls of the Second Floor Front," during the war.

Nancy Reagan had an elegant office, beside the family gym, overlooking Pennsylvania Avenue. From this vortex, she kept in constant touch with the West Wing with her famous white telephone, plugged into a private line that couldn't be tracked by government operators.

During the Franklin Roosevelt administration, the East Wing was built as a control center for the military. Military aides also served as escorts at social events, and thus the social office and growing First Lady's staff was soon based here. After Jackie Kennedy saw the mayhem there of frantic aides, jingling telephones, and clacking typewriters, she said it was like "an old Rosalind Russell movie," and established her office in the family floor Treaty Room. From the Grant cabinet table, she scribbled out memos for her staff on legal-sized yellow notepads, taking an hour break daily for her children. Rosalynn Carter broke precedent by taking her own office in the East Wing near her staff. Wearing a business suit and carrying a briefcase, to avoid the tourists who daily marched through the East Wing hall, she had to skirt across the lawn or duck into an underground tunnel. Hillary Clinton was the first First Lady to have an office in the West Wing, directly above the Oval Office. As she was so involved in helping to formulate policy, her small office space gave her quicker access to aides and advisers, and for meetings.

Even away from the mansion, presidents keep up manic work hours. When they travel, staff and office equipment go with them. Throughout his 1990 summer "vacation" at his Maine home, George Bush was breezily relaxed in front of the press when he took a break to play some golf; in reality, he worked many hours a day on the Gulf War crisis. While in France during the Versailles Treaty talks, Wilson began his day before dawn and later held a series of intense fifteen-minute meetings with European leaders, back to back, starting at eleven and

Powers Fillmore, one of many presidential sons who put his own legal career on hold and came to work for his father in the White House. His father was known to criticize his posture and clothing.
BUFFALO AND ERIE COUNTY HISTORICAL SOCIETY

ending at three-thirty. When he returned to the United States, he promoted his League of Nations on a 9,981-mile train tour with twenty-six stops in twenty-seven days, speaking endlessly in smoky halls and from the train's back platform. Despite severe headaches, sleeplessness, and slurred speech, he defied doctor's orders and forged ahead. On September 25, 1919, he suffered the first of two strokes that would permanently incapacitate him.

Several other workaholics paid a heavy toll. James Polk so believed in his vow to work for the nation that when protocol demanded that he attend a function, he would later return to the office to make up the time he spent socializing, not wanting to cheat the nation of his productivity. On the last day of his grueling term, by the end of which he had aged shockingly—his hair gone white, his eyes sunken in his gaunt face—Polk wrote, "I feel exceedingly relieved that I am now free from all public cares. I am sure I shall be a happier man in my retirement than I have been during the four years I have filled the highest office." He died 103 days later.

Certainly there are momentary crises that keep a president at work. In his last days in office, as he negotiated the release of American hostages in Iran, Jimmy Carter did not go to sleep for

James Buchanan "Buck" Henry, nephew of James Buchanan and the first presidential secretary to be federally salaried. He left the house and job in anger when his uncle insisted he shave a mustache he later grew.
WHEATLANDS, HOME OF JAMES BUCHANAN

many of the nights, and not at all on his last night in the White House. He got through Reagan's inaugural on the adrenaline of the crisis and the euphoria of knowing the hostages would soon be freed. More than any other modern president, Lyndon Johnson maintained a killing pace. He took phone calls at three in the morning, waking his light sleep, and would meet with people at any time, any place—even in the rest room if necessary. A decent meal was something simply to be squeezed in between meetings, often brought in by his solicitous wife herself. Lady Bird Johnson recalled the cursed package of priority memos, correspondence, decisions, and Vietnam War reports that was bundled and placed on the pillow of his bed every night before he went to sleep. She pleaded with him to "let it rest until morning," but he knew there would be more work as soon as he awoke. Toward the end of his administration, he worked even later into the wee hours of the morning. Lady Bird "kept on counting the days that were left to his term," and attempted to have him "measure his strength. Unfortunately, Lyndon's health began to deteriorate markedly." Johnson lived barely four years after leaving office.

When it came to an astounding work schedule, however, perhaps none compares with the one Eleanor Roosevelt sustained over twelve years. She never waited for elevators: it wasted time. As she hurried up and down stairs, her fur piece swinging in her whirlwind, the First Lady often dictated her daily newspaper column, "My Day," to her secretary—even as she hopped into a car to go across town for a meeting or to catch a plane across the country. When she was in residence, Mrs. Roosevelt took a daily seven A.M. canter on her horse in the park, then held meetings over breakfast with members of Congress or labor leaders or political advisers. Then it was to her office, where she and her secretaries responded to tens of thousands of letters. Lunch was often another political meeting. Afternoons, she might be found at a ceremonial function, giving a speech, or pre-

siding over a New Deal conference, sitting in the front row taking notes or clicking her knitting needles as she missed not a word. If she dined apart from her family, her meal was over another meeting. Her day often wound down at about three in the morning, when she wrote personal letters by hand. Sistie Dall recalled that her grandmother's only respites were frequent catnaps, snatched during traveling time (Hillary Clinton, often compared to Mrs. Roosevelt, kept a similar work pace, and managed catnaps in which she simply shut down into a half-sleep for ten-minute intervals—even while sitting).

When Eleanor Roosevelt traveled, she was in constant motion. One travel day had her arriving by train in West Virginia by six-thirty in the morning, then making a 50-mile car trip to deliver three speeches—all before nine in the morning. After a college commencement, tours of two farming communities and a battlefield, eight more speeches, and another 150 miles by motorcade, Eleanor Roosevelt wrapped up her nineteen-hour day.

Eleanor Roosevelt became the only First Lady to take a job outside the mansion. In 1940, as America prepared for war, she assumed the unsalaried post of deputy director of the Office of Civilian Defense. The sight of the tall First Lady in the blue-gray coverall uniform of the OCD, striding up Connecticut Avenue to the Dupont Circle Building stopped early morning workers in their tracks. At the OCD, the First Lady worked from her office desk on the top floor, organizing a national volunteer network. Outside the building, the curious gathered daily to see her or one of her special visitors—even the Duchess of Windsor came with her little dog to meet with Mrs. Roosevelt. One afternoon, when some African-American friends were refused seats in the restaurant on the ground floor, the First Lady announced, "Very well, we'll all eat in the lobby." She did so for several days until the restaurant was integrated. But

Like many First Ladies before and since, Pat Nixon worked in her bedroom and sitting room suite. Her daughter Julie is here with her in the bedroom.
NIXON PRESIDENTIAL MATERIALS

when she hired her friend dancer Mayris Chaney to teach calisthenics on the building's roof in the afternoons, a hue and cry went up in Congress about the "fan dancer" and provoked what Eleanor said was "more or less abusive" public mail.

Her conclusion was that it was "unwise" for a president's wife to work outside the mansion and "try a government job."

No matter where he is, a president cannot escape work. Here George Bush reads—and fishes—on his speedboat Fidelity.
GEORGE BUSH PRESIDENTIAL LIBRARY

13

Pets and Pastimes

As to his two hobbies being fishing and chess in that order, I cannot remember. . . . On the other hand, my mother was a devoted fisherman—and I used to say she would fish from sunup to sunset whether she caught anything or not!
—First Daughter Fanny Hayes

Any man who does not like dogs and want them about, does not deserve to be in the White House.
—President Calvin Coolidge

No vacations, card games, horse races, billiards, dancing and—on Sundays—no music. Sarah Polk felt that in both her public and private life she must indulge in no frivolity. The religious press praised her highly: "Mrs. Polk deeply realizes the responsibility of her position."

She was the rare exception. As they sought diversion from work in and out of the White House, and simply indulged a pastime, First Families have usually done so with gusto. Certainly there were those like Nellie Taft who feared newspaper publicity about playing cards on a Sunday, but most have been willing to risk a little criticism for pleasure. Although Adams and his sons had been rebuked in Congress and the press for playing billiards, forty years later Grant created a new billiards room. Under Jimmy Carter, a billiards room was created on the third floor, the walls lined with wood panels crafted from one of their old family barns. The Hardings kept a large Chinese bureau in the Yellow Oval Room filled with checkers, chess, and dominoes.

Cards have been the most popular recreation among the families. As Mamie Eisenhower

FDR plays solitaire as his devoted cousin Margaret Suckley looks on, holding dog Fala, which she gave him.

FRANKLIN D. ROOSEVELT LIBRARY

had cherished her bridge games with old friends in the Solarium, Hillary Clinton played pinochle in that same room with her husband, daughter, and brothers. Many early presidents played for stakes. FDR did so only occasionally, but his successors indulged freely, poker having lost its sinful overtones. Harry Truman was famous for having his bourbon and branch water at hand during his sessions. Eisenhower held stag poker nights in the present-day Treaty Room after a dinner of venison, his favorite quail hash, or other wild game. No president played more poker than Warren Harding, who once even wagered a barrel of Harrison-era china—and lost it. He played twice a week in the White House with a group drawn from four dozen or so regulars, mixing business with pleasure over the chips, cigars, and whiskey cocktails mixed by his wife.

Hoover's dislike of cards was actually due to Harding's obsession with them. As his commerce secretary, Hoover was invited for poker but took offense at what was technically gambling in the White House. On a western junket Hoover recalled: "As soon as we were aboard ship [Harding] insisted on playing bridge, beginning every day immediately after breakfast and continuing except for mealtime often until after midnight. There were only four other bridge players in the party, and we soon set up shifts so that one at a time had some relief. For some reason I developed a distaste for bridge on this journey and never played it again."

Few First Ladies played cards with more tenacity than Ida McKinley—though her husband often just let her win. She was renowned, however, for her needles. Ida turned her pastime of knitting slippers into public good by donating them to the needy or to charities as fundraising items. Quite a few women did handiwork. Whether on an army transport to the South Pacific or in the front row of congressional hearings, Eleanor Roosevelt kept clacking her knitting needles. Julie Nixon did a crewelwork of the presidential seal for her father. Barbara Bush's needlepoint rug was used in the family room adjacent to the presidential bedroom. Perhaps the most personal gift given to the White House was the blanket for the Lincoln bed, crocheted by Grace Coolidge.

While Ike played poker with his men friends in the Monroe Room (now the Treaty Room), his wife, Mamie, played bridge with her friends in the Solarium.

Dwight D. Eisenhower Presidential Library; private collection

Harry Truman reading in the garden at Blair House.

A permanent library was established at the White House only in 1961, by Jackie Kennedy. Although Abigail Fillmore had Congress appropriate funding for the first library, the books disappeared over the years and families had to bring their own. Many had specific preferences: Bess Truman loved murder mysteries, while her husband indulged in ancient and American history. Clinton read through biographies of his predecessors, while Pat Nixon and Grace Coolidge were known to read biographies of *their* predecessors. When word got out about Lou Hoover's collection of Washington history books, she was inundated with hundreds more. Jackie Kennedy pored through art, fashion, architecture, history, and philosophy books and magazines. Ike liked Zane Grey westerns; Lincoln stunned visitors by his ability to quote lengthy passages of *Hamlet* and *Macbeth*, which he read and reread; Reagan enjoyed newspaper comics. TR read voraciously—everything from Sinclair's shocking novel *The Jungle* to Milton and Tacitus. "I find it a great comfort to like all kinds of books," he said, "and to be able to get half an hour or an hour's complete rest and complete detachment from the fighting of the moment." It was said TR could skim a page and absorb it all. When his family took a speed-reading course, President Carter managed to take in about 2,000 words a minute with a nearly 100 percent comprehension rate.

Numerous family members were published during their tenure, but Quincy Adams, Polk, Mollie Garfield, Barbara Bush, Nancy Reagan, and Lady Bird Johnson, to name but a few, kept diaries. Robert Tyler published a grim tract of poems about death. Many others found poetry to be an outlet for their emotions. George Adams exchanged poetry with his mother on the frustrations of public expectations. When John Tyler Jr. sent vaguely romantic poems to his stepmother, Julia, she said she forgave "bad poetry when it is flattering." Presidential sister and hostess Rose Cleveland spent much of her private time writing and editing her book on George Eliot's poetry, which, she admitted, "is not of a kind to suit the masses." Still, her celebrity helped her sell the book—her first royalty payment was $25,000. She soon after became editor of *Literary Life* magazine, wrote three novels, and went to law school. Wilson's compositions were limericks he jotted and performed for his daughters' amusement, often in dialects. His signature work: "For beauty I am not a star,/There are others more handsome by far./But my face I don't mind it,/For I am behind it,/It's the people in front that I jar."

So scholarly were John Quincy Adams's published studies on Shakespeare that when actor James Hackett asked for a copy of his *Othello* article, Adams replied, "This extension of my fame is more tickling to my vanity than it was to be elected President." The Monroes were the first family to attend the Washington theater, an 1819 performance of *School of Reform*, but many made theater their favorite outing. Even workaholic Cleveland, enchanted with the comic operas of Gilbert and Sullivan, relaxed enough to let his sister Rose treat him and friends on his birthday to *The Mikado* at the National Theater. Bob Taft took dates to "all the melodramas," but discovered that as a president's son he still "found myself paying as usual from my none too large allowance."

Reserved boxes at the Keith's, National, and Belasco theaters were held for earlier First Families. Grace Coolidge, the most frequent theatergoer, took an orchestra seat in the fifth row instead, attending matinees of everything from Ethel Barrymore in *The Kingdom of God* to the frothy musical *No, No Nanette.* The Kennedys took Alice Longworth with them to the premiere of Irving Berlin's musical spoof of First Family life, *Mr. President*, and Mamie Eisenhower went to *The Music Man* several times because it evoked her Midwestern youth. Harding did occasionally slip into a private box at the Gaiety burlesque, but he most enjoyed vaudeville comedians like Eddie Cantor, Al Jolson, and Fanny Brice. When Will Rogers did a routine of Harding talking to his cabinet by phone from the golf course, however, the insulted president canceled his plans to see the humorist. His letters show his interest in each year's new Ziegfield Follies girls, and at the musical *Mary*, he unconsciously shouted to a friend at intermission, "Hey, John, how do you like the girls?" Coolidge avoided what he called "leg shows."

Dance is a rare favorite in the White House. The wives of both Harding and Coolidge went to see Anna Pavlova dance. Jackie Kennedy had a passion for ballet, while Betty Ford, formerly of the Martha Graham troupe, related best to modern dance. Since the Nixons, families have had the Kennedy Center presidential box at their disposal for any type of performance.

Chelsea Clinton not only went to the ballet but performed in the *Nutcracker Suite* with her class; several other children performed publicly during their residency. Trained at Baltimore's Peabody Institute in piano and voice, Margaret Wilson gave concerts and even made a record album during World War I. She and her sister Eleanor joined a benefit performance of "Bird Masque" during their summer vacation, the former as the Bird Spirit's voice, "singing from a bush," the latter dancing as Ornis, the Bird Spirit. With popular hits like "Nona from Arizona," McKinley's niece Mabel sang for guests one night. The Lincoln boys put on skits and shows on a small stage made for them in the White House. Margaret Truman sang on radio and television.

While many wives, such as Mary Lincoln and Nellie Taft, went to the opera, so too did some of the men, including Jefferson. "Very often," FDR wrote the Metropolitan Opera's radio chairman, "on Saturday afternoons, when my work is done I have listened to the opera broadcasts." Lincoln went often to the opera, once explaining, "I must have a change of some sort or die." The Fillmores were so taken with popular singer Jenny Lind at her concert that they invited the "Swedish nightingale" to dinner at the White House.

"Now sing, Letty," President Tyler asked his daughter Letty, requesting his favorite Scotch ballads as they escaped, she recalled, "from the maddening crowd [to enjoy] the quiet of some country road." Only Fillmore, who enjoyed Stephen Foster's "Old Folks at Home," and Wilson, who delighted in his ability to hold the high note of the "Star-Spangled Banner," had decent singing voices. Jimmy Roosevelt said that, with his "robust voice [which] ranged between baritone and tenor," his father "sang so loudly that we children were just a little embarrassed."

Among his numerous pastimes—architecture, botany, mechanics, to name but a few—Jefferson said that playing or listening to music was the "favorite passion of my soul." Music drew many families together. The first documentation of an instrument in the mansion was a piano ordered for the Madisons, though there is no evidence the president or his wife played. Abigail Fillmore and her daughter Abbie sometimes entertained friends with duets on the piano and harp, respectively. Willie and Tad Lincoln took piano lessons in the Red Room with a professor Alexander Wolowski. Minnie Doud played the harmonica—sometimes accompanied by her daughter Mamie Eisenhower on her electric organ in the West Sitting Hall. "President Arthur is no mean banjo player and can make the banjo do some lively humming when so disposed," recorded one newspaper. "His son is also conceded to be an excellent player." On some nights, as the Watergate scandal worsened, Nixon would play the piano. "Playing the piano," he later wrote, "is a way of expressing oneself that is perhaps even more

Margaret Wilson poses with record album she made, in front of her piano.

fulfilling than writing or speaking."

Popular contemporary music was a preference for younger people, although it was Florence Harding who first asked a navy band to play jazz. Alice Roosevelt loved the "Maple Leaf Rag." When a Marine Band conductor claimed it was not in their repertoire, she snapped, "The band boys have played it for me time and again. I'll wager they all know it without the music." When John Coolidge and his cousin Marion blared a jazz tune on the player piano, she recalled, "Cousin Calvin made us stop and sent us off to bed." On another occasion, however, they foiled the president, and John Coolidge banged out fraternity songs on the East Room piano as Marion sang.

Several other families used their mechanical or electronic musical devices in the family quarters. Nellie Taft bought her husband many of the clay record disks for his Victrola phonograph, which he kept in the Blue Room. His favorite recording was Caruso's *La Boheme*, to which he hummed along with his eyes closed. On the Kennedys' hi-fi set, installed in the West Hall, the president enjoyed the score of the musical *Camelot*, while his wife played modern jazz, bossa novas, and allegedly even a 1963 Beatles import. Truman took his large classical music record collection seriously, often contrasting the performances of the same work by various musicians.

With Nixon's great breadth of enjoyment from classical to bluegrass, big band to movie scores, came a Recording Industry Association of America donation to the White House of some 2,000 albums and the latest technology in stereo equipment. Carter, a classical music aficionado, fully utilized the collection, having his office study wired for about ten hours of music a day. Besides Bach and Vivaldi, he enjoyed Bob Dylan and the Allman Brothers. When he played his country music records of singer Willie Nelson too loudly in the family quarters, however, Mrs. Carter insisted that the volume be lowered so she couldn't hear it.

Ever since Theodore Roosevelt screened "moving picture shows" of wild animals killing

each other and his wife showed films of butterflies, movies have been popular with the families. "It is like writing history with electricity," Woodrow Wilson told director D. W. Griffith about film, after viewing Griffith's *Birth of a Nation*. After his stroke, Wilson sat for hours in the darkened East Room watching silent films lent by a local theater. The Hardings not only welcomed movie actors as regular guests, but used movies as after-dinner entertainment; for their showing of *Covered Wagon*, they had a live orchestra provide the score. The Coolidges loved movies so much they had a screen rigged for the presidential yacht, *Mayflower*, and watched at night, with the black sky and stars as a backdrop to the screen. Lou Hoover had a small-size professional movie screen installed in the hall of the family quarters, and here the Roosevelts also showed a wide variety of movies—from government information films to Disney pictures to saucy Mae West vehicles, after viewing one of which FDR joked that it was "considerably warmer" than the short on Antarctica shown just previous. With the Truman renovation, a movie theater was built in the East Wing (Margaret Truman had been so enchanted with *The Scarlet Pimpernel*, she watched it three times.) The Reagans indulged weekly in old movies at the White House and Camp David, always with "big baskets of popcorn." Reagan said that although new and recent Hollywood films were shown, he began to sneak in "golden oldies" starring Gable, Bogart, Cagney, "and a couple of actors named Reagan and Davis."

The Trumans were the first to have a television set, but the Eisenhowers were addicts. With two porthole sets installed in the wall of the west sitting hall, Mamie always watched *I Love Lucy*, as Ike—seated right beside her—watched westerns on *his* set, and they both ate dinner. Lady Bird Johnson was a *Gunsmoke* fan but was crestfallen when she discovered that the actress who played Miss Kitty was a Republican. The Carters were the first to have a videotape machine. The Reagans frequently watched programs taped for them—including the *Saturday*

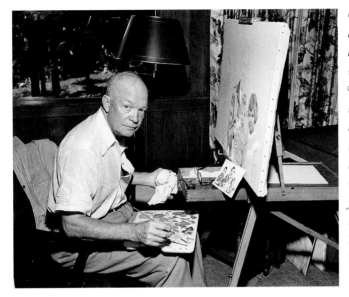

Of his painting, Eisenhower recalled, "I attempt only simple compositions. My frustration is complete when I try for anything delicate. . . . I refuse to refer to my productions as paintings. They are daubs, born of my love for color, and in my pleasure in experimenting, nothing else. I destroy two out of three I start. . . . In spite of this, I have frequently wished for more daylight hours to paint. . . . In the White House, in bad weather, painting was one way to survive away from the desk. . . . Often, going to lunch, I'd stop off for ten minutes to paint."

DWIGHT D. EISENHOWER
PRESIDENTIAL LIBRARY

Night Live episode hosted by their son Ron, who did a sendup of the popular movie *Risky Business*, dancing in his skivvies on a set made to resemble the White House family rooms and appearing with an actor who impersonated his mother. Bush liked *America's Funniest Home Videos* and *Murder, She Wrote.* Mrs. Bush called the adult cartoon *The Simpsons* "the dumbest thing" she ever saw. Hillary Clinton confessed that she was a longtime fan of the comedy series *The Three Stooges* and the cartoon series *The Flintstones.*

There have been relatively few artists among presidential families. Jackie Kennedy drew satirical ink sketches posing friends, family, and herself in wild predicaments, and painted in watercolors and oils, as did Caroline Harrison. Mrs. Harrison also held china painting classes in the White House and fired creations in her kiln, her interests leading her to design a set of state china. Only Ellen Wilson was a professionally trained artist. A month before moving into the White House, she had her first one-woman exhibition of fifty landscapes, and a year earlier one of them had placed twenty-fifth in a Chicago Art Institute showing. She set up a painting studio on the third floor. In what is now the cosmetology room, Eisenhower painted his numerous portraits and landscapes.

There have also been numerous collectors in the White House. Adams and Jefferson both spent years discerningly building their libraries. FDR took great pride in the many rarities among his antique print collection. His collection of about 25,000 stamps filled forty albums, aided by the postmaster general, who always sent him the first sheet of new commemoratives. TR placed his gruesome collection of animal heads on the State Dining Room walls. Kennedy had an autograph collection featuring his predecessors, while his wife acquired a collection of antique French and English prints, drawings, and watercolors featuring court life, costumes, landscapes, seascapes, and horticulture, as well as Audubon prints of plant and animal life. Nancy Reagan displayed her small porcelein battersea boxes in her bedroom. Hillary Clinton kept her varied collection of angel images and figures in her West Wing office.

"If you want a friend in Washington, get a dog." So said Truman, implying that politics does not breed genuine loyalty. In fact, pets have proven valuable to First Families, not only for companionship but great publicity.

Hillary Clinton compiled a book to benefit charity, containing letters sent by children to her family pets, Buddy, the chocolate Labrador retriever, and Socks, the cat; and Barbara Bush penned a humorous "memoir" of her dog Millie's White House life, to raise funds for literacy. The first family to utilize a pet was the Hardings: Florence sent their famous Airedale, Laddie Boy, out to fund-raising events she supported as an animal rights advocate, while Warren ghostwrote Laddie's responses to letters and a news interview. So popular was Laddie that he was regularly featured in political cartoons, had a dog food company named for him, and was replicated as a stuffed toy. FDR traveled the world with his Scottie, Fala, and made humorous reference in a political speech to his Republican opponents' criticism of his using a naval destroyer—at a cost of $15,000 to the government—to retrieve Fala, who had been left on the Aleutian Islands. The Fords were even criticized for letting their golden retriever, Liberty, have puppies when there were many unadopted ones at the ASPCA.

Beyond image enhancement, a pet can soothe the isolation that often sets in at the White House; pets serve a real purpose. "One of the ways I really relaxed when I was President was walking with my dog. I bonded with my dog," said Bush of his springer spaniel Ranger, a puppy of Millie's. "It didn't matter rain or shine, he was at my side or sleeping on our bed . . . He was my friend and companion." At Camp David, Bush had a dog biscuit dispenser shaped like a gumball machine; the dogs would "mill around, wagging their tails making clear that they were desperately hungry" and leave only when they got a treat. Jefferson taught his mockingbird "Dick" to peck food from his lips, doting on it, recalled his friend Margaret Bayard Smith, "as if a child." TR used his mutt Skip for hunting, but was comforted in having the dog jump into his lap as he read in his study. After the sudden death of his famous beagles,

Bill Clinton playing the saxophone at the 1993 inaugural. His wife outfitted a room on the third floor for his music—complete with soundproof walls—as a birthday gift.

THE WHITE HOUSE

Him and Her, LBJ found solace in the company of his white mutt, Yuki, found by his daughter Luci at a gas station.

Before a Mr. Jackson of the household staff looked after Laddie Boy, families took responsibility for the pets, although dogs and horses were kept in the doghouses or stables. As curiosities they lived at their own peril. The Clevelands' dog Hector, for example, was fed a rotten egg at an Easter egg roll and was found sick in a corner. Jesse Grant suspected his yipping dogs were poisoned by perturbed servants. Alice Roosevelt's snake Emily Spinach (named for Alice's spinster aunt and because she was green) often got loose in the house, terrorizing servants. When Alice found it limp under a bed, she knew instantly it had been murdered. Perhaps there was no crueler fate than that met by "Old Whitey," Taylor's fat, aging horse kept in the garden, where tourists openly clipped souvenir strands of his yellowed tail. By Hoover's day, outside pens were built and a household staff member was assigned to care for the pets. Under Truman, electrician Traphes Bryant took on dogkeeping duty, a role he fulfilled through the Nixon years.

In recent administrations, those that began with just a cat ended up with a dog as well:

Amy Carter practices violin under her mother's watchful eye.

Ford, Carter, and Clinton. The Clinton cat, Socks, managed to survive through not only the president's allergy to him but the arrival of Clinton's dog Buddy in 1997. Mrs. Hayes was the first American to be sent a native cat of Siam—which she called, prosaically enough, Siam. Fillmore himself brought a plate of milk for several stray kittens that nested in an unused East Room fireplace. Not all felines fared so well. Ida McKinley named the two weaklings of her Angora's litter after the Cuban governor and the Spanish ambassador; when Spain gained the upper hand during its war with America, the First Lady ordered her maid to drown the two kittens.

Birds did well. One of the few treasures Dolley Madison made certain to rescue before the British burned the mansion was her old green parrot. Lou Hoover and Grace Coolidge let their birds fly free through the west sitting hall. Florence Harding had her canary, "Pete," stuffed after his premature death, and when a same-named canary—which Mamie Eisenhower kept in the Solarium for her grandchildren—died, he had a Rose Garden funeral.

Many other sorts of animals have been fond companions for family members. The Harrison grandchildren had a goat, "Old Whiskers," that pulled them in a cart on the lawn— until the day it bolted onto the street, chased by the president. Tad Lincoln's turkey "Tom" ran around a polling booth set up on the South Lawn for Union soldiers to vote in during the 1864 election. Woodrow and Edith Wilson had sheep and a ram, "Old Ike"—who was addicted to chewing tobacco—to graze the South Lawn. The Coolidges' declawed raccoon "Rebecca" was walked like a cat, on a neck chain. William Henry Harrison was the first to buy a bovine for his dairy, a cow named Sukey, purchased from a Maryland farmer. After Nellie Taft espoused the virtues of fresh dairy products to Wisconsin senator Isaac Stephenson, he sent her a four-year-old 1,500-pound Holstein-Friesian by boxcar from a Marinette farm. The cow (not Nellie) was kept in the old stables—no longer needed after the advent of automobiles—where the Tafts hired someone to milk "Pauline Wayne" twice daily. The famous cow was even to be sent by Taft for exhibition at the International Dairy Show in Milwaukee—-until it was discovered she was about to calve. Pauline also grazed the White House lawn.

The White House family pets were not immune to common problems. Although given as

Musical Instruments Played by Some Family Members

violin: Thomas Jefferson, John Tyler, Andrew Stover (Andew Johnson's grandson), Nicolas Longworth (son-in-law of Theodore Roosevelt), Amy Carter

piano: Martha Jefferson Randolph, Maria Jefferson Eppes, Louisa Adams, Mary Catherine Hellen Adams, Abigail Fillmore, Abbie Fillmore, Jane Pierce, Harriet Lane (Buchanan's niece), Willie Lincoln, Tad Lincoln, Martha Johnson Patterson, Belle Patterson, Mary Johnson Stover, Julia Grant, Lucy Hayes, Harry Garfield, Alan Arthur, Nell Arthur, Caroline Harrison, Mary Harrison McKee, Nellie Taft, Margaret Wilson, Florence Harding, Grace Coolidge, Sara Delano Roosevelt, Harry Truman, Martha Truman, Margaret Truman, Richard Nixon, Rosalynn Carter

mandolin: Franklin D. Roosevelt

banjo: William Waller (Tyler's son-in-law), Chester Arthur, Alan Arthur

castanets: Tazewell Tyler

electric organ: Mamie Eisenhower

harmonica: Calvin Coolidge, Minnie Doud (Eisenhower's mother-in-law)

cornet: Warren Harding

harp: Eliza Monroe Hay, Louisa Adams, Abbie Fillmore

guitar: Martha Jefferson Randolph, Maria Jefferson Eppes, Sarah Yorke Jackson, Julia Tyler, Abbie Fillmore

saxophone: Bill Clinton

a gift to Nixon, Irish setter King Timahoe was better disciplined by his wife. FDR's grandson Johnny Boettiger frequently fed his Jell-O to his retriever Ensign under the table, until the dog's appetite was spoiled. If David Eisenhower was visiting his grandparents with his mutt Spunky, Ike's weimaraner Heidi would have to be shut away to prevent a fight. The chef also disliked Spunky, who begged for scraps at the kitchen door. And there have been runaways: when Edith Roosevelt's dog Tip disappeared, she went down to the local pound with one of her sons to get another similar-looking mongrel to fill the void.

On the other hand, some pets just don't fit in. Little Rachel Jackson was terrified of her grandfather's bloodhounds Leon and Diane. Screaming from a nightmare in which the dogs were attacking her, she awoke the president, who grabbed her to his chest, she recalled, and "paced back and forth across the room until every fear was quelled." Although he thought a "dog is one of the most affectionate of all the animal species," Jackson gave the dogs away.

Mamie Eisenhower takes in a movie with her three granddaughters Anne (far right), Susan Elaine (left), and Mary Jean (on her lap).

George and Barbara Bush and their grandson Jebby in the White House movie theater.

Eleanor Roosevelt's terrier Meggie bit a reporter's nose, and maids had to fight off her aggressive police dog Major with broomsticks. Both dogs were banished. Harding's bulldog Oh Boy, kept from his feedbowl by the jealous Laddie, was given away. Grace Coolidge's ducklings could grow only so big in her bathtub before she had to donate them to the National Zoo, a fate shared by baby deer given to the Kennedys.

Nearly every family has had a pet, using them for all imaginable purposes. Julia Tyler's greyhound Le Beau came from the consul at Naples "to grace the White House lawn," perhaps because Julia found he

Some Favorite Movies of Presidential Family Members

Woodrow Wilson: D. W. Griffith's *Birth of a Nation*
Warren Harding: silent film *The Covered Wagon*
Florence Harding: Mary Pickford in *Little Lord Fauntleroy*, Charlie Chaplin in *The Gold Rush*
Grace Coolidge: Valentino in *The Sheik*
Franklin D. Roosevelt: Mae West in *I'm No Angel*
Margaret Truman: *The Scarlet Pimpernel*
Dwight Eisenhower: Gregory Peck in *The Big Country*
Mamie Eisenhower: Maurice Chevalier in *Gigi*
Jack Kennedy: Kirk Douglas in *Spartacus,* Spencer Tracy in *Bad Day at Black Rock*
Jackie Kennedy: Fellini's *La Dolce Vita*
Richard Nixon: George C. Scott in *Patton*
Pat Nixon: Anthony Quinn in *Shoes of the Fisherman*
Ronald Reagan: Clint Eastwood in *Dirty Harry,* Sylvester Stallone in *Rambo*
George Bush: *Chariots of Fire*
Bill Clinton: *High Noon* and *Casablanca*

was "very rough" on the rugs. Hoover trained his police dog King Tut to sit on piles of papers while the president read outside, to keep them from blowing away. The Hoovers counted on their Irish wolfhound Patrick to bound into the bedroom and wake them up. Jackie Kennedy found that Clipper, the German shepherd given to her by her father-in-law, protected her from what she felt was the greatest threat. When journalists kept sending her questions she considered ridiculous, she became exasperated. At the question "What does Clipper eat?" Jackie scribbled back one word, "Reporters." There were no more questions.

Some pets became legendary to the public as well as the family. When the Hayeses' greyhound Grim died, "The whole country knew him, and respected him," the president noted solemnly. The Theodore Roosevelt menagerie included a badger, a kitten that attacked the Speaker of the House, a six-toed cat that lay in the middle of the hall during a state dinner, a one-legged rooster given a crutch by the children, parrots, kangaroo rats, an owl, guinea pigs, dogs, horses, and ponies. Quentin and Kermit sneaked the pony Algonquin up in the elevator

Zachary Taylor on "Old Whitey."
LIBRARY OF CONGRESS

Warren and Florence Harding greeted by Laddie Boy as they return home from a trip. 1923.
SCHERMER COLLECTION

Lucy Hayes feeding her chickens.
HAYES PRESIDENTIAL CENTER

Some Favorite Family Games

blindman's buff: Scott and Fanny Hayes

hide-and-seek: Scott and Fanny Hayes; Quentin and Archie Roosevelt; the Taft children

charades: Alice Roosevelt Longworth; the Taft children; the Kennedy family

twenty questions: the Taft children; Eleanor Roosevelt

jigsaw puzzles: Calvin Coolidge

Boggle: the Clinton family

mah-jonng: Florence Harding

dominoes: the Hardings; Lyndon B. Johnson

billiards: sons of John Quincy Adams; Abraham Lincoln; the Grant family; Garfield and his sons; the Benjamin Harrison family; Woodrow Wilson; the Carter family

chess: Abraham Lincoln, James Madison, James Garfield, Rutherford Hayes, the Hardings, Rosalynn and Amy Carter

checkers: Andrew Johnson, the Hardings

Bolivia (card game): Bess Truman, her brothers and sisters-in-law; Mamie Eisenhower and her mother

whist (card game): Dolley Madison, John Quincy and Louisa Adams, James Garfield

loo (card game): Dolley Madison; Elizabeth Monroe and Eliza Monroe Hay

cribbage: Grover Cleveland; the McKinleys

pinochle: Grover Cleveland; the Clinton family

euchre: James Garfield; Grover Cleveland; William and Ida McKinley

gin rummy: Anna Roosevelt

solitaire: Woodrow Wilson, Franklin Roosevelt, Mamie Eisenhower

poker: Warren Harding, Franklin Roosevelt, Harry Truman, Dwight Eisenhower, Richard Nixon

bridge: The Tafts; Edith Wilson and her sister Bertha Bolling; the Hardings; Bess Truman; Dwight Eisenhower, Mamie Eisenhower, her mother, Elvira Doud, and sister Mike Moore; Lady Bird Johnson, Luci Johnson Nugent, Lynda Johnson, and Chuck Robb

Eleanor Roosevelt getting Fala to do tricks.

FRANKLIN D. ROOSEVELT PRESIDENTIAL LIBRARY

to cheer their sick brother Archie in bed. The "most absolute pet of all," the president said of the pony. Caroline Kennedy's pony Macaroni pulled the First Lady and her children in a sleigh across the snow-covered South Lawn. He had been a gift from Vice President Johnson.

Many White House pets have been gifts from foreign dignitaries: the U.S. consul at Southampton sent Harriet Lane a toy terrier she named Punch; the queen of Italy gave Helen Taft a large caramel poodle she named Caro, or "love" in Italian, but her brothers renamed it Caruso; the empress of China gave Alice Roosevelt a black Pekingese—which she claimed danced on its hind legs in the moonlight; the president of Ireland gave the Kennedys Shannon, a spaniel. Some gift pets had poignant and historic significance. A poor mountain boy who lived near the Hoovers' retreat brought a possum to the president as a birthday gift. Touched, Hoover decided against having it killed for stew, giving it instead to his son Allan—

Archie Roosevelt on his pony,
Algonquin.
LIBRARY OF CONGRESS

Caroline Kennedy on her pony, Macaroni, a gift from Vice President Lyndon Johnson. President Kennedy is at far left.
JOHN F. KENNEDY PRESIDENTIAL LIBRARY

As an adult, John Kennedy Jr. recalled of his family dog Pushinka, "We trained it to slide down the slide we had in the back of the White House. Sliding the dog down the slide is probably my first memory."

who promptly "gave" it back to his parents; the animal had its own White House treehouse. The boy was later invited to stay in the White House with the Hoovers—and the possum. A symbol of friendship in the midst of the cold war was Soviet premier Nikita Khrushchev's gift to the Kennedys of Pushinka, a puppy of the first dog to orbit in space. When the dog was bred with their Welsh terrier Charlie, the family was inundated with requests for the offspring. The First Lady finally settled on a national essay contest for children, the prizes being the puppies.

No family outdid the Coolidges in numbers alone: eleven dogs, seven birds, three cats, two raccoons, and assorted other odd gifts—from a wallaby to a bobcat to a donkey. Coolidge

Aboard the presidential yacht Sequoia, *Pat Nixon tries to coax the family's Irish setter,* King Timahoe, *to his food dish.* NIXON PRESIDENTIAL MATERIALS, NATIONAL ARCHIVES

indulged the house pets at the table. At lunch with the secretary of state, he put a full plate of oysters on the floor for his kitten. At a breakfast, his beautiful white collie Rob Roy sat upright next to a seated senator who was eating breakfast. Trying to get through his meal, the man was clearly disconcerted by the intently staring dog. "Senator," Coolidge cracked, "I think he wants your sausage." The senator relented.

There has been only one White House pet that brought nothing but bad press. When three servicemen were bumped from a flight home on an army transport for a large box carrying a mastiff, the irate GIs examined the box to discover Blaze, Elliott Roosevelt's dog, being sent from the White House to his wife, actress Faye Emerson, in Hollywood. The story made overnight headlines, and as "a subject of discussion from coast to coast is a strong rival," said the *New York Herald Tribune,* of the Russian offensive in the third week of January 1945. The Senate military affairs committee began a formal investigation; when it was discovered that Blaze had been flown across the Atlantic during wartime limitations the debacle further enraged the public. It was finally learned that Anna Roosevelt had phoned the air transport command to get her brother's dog out of the White House—but that the assistant chief had given Blaze an "A" rating. The *Tribune* declared finally that Blaze's trip was a "scandal to which a democratic society is most sensitive."

A Sampling of Leisure Activities of Some First Family Members

knitting: Frances Cleveland, Ida McKinley, Edith Roosevelt, Eleanor Roosevelt, Mamie Eisenhower

crewelwork: Julie Nixon

needlepoint: Barbara Bush

crocheting: Grace Coolidge

sewing: Eliza Johnson, Edith Wilson, Florence Harding, Grace Coolidge, Rosalynn Carter

gardening: John Quincy Adams, Caroline Harrison, Peggy Taylor, Grace Coolidge, Bess Truman, Lady Bird Johnson, Pat Nixon, Rosalynn Carter, Barbara Bush, Hillary Clinton

furniture making: Jimmy Carter

wood-chopping and fence-making: Ronald Reagan

roller-skating: Amy Carter

table tennis: Warren Harding; Bess and Margaret Truman

croquet: the Hayes family

squash: Bob Taft

tennis: Fanny Hayes, Ruddy Hayes; the Garfield children; Alan Arthur; the Theodore Roosevelt family; the Taft children; the Wilson daughters; Warren Harding; the Coolidge sons; Jacqueline Kennedy; the Carter family; Gerald Ford; the Bush family

hunting: John Adams, James Monroe, John Tyler, James Buchanan, Rutherford Hayes, Chester Arthur, Grover Cleveland, Benjamin Harrison, Theodore Roosevelt, Calvin and Grace Coolidge, Dwight Eisenhower, Lyndon Johnson, George Bush

foxhunting: James Monroe, Jacqueline Kennedy

riding horseback: John Adams; Thomas Jefferson; James Madison; James Monroe; John Quincy Adams, John Adams II; Andrew Jackson, Andrew

Jackson "AJ" Donelson (great-nephew); Martin Van Buren; William Henry Harrison; John Tyler, Julia Tyler; Zachary Taylor and son-in-law William Bliss; Franklin Pierce, Jane Pierce; Mary Lincoln, Tad Lincoln; the Grant family; Alan Arthur; Benjamin Harrison; the Theodore Roosevelt family; William Howard Taft, Charlie and Helen Taft; Woodrow Wilson, Edith Wilson; Warren Harding; Calvin Coolidge, Calvin Coolidge Jr., John Coolidge; Herbert Hoover, Lou Hoover, and her sister Jean Large; Eleanor Roosevelt, Franklin Roosevelt Jr., Anna Roosevelt; Dwight Eisenhower; Jacqueline Kennedy, Caroline Kennedy; Lyndon Johnson; Steve Ford; the Reagan family; the Clinton family

rowing: Franklin Roosevelt, Jimmy Carter

medicine ball: Herbert Hoover

golf: William McKinley, William Howard Taft, Woodrow Wilson, Warren Harding, Dwight Eisenhower, John and Jacqueline Kennedy, Richard Nixon, Gerald Ford, George and Barbara Bush, Bill Clinton

horseshoes: Harry Truman, the Bushes

jogging: Jacqueline Kennedy; Gerald Ford; Jimmy, Rosalynn, and Chip Carter; George and Doro Bush; Bill and Hillary Clinton

bowling: Lady Bird Johnson, the Nixons, the Bush grandchildren, the Clintons

bicycling: Abram Garfield, Nell and Alan Arthur, the Theodore Roosevelt children, Charlie Taft, Woodrow Wilson, the Eisenhower grandchildren, Jacqueline Kennedy, the Carter family, Nancy Reagan and son Ron Reagan, Barbara Bush, Hillary and Chelsea Clinton

sailing: the Theodore Roosevelt family, the Franklin Roosevelt family, the Kennedy family

polo: Theodore Roosevelt

boxing: Theodore Roosevelt

jujitsu: Theodore Roosevelt

Richard Nixon, his daughters Tricia and Julie, and son-in-law David Eisenhower row out in a glass-bottom boat at Key Biscayne, Florida.

Nixon 1968 Yearbook

14

Recreation

Without Camp David, you'll go stir crazy.
—First Lady Pat Nixon

Today, Memorial Day and Labor Day weekends are the parameters of the summer season in America. Before those holidays were created (1868 and 1882, respectively), the "summering" period for First Families was longer. They were in Washington often only for the social season but left when the congressional session ended, and returned in the autumn when it began again. In 1816, for example, the Madisons were gone from May to October—the record length of time a family was away from the White House.

The Madisons, like other early families, spent summer at their private home. There, since so many early presidents used relatives as aides, they were able to keep working. Staff of later presidents worked in rented facilities or those built especially to accommodate them, near the families' homes. Summer also meant national tours for some presidents such as Monroe and Polk, who spent weeks traveling the East making speeches but relaxing at the homes of supporters. Male relatives usually went along. Until Martha Johnson Patterson joined her father, only one woman, Priscilla Tyler, made such a tour.

Theodore Roosevelt reading at his summer White House, his home Sagamore Hill.
Library of Congress

William Howard Taft out for a ride with his son Charlie and daughter Helen.
LIBRARY OF CONGRESS

Since Coolidge, no president has left the White House for an entire summer: flying permits him to be anywhere any day. In earlier days, a family would sometimes flee hot Washington, leaving the president alone. Any time of the year Coolidge's wife was gone, he often waited in the mail room for the arrival of her letters to him. Jackson grew despondent, writing his daughter-in-law Sarah, "I have not rested well at night since you left me—every thing appeared silent & in gloom about the House, and when I walked into your room—found it without its occupants—everything changed, the cradle of my little pet without it, and its little wagon there—my feelings were overcome for the moment."

To avoid such separations, Jackson became the first president to rent a retreat not far from the White House. By 1833, he was making an annual August sojourn down the Chesapeake Bay to "the Rip Raps," a small, breezy island in Hampton Roads, Virginia. For twenty-seven days his large family and five servants bathed in the ocean and played games on the beach. The hotel bill, which Jackson paid by personal check, was $395.75. His confidant Francis Blair observed the importance of Jackson's adoptive granddaughter to him: "Rachel he takes to his bosom whenever brought within his reach. I never saw this little bantling in his presence that his eyes did not brighten and his affections rise. He says she is the solace of his waning life."

Van Buren rented a nearby estate, Woodley. The Tylers made a honeymoon of their summer stay in Old Point Comfort, Virginia, at a government-owned cottage on the grounds of Fortress Monroe. At war department expense, commanding officer Colonel Gustavas DeRussy had a four-room cottage decorated for them. Julia Tyler described their bedroom: "A richly covered high post bedstead hung with white lace curtains looped up with blue ribbon . . . new matting which emitted its sweet fragrance, two handsome mahogany dressing tables, writing table, and sofa . . . True love in a cottage—and quite a contrast to my dirty establishment in Washington [the White House]. It seemed quite as if I had stepped into paradise."

After their stay, and a visit to their estate, the Tylers went to White Sulphur Springs, West Virginia, staying in "The President's Cottage," where Van Buren, Fillmore, Pierce, and Buchanan also spent part of their summer vacations. Buchanan also had the government underwrite his summer home by staying at Anderson Cottage, on the grounds of a soldiers' retirement home. With a 300-foot elevation, it was a short drive from the White House, just within the District of Columbia line. Except for a two-week excursion in August 1861 to the Jersey shore, Saratoga, and Niagara, Mary Lincoln and her sons joined her husband at Anderson Cottage every summer of their tenure. Hayes and Arthur also used the cottage.

Hayes revived the presidential tour by visiting regions that rarely saw their leader. At the end of August 1880, Hayes, his niece Laura Mitchell, his wife, and their sons Birch and Ruddy became the First Family to travel to the West Coast. Passing through Utah's Echo Canyon, Ruddy Hayes rode on the locomotive cowcatcher, and when they steamed from San Francisco to Oregon, Hayes marveled at whales "tossing up their sun-lit spray." As the Hayeses went through Yosemite, down to Los Angeles, and across to Santa Fe, however, newspapers sniped that a president should not be away from business for so long.

Arthur tried to avoid such criticism by announcing that his summer excursion to Yellowstone was to "inspect" the recently designated national park. Democrats blasted the government cost, and a reporter asked Arthur point-blank, "Will your western trip form a portion of your vacation?" To this the president snapped, "Vacation, eh? That is the way all the newspapers talk. They speak of my journeys as junketings. I need a holiday as much as the poorest of my fellow citizens." Arthur "inspected" as he hiked, fished, and hunted.

Arthur's family liked to rove. His son and sister, Alan and Molly, made an unprecedented trip to Cullbackey, Ireland, in the summer of 1882 to visit the birthplace of the president's father; it was the first of several such trips for families of Irish ancestry (John Kennedy, Richard and Pat Nixon, Ronald Reagan, and Bill Clinton would do so in the next century).

When the Arthur clan arrived in 1883 at Lake Mohonk, New York, they rather embarrassingly found that in order to enter their hotel, they had to pass under an arch of flowers and evergreens held up by forty girls dressed in white. Past presidents had been similarly doted

Jessie Wilson on the tennis court.

upon, but now even when family members vacationed apart from the president, they received
detailed media coverage. As little Nell Arthur,
the president's brother William and his daughter Alice, the president's sister Molly and her
daughters May and Jessie took off for a vacation that newspapers said would be of length
"depending upon the wishes of Miss Nell,"
their every pleasure was reported. At Cape May,
they were "somewhat fatigued of the festivities
in which they have participated on shore." At
Block Island their use of plush carriages offered
them for free to attend social events, left them
"in good spirits."

It was their use of the government steamer
Dispatch as "a summer house" with easy chairs,
rugs, books, and needlework on deck which
brought swift rebuke. As the August 16, 1883, *New York Sun* editorialized, "When in the
absence of the President, the ladies of his family take possession of a government ship, with
its officers and crew and running expenses all paid out of the Treasury . . . they take for themselves that which is not theirs . . . In monarchical countries . . . it is thought proper; but in this
country a different system has prevailed. . . . there are certain perquisites provided for him,
such as a house, a garden, and servants, and these are also for the use of his family, but when
he goes beyond the limits of the law and sets up a sort of royal prerogative . . . to take the
public vessels of the country . . . for his own personal entertainment . . . he commits a wrong
and descredits his exalted station."

There were other problems with First Families roaming about. In 1901, an exhausted Ida
McKinley nearly died of an infection on a western tour. Luckily, her accompanying niece
Mary Barber assumed her aunt's commitments. With the publication of Harding's 1923 western tour route, he was stalked in three cities by a would-be woman assassin. Earlier security at
presidential retreats came at the insistence of Edith Roosevelt, who arranged for agents to
guard the woods around Pine Knot, the family's Virginia getaway. So determined was
Theodore Roosevelt to have privacy on a visit to Yellowstone National Park that when a
reporter rode nearby, with a dog alongside, the reporter was arrested, the horse was confis-
cated, and the dog was shot. A decade earlier, guards were employed only after Frances

Herbert Hoover (center) playing medicine ball at the White House. His German shepherd Weegie is behind him.
HERBERT HOOVER PRESIDENTIAL LIBRARY

Cleveland had written with alarm to her husband in Washington from their Cape Cod home about a suspected kidnapper who came onto the grounds as her three daughters played.

Annoyed by public attention even away from the White House, many older children vacationed apart from their parents; they still brought publicity. Reports that Helen Taft put on warpaint and staged a fake Indian raid on fellow campers out west trickled into the eastern papers. Her brother Bob thought he could escape notice on a transatlantic voyage; on the second day at sea the captain made his identity known to other passengers. Webb Hayes was enjoying a geese and quail hunt on the James River until locals learned he was there, came to camp, and, said a fellow hunter, "sit around near the fire and look at Webb, and look, and look, without question or comment."

Although Coolidge worked when he took his entire summer in different regions each year

The Roosevelt First Ladies were avid horsewomen. Edith Roosevelt (below) mounting a horse in Washington for a ride. Her niece Eleanor (right) takes a jaunt with her son, Franklin D. Roosevelt Jr.
LIBRARY OF CONGRESS; FRANKLIN D. ROOSEVELT LIBRARY

William Howard Taft on the golf course.
LIBRARY OF CONGRESS

(Massachusetts in 1925, then New York, South Dakota, and Wisconsin), it proved exhausting for the executive staff who had to establish new headquarters, the housekeeping staff who had to transport supplies, and the family. Presidents could no longer truly escape. "Hoover seemed to feel that he would be unfavorably criticized if he took a vacation," said the chief usher. "He felt that the people would think he was neglecting his duty." Consequently, the

Grace Coolidge (at left) at a Washington Senators baseball game.
LIBRARY OF CONGRESS

Hoovers created their own retreat, Camp Rapidan in the Shenandoah Mountains, within 100 miles of Washington. Used all year, it was conceived by Lou Hoover, who had been going camping, hiking, riding, fishing, and mountain climbing since childhood. In this sylvan setting, Herbert Jr. ("Bub" to the family) finished his long recuperation from tuberculosis. The Hoovers owned the property and buildings but donated it all to the government, for future First Families. FDR visited once but realized that "the terrain was too rough" at that location for him to get about with his disability.

Undeterred, FDR established a government-owned retreat in the Catoctin Mountains of Maryland, dubbed "Shangri-La." It was initially spartan. FDR slept on a narrow iron-frame bed, and the door to the connecting lavatory never closed properly. Bess Truman came once to use the pool with friends, but the Eisenhowers gave it the touches which made it, as Tricia Nixon later said, "like a resort hotel where you are the only guests." Mamie appropriated military funds to decorate the cabins that formed the compound in contemporary fifties style and put in a barbecue pit, flagstone terrace, rattan chairs, and a putting green for Ike. He renamed it Camp David after their grandson. All succeeding First Families spent weekends and holidays there. With its horse trails (Reagan put in stables), skeet shooting, bowling alley, swimming pool, golf course, archery range, and tennis and badminton courts, it encouraged family togetherness.

When Kennedy finally spent time at Camp David, he regretted that his wife had first rented and then built homes in the Virginia horse country. There, Jackie spent her famous "Thursday-to-Tuesday" weekends away from the White House, living a normal life with her children. So much time away from the mansion provoked criticism ("She should be home with her husband, not with her horses," one citizen complained). Jackie later revealed that the family planned to spend all of the summer of 1964 together, part of it out west in Montana so she could see more of America and because it would be good politics in that reelection year. Similar thinking later prompted advisers to suggest that Clinton forgo his usual Martha's Vineyard vacation and go to Wyoming in his reelection summer of 1996. When the family spent part of their 1999 respite in the Finger Lakes region of New York State, where the First Lady would be a Senate candidate, the Republican National Committee chairman attacked the choice as "politically motivated."

A presidential vacation site, and from whom the family rents, buys, or borrows the home, has always been an issue of public debate. In 1889, after Benjamin Harrison accepted from several businessmen a Cape May, New Jersey, cottage in his wife's name, it raged as a lead story with an implication of quid pro quo. It was even lampooned in Gilbert and Sullivan verse at a vaudeville performance attended by the humiliated president's son Russell. "The President said a vacation he'd take," ran the lyrics. ("Down by the blue sea, where the high breakers break . . . And my friends who belong to the real estate ring,/have promised a cottage to which I shall cling.") Harrison finally bought the place outright.

Family Homes Used as "Unofficial White House" During Summer and Other Vacations

John Adams and John Quincy Adams: "Peacefield," later called The Old House, Quincy, Massachusetts

Thomas Jefferson: "Monticello" and "Poplar Forest," Charlottesville, Virginia

James Madison: "Montpelier," Orange, Virginia

James Monroe: "Oak Hill," Loudon, Virginia

Andrew Jackson: "The Hermitage," Nashville, Tennessee

Grover Cleveland: "Grey Gables," Buzzard's Bay, Cape Cod

William McKinley: mother's home, and his own repurchased home, Canton, Ohio

Theodore Roosevelt: "Sagamore Hill," Oyster Bay, New York

Calvin Coolidge: family farmhouse, Plymouth Notch, Vermont

Franklin D. Roosevelt: "Springwood," Hyde Park, New York

Harry Truman: the Wallace "mansion," Independence, Missouri

Dwight Eisenhower: mother-in-law's home, Denver, Colorado, and own home, Gettysburg, Pennsylvania

John F. Kennedy: family compound, Hyannis Port, Cape Cod, Massachusetts; Palm Beach, Florida; and mother-in-law's home, "Hammersmith Farm," Newport, Rhode Island

Lyndon B. Johnson: "The LBJ Ranch," Stonewall, Texas

Richard Nixon: "La Casa Pacifica," San Clemente, California, and home in Key Biscayne, Florida

Jimmy Carter: family home, Plains, Georgia

Ronald Reagan: "Rancho del Cielo," Santa Barbara, California

George Bush: "Walker's Point," Kennebunkport, Maine

Bill Clinton: family home in Chappaqua, New York; Little Rock, Arkansas, home owned jointly with mother-in-law

Theodore Roosevelt and his bloodhound dogs inspect a bear he shot.
LIBRARY OF CONGRESS

The fact that the Tafts had long summered at their property on Murray's Bay, in Quebec, Canada, was moot when he became president. At that time the only president to have left the United States was Theodore Roosevelt. Instead, the Tafts rented a home in Beverly, Massachusetts, looking across Salem Harbor. Although his aunt Delia came to visit, and his children Bob and Helen often joined him at ceremonies, Taft longed for his brothers in Canada. "If I only have one term," he said, "one of the great consolations will be that I can go to Murray Bay in the summers thereafter." His brother Charles's wife, Annie, found the limitation ridiculous: "By the way, if the Czar of all the Russias can go to Cowes why cannot you come to Murray Bay?"

In the late winter of 1922 and 1923 the Hardings took an entourage of congressional friends and poker cronies for several weeks of golf, sun, and yachting in Florida (which sparked so much publicity it helped the Miami building boom), setting a tradition for winter junkets. Whether it was the Coolidges' turkey hunting in coastal Georgia or the Fords' skiing in Colorado, most twentieth-century First Families took a winter vacation.

In winter or summer, at the shore or mountains, most First Families have engaged in sports as a form of leisure—not merely for the health benefits. Horseback riding, tennis, jogging, horseshoes, and badminton have been the primary activities which drew the families into

Grover Cleveland duck hunting. He named his gun "Death and Destruction."
LIBRARY OF CONGRESS

Lady Bird Johnson and Richard
Nixon try their skill on the White
House bowling alley lanes.
LYNDON B. JOHNSON PRESIDENTIAL
LIBRARY AND NIXON PRESIDENTIAL
MATERIALS, NATIONAL ARCHIVES

Jack Ford (at left) taking scuba-diving lessons in the White House pool.
GERALD R. FORD PRESIDENTIAL LIBRARY

activities together. At the White House, of course, there are tennis courts added under TR, a bowling alley created under Nixon, a pool installed by Ford, a basketball hoop and horseshoe ring put in during Bush's term, and a jogging track laid down for use by Clinton. It was a rare sport that could not be enjoyed on the property; the Hayses even played croquet on the lawn. Only poor Bob Taft had to find local facilities for a squash game.

Although Carter and Bush played softball with their staffs on several occasions—and Betty Ford coached a game of tag football between Secret Service agents—many more families have been spectators at sporting events. Taft was the first to throw out a baseball, to begin the Washington Senators' 1910 season, and they were the hometeam for generations of First Families. Its most avid fans were Grace Coolidge and Bess Truman, the former keeping her own scorecard and the latter insisting on sitting through a game even in the rain. Bush was a staunch fan of the New York Mets, a team once partially owned by a relative.

Harding followed prizefights—but his wife wouldn't let him go to an arena. He was also the first to attend a football game, played by the Army and Marines. Through most of the twentieth century, families attended the annual Army-Navy game. Pat Nixon told a reporter

that she joined her husband watching Sunday afternoon football games on television. As Super Bowl Sunday took on the feeling of a holiday in the 1980s, Maureen Reagan helped make it a family event by joining her father to watch the game—and making the requisite chili herself in the large ground-floor kitchen. Clinton invited governors Mario Cuomo and Ann Richards, of New York and Texas, respectively, to watch the 1993 Super Bowl game with him and other guests.

If golf is the most popular sport among presidents, then fishing holds the record for the whole family. FDR liked to watch birds rather than shoot them, for example, but he was an avid deep-sea fisherman with his sons. Hoover explained, "One of the few opportunities given a President for the refreshment of his soul and the clarification of his thoughts by solitude lies through fishing." Many couples (the Hayeses, Clevelands, Hardings, Coolidges, Carters) and families (the Coolidges and their son John; the Trumans and their daughter, Margaret; Arthur and his son, Alan) fished together—and separately. "When you're out fishing," Rosalynn Carter explained to historian Bill Mares, "it totally clears the mind. I don't think about work or anything that is pressing. . . . It's so different from being in public and being conscious of all the people around you. . . . We did have to teach the Secret Service not to 'advance' the stream . . . by walking right down to the bank and scaring the fish. . . . When we were fishing we were not public property."

Whether fishing or hunting, however controversial, everyone who shot fowl or game—except perhaps Theodore Roosevelt—used it for family meals: Eisenhower, who shot pheasant; LBJ, who bagged deer; and Bush and his son George, who annually hunted quail in Beesville, Texas. Certainly having a forest or an ocean area cleared by security reduces the competition of fellow hunters and fishers.

Amy Carter roller-skating at the White House.

Naval vessels or private yachts of wealthy friends were used for pleasure or travel by early First Families. Buchanan's niece was the first member of a presidential family to be chastised for using a naval vessel for pleasure, but when TR commissioned the first official presidential yacht, *The Mayflower,* in 1902, there was no criticism. Nellie Taft suffered her stroke on the vessel, and the Hardings were the first to entertain the public on it, its staterooms done in ubiquitous "Harding blue." A second vessel, *The Sequoia,* was briefly used by Hoover and FDR, and a third, *The Potomac,* was regularly used by FDR, refitted to hide an elevator in an artificial smokestack for the wheelchair-bound president. Truman had *The Williamsburg* commissioned and took visiting family members on leisurely summer cruises, but it proved too slow. He revived *The Sequoia,* which was used through the Nixon administration. Reagan, for one, liked to paddle a canoe with his wife on their man-made lake.

The entire extended Kennedy family loved yachting, sailing, and any other kind of boating on Cape Cod. The president, his wife, and their daughter often swam together in the Atlantic off the family yacht, *Honey Fitz.* Swimming has tended to bring together young and old in First Families. The Madisons and Monroes were regulars at the hot mineral springs that dotted the western portion of Virginia. John Adams took the waters in Connecticut, paying eight pence twice a day to join the "lame, the vapory, hypochondriac, scrofulous." In oilcloth cap, flannel

In a rare, previously unpublished photograph showing his
legs ravaged by polio, Franklin
D. Roosevelt sits at the side of
the pool at the Val-Kill cottage
used by his wife. Eleanor
Roosevelt at the same pool, in
her bathing suit.
FRANKIN D. ROOSEVELT
PRESIDENTIAL LIBRARY

The Hardings relaxing during their yacht trip through coastal Florida.

gown, and socks, Abigail had first gone went swimming in England, enjoying the experience but scornful of the fact that it seemed to promote "dissipation, [and] mixes all characters promiscuously," and drew "the most unprincipaled female characters." While their son John Quincy Adams took his famous nude swims in the Potomac, his wife Louisa particularly enjoyed her separate vacation from him in the summer of 1825 at Bordentown, New Jersey, where—without the presence of male swimmers—she was free to wear loose muslin bodice dresses to more comfortably bathe. The entire Grant family publicly emerged from their large cabana in Long Branch to plunge into the ocean together. Grace Coolidge, a good swimmer, took "Australian crawl" lessons to improve her skills in the pool of the rented summer 1925 White House in Swampscott, Massachusetts.

Swimming afforded FDR, disabled with polio, his only free movement. Throughout his presidency he made trips to the "Little White House" in Warm Springs, Georgia, which he helped turn into a therapeutic center for paralysis patients. Here, he reported, he could "walk around in four-foot-deep water without a brace or crutches almost as well as if I had nothing to do with my legs." Children across the country sent in their pennies to build him a White House pool, used by families until it was cemented over by Nixon. Joe Kennedy had hired artist Bernard Lamotte to paint a nautical mural on the walls around the pool, where his son and his family, many Kennedy nieces and nephews—even the "First Dog," terrier Charlie—spent hours swimming. Ford's installation of the outdoor pool at the White House was a godsend to swimmers like the Bushes, Clintons, and Carters. Betty Ford recalled, "Jerry used the new pool all year round. No matter how late he worked, if he had a chance, he'd take a swim afterward."

During their Key West winter vacation, Margaret Truman plays volleyball, and then deep-sea fishes with her mother, Bess.
HARRY S. TRUMAN PRESIDENTIAL LIBRARY

President Kennedy, friends, and family on the Kennedy yacht, Honey Fitz; *the First Lady is at far right, in large hat. 1963.*
JOHN F. KENNEDY PRESIDENTIAL LIBRARY

When the Reagans went swimming while at the Barbados home of their friend Claudette Colbert, the Secret Service had to clear the water of other swimmers. Reserving an ocean for a president, however, was nothing new. When 300-plus-pound Taft dipped into the Atlantic, other swimmers pulled out in respect to him. "The President is using the ocean," observed one woman without any irony about the obese executive, "and nobody else can get in." Some papers more seriously considered it highly undemocratic that citizens be expected to leave the ocean for the chief executive.

Of course, there was criticism of how and where presidential families relaxed. Jackie Kennedy got it from all sides: conservative preachers pilloried her for wearing a bathing suit

Calvin and Grace Coolidge at pier, boarding presidential yacht Mayflower.
LIBRARY OF CONGRESS

The Jimmy Carters went fishing frequently, together and separately.
JIMMY CARTER PRESIDENTIAL LIBRARY

when she went swimming (without suggesting what it was that she should have worn); a group of picketers carried signs decrying her having vacationed in Europe without her husband. Some women wrote her that it was reckless to be jumping hurdles on her horse, and animal rights groups protested her participation in foxhunting. The clergy rebuked Hoover for fishing on Sundays, while FDR got letters mocking the fact that for all the time he spent fishing he didn't catch that many fish. Reagan was often criticized for the frequency of his vacations, and Cleveland for the length of his. Defending his seeking of "relief from the wearing labors and perplexities of official duty," Cleveland said the best revenge he had for the "petty" criticism was receiving "the mental and physical restoration" of vacation time. He was unapologetic: "[S]o far as my attachment to outdoor sports may be considered a fault, I am . . . utterly incorrigible and shameless."

Some Winter Presidential Vacation Sites

The Hardings: train and sea trip through Florida, south to Miami

The Coolidges: Sapelo Island, Georgia, for turkey hunting; Cuba

The FDRs: personal cottage in Warm Springs, Georgia; Bernard Baruch's South Carolina estate; and south Florida

The Trumans: Key West, Florida

The Eisenhowers: "Mamie's Cabin," grounds of Augusta National Golf Course, Georgia; Palm Desert, California

The Kennedys: JFK's parents' estate in Palm Beach, Florida

The Nixons: Key Biscayne, Florida, home

The Fords: Vail, Colorado

The Carters: Sapelo Island, Georgia; Cumberland Island, Georgia

The Reagans: home of Claudette Colbert in Barbados

The Bushes: Bush's mother's home in Hobe Sound, Florida

The Clintons: Utah, for skiing

15

Hospitality

The profusion of my table so repugnant to foreign customs arises from the happy circumstances of abundance and prosperity in our country.
—First Lady Dolley Madison

I'm the President of the United States and I should be able to have some music I can dance to.
—President Gerald R. Ford

There are two sorts of guests at the White House, those of the President of the United States, or those of Ike and Mamie, Jack and Jackie, George and Bar, Bill and Hillary. . . .

Each family treated their guests differently. George Bush had so many friends upstairs that his wife called him Perle Mesta, after the legendary society hostess. The Reagans invited only their closest friends into the private rooms. Lou Hoover drove her visitors in her own car to see the cherry blossoms and even had a small bedroom outfitted just for the children of guests, filled with toys. The busy Franklin Roosevelts expected to see their personal guests only at dinner—if then—and simply told them to check with the usher's office for information on tourist stops. So many friends, family, and colleagues were coming and going, in and out of bedrooms and suites, for overnight stays or for visits of several weeks, that the staff felt the house resembled a hotel.

Dwight Eisenhower loved barbecuing and often willingly donned an apron to do it. He is seen here, on the White House "roof," the small terrace outside the solarium.
Dwight D. Eisenhower Presidential Library

The publicity of the presidency will often test the loyalty of true friendships. Three that were lifelong (clockwise fr. top): Eleanor Roosevelt and Earl Miller; Richard Nixon and Bebe Rebozo; Nancy Reagan and Betsy Bloomingdale.

FRANKLIN D. ROOSEVELT PRESIDENTIAL LIBRARY; NIXON PRESIDENTIAL MATERIALS, NATIONAL ARCHIVES; RONALD REAGAN PRESIDENTIAL LIBRARY

Today, there are cards left for overnight guests to indicate what they would like to eat when they are dining in their rooms. Government cars are often at their disposal. Most stay in a third-floor room. Overnight guests are not as frequent as they were when traveling conditions were more arduous, so it is usually only the closest friends who stay in the Lincoln or Queen's Suites, down the hall from the First Family. The Clintons had numerous political supporters spend the night, but would allow only married couples to stay in a room together. Nancy Reagan did not feel comfortable permitting her stepdaughter to share a room with her fiancé during the 1981 inaugural festivities, yet soon afterward let her friend Ted Graber do so with his partner.

If being a close friend of the family provides access to the mansion, it can also bring unwanted scrutiny and criticism, the presidency testing many a friendship. In early 1803, Jefferson courted trouble by insisting that his friend Thomas Paine stay there with him. Paine's recently published *Age of Reason* had just been attacked as a call for atheism, and while he was a guest of Jefferson's, *Port Folio* magazine dubbed Paine "the greatest infidel on earth." By April of 1803, Boston and Philadelphia newspapers were printing a scurrilous poem called "Black and White," in which they falsely described the White House guest Tom Paine seducing Jefferson's slave Sally Hemings while the president was out of the house.

Many of those close to presidents were themselves distinguished individuals. The Polks were longstanding confidants of Supreme Court justice John Catron and his wife. Franklin Pierce and Nathaniel Hawthorne had been companions since their days together at Bowdoin College, and when he was a houseguest, Hawthorne was the only person who could coax Jane Pierce out for a cruise down the Potomac. Grover Cleveland suffered none of his era's scorn

On a rare night out, the Nixons, their daughter Julie, and her husband, David, join friends including Gerald and Betty Ford, at the family's favorite restaurant, Trader Vic's.

NIXON PRESIDENTIAL MATERIALS, NATIONAL ARCHIVES

for stage performers, and his closest friend was his fishing companion, famous actor Joe Jefferson. Millard Fillmore's only real confidants were his former Buffalo law partners; that city's mayor, a former three-term congressman Solomon G. Haven, and Nathan Hall, who was made postmaster general by Fillmore. FDR was the only president to have his closest advisers who were not relatives, Louis Howe and Harry Hopkins, live in the White House with him.

The presidency broke other friendships: a close friend of Wilson and his first wife, Colonel Edmund House, alienated the second Mrs. Wilson, who felt he was disloyal. The Grants shared opera boxes, carriage rides, and sumptuous meals with financiers Jim Fisk and Jay Gould until it was learned that they were trying to corner the gold market by using their friendship with Grant. In politics, it is sometimes hard to distinguish friends from opportunists, but First Families as well as their friends must be especially conscious of motive.

On the other hand, there is often an unspoken understanding that a First Family will depend on their friends for political help. There was not even a vague suggestion of objectivity in the coverage of the *Washington Globe*, owned and edited by Kentuckian Francis Preston Blair, friend, creditor, and adviser to Andrew Jackson. The two frequently conferred over dinner, Blair having only to cross the street from his Pennsylvania Avenue house, which now bears his name. Jackson trusted Blair enough to lend him a prize racehorse. The Hardings' best friends, *Washington Post* owner Ned McLean and his wife, Evalyn, were constantly attacked for turning their traditionally Democratic paper pro-Harding. Unknown to the public was that the *Post* owner was also an FBI agent, part of a covert intimidation squad that sought to prevent revelations of the president's personal life. The acquaintance of JFK and Ben Bradlee of *Newsweek* resulted in White House dinner invitations and a weekend at the family's private home in Virginia, but Bradlee picked up few scoops and got a scolding from JFK when the magazine criticized Jackie's trip to India.

Some friends served as unofficial advisers (the Clintons' friends, television producers Harry and Linda Bloodworth-Thomason), were given government positions (the Reagans named their old friend producer Charles Wick head of the U.S. Information Agency), or simply provided relief from politics (Nixon befriended low-key millionaire Bebe Rebozo, with whom he often slipped away for Florida cruises) or provided a stabilizing reality check (Calvin Coolidge's friend merchant Frank Stearns practically lived at the White House).

Most wives have had close friends outside of their husbands' circle. Jackie Kennedy so trusted her old school chum Nancy Tuckerman that she hired her as social secretary. Eleanor Roosevelt found new friends during her tenancy in reporter Lorena Hickok and young student Joseph Lash, both of whom were long-term guests at the White House; she also continued her close relationship with former New York state trooper Earl Miller, Marion Dickerman, and Esther Lape. Dolley Madison's closest confidante was her girlhood friend Eliza Collins Lee. For Nancy Reagan, the loyalty and support of Betsy Bloomingdale helped

her through difficult times in the White House.

Many nineteenth-century presidents had their closest friends come to the White House because it was considered improper to accept invitations to dine in the homes of private citizens, and even more a breach of respectability to dine in a public restaurant. When widower Chester Arthur's sister served as his hostess, however, she was not given the protocol status that

Chester Arthur (right) at a picnic, finished with his muskmelon.
LIBRARY OF CONGRESS

would have been accorded to a spouse; thus she felt she need not worry about these unwritten prohibitive codes. It was nevertheless a startling moment to receive a visit from her. In August 1884, after Molly McElroy visited the private home of one Alfred McKinney at Lake Minnewaska Mountain House in Ulster County, New York, the man was taken aback "that the first lady of the land should make me half forget the difference in our station and cause me to think of her smiling as a very agreeable woman."

Perhaps not since Monroe—and not again until Mrs. Kennedy—was there such a precise host as Chester Arthur. "Arthur was the highest liver in the White House," recalled a local market proprietor who had long serviced the White House. "He paid more attention to food than any other President in the last fifty years and gave a lot of personal attention to his dinners . . . [he] would see that the correct wine glasses, flowers, china, table linen . . . were in use, and that a perfect menu had been prepared. He was a connoisseur of wines."

Arthur's successor, Grover Cleveland, continued Molly McElroy's habit of visiting the private homes of friends but did not feel he should go to a public restaurant. He complained of the French food initially served to him in the White House, "I must go to dinner. I wish it was to eat a pickled herring, Swiss cheese, and a chop at Louis', instead of the French stuff I will find." By the time Theodore Roosevelt ate breakfast in Nashville's Maxwell House and declared that the coffee there was "good to the last drop," the ban on outside dining was finally broken. Even his more proper wife, Edith, was known to slip unnoticed into a rowdy F Street oyster house with her secretary. Jackie Kennedy enjoyed having lunch with old friends in familiar restaurants like Martin's steakhouse or Rive Gauche, which she had frequented in her Georgetown neighborhood as a senator's wife. Richard and Pat Nixon were longtime fans of Trader Vic's Polynesian eatery, while Gerald Ford took his wife to San Souci, a nearby restaurant popular with famous journalists. Betty Ford also once sneaked out to McDonald's. Nancy Reagan had a favorite corner table in the discreet Jockey Club restaurant, located in a

When he and his wife entertained the king and queen of England, FDR (at right) was criticized for serving hot dogs to them at a picnic—but they were a family favorite.

hotel, while the Bushes often went to a favorite Chinese restaurant in suburban Virginia.

By the end of the twentieth century, the idea of a president or his wife dining out was again a novelty—now because of security concerns, not broken protocol. Dining in a private home means the site must be cleared and secured, with special phone lines installed. Certainly the children of presidents have greater freedom than do their parents. Chelsea Clinton often slipped into a bagel and sandwich shop near her school, much as Susan Ford had done at a watering hole popular with college students. In New York, the Roosevelt boys were always swept to a table at "21" when they were at the door. The likes of Alan Arthur, Alice Roosevelt, Margaret Truman, and Chip Carter, who all basked in the limelight, were given immediate attention and service when they appeared at clubs and restaurants.

Friends and food, drinking and dancing, even the seemingly simple economics of keeping house, have all taken on politically explosive proportions for the families of presidents. Jefferson was perhaps the most sophisticated epicurean to live in the White House. The first president to have truly explored Europe, he enjoyed experimenting with different vegetables and other foods he was first exposed to on the Continent, whether it be pasta, artichokes, and the predominantly French sauces and creams served with them; he even kept his own cookbook of food specialties he preferred. As president, he was in correspondence with various consuls who sent him vegetable and fruit plants and seeds, and many of these he distributed to a local farmer with fields on the Potomac banks, a Scotchman by the name of Mayne.

Gerald Ford famously made his own breakfast of English muffins—at least in the beginning. Seen here with his daughter Susan at breakfast in family kitchen on second floor of White House.

GERALD R. FORD PRESIDENTIAL LIBRARY

Jefferson instructed his steward to pay premium prices for the first and the finest crops from Mayne. He had been attacked for this preference for foreign food by Patrick Henry, who accused Jefferson of being an American who "abjured his native victuals."

The personal taste of First Families inevitably became a political issue. James and Dolley Madison dealt directly with the "importer of everything" himself, John Jacob Astor, in procuring everything from Canton tea to "wine from the northwest coast of this continent." Still, a snobbish ambassador's wife sniffed to Dolley that her buffet tables were like a "harvest home supper." In the 1840 campaign, a political attack on Van Buren in Congress included reference to his regal dining on "salade à la volaille from a silver plate with a golden knife," while his opponent William Henry Harrison would eat "hog and hominy." Attacking a president for his food preferences seemed to stop when Taylor was said to have died from a gastric attack caused by too many cherries and iced milk. Still, when the FDRs served hot dogs to the king and queen of England in 1939, his mother took pleasure in forwarding to her daughter-in-law letters sent to her criticizing such a "disgraceful" menu. When George Bush publicly declared his dislike of broccoli, farm associations sent him the vegetable by the truckload in protest.

James Madison spent lavishly on food, which often had to be imported at great expense.
LIBRARY OF CONGRESS

Truman, like Lincoln, favored sorghum syrup to sweeten his food. Indeed, regionality strongly influences the tastes of the families: Theodore Roosevelt, from Long Island, liked the fresh wild greens that grew in the bogs of the North Shore there; JFK had a penchant for New England chowders and fish, while his wife liked French haute cuisine; the Carters frequently asked that the cheese grits and peanut pie of the rural South be served; the Hardings, said one reporter, "have openly stated that they 'just adore green onions,'" an old Ohio country staple for snacking. LBJ relished the likes of grilled deer sausage of his Texas and the tapioca made by his family cook. During one state dinner, he sent back to the kitchen a plate of beef, carping that it was rotten. The French chef responded that it was just as filet stuffed with pâté should taste. "Don't ever serve that stuff in this house again," the president snapped. Where once cooks privately hired or brought from home prepared the daily meals for presidential families, government-salaried chefs now do so.

Presidents pay for all food consumed by their family and friends, so gifts of food were often gratefully accepted. Jefferson, Jackson, and Van Buren were all sent mammoth wheels of cheese. Tyler served a 300-pound turtle sent to him from admirers in Key West; the Hardings, a vanilla pound cake sent from fans in Virginia. Once when the Hoovers were given a salmon, they had it sent right to the kitchen for preparation. When the group presenting it suddenly appeared to be photographed with the president and the fish, the salmon's head had to be quickly sewed back on. LBJ was steamed when the Secret Service destroyed his favorite cheese blintzes—brought by Defense Secretary McNamara himself, from his wife: "What in the hell happened to my cheese blintzes? You leave my food alone." Food is still sent to First Families, though security concerns now prevent its consumption.

On their first night in the White House, Nixon asked for cottage cheese and his daughter Tricia requested a hot dog. Kitchen staff had to run out to a local deli to get the items, but they were never out of stock again. With the First Lady generally devising or approving her family meals, food preferences are quickly learned. Although his wife's office mistakenly sent a recipe for a pricey crabmeat-stuffed artichoke to a woman complaining about feeding her family on food stamps during the recession, Reagan had simple tastes. He loved macaroni and cheese, and any dessert with coconut. Hillary and Chelsea Clinton loved chocolate, but the

Dancing

There is a long and rich history of dancing in the White House. *(clockwise from far left) LBJ's daughter "Watusi Luci" does a sixties frug. Jacqueline Kennedy waltzes with the man she called "my favorite dance partner," Vice President Lyndon Johnson. Lynda Bird Johnson cuts it up with her date, actor George Hamilton, in the East Room. Jimmy Carter square-danced with performers on the South Lawn. The Reagans do an elegant two-step. Betty Ford did the seventies disco "bump," with singer Tony Orlando in the East Room. The Clintons slow-dance.*

Lyndon Baines Johnson Library (2); John F. Kennedy Presidential Library; Jimmy Carter Presidential Library; Ronald Reagan Presidential Library; Gerald Ford Presidential Library; The White House

president was allergic to it, as well as to wheat and dairy foods. Theodore Roosevelt so loved fresh mint that he had a bed of it planted. Coolidge had fresh chicken served to him from birds kept in a coop on the lawn, but when it was noted the flavor was unusual, it was discovered that the coop was on Roosevelt's old mint bed. Bush drank endless cups of coffee every day. Next to his White House bed and Camp David desk, he kept an electric mug warmer. A "marvelous device," he called it.

The main kitchen was always located in the basement, so it was rare for members of the president's family to go there other than to give orders on food preparation or preferences. While entertaining at dinner one night, Van Buren was told by a whispering servant that the kitchen was on fire. Calmly excusing himself, he organized a systematic relay of water buckets to extinguish the flames. It was the only time he went into the kitchen. Fillmore finally got rid of the old open woodstoves when he brought in a coal-operated range. When the cook complained about the draughts, the president himself went down to the patent office to learn how the stove worked. Jefferson put in an icehouse where the present West Wing sits. Theodore Roosevelt had oak-lined iceboxes installed. Taft put in the first gas range. Refrigeration came to the White House in the early twentieth century. The kitchens were remodeled in 1935 with ceramic fixtures and stainless steel, modernized again in 1953, and updated several times since.

FDR so detested the constant serving of chicken in wartime that he wrote a humorous memo to his wife: "chicken six times a week" got him "to the point where my stomach rebels, and this does not help my relations with foreign powers. I bit two of them today." In the small kitchen FDR finally had installed on the attic floor, Eisenhower—who read cookbooks—prepared his soups and stews made from fowl he bagged; that is, until Mamie grumbled, "I smell garlic and onions in my house!" In the private kitchen created by Jackie Kennedy on the second floor, Ford made his breakfast and the Clintons prepared enchiladas.

Some families were not complete strangers to the kitchen. Bess Truman made her family dinner on a cook's day off. Grace Coolidge enjoyed baking—muffins, custards, pies. "Don't you think the road commissioner would be willing to pay well for Mrs. Coolidge's pie crust recipe?" her husband had once joked to friends. The hefty Grover Cleveland often supplemented the food orders: in his first term alone, he was said to have shot about 4,000 ducks while hunting! While awaiting a plate of broiled duck livers, he flicked his cigar and the ash ignited some gunpowder grains, causing a brief explosion. "Great God!" said the cook. "I knew it was bound to happen. He done bust!"

Since Jefferson's day, dining rooms were downstairs on the state floor: one for public entertaining, the other for the family. Pulleys brought up the food from the kitchen. Most families breakfasted in their suites. The Coolidges, dressed formally for evening, ate at the long table in the large State Dining Room; their house guests joined them upstairs before coming down to dinner. Coolidge cousin Marion Pollard was crestfallen by the menus: ham and eggs

Mamie Eisenhower, keeping account in the pantry, said she could "squeeze a dollar so tight, you can hear the eagle scream."
WASHINGTON POST; WASHINGTONIAN COLLECTION, MARTIN LUTHER KING LIBRARY

for breakfast; a souffle for lunch; soup, meat, potatoes, and salad for dinner. One morning, fish cakes were served. "I just about died! Fish cakes at the White House," she recalled. "I'd been thinking of Virginia ham and hothouse fruit."

Some families, like the McKinleys, ate in the west hall of the private quarters, but with the 1961 creation of a dining room there, the "Family Dining Room" on the state floor was essentially abandoned. No matter where they eat, each family has their own rituals. Jackson broke the precedent of being served dinner first, explaining of the children, "Let them be served first. They have better appetites and less patience and should not be required to wait until their elders are served." The Monroes ate formally, with a servant for each guest. Sarah Polk sometimes got so caught up in conversation, she never touched her plate. FDR was always given the honor of carving turkey at the table. The Truman trio teased one another by throwing bits of bread across the table or having watermelon-seed-spitting contests. The Eisenhowers and the Reagans watched television while they ate from trays. Coolidge tried to crack up the proper servants. "What's this," he'd tease when they put down a plate of chicken, "ham?" As ice cream was served, he piped up, "What's this—tapioca?" The servant solemnly replied, "Ice cream, Mr. President." It was a nearly daily ritual, which sent his wife and sons into gales of laughter.

Nearly all of the nineteenth-century families drank and served alcohol to their guests, the Polks and Hayeses being the exceptions. While the Polks would serve wine at formal dinners, the Hayeses—both abstainers—instituted a ban on all alcoholic beverages. For this, Mrs.

Hayes was ridiculed with the epithet "Lemonade Lucy." In fact, her decree also served a more important political purpose for the president—a large faction of his support in the election had been from the Prohibition Party, and he was rewarding them in kind. "My kingdom for a glass of whiskey," complained an exasperated Senator Blaine after dining with the Hayeses. Like Lucy, Frances Cleveland did not drink alcohol herself; she simply turned over her wine-glass during dinner, and permitted her guests to have the choice of going wet or dry.

Lucretia Garfield not only ignored the pleas of temperance advocates to continue the Hayes policy but, as she confessed in a letter to her husband, imbibed a bit herself—to help her sleep. "For two nights I have taken a glass of port wine, and conclude that is one reason I have slept better, but I have only a little more wine and if you can bring me a little more that you can trust as pure port, I think it may be of advantage to me." Nellie Taft, on the other hand, enjoyed a good drink. "I have only drunk one bottle of Scotch," she wrote her daughter during a trip, "and have to begin on rye and bourbon." Taft chuckled, "You should see Nellie's lip curl at the suggestion of Sunday high teas and dinner parties without champagne."

No president was a heavy drinker. When Theodore Roosevelt quickly sipped some champagne, thinking it was "fizzy water," his wife noticed that "it took no effect." While there was no evidence to support the claim that Grant had a drinking problem, he did imbibe and freely served his guests the heavily intoxicating concoctions of his era, like "Roman Punch," a champagne, Cointreau, and rum drink. His drinking—and smoking cigars—did not escape censure, one bitter ditty running in part, "Old Grant! We've had enough. We've seen you drink and heard you puff." No Gilded Age resident was more lavish with liquor than Chester Arthur. His private midnight bacchanalia featured society figures drinking champagne, liqueurs, and imported wines, smoking fine cigars, gorging on feasts of pheasant, mussels, mutton, and sweetbreads. "Nothing like it ever before has been perpetrated in the Executive Mansion," former president Hayes observed of the "liquor, snobbery, and worse."

During Prohibition, although the Hardings made alcohol available to guests in the private quarters, Florence Harding did not indulge—and her husband never overindulged. Hoover and FDR balked at the Prohibition ban of alcohol in their private homes, but toed the line drawn by women in their families and did not serve spirits at official functions. When Prohibition ended under Roosevelt, however, he reveled in his cocktail prowess. In 1939, as FDR served the king of England a martini, he suggested what a small battle it had been: "My mother does not approve of cocktails." The king sighed, "Neither does my mother." After work hours, FDR also liked to make his "Haitian libation," his own concoction of rum, orange juice, and brown sugar. The Trumans both enjoyed a drink. When repeated efforts to mix an old-fashioned failed to please Bess Truman, a waiter simply poured straight bourbon in a glass with an orange slice and cherry. "Now that's what I call an old-fashioned," said the First Lady.

In the later twentieth century, there was less drinking among First Families. The Kennedys

Rosalynn Carter presides over family meal, feeding her granddaughter Sarah, joined by her son Chip, daughter-in-law Judy, and mother-in-law Miss Lillian.
JIMMY CARTER PRESIDENTIAL LIBRARY

enjoyed daiquiris. Nixon was a connoisseur of wines and served the finest Californian as well as French wines, as did the Reagans. Under Carter hard liquor was banned at official functions but served privately to the family in moderation. In contrast to the teetotaler image fostered by her son-in-law Jimmy, Allie Smith declared that while her Christmas cake used wine as an ingredient, "it's better with bourbon."

Along with alcohol, tobacco use was often cast as a political "character" or religious issue. Although many presidents smoked cigars, other habits proved more controversial. Harding received critical letters when it was correctly implied in print that he chewed tobacco. Jackson's spittoons were ridiculed as undignified, and even Dolley Madison had what a friend admitted was "that unfortunate propensity to snuff-taking." When Alice Longworth smoked a cigarette at a Taft reception all hell broke loose: ladies never smoked in public, but nobody had the guts to ask her to leave—or put it out. During her husband's campaign, Ellen Wilson even issued a press release denying the rumor that she approved of it. Grace Coolidge smoked only in the family quarters. Eleanor Roosevelt openly lit and puffed on a cigarette after dinner to let women feel they could do so if they wished, but Mamie Eisenhower and Jackie Kennedy continued to smoke only in private. When Pat Nixon was spotted smoking in a restaurant, her press secretary clarified that she did "not inhale." Betty Ford sometimes put her cigarettes in the fingers of figurines—to make sure the maids were cleaning. The Clintons enforced what had been the unwritten rule under Bush: no smoking inside.

Like smoking and drinking, dancing proved controversial. Abigail Adams permitted her son Thomas to host a dance party for his young friends in the Philadelphia presidential mansion, and there is record of a private dance hosted by Dolley Madison, and of John Quincy Adams's dancing at his son's wedding. By the time of the great religious revival movement in the 1840s, the notion of a man and woman touching publicly and moving together to music was thought sinful by the pious. John Tyler had earlier warned his daughter Mary that the waltz was "rather vulgar," and something "which I do not desire to see you dance," but abandoned all protest when his second wife, Julia, insisted on "opening" balls with the first waltz or polka. "'Have you seen the Julia Waltzes which are just out, dedicated to Mrs. Tyler?'" the

First Lady told her sister Margaret to ask people. "[A]lmost everything in the polka depends upon the fascinating expression of countenance," she further explained. Ten months after he left the White House, John Tyler was still answering letters from ministers attacking his wife for popularizing dance.

In dramatic contrast, Julia Tyler's immediate successor Sarah Polk considered dancing so ungodly that she would not even enter a room where it was going on. James Buchanan not only asked his niece Harriet to remove her portrait from the room in which the visiting Edward, Prince of Wales, would be sleeping and not to play cards after dinner, but also refused her request to host a dance for him. Annie Buchanan said her uncle "thought that it would cause a scandal to the religious people of the country, if there were to be a dance there in the White House." It was not just at public events, however, that there was a harsh judgment. When word leaked out that teenager Nellie Grant was out dancing "the Germans," a fast-trotting polka, until three in the morning, even society leaders gasped at the scandal of it all.

Not until Benjamin Harrison's daughter Mary and her husband, Bob McKee, hosted a late-night party for friends on April 23, 1890, did a president dance again. Ironically, he had refused to let them take dancing lessons as young children, but ever since he had become a senator his daughter had dreamed of dancing in the East Room. Harrison liked the fast-paced "Germans," but his indulgence in them inspired attacks from some elements. One newspaper excoriated the president:

> "The German" is a dance in full party snobocratic dress, where the hugging process is the chief ingredient. . . . no such ridiculous performance has occurred at the President's mansion since the days of President Tyler. It is considered an offense to good taste, and the fringe or border on the cloak of lewd immorality . . . [Have] not the christian people who supported him . . . a right to complain when he throws open the parlors of the executive mansion for a dance the depravity of which is found in the underground variety halls of the slums of the larger cities. . . . Have the christian people of the Nation been deceived in President Harrison or has he backslidden since he went to the "White House"?

Coolidge refused to permit his wife—who took dance lessons—to dance in public. When his cousin's young daughter Marion was visiting and attended a ball with the Coolidges, Treasury Secretary Andrew Mellon offered to escort her to the dance floor, but the president broke in. Marion recalled, "He said that he did not want either Cousin Grace or me to go on the ball room floor *at all*." Only in private, recalled a maid, did Grace Coolidge get to try the Charleston, when a butler taught it to her and her son John.

Private holiday parties under Roosevelt, Taft, and Wilson permitted dancing for young people, and Alice Longworth was particularly good at the sinewy steps of ragtime. At his daughter Helen's debut party, the overweight President Taft proved particularly nimble on his feet: it was later discovered that he had been having private lessons in advance. Upstairs, in the

oval study, Wilson danced jigs to Scottish and Irish music his wife Edith put on their Victrola. After guests at a 1921 lawn party were invited to stay and join an impromptu party in the East Room, the Hardings waltzed to the "Blue Danube" and became the first presidential couple to do so publicly. Reports of this came at the same time as news that they had instructed a navy band to play jazz music. When it was mis-reported that they had danced to jazz, it caused a fury with the press. But by the twenties the mainstream media had relaxed, pointing out that "it is well that we have a President who knows that his dignity does not require the constant maintenance of solemnity . . . Harding . . . is distinctly 'human' and not afraid of showing it." The tide had turned.

Herbert Hoover admitted, "I cannot dance because of both my faith and my ignorance," but his son Allan hosted a holiday dance. While they were expert at jitterbugging, the Roosevelt sons—who held numerous holiday dances for their friends—were matched in dancing skill by their mother, who indulged in swing music as well as the traditional Virginia reel. Not until the 1960s, however, was dancing something First Families openly and regu-larly enjoyed. Jack Kennedy watched a young man at a party illustrate the moves of "the twist" but kept to the traditional dance numbers played that night. Jackie Kennedy loved to waltz— she described LBJ as "my favorite dance partner"— but she was also known, in the words of her mother's friend Molly Thayer, to be a "wicked twister."

Certainly no president loved dancing more than LBJ. In any one turn on the floor, he would switch partners several times. "He was a marvelous dancer, a strong lead," recalled one guest, chanteuse Edie Adams. "This is a strong man we've got up here running the country." LBJ even briefly tried to keep up with his frug-dancing daughter, who was so energetic that she was nicknamed "Watusi Luci" in the press. The Fords also loved to dance; he often requested the Swing era music of their youth. A Martha Graham–trained dancer, Betty Ford was the most adept First Lady in the ballroom—whether trying a soft shoe routine, modern dance, or even the disco "bump" of the seventies. Although presidential daughter Tricia Nixon hosted a party where the rock group The Turtles performed, it was not until the Clintons celebrated Hillary's 1993 birthday at a private party for friends and family that a presidential couple danced to rock and roll in the stately old East Room. With the first generation of the rock era to preside in the White House, contemporary and often raucous dance music frequently rang from the house.

The cost of feeding personal guests or even those at a strictly political event is paid out of pocket by the presidential family, or underwritten by a private donor. This can be exorbitant, even for those with great family wealth like Hoover and Kennedy, both of whom donated their salaries to charity. Even in the midst of the Depression, the Hoovers never let money stand in the way of sending for the most exotic California fruits as centerpieces or dessert. Jackie Kennedy, on the other hand, so ran up private entertaining and clothing costs in her first year as First Lady that her husband chided her about her budget.

Congress raised the presidential salary to its present $200,000 annually in 1969, under Nixon, but Taft was the first to be given money for discretionary use beyond his flat earnings. He was not only the first to get a salary raise to $75,000, but had an additional expense account of $25,000 for travel and $60,000 for entertaining. While his family spent about $50,000 a year on their clothes, private entertaining, and meals—including the meals of the servants—Taft still saved money. He explained to his successor Woodrow Wilson, "You have all your transportation paid for, and all servants in the White House except such valet and maid as you and Mrs. Wilson choose to employ. Your flowers . . . are furnished. . . . Music for all your entertainments . . . is always at hand. . . . when you leave in the summer you may at government expense take such of the household as you need. . . . Your laundry is looked after. . . . Altogether, you can calculate that your expenses are only those of furnishing food to a large boardinghouse. . . . I have been able to save from my four years about $100,000."

Before the Tafts, First Families could find themselves broke after living in the mansion. Servant salaries, food for all guests, even bills for horses and carriages, were paid out of their pocket. In his two terms as president, Jefferson spent a total of $11,000 on wine alone. He spent about $6,500 a year on food, paying his French chef an annual salary of $300. Jefferson's own annual salary was $25,000. He never recovered from the debts he compounded as president, dying in near poverty.

When it came to managing the accounts of the household, most families relied on housekeepers or the chief usher. The day before the inauguration, Nellie Taft went down to the market with Elizabeth Jaffray, the housekeeper she had appointed, and showed her what sort of food she wanted for her family—and how much she wanted to pay. A few later residents took a direct role in household expenditures and gave Jaffray a hard time. Florence Harding insisted that she get sixty cups from one pound of coffee. While the Hardings were successful at keeping government costs down—closing unused rooms, turning off every other electric lightbulb, running the fountain only when there were lawn guests, reducing the amount of coal—their personal accounts were high. From entertaining guests at lunch and dinner every day, for example, the Hardings' beef bill alone for February 1922 was $377.85. Coolidge—who kept his family accounts—finally got rid of Jaffray, insisting that she wasted money by having more than six hams to feed sixty people. After housekeeper Henrietta Nesbitt told Bess Truman that under wartime restrictions, she could not have a stick of butter to bring to one of her Spanish cooking classes, she too "retired."

Several wives have prided themselves on keeping a tight account. Edith Roosevelt even doled out a twenty-five-dollar-a-day allowance for her husband. Bess Truman and Mamie Eisenhower both kept their own family finances. The latter was particularly precise on what went "on the eagle," meaning the government accounts. Mamie was aware of how much food her family ate, and wanted all leftovers kept and re-served. She scanned newspapers for sales on everything from canned peaches to mink stoles. Items were often sent from stores for her inspection before she decided to make a purchase, which could create problems. When Marion Pollard went shopping for some inexpensive lingerie for cousin Grace Coolidge, she felt embarrassed examining items in view of her Secret Service escort. She asked that several pieces be sent to her at the White House to consider. The store sent up dozens of boxes with nearly $1,000 worth of items.

Generally, most presidents and their wives do not carry cash. Kennedy was forever having to borrow money from aides accompanying him—and often forgot to pay them back. This does not mean they don't enjoy shopping. William Henry Harrison frequented open-air markets with his grandsons, carrying food home to the White House in a basket. Nancy Reagan enjoyed popping into a nearby stationery store to buy greeting cards. Rosalynn Carter shopped in a local grocery as a brief excursion back into real life.

It is most often at Christmas that the families indulge their shopping instincts—although it can be difficult. When Herbert Hoover went shopping for his grandchildren on Christmas Eve, photographers swarmed him and revealed every gift he bought. Pat Nixon and her daughter Julie were mobbed at a local Sears, followed by reporters and cameras in the store, asking them questions. In modern times, Clinton managed frequently to get out to shop. On a Christmas Eve 1999 spree accompanied by his daughter, shaking hands and holding babies along the way, and stopping for a coffee, the president browsed and bought items in a bookstore, the U.S. Mint gift shop, and a jewlery store. Being president has shopping perks. While shopping in a store out west, Clinton produced his credit card only to learn that the account for "W. J. Clinton" had expired. The clerk bent the rules to take a personal check, she said, because, "I know where to find him if it bounces."

16

Young Life

*I feel much more deeply the humiliation of having
my name connected with a failure.*

—*Fred Grant*

*Children of men in public life—somewhat like the
children of preachers—learn early in life that people
expect them to be adults before they are even adoles-
cents.*

—*Lynda Bird Johnon*

*L*incoln was meeting with his cabinet when there came three short raps and two slow thumps on the door. The president opened it, explaining, "I've got to let him in, because I promised never to go back on the code." There stood his lilliputian son Tad, famous for his terrorizing pranks around the house, now looking deadly serious. "Ma says come to supper!" he shouted. The president broke up the meeting and did as he was told.

The routine of young and older White House children is often lived on a plane separate from their famous parents. Their existence could be as private as they and their parents chose, although not all the young people wished to live an insular life. Some have been central to a presidency and became celebrities; others made the news by simply going to school, dating, playing, working—or behaving poorly.

In the hothouse globe of the White House, it has most often been children who seem intent on functioning as normally as they can, seemingly ignoring the trappings of the man-

Caroline Kennedy (at right) clowning for the camera on the yacht Honey Fitz, *with her cousin Maria Shriver.*
JOHN F. KENNEDY PRESIDENTIAL LIBRARY

sion. "As a seven-year-old," recalled FDR's granddaughter Sistie, "you have no cognizance of where it is. It could be a palace or it could be a shack. But you lived very happily wherever there was love and warmth and food. You really don't notice your surroundings. You notice your family."

Sistie and her brother Buzzie briefly joined their grandfather as he had breakfast in bed for a hand game called "Whiffenpoof." They were encouraged by their grandmother to speak out to adults, during her afternoon tea for guests and visitors in the west sitting hall. "This is Mrs. Roosevelt's version of The Children's Hour," cracked a secretary. The children rolled with the punches in the frenetic household. Sistie sneaked into the hall to watch a premiere viewing of *Gone With the Wind*, until she was caught and marched off to bed. When Buzzie got into a crying jag, his exasperated grandmother told him to bottle it and "find a bathtub you can cry into." She later found him curled up outside FDR's bedroom, still crying. "Well, Grandma, I tried to find one," he said through his tears. "But they were all full."

Despite their mother Anna's best efforts, publicity was inevitable. Buzzie was immortalized in a *New Yorker* cartoon, and Sistie was a mini-hostess at the Easter egg roll—where a magician once pulled purple eggs from her mouth—and for a visiting Shirley Temple. She recalled that the fussily dressed child movie star "bowed to us rowdies." When Anna's husband enlisted during World War II, she returned to live in the mansion with her five-year-old Johnny. Once he was found running the seamstress's measuring stick along the posts of the Grand Staircase to make a noise, and another time walked into an idling limousine on an "errand" for his grandmother—until, several blocks away, the driver realized he was playing. If his mother, who worked as her father's aide, was free, they went swimming or played table tennis together. Otherwise, he roamed the grounds, a buddy to all the guards and household staff.

"If I could only walk about a little with my children sometimes in the grounds without being stared at, and really enjoy the comfort of an old dress and a little privacy," Martha Patterson told a reporter, "it would be very pleasant." Her children, nieces, and nephew, however, were blissfully unaware of such a strain. The five Andrew Johnson grandchildren were the core of a tight family that kept outsiders at bay during his impeachment trial. The three girls did needlework with their grandmother, but it was especially critiqued by the president, a former tailor. Lillie and Sarah Stover played the piano as their brother Andrew played the

guitar or violin, to entertain
the family. All five went to the
prestigious Marini dance studio and were tutored in other
subjects; their mothers supervised their studying. After
class each late morning, they
made a beeline into their
grandmother's room.

There has been a strong
effort to protect the very young from the damage of publicity. Her father allowed nine-year-
old Nell Arthur to attend receptions only when accompanied by her older cousins May and
Jessie. In the summers, "Aunt Molly" watched over her. As the president wrote his sister on
July 20, 1883, "I will be very glad if you will take charge of Nell during the month of August
(and probably the first week of September) . . . I plan . . . to be absent the whole of that
time . . . I want Nell to stay in New York a day or two, so that she can go to the dentist and
have some shopping done for her . . . would you come to New York."

Cleveland had infant children and was extremely protective of their well-being. While he
once let baby Marion press a button to start Atlanta Cotton Exposition machinery, and permitted some boys to "serve" as his toddler Ruth's "honor guard," he raised them mostly in a
private home, Red Top. While in the White House, the First Lady created a kindergarten for
the little girls and children of her friends. "My mother did not want us to grow up dwelling
on the fact that we had been White House children. She trained us for living on our own
account," Marion later recalled.

The passage of time and increased sophistication of the media did not alter this impulse,
for Jackie Kennedy also created a kindergarten class in the Solarium for her three-year-old
daughter Caroline—and kept all the "Caroline" dolls and coloring books away from her. "I
think it's hard enough to bring up children anyway, and everyone knows that limelight is the
worst thing for them," she explained. "They either get conceited, or else they get hurt." For
her, this meant more than just shielding her children from public exposure to crowds or the
press. Despite the existence of a live-in nanny, Maude Shaw, it was Jackie who read to, played
with, and fed the children in what she called the family's "real" home, in pastoral Virginia.

Amy Carter in public school in Washington, D.C.
JIMMY CARTER PRESIDENTIAL LIBRARY

Jackie Kennedy passed on her parenting advice to Hillary Clinton, who brought her twelve-year-old daughter, Chelsea, to the White House. Hillary recalled: "She gave that constant kind of instilling of family pride . . . and that even if other people are writing silly stories about you, you don't have to let that affect you, you can keep your head up high and keep going . . . [W]e talked a lot about the effect of the press on children . . . and [of] adults . . . who cater, or play up, protect or give them all sorts of benefits, whether they earned them or not." Similarly, Hillary made sure that Chelsea cleaned her own room, and swept up the popcorn on the floor of the movie theater after she had friends in to watch a film. The effort to maintain normality was evidenced by Hillary's arranging for Chelsea's birthday wish to have her friends in for bowling, and riding a bike to the National Zoo to help chaperone a trip for Chelsea and her classmates.

Arresting a daughter's development of what Margaret Truman called "belleship" is nothing new. Susan Ford complained that despite all the servants in the White House she still had to make her own bed. Her mother insisted she do it. The Fords were equally clear with their sons Steve and Jack not to make any excessive demands on the staff—and to learn how to cook their own breakfasts. Parents can take even presidential children down a notch. Quentin Roosevelt was shaken out of his bed by his angry father and made to remove the spitballs the boy had put on the eyes of First Lady portraits. It was a "double disgrace," said TR, to "behave like this in the house of the nation." Quentin raised his chin and said it didn't matter because one of his gang was Charlie Taft, the son of the president-elect, and it would "soon be his house anyway." Eleven-year-old Charlie soon came in for his share of punishment—for carving his initials in the presidential yacht and driving the presidential electric car into a tree.

Even adult children do not escape parental dictates. Mamie Eisenhower often complained about her grown son, "He's cutting his hair much too short!" Outspoken in defense of his father's honor, George W. Bush called himself the "loyalty enforcer," but his mother, to ensure he didn't say anything inappropriate to the queen of England, wouldn't seat him next to her at a state dinner. When Buck Grant snapped a carriage whip, he startled the horses, and it nearly threw his old grandfather to the ground. "That was careless," the president quietly remarked. With the gentle rebuke, the highly sensitive Buck admitted, "[I]t hurt me. It nearly broke my heart." Rarely has parental dictate been publicly questioned by the press: only when Edith Roosevelt replaced antique beds with stern iron bedsteads for her sons to use was there a "howl," as one reporter put it. When it was explained that she did it to save the antiques from the boys, the hubbub died out. Said Lynda Johnson, "Once you get upstairs on the second floor you really are free. But, of course, you have your parents, so it is not much better."

With its nooks, crannies, hidden staircase, and storage rooms, most young people have made good use of the mansion. Irvin Garfield sped his bike straight down the family staircase, through the hallway, and into the East Room, while his brother Jim jumped a springboard in the high-ceilinged room. Charlie Taft and his pals played hide-and-seek among the stored gold dinner chairs in the attic and "sardines" in the dank basement. He loved taking over the switchboard when the operator went to lunch. Scott and Fanny Hayes roped visiting justices and senators into their game of hide-and-seek in dimly lit state rooms. When FDR Jr. and his brothers Elliott and John were together in the mansion, they enjoyed roughhousing. Their uncle Hall, the First Lady's brother, whom they always teased as "just a boy at heart," joined in one rowdy pillow fight, piled on by his tall and strong nephews, until the commotion was heard down the hall. FDR told his son Jimmy, "Go and see if you can arbitrate among those battling warriors!" When Jimmy entered, everyone jumped on him. Margaret and Eleanor Wilson played their shenanigans on a city tour bus, posing as midwestern visitors. When they got to the White House, Margaret cried to the guide, "Oh, mister, can't we go in? I want to see where the Wilson girls sleep."

Unlike his brother Tad, who smeared ink on the telegraph desks and hammered nails into the desk of the president's secretary, Willie Lincoln was, in the words of his mother, "a very beautiful boy with a most spiritual expression of face." He was sensitive about being the president's son: "I wish they wouldn't stare at us so. Wasn't there ever a President who had children?" Willie had a studious quality. When family friend Edward Baker was killed in the Civil War, the eleven-year-old wrote a poem about the man's death which was published in the

Quentin Roosevelt, who went to local public school for a time, with one of his friends, whom his mother said she disapproved of.
LIBRARY OF CONGRESS.

Washington National Republican. Like Tazewell and Alice Tyler—the last young children of a president to live in the mansion—Tad and Willie Lincoln were tutored at home. Their father could not bear the idea of sending them out of the house for school, let alone to boarding school.

The Grants were extraordinarily close to their son Jesse and daughter Nellie, ten and thirteen years old, respectively, when they came to the White House. Soon after both were sent to boarding school the parents became heartsick. When Jesse wrote the president, "I want to come home," the father wired back, "We want you too. Come at once." Both children returned, and neither studied hard in local schools, lacking parental pressure to do so. Permitted to roam about freely at receptions, the unsupervised Jesse recalled swiping enough food from the buffet tables to make up several meals. Still, Jesse exercised some self-discipline, for he got into Cornell University by the end of the administration, his father proudly pointing out, "although he has never attended school but three years."

Studying has its benefits and drawbacks in the White House. Lynda Johnson, a student at nearby George Washington University, said the noise outside her bedroom window was worst when the tourists filed out of the North Portico and yelled to each other where to pose for pictures. "I am dying to go [out] there and say, 'Be quiet!'" she cracked. Margaret Truman, also a GWU student, hosted her history seminar in the State Dining Room every Thursday because, she said, "it was the only place we could get any privacy." Hal and Jim Garfield spent months burrowed in the small hideaway room that is now the Queen's Sitting Room, reading in preparation for their first year of college. On many occasions, President Clinton helped his daughter with homework—once asking an aide to locate some government research for her studies. Similarly, when Rosalynn Carter requested some government data through her office over a weekend, the request was assumed to relate to federal business. The Carters were mortified when a truck pulled up with loads of government reports and statistics—all for their grammar school daughter Amy's term paper.

The three elder Hayes sons in the conservatory with friends. Ruddy, standing on far left; Webb, standing, fourth from left; Birch, seated at far left.

HAYES PRESIDENTIAL CENTER

Numerous children attended both public and private local grammar schools, high schools, and colleges during their White House residency. Quentin Roosevelt, who attended the local public school, made a great pal in a small African-American boy who often came to play with him at the mansion. Sometimes Quentin walked to school with a security agent, but most often he did not.

There is no disguising one's identity in school, and the president's children learn how to deflect attention from themselves. When a fellow student asked for her autograph, for example, Chelsea Clinton instead sketched a face on the girl's fingertips so when she wiggled them they became finger puppets. The chance to have sleepovers in the Lincoln bed is a definite plus. When pals of Archie and Quentin Roosevelt came over for a slumber party, they slept four crosswise on the bed, which is eight feet wide and seven feet long. Margaret Truman's father, however, did not go through with his scheme—to have her and her friends frightened one night in the room by a nearly seven-foot-tall butler dressed as Lincoln's ghost. The Taft children and their friends had permission to raid the kitchen for snacks. Overnight friends, recalled Bob Taft, often stayed up writing letters on White House stationery.

There are hazards to having classmates all know where you live, however. At a class reunion Tricia Nixon hosted, fellow alum Grace Slick, singer of the sixties rock group Jefferson Airplane,

and her date, the radical activist Abbie Hoffman, were not permitted into the White House party; only later did Slick reveal that she had planned to put LSD into the punch.

As children become teenagers, the potential for public exploitation is greater. In reaction to one of her spontaneous sixteen-year-old daughter Luci's emotionally honest answers to reporters, Lady Bird Johnson admitted, "I find this both frightening and interesting." After respecting her privacy while she lived in the mansion as a high school student, the media began to cover Chelsea Clinton once she left for Stanford University. When it was learned that Hal and Jim Garfield were going to Williams, applications to the college shot up and enrollment increased. Sometimes it is not just publicity which is embarrassing to presidential children away in school. When Ted Roosevelt got sick, his mother rushed up to his Connecticut boarding school to see that he was nursed back to health. It made national headlines, causing the prince of Germany to postpone a trip to America. She did the same thing when Archie came down with diphtheria at Groton, and Kermit had scarlet fever.

One might assume that being away from the White House would make it easier for the children to date. This is not necessarily the case. While he was at Amherst, there was constant speculation that John Coolidge might elope with his girlfriend, and there were articles such as the one in the *New York Times* headlined, "John Coolidge a 'Peach,'" in which Mount Holyoke girls recalled their swooning over him at a dance. Alan Hoover found that if he was just photographed next to a girl, they were "engaged."

"I deeply resent the treatment the ladies of my household are receiving at the hands of the papers . . . they are not servants of the government," Woodrow Wilson angrily told the press corps after their stories had his daughter Margaret engaged to any number of men she had never met. Her sister Nell's engagement broke in the news after one of her love letters was opened in a post office. After going through the trauma of breaking her engagement to one man, Nell was then confronted by her father's press secretary when he learned that she was mar-

Jack Ford with his parents in the family room.
GERALD R. FORD PRESIDENTIAL LIBRARY

rying an older, divorced man, Treasury Secretary William McAdoo, telling her it put him and the president in "an awkward position." The eldest sister, Jessie, managed to keep her engagement secret by accepting Frank Sayre's marriage proposal while wearing a cloak in a misty garden by the light of the moon. She and Frank would surreptitiously rendezvous at the C&O Canal and slip off in a canoe.

Once Secret Service protection became a permanent fixture it wreaked havoc on romance. Patti Davis chafed at the possibility that her agents would report details of her love life to her parents. Lynda Johnson said it was often difficult to have genuine romantic privacy outside of the family rooms, all the while knowing the agents would always be part of any potential marital life: she planned to write a memoir called *Three on a Honeymoon.* Privacy is no easier to achieve for young men. Jack Ford's meeting of tennis champion Chrissie Evert, their subsequent date—even their jog and bike ride together—all made *People* magazine. Divorced but dating, Doro Bush screened out suitors by reminding them of her real life with two children.

Most young adults have been cautious in deciding whom to date—especially when so many opportunists seek them out. Webb Hayes, serving as his father's secretary, was also enlisted by his mother to squire an endless stream of Ohio girls she invited for lengthy visits. At one point he had eight belles to corral. Finally, after too many nights of flirtatious chatter, he went upstairs and dropped a massive dictionary on the floor, resounding to the Red Room below. The girls got the message and went to bed.

No family was more dominated by an endless parade of young people dating and pairing off than that of Andrew Jackson; all of them were blood nieces and nephews of his late wife. Niece Emily Donelson—married to her cousin Jack—served as official hostess, and was quickly joined by cousins Mary Coffee, Mary McLemore, Mary Eastin, Elizabeth Martin, Andrew Hutchings, Samuel Hays, and Daniel Donelson. All enjoyed being in the social apex. "I have a [bed]room fit for a Princess," wrote Mary Eastin, "with silk curtains, mahogany furniture, a carpet such as you Tennesseans have in your parlor, and a piano." Just before dinner,

As part of the circle of young Donelson cousins who lived in the Jackson White House, Mary Coffee and Andrew Jackson Hutchings dated and married. Jackson told one of his great-nieces, "With love, marriage is heaven. Without it, hell."
LADIES HERMITAGE ASSOCIATION

the beaux, belles, and their friends had a social hour in the Red Room, with wine and hors d'oeuvres. One intra-family marriage resulted when Andrew Hutchings wed Mary Coffee. Jackson had sent his troublesome nephew to the strict Catholic college at Georgetown, but Hutchings still ran up huge bills and was expelled. Jackson patiently advised the young man on plantation management and, when his behavior improved, paid a great sum for his wedding.

Coming into this atmosphere in the next administration, chaperoned by her maternal grandfather's elderly cousin, Dolley Madison, was one Angelica Rebecca Singleton. "Despite all preconceived notions about the heartlessness and worthlessness of this great metropolis, I find it a mighty pleasant place," she wrote her sister Marion. "Matrimony . . . is at the very end . . . of very many who profess to be mere lookers on . . . But such things I believe to be preordained and . . . the mate designed for me . . . has not yet crossed my path." She was bored by a courting senator who talked only of drinking, and a Georgian who became "excited and shocked" at seeing a "Georgia girl" whose dress was "draped so indecently low." But when she met Abraham Van Buren, she managed a quick courtship—and married the president's son.

Many a young adult refused to be lured by a glamorous life. Eleanor Wilson often danced at parties until three in the morning, for example, but her sister Jessie worked at the YWCA. Mary Abigail Fillmore, fluent in German, French, and Spanish, and a graduate of the Sedgewick Seminary in Lenox, Massachusetts, sought professional employment as a teacher.

Allan Hoover leaving his dormitory building at Harvard Business School.
LIBRARY OF CONGRESS

She worked into the early months of her father's presidency, fulfilling a New York State requirement to teach after graduation before finally agreeing to live in the White House and aid her mother in social duties.

For many sons, the White House is problematic. When he graduated first in his class at Yale, Bob Taft desperately hoped that people understood that he earned the grades by his genuine effort, not his status. "Being the President's children brought few extra privileges for us," he said. Buck Grant so disliked publicity that he became the only presidential child to study outside the country while his father was president, taking a year in Germany at the University of Göttingen. When he returned, and graduated, he spent little time in the White House, heading out west instead for a lengthy vacation.

Similarly, Steve Ford found life in the mansion so confining that he headed out west to study, packing up his Jeep and driving himself. Still, even when they try to live normally, outside of Washington, it is impossible for them not to be treated as special. Despite the fact that Ted Roosevelt took off a year to work in a steel mill, he ended up marrying the corporation president and chief stockholder's daughter.

Allan Hoover managed to elude press in his last year at Stanford, but by the fall of 1929, when he came east to Harvard Business School, he was a media commodity. Newsreel cameramen, photographers, and reporters gathered to meet him outside his dormitory. When the young man stepped grinning into the fray, some

Mary Abigail Fillmore, called Abbie, was a studious but humorous young woman.
BUFFALO AND ERIE COUNTY HISTORICAL SOCIETY

"Little Nell" Arthur, the president's daughter (above), spent most of her good times in the company of her cousins Jessie and May McElroy in the White House. Jessie stands, May is seated on the lap of a cousin (below).

PRIVATE COLLECTION

reporters doubted it was the president's son. He silently pulled out a White House telegram from his father which stated that he could pose for the cameras but that he "must not speak."

"My children are not freaks," Theodore Roosevelt once insistently lectured reporters. "When I go out to play tennis with my children, it is not a matter of public interest."

No matter how much children are protected by their parents, simply living in the White House and/or being a presidential offspring brings inevitable media and public interest in them. Even President Arthur's nieces May and Jessie McElroy, who lived in the White House, received requests and appeals, one addressed simply "For the Daughter of the Sister of the President of the United States." May got a letter in February 1882 warning her not to let her uncle leave the city "and he may be able to imagine the reason why this is said," it ominously stated. A nasty poem scorning young girls who wore gloves and jewelry came for Jessie. Meanwhile, one woman incessantly wrote their mother wanting to know when she could come to the family quarters to see the president's daughter's dollhouse.

Today, even married adult children, like Chip and Jeff Carter, who come to live back "home" in the mansion are assigned security agents. "I have to say," admitted Hillary Clinton when she was asked how she had managed to regulate what sort of video games Chelsea played, or films and television shows she watched, "one of the best things about Bill being president is that she was surrounded by Secret Service agents." Protection for children was informally phased in for the young sons of Theodore Roosevelt and officially under Taft, but it remained fairly lax until the

Once he left the White House for St. Mary's Catholic College in Baltimore, Madison's stepson Payne Todd began stepping out into society under the wing of his mother's friend Elizabeth Patterson, the flighty and bawdy abandoned wife of Prince Jerome Bonaparte. Seeking to pull him away from this influence, the Madisons sent him along as a non-official with peace negotiators during the War of 1812. In Czarist St. Petersburg, his status was comprehended only as "The American Prince." As Henry Clay recalled to him, "Do you remember when we were in Russia together how . . . all the rest of us sat apart in a gallery and watched you dance with the Czar's sister, we being debarred because we were not of the blood royal?" Upon his return, Payne Todd took one of his cousins to a tavern and slipped brandy into the berry bowl of the young boy, who came back to the mansion with his first experience of intoxication.

Although three presidents' sons of the same era suffered from the same "Prince" complex as Payne, they did so because they believed they had to be their fathers' most vociferous defenders. As if being the grandson of the second president wasn't enough, young John Adams was also the son of the sixth president. However arrogantly, he was only defending his father when, at one of his mother's receptions, he insulted a snide anti-Adams reporter, Russell Jarvis. Some days later, when Jarvis saw Adams delivering documents in the Capitol Building, he shoved him. The ensuing fight provoked a full-blown congressional investigation. Swashbuckling John Tyler Jr. reacted similarly when he read attacks on his father's policies in a Richmond paper. Priding himself on being the family's best editorial defender, Tyler nevertheless decided to challenge the writer to a duel. He appeared at the field, waiting. Word came that his opponent had been told the wrong time. Considering his honor intact for showing, Tyler left the field. The *Norfolk Herald* found the chivalry hilarious and headlined its story, "Another Silly Affair."

There was no grander a son than "Prince John" Van Buren. An astute lawyer, he was hosted in England by the Duke of Wellington and attended a ball held by Queen Victoria. The *London Chronicle* published his name and status alongside those of lords, counts, and nobility who were also guests. In his famous harangue against the royal Van Burens, Congressman Charles Ogle took to the floor of the House declaring ominously, "There was a time when you would not find the son of the President . . . invited and set down to the royal table . . . Just look at it! . . . I tell you we are growing in favor of crowned heads!" The same year that his father was defeated for reelection, in large part because of Ogle's speech, "Prince John," now a celebrity, was elected to Congress.

Some parents guarded against their children's using their status for personal benefit. Taft refused to let his daughter Helen attend King George V's coronation with his designated representative because "people might think I appointed a friend so my daughter could be escorted." Sometime in the spring of 1841, John Tyler gathered his sons, daughters, and daughter-in-law to deliver what could still be held as a code for presidential children: "Now

One of the press photographs long unpublished and originally suppressed by her father from being printed in newspapers: Alice Roosevelt gets paid winnings from her bookie at the racetrack.
LIBRARY OF CONGRESS

my children, during the next few years, I hope that you will conduct yourselves with more than usual propriety and decorum . . . You are to know no favourites . . . You are to accept no gifts whatsoever . . . You are to allow no one to approach you on the subject of office or favors." In the end, none of the Tylers did anything wrong. Although the dreamy Robert, who loved theater, poetry, music, art, and literature, did charm Dickens and Irving when he got the chance to meet his role models, he could not place his hero Edgar Allan Poe in the U.S. Customs Office at Philadelphia. The president, it was written, was "not in favor of the dispensing of political plums by his son."

The argument can be made that inevitably most children have benefited from having a president for a father. Robert Lincoln would not have been held back from the front line of the Civil War had his father not been president. On the other hand, Neil Bush's debacle in the failed Silverado Savings and Loan would not have received the international attention it did had he been someone else's son. What the presidential child should do to earn his own wage has always been a question fraught with conflicts, creating potential political fodder and public interest. No sooner had John Coolidge graduated, for example, than the *Indianapolis Star* carried a headline story, "Will Ask Dad What to Do." Several children were accused of benefiting financially from their fathers' positions. In some cases there is proof to support such claims. Russell Harrison multiplied his wealth by taking huge gifts of stocks from influence-buying companies, and his wife, Mamie, was discovered to be drawing a federal salary of $5,000 annually on the "Utah Mission"—which required nothing of her. The only child ever charged with a crime, however, was Fred Grant. He punched a columnist who wrote disparaging remarks about his wife. Fred gladly paid the hundred-dollar fine for battery.

More often than not, the publicity comes in reaction to something parents do—not the children's deeds. Reporters asked Susan Ford about her intimate life only after her mother addressed speculation about it in front of millions of Americans on *60 Minutes*. "Ask Amy" buttons were coined after Carter mentioned that he discussed nuclear armament with his preteen daughter during the 1980 debates. Ronald Reagan's refusal to endorse his daughter Maureen Reagan's race for the Republican nomination of a California U.S. Senate seat provoked as much news as the race itself. In the midst of President Clinton's impeachment trial his daughter's name was invoked on the Senate floor by former senator Dale Bumpers. "Kids go through hell if their folks are in politics," offered President Clinton. "They get all of the burdens and none of the benefits."

Many parents wanted to protect their children in public life, yet encouraged their use for political purposes. Even though Margaret Truman had a very public role on the lengthy 1948 campaign whistlestop tour, and assisted her mother at receptions, her father nevertheless publicly rebuked music critic Paul Hume, who suggested that she wouldn't have a singing career had she not been First Daughter. Recalled Truman: "I wrote [Hume] a letter saying that if I could get my hands on him I'd bust him in the jaw. . . . When Margaret and Bess found out, they both wept and said that I'd ruined Margaret. . . . I said 'Now, you wait and see. Every man in this United States that's got a daughter will be on my side,' and it turned out they were." Truman thought presidential children were like "the offpsring of hereditary rulers . . . expected to be out of the ordinary and to maintain a special prominence. . . . even in a republic where people vest authority in a President, they want to glamorize not only him but his family."

Perhaps, in the end, kids will be kids. John Coolidge cringed whenever his father called his mother "Mummer" in front of other people. Robert Lincoln was embarrassed among his prep school pals when they heard his father's western twang. At a mother-daughter dinner, Hillary Clinton and other mothers had to dress up and perform as they imagined their chil-

dren to be. Costumed as "Chelsea" in her ballet tutu, the First Lady turned to another mother playing daughter and quipped, "Your mother embarrasses you in front of maybe a couple hundred people. *My* mother embarrasses me in front of *millions.*"

And too, parents will be parents—even at 1600 Pennsylvania Avenue. When Tricia Nixon got huffy after learning that her mother would discuss her in an interview, Pat Nixon shot back, "Twenty-four-year-olds don't run the world!"

Susan Ford washes her car at the White House.

Education of Some "First Children" During Their Fathers' Presidencies

Payne Todd, Madison's stepson: St. Mary's College, Baltimore, Md.

Charles Adams: Harvard College, Cambridge, Mass.

Andrew Jackson Jr.: Cumberland University, Cumberland, Tenn.

Smith Van Buren: private law apprentice, Albany, N.Y.

Tazewell Tyler: privately tutored in White House

Alice Tyler: privately tutored in White House

Mary Abigail Fillmore: Miss Sedgewick's Academy, Lenox, Mass.; State Normal School, Albany, N.Y.

Thomas "Tad" Lincoln, privately tutored in White House

William "Willie" Lincoln, privately tutored in White House

Robert Lincoln, Harvard College, Cambridge, Mass.

Robert "Frank" Johnson, Georgetown College, Washington, D.C.

Nellie Grant, Miss Porter's School, Farmington, Conn.

Jesse Grant, Cheltenham Academy, Penn.; Cornell University, Ithaca, N.Y.

Ulysses S. "Buck" Grant, Harvard College, Cambridge, Mass.; Columbia University Law School, N.Y.

Fred Grant, West Point Academy, Poughkeepsie, N.Y.

Scott Hayes, privately tutored in White House

Fanny Hayes, privately tutored in White House; Madame Burr's School, Washington, D.C.

Webb Hayes, Cornell University, Ithaca, N.Y.

Rutherford "Ruddy" Hayes, Cornell University, Ithaca, N.Y.

James "Jim" Garfield, privately prepared for Williams College in White House

Birchard Hayes, Harvard Law School, Cambridge, Mass.

Harry "Hal" Garfield, privately prepared for Williams College in White House

Mollie Garfield, privately tutored in White House; Madame Burr's School, Washington, D.C.

Abram Garfield, privately tutored in White House

Irwin Garfield, privately tutored in White House

Nell Arthur, Madame Burr's School, Washington, D.C.

Alan Arthur, Princeton University, Princeton, N.J.; Columbia University Law School, N.Y.

Ruth Cleveland, attended private kindergarten in White House

Esther Cleveland, attended private kindergarten in White House

Marion Cleveland, attended private kindergarten in White House

Quentin Roosevelt, public school, Washington, D.C.; boarding school in
   Alexandria, Va.
Archie Roosevelt, public school, Washington, D.C.; Groton School, Groton,
   Mass.
Kermit Roosevelt, Groton School, Groton, Mass.; Harvard College, Cambridge,
   Mass.
Theodore Roosevelt Jr., Groton School, Groton, Mass.; Harvard College,
   Cambridge, Mass.
Alice Roosevelt, refused to attend school of any kind
Ethel Roosevelt, National Cathedral School, Washington, D.C.
Helen Taft, National Cathedral School, Washington, D.C.; Bryn Mawr College,
   Bryn Mawr, Penn.
Charlie Taft, The Taft School, Watertown, Conn.
Robert Taft, Yale University, New Haven, Conn.; Harvard Law School,
   Cambridge, Mass.
John Coolidge, Mercersburg Academy, Penn.; Amherst College, Amherst, Mass.
Calvin Coolidge Jr., Mercersburg Academy, Penn.
Allan Hoover, Stanford University, Palo Alto, Calif.; Harvard Business School,
   Cambridge, Mass.
Franklin D. Roosevelt Jr., Groton School, Groton, Mass.; Harvard College,
   Cambridge, Mass.; University of Virginia Law School, Charlottesville, Va.
John Roosevelt, Groton School, Groton, Mass.; Harvard College, Cambridge,
   Mass.
Margaret Truman, Gunston Hall, Washington, D.C.; George Washington
   University, Washington, D.C.
Caroline Kennedy, attended private kindergarten in White House
Luci Baines Johnson, National Cathedral School, Washington, D.C.; Georgetown
   University, Washington, D.C.
Lynda Bird Johnson, University of Texas at Austin; George Washington
   University, Washington, D.C.
Julie Nixon Eisenhower, Smith College, Northampton, Mass.
Susan Ford, Holton-Arms School, Washington, D.C.; Mount Vernon College,
   Washington, D.C.; University of Kansas at Lawrence
Jack Ford, Utah State University, Logan, Utah
Amy Carter, Thaddeus Stevens public school, Washington, D.C.; Sidwell Friends
   School, Washington, D.C.
Chelsea Clinton, Sidwell Friends School, Washington, D.C.; Stanford University,
   Palo Alto, Calif.

James Monroe was the last president to wear silk breeches and knee stockings.

17

Looking the Part

Sometimes I feel as if I am dressing the Washington Monument.
—First Lady Eleanor Roosevelt

I must dress in costly material. The people scrutinize every article that I wear with critical curiosity.
—First Lady Mary Todd Lincoln

Formality and style. Comfort and naturalness. There are constantly conflicting views of how a presidential family should dress. While none have appeared publicly in radical attire, almost all draw the line about public comment on what they wear when they are relaxing, or "off duty," so to speak.

Perhaps inevitably it was egalitarian Jefferson who caused the first political controversy over style simply by dressing as he did when he greeted British minister Anthony Merry in the White House. The president was "not merely in undress, but actually standing in slippers down at the heels and both pantaloons, coat and underclothes indicative of utter slovenliness," Merry informed his king, taking it as a brazen insult of international proportions.

From the beginning of the presidency, most who served were conscious of their clothes. When George Washington, John Adams, and James Madison were inaugurated, for example, it was well publicized that their cloth suits were American made. Most have dressed so conservatively as to be utterly unfashionable. James Monroe, for example, insisted on wearing satin knee breeches, white silk stockings, and buckled shoes long after most men wore long trousers. Not all cared about clothes. "Never judge a stranger by his clothes," said Zachary Taylor, who lived up to his motto. Having become recognizable in his long linen duster and battered straw hat, the president was mistaken for an "old farmer going to market with eggs"

Mary Todd Lincoln, who was close friends with her dressmaker, the former slave Elizabeth Keckley, compulsively purchased clothes and raw materials, which she carried with her for nearly two decades in trunks.
Washingtonian Collection, Martin Luther King Public Library

when he appeared in a dingy green coat and cotton pants.

Most presidents have had their clothes tailor-made, while their shoes, ties, and casual clothes might be purchased from stores by a valet, a friend, or, on rare occasion, themselves. Since World War II, as the middle class emerged and leisure time increased, some presidents became role models for casual yet proper dress, and more attention was focused on what they wore. Kennedy's loafers, white chinos, polo shirt under a two-button blue blazer, and Wayfarer sunglasses all suggested a nautical look that took hold in the early sixties. If Ike could be seen in his cooking and barbecue apron, or rubber gaiters as he fished, so could any red-blooded American man. Others enhanced their public persona without setting a trend: LBJ in cowboy hat and boots, Jimmy Carter in cardigan sweater or T-shirt and cut-off blue jean shorts, Reagan in riding jodhpurs and white turtleneck sweater.

Although the fashion crowd might have hailed some wilder presidential tastes, at home it was often a different story. Truman's loud Hawaiian shirts in bright colors and wild prints were despised by his wife. She proved successful only in preventing him from wearing his red trousers in Florida. Nancy Reagan conspired with a presidential adviser to throw out a plaid suit of her husband's. Grover Cleveland finally got rid of a button-busting orange suit when he married: his wife insisted that the distinct color would alienate the vital block of "green" Irish—meaning Catholics—by showing preference for the orange color of Protestant Irish.

While many wives have dictated their husbands' fashions, several men developed their own distinct style. McKinley always wore a pink carnation in his buttonhole, set off by a black cravat and an immaculate white six-button vest, which he changed several times a day. Reflecting his era's love of sports celebrities like Bill Tilden, Jack Dempsey, and Knute Rockne, Harding was the first to bring a sporty look to work, often meeting with the press in his "plus-fours" (light wool golf knickers) and a jauntily tilted cap or a white boater. He also wore pinky diamond rings and a scarf pin. Herbert Hoover's starched, high-necked, rounded size 17 "Hoover collar" was more a function of convenience: when he had to change rapidly from work clothes to formal reception attire he could keep on the rather ambiguously styled shirt collar.

No president had a more particular sense of style than Chester Arthur. He ordered twenty-five coats at a time from his New York tailor, and once tried on twenty different trousers before he found a pair he deemed perfect. Whether in his tuxedo, gray silk vests, or fine tweeds, Arthur was described by one reporter as "the metropolitan gentleman, the member of clubs . . . who wears a scarf and a pin in it and prefers a sack coat to the long-tailed frock coat that pervades politics, and a Derby hat to the slouch that seems to be regarded . . . as something no statesman should be without—this is a novel species of President."

Arthur always made certain that his side-whiskers were trimmed neatly by his finicky valet, Alec Powell. John Adams was the only White House resident who wore a powdered wig. Jefferson left his hair gray and growing down his neck. Madison wore his white hair in a long queue, tied by his wife. Lincoln was elected without a beard but grew one to fill in his gaunt face in time for his inaugural. Grant shaved his beard only once, for a picture requested by his wife.

Most presidents in the nineteenth and early twentieth centuries were groomed by valets or

> ## Bearded and Mustached Presidents
>
> Abraham Lincoln, beard
> Ulysses Grant, beard and mustache
> Rutherford Hayes, beard and mustache
> James Garfield, beard and mustache
> Chester Arthur, sideburns and mustache
> Grover Cleveland, mustache
> Benjamin Harrison, beard and mustache
> Theodore Roosevelt, mustache
> William Howard Taft, mustache

other servants. Harrison put his Indianapolis barber on the federal payroll as a messenger; his only task was to cut the president's hair. Theodore Roosevelt was trimmed and shaved in his office before lunch, often receiving callers while he was being cleaned up. Coolidge sometimes had his hair cut while eating breakfast. Starting with Wilson, doorman John Mays began performing the task for presidents through Truman. Soon after, Washington barber Milton Pitts was on call for presidents from Eisenhower to Reagan. Perhaps the most famous incident involving a president's haircut occurred in 1993, when President Clinton had his hair trimmed on an idle Air Force One at the Los Angeles airport tarmac by a local stylist, while security prevented other planes from departing. The grooming habits of numerous presidents have

Gerald Ford putting away his tie in the presidential clothing closet.

GERALD R. FORD PRESIDENTIAL LIBRARY

managed to get into the news and have been used for political purposes: Reagan's claim that he never dyed his full head of dark hair provoked some critics to charge that he was lying; Jimmy Carter's decision to change the part in his hair at a time of high unpopularity led some commentators to conclude that he did so to change his image.

Not surprisingly, the presidents' wives' hairstyles were critically reviewed by the public. An Oregon politician ridiculed Mary Lincoln's rose headdress by saying she walked around with "a flower pot on her head." Frances Cleveland's girlish mistake of having shaved the nape of her neck clean to heighten her auburn bun became a national sensation for young women. One reporter recorded that women were spending up to ninety dollars a month to have their hair "à la Cleveland," and that the First Lady was hailed for setting the "example of simple and becoming hairdressing." Some women, like Edith Roosevelt, paid no attention to their hair; hers was always astray and falling out of its clips and combs.

With the increased attention on glamour that came with the film era, First Ladies took their hairstyles seriously. White House maid Maggie Rogers dressed Florence Harding's "marcelled wave" so tightly that the First Lady was rumored to wear a wig. Grace Coolidge was one of the few wives who went out to be shorn, getting her "horseshoe marcel" at the shop of Leon and Jules. She wanted to get a twenties "bob" but admitted "the President has his own ideas." When Bess Truman returned from Jill's Beauty Shop with a youthful forties "poodle cut," it was ridiculed in social columns until her husband angrily declared, "*Real* gentlemen prefer gray." Mamie Eisenhower's seemingly simple bangs and pixie cut were actually a complicated bit of engineering, carefully drawn by the head of the salon chain Elizabeth Arden herself, in a series of top-secret six-step drawings to be strictly followed by any Arden stylists who serviced the First Lady. When one *Life* photographer suggested that she alter the look, Mamie said she had "great respect for the judgment of photographers," but the bangs stayed because, she told a friend, "the whole nation is imitating me."

It was not long before hairstyling became an annoyance. Jackie Kennedy, whose much-copied bouffant was created by her New York stylist Kenneth, also found her long tresses criticized as looking "like a mop." Bewildered, she asked a reporter, "What does my hairdo have to do with my husband's ability to be president?" Under Pat Nixon came the "cosmetology room" in the family quarters, allowing for grooming in privacy, but it didn't end public interest. Hillary Clinton changed her hairstyle several times during her residency and was shocked at the press coverage it received. "If we ever want to get Bosnia off the front page," she cracked, "all I have to do is change my hair."

Barbara Bush's three-strand faux pearls provoked several manufacturers to copy them for

Lyndon B. Johnson getting a haircut in the presidential lavatory. The glass door to the shower he installed with the high-powered spray is in background, at left; entrance to commode is at right.

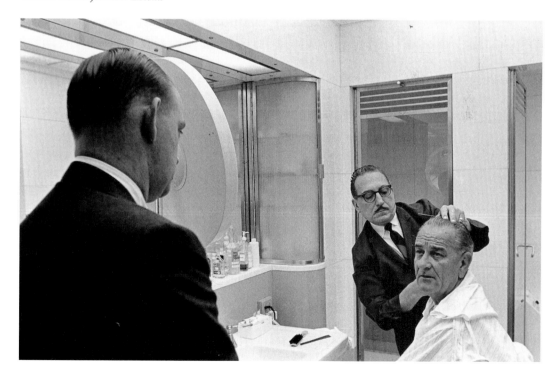

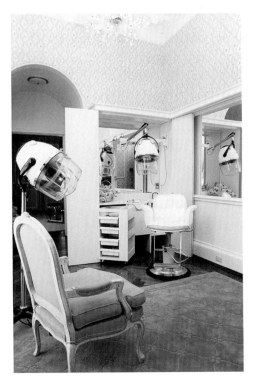

The "cosmetology room" created under the Nixons, where members of the First Family can have their hair styled and makeup applied before being photographed. As the room looked under the Reagans, 1981.
RONALD REAGAN PRESIDENTIAL LIBRARY

sale, but the jewelry tastes of most wives have been so sedate as to be hardly noticed: Mary Lincoln wore a cameo of her husband at her neck, set in jet stone; Lou Hoover wore no jewelry save for an occasional string of beads or stones; Mamie Eisenhower wore clip-on earrings from Woolworth's. It was their clothing that provoked public interest from the beginning. For women in nineteenth-century presidential families, their attire was usually made by servants working from fashion magazines. Certain accoutrements were ordered from specialty shops. Mary Todd Lincoln famously depended upon her friend and dressmaker, the former slave Elizabeth Keckley, to make her clothes. Even sickly Eliza Johnson, who rarely appeared in public, according to one employee, "always wore clothing of rich, expensive material . . . and employed the best dressmakers. . . ."

Other women took their chances by sending away for items. Jefferson's daughters Maria and Martha had wigs purchased for them by Dolley Madison, who, as First Lady, ordered many gowns for herself from France, through the American consul there. Sarah Polk and Edith Wilson both ordered gowns from Worth of Paris. Others, like Edith Roosevelt and Florence Harding, insisted on wearing only American-made clothing; by World War II, it was expected. Even then, there was criticism. When, for example, in the midst of recession and unemployment, it was learned that Nancy Reagan had unwittingly violated the Ethics in Government Act by accepting gifts of gowns from American designers, there was a firestorm of ridicule.

Attacks on First Ladies for what they wore were common. Ida McKinley was censured by the Audubon Society for wearing the feathers of the endangered egret in her hair. Abigail Adams criticized what an observer delicately described as Dolley Madison's "sylphic form 'thinly veiled' [which] displays all the graces of a Venus . . . " Reporters trailed Mary Lincoln on her shopping binges in New York department stores—though they did not discover her huge clothing debt. Fearing it would be disclosed and used against her husband's reelection

Margaret Taylor, whose photograph is previously unpublished, and the public engraving later adapted from it.
PRIVATE COLLECTION; LIBRARY OF CONGRESS

joked about his wife's expensive tastes but took pride in his increasing ability to spot a particular designer's creation. Carter bought his sentimental wife a red sweater on his first overseas trip as president—a present she cherished for decades. Taft even urged his wife to spend more money on gowns and less on street clothes. Grace Coolidge bought clothes only after getting her husband's advice, explaining, "I always like to have him with me when I am shopping. Oftentimes when I would be ready to quit and take a garment or hat, he would insist upon looking further and would encourage me to hold off until I found just what I wanted." Coolidge was famous for his window shopping, but Grace enjoyed poking into stores to see if she could go unnoticed. When asked if she knew that she looked like the First Lady, she replied honestly but briefly, "Yes." Margaret Truman enjoyed a similar game. In one store, she delighted in giving the address to which her purchases should be sent: 1600 Pennsylvania Avenue.

As with all families, those of presidents like to preserve their memories and lives in pictures. Many captured their own private moments in the White House. Ike renewed his earlier interest in photography, fascinated by a special 3-D camera. Jackie Kennedy, Frances Cleveland, and Grace Coolidge were among several First Lady shutterbugs. Lou Hoover made home movies, even editing them in a small White House room. More often children indulged in

Frances Cleveland posing for a bas-relief portrait by Augustus Saint Gaudens, summer of 1887.

ORIGINALLY APPEARED IN *Grover Cleveland*, 1910

photography, perhaps because they had more time, or could do so less conspicuously. Mary McKee's pictures of her children and niece provided a glimpse of a child's life in the Gay Nineties White House. Susan Ford apprenticed with the presidential photographer David Kennerly, transferring to the University of Kansas, where she studied photography, and even sold some of her work to a national magazine. Alan Arthur took many of the rare pictures that exist of his sister, once placing her on a horse on the South Lawn for a series of humorous images. Margaret Truman was her family camerawoman—until her father complained, "It's not enough that my homely countenance is at the mercy of the press—I have to have a photographer in the family?!"

It was not long before images of a president's family life were out of their control. John and Julia Tyler were the first incumbents to be photographed, in 1844, but within seven years images of the Fillmores were being reprinted en masse and sold through the studios of photographers like Mathew Brady, the most famous chronicler of mid-century presidential families. The "carte de visite," a small cardboard picture that the purchaser could place in a photo book—as if the president's family were their own—and then the larger "cabinet photo" and "stereographic cards" became popular items in American homes. Harriet Lane in the conservatory, Lincoln reading to his son Tad, Scott Hayes in costume, a group of Garfields: all were suddenly recognizable celebrities, quite literally public property. Already the manipulation of image was taking place. When Brady pulled up Lincoln's collar before taking a picture, the president cracked, "I see you want to shorten my neck." The Lincolns, then the Grants and their successors soon found that individual family photos were pasted into a photomontage suggesting blissful domesticity—and sold by the thousands, worthy of framed exhibition in the parlor. Soon the weekly illustrated

Margaret Truman snaps a picture of herself in her White House bedroom mirror.
HARRY S. TRUMAN PRESIDENTIAL LIBRARY

newspapers were carrying scenes of Nellie Grant's wedding—or creating imaginary scenes of Chet Arthur reading to his daughter. Each week, America could now seemingly peek into the family rooms for a homey moment. The Grants even let them. In posing at their vacation cottage for G. W. Pach, they became the first First Family to cooperate for a "candid" family group shot.

It was not long before the families attempted to regain some privacy. Mary Lincoln made certain she had the right to refuse any photographer from selling her image on cartes de visite until she gave her approval of the picture. Chester Arthur refused to let studios release any pictures of his children. Grover Cleveland banned almost all pictures of his three baby daughters—period. With the mobility of the camera, however, it became impossible to prevent the public from snapping pictures of the children in their daily lives. Edith Roosevelt devised a solution: she hired photographer Frances Benjamin Johnston to photograph what were

Dwight Eisenhower with a special Fifties "3-D" camera he used for family gatherings. Flanking him are wife, Mamie, and her mother, Elvira "Min" Doud.
DWIGHT D. EISENHOWER
PRESIDENTIAL LIBRARY

essentially straight portrait shots of the First Family—but in the halls, on the lawn, and behind the furniture of the private White House, providing an illusion of intimacy. These were then released on Mrs. Roosevelt's approval. Such arrangement proved evanescent. By the Taft era, the day of the White House press photographer had come and all semblance of a barrier between a president's private life and public life vanished. When William Howard Taft, in rumpled hat with his gut overhanging his belt, was photographed on the golf course, scribbling his scorecard, a president was captured disheveled, in shirt sleeves—enjoying himself. Just a few years earlier, Roosevelt was able to order a newspaper not to print candids of his daughter Alice getting her cash winnings from a bookie at the track. No more.

In Harding's first year the White House News Photographers Association was created. By Hoover's first year they were given their own room in the West Wing. Most covered presidents in official duties, but Florence Harding realized the power of a single image, and "photo opportunities" were now available for the "picture boys"—the Hardings with their dog, Mrs. Coolidge's grim mother walking down the driveway, Mrs. Hoover on horseback. The convergence of newer and lighter cameras—making for more candid shots—and FDR's concealment of his disability, brought a ban on the use of the new cameras. During World War II, military and other government agency photographers began chronicling official events and releasing photos to the press; many such events included family. National Park Service photographer Abbie Rowe became the first real, though unofficial, White House photographer, capturing many pictures of the Trumans and Eisenhowers—often self-consciously posed.

Florence Harding using a hand-cranked "moving picture" camera.
LIBRARY OF CONGRESS

Jackie Kennedy sought to control photographs of her family, thanking one press photographer for the "incredibly decent gesture" of not snapping Caroline. *Look* photographer Stanley Tretick—who had been given access to the family by the president—recalled that she "struck terror" by firmly asking, "Oh, now you're not here to photograph us, are you, Stanley?" As a former newspaper photographer herself, Jackie loved the visual and worked closely with Army Signal Corps photographer Cecil Stoughton on setting up family shots and giving him access for spontaneous moments, resulting in intimate color pictures. But, "despite the constant entreaties of the photographers, the president was never seen to kiss his wife in public," recalled a member of the White House press corps. "Such displays of affection before cameras he considered to be in bad taste."

Not so for LBJ or Gerald Ford. Both hired professional photographers, Yoichi Okamoto and David Kennerly, respectively. It had not been long after the end of World War II that wire service photographs captured Truman in his swimming trunks; the same happened to JFK, LBJ, Ford, Reagan, and Clinton (Nixon never took his shirt off, and Bush always wore at least a T-shirt), simultaneously demystifying and humanizing them. LBJ and Ford regained the upper hand by having their photographers take most of these sort of images, and then themselves selecting the best of the intimate moments for the press: Ford is seen at his wife's bedside after surgery or hugging his son before he leaves home; LBJ gets his hair cut in the bathroom and watches television in bed with his wife. Unparalleled access by official White House photographers did not mean the family couldn't still censor a cigarette, a drink, or an unflattering profile from pictures.

Bill Clinton and his brother Roger capture each other on videotape at a family Christmas gathering in the Yellow Oval Room.
THE WHITE HOUSE

Soon enough, the White House manipulated such images for political purposes. Under the expertise of Reagan photographer Michael Evans, formerly of *Time,* former actors Ronald and Nancy Reagan brought a new sophistication to the photo op. For the couple, holding a smile or pose or grimace or some other emotional expression for the sole purpose of being photographed was easier than it had been for their predecessors: they'd been trained earlier to do so. The color coordination of clothes with backdrops, lighting, and often even a small "X" to mark where the Reagans should stand all resulted in evocative and stirring pictures without the couple having to sacrifice their real privacy. "Reagan likes his time alone, to read or be with his wife," Evans confessed. "He doesn't want me spending every waking moment with him."

Earlier families had similar problems. Reproduction engravings were copied from the oil portraits of presidential family members, etched into wood and later steel plates, then put through a printing press. Thousands of cardboard prints were mass-produced—and sold to the public. Thus the images of presidents' relatives like Tyler's daughter-in-law or Van Buren's son were soon made available to the public by engravers like Henry Inman. Painters profited by the proliferation of their portrait adaptations of First Families, notably Gilbert Stuart. Abigail Adams, for one, was angry with Stuart for concentrating on his profitable copies rather than completing her portrait. A woodcut engraving of Dolley Madison made her the first First Lady to appear on the cover of a national magazine, the *Port Folio.*

Presidents took firmer control with the portrait artist, devising the image they wanted to have preserved—knowing that engravings would be struck. Tyler, Polk, Fillmore, Pierce, and Buchanan appeared with important documents rolled in their hands or maps in the background. First Ladies were posed in White House chairs and sofas. A water fountain is painted beside temperance advocate Lucy Hayes, a Daughters of the American Revolution pin is on its first president, Caroline Harrison. It was perhaps little wonder that Jefferson destroyed images of his late wife to truly preserve her as his own—or that Andrew Jackson placed a larger-than-life swashbuckling portrait of himself on public display in the East Room, when in reality he was a sickly, broken old man, often unable to rise from his bed or chair.

Even after photography captured what they really looked like, families persisted in shaping their images through the context in which they had their *official* portraits painted. Presidential portraits had been hung as early as the Madison administration; Julia Tyler donated her portrait to Andrew Johnson to begin a collection of First Ladies. The Grants placed an over-

First Lady Hillary Clinton being photographed by Annie Liebovitz for the cover of Vogue, *in the Red Room.*
THE WHITE HOUSE

Not yet three years old, John Kennedy had practically been born with a camera before him, despite his mother's efforts to shield him from publicity.

JOHN F. KENNEDY PRESIDENTIAL LIBRARY

poweringly large group portrait of themselves in the Red Room as the quintessential wealthy, healthy Gilded Age dynasty. Mrs. Bush and Mrs. Coolidge included their pets in their portraits (the Coolidges' dog, a white collie named Rob Roy, had to be held in place by friends and fed candy). Florence Harding and Mamie Eisenhower, both looking younger in oil, sent out pictures of their portraits on request—instead of photographs. Reagan and LBJ rejected their first portraits. The second attempts projected the images they wished to convey. No amount of paint, however, can cover the physical cost of being president. "It would belabor the obvious," wrote Lady Bird Johnson, "to say that every time I pass the portrait of President Woodrow Wilson—painted when the strains of office lay heavily upon him—it says to me: 'Have his [LBJ's] portrait painted soon.'"

Not every family worried about the invasion of their privacy at the hands of the "ghouls," as Cleveland called the press. As he was being chased by a cameraman one day and asked to stop and pose, only when Coolidge got into his limousine did he acknowledge the man. Then he calmly leaned out the window and said, "Next time, George, take the cap off your lens."

18

Farewells and Reunions

I am heartily rejoiced that my term is so near its close.

—President James Polk

That the White House will be left willingly by both Mrs. Hayes and myself is perfectly true. Indeed, "gladly," might truthfully be substituted for "willingly." We have on the whole enjoyed our four years here. But the responsibility, the embarrassments, the heartbreaking sufferings which we can't relieve, the ever present danger of scandals . . . and a thousand other drawbacks . . . leave us no place for regret upon retiring from this conspicuous scene.

—President Rutherford Hayes

Few of them like to leave. From the moment they know they will be coming to live in the White House, however, First Families also realize that their occupancy will be eight years at most. Even though the Eisenhowers were the first limited to that time by law, all presidents except FDR honored the two-term tradition.

A skilled diplomat, Buchanan was exhausted and frustrated by the onset of civil war and only too relieved to leave the presidency to Abraham Lincoln.

GEORGE EASTMAN HOUSE

Presidents Who Served One Term or Less, by Defeat, Choice, or Death

John Adams, defeat
John Quincy Adams, defeat
Martin Van Buren, defeat
William Henry Harrison, death
John Tyler, choice
James Polk, choice
Zachary Taylor, death
Millard Fillmore, choice
Franklin Pierce, choice
James Buchanan, choice
Andrew Johnson, choice
Rutherford Hayes, choice
James Garfield, assassination
Chester Arthur, choice
Benjamin Harrison, defeat
William Howard Taft, defeat
Warren Harding, death
Herbert Hoover, defeat
John F. Kennedy, assassination
Gerald Ford, defeat
Jimmy Carter, defeat
George Bush, defeat

*Grover Cleveland served two terms but was defeated after his first term and chose not to run after his second, non-consecutive term; Abraham Lincoln, William McKinley, and Franklin Roosevelt were elected to more than one term but did not live to completion of it.

Understandably, those who left with the most bittersweet emotions were the families of presidents who failed in their bid for reelection. John Adams only half-jokingly sniped at Jefferson, when the two first saw each other after the 1800 election, "You have put me out!" The political struggle between Grover Cleveland and Benjamin Harrison through two election cycles resulted in triumph and defeat for both men. Incumbent Cleveland had to relinquish his residency to Harrison in 1888, claiming that there was "no happier man in the United States" than himself. Perhaps, but four years later he came back and beat Harrison, thus becoming the only man to occupy the White House for eight years with a four-year hiatus in between. By 1892, with his wife having died just weeks before the election, Harrison, according to the chief usher, "felt his defeat coming on" and was in an "almost indifferent mood" about moving out. Often wives are more insulted at defeat. Throughout the morning of her departure, Lou Hoover felt bruised, but defiantly predicted that her husband "will live to do great things for his country." After her husband's defeat, Rosalynn Carter said she was "bitter enough for the both of us."

Save for the Clevelands' first vacancy, only twenty-one of the forty White House families left the mansion as hoped; the others departed by defeat, death, and resignation. Most who left by their own design, on schedule, were satisfied with their turn at history but eagerly anticipated a break with public life and obligations. There are notable exceptions. Although they did not seek immediate reelection, Tyler, Grant, and Theodore Roosevelt—and their families—still wanted to

live in the White House; the latter two would later unsuccessfully attempt to win back the presidency. Andrew Johnson fought to nullify his Senate impeachment trial—by being elected to that body and returning to Washington. Elizabeth Monroe, Jackson, Polk, Abigail Fillmore, Jane Pierce, Arthur, Wilson, Coolidge, Eisenhower, and LBJ all left with health problems. Reagan spoke of wanting a third term and promised to work to amend the Constitution to permit his successors to do so. Clinton, a relatively young man, was left with great energy but no more official position toward which to direct it.

As the final months wind down to the final days, First Families have naturally experienced a full range of emotions. The entire congregation of Sarah Polk's church came en masse several days before she left the mansion to hail her. In her waning days, Mamie Eisenhower put all her energy into creating the most spectacular holiday season of her eight years, inviting friends and associates from all walks of life to come see her and Ike before they left. As they were preparing to leave, the modest Andrew Johnson family, who had made no social sparks, suddenly found themselves deluged with praise from all directions. "No better persons have occupied the executive mansion," Navy Secretary Gideon Welles wrote in his diary. "They leave Washington with spotless reputations," editorialized one newspaper. "They have received no presents, no carriages, no costly plate, they have dispensed a liberal hospitality."

Other families were virtually ignored. John Quincy and Louisa Adams had a grim time in the weeks preceding their forced retirement from the mansion, in 1829. "The year begins in gloom," he noted in his diary on January 1. "My wife had a sleepless and painful night. The dawn was overcast, and, as I began to write, my lamp went out, self-extinguished. . . . The

Pat Nixon kisses Luci Johnson Nugent after completing her tour of the private quarters with Lady Bird Johnson. Her daughter Tricia Nixon is at far left.

notice of so trivial an incident may serve to mark the present temper of my mind." Adams felt that his "character and reputation [are] a wreck," and that the "sun of my political life sets in the deepest gloom." He planned to go "into the deepest retirement and withdraw from all connections with public affairs." Perhaps most forlorn was stroke victim Woodrow Wilson, who was further depressed by the overwhelming Republican victory in the Senate, which rejected his vision of a League of Nations. Edith Wilson distracted herself from the pain of what seemed like a crushing end by overseeing the decorating of the local house to which they were retiring.

First Ladies are left with the brunt of packing and shipping their family possessions before the new First Family moves in on Inauguration Day. Part of that ritual now includes a tour of the private quarters for her successor. When the guest happens to be the spouse of the man whose election is forcing the incumbents to leave, it can make for a tense afternoon. After taking Eleanor Roosevelt all through the house in 1932, Lou Hoover stopped at the doors of the kitchen—which the incoming First Lady specifically wanted to see. "I'm sorry, but the house-

In the Solarium, Richard Nixon hugs his daughter Julie after affirming his decision to resign the presidency. His daughter Tricia and her husband, Ed Cox, at left.

NIXON PRESIDENTIAL MATERIALS, NATIONAL ARCHIVES

keeper will have to show you the kitchens," said Mrs. Hoover. "I never go into the kitchens." They shook hands, and Eleanor went through the swinging doors to speak with the help. Nancy Reagan detected a "chill" in Rosalynn Carter's reluctance to take her into the family rooms in 1980, scattered with shipping boxes, but said she understood given the loss of the election.

Even those presidential wives whose husbands had not sought reelection found it difficult to accommodate the women who would shortly be running "their" house. A condescending Edith Wilson found an uncertain Florence Harding "so effusive, so voluble, that after a half-hour over the teacups I could hardly stem the torrent of words to send for the housekeeper." Resentful that Edith wouldn't personally guide her through, Florence told the housekeeper right there that she'd be fired—but she backed down later. Recovering from cesarean surgery, Jackie Kennedy was told by her doctor that she could tour the White House only in a wheel-chair. Informed, Mamie Eisenhower had a chair available for use—but only if Jackie asked for

In the family room, watching presidential election returns, election night 1976, Betty Ford seated on floor with Pearl Bailey, son Steve Ford in foreground drinking coffee, son Mike at far left, vice presidential candidate's wife Elizabeth Dole on ottoman. In the same room, some ten weeks later, Gerald Ford sits with all the family possessions now packed on the last day of his presidency.
GERALD R. FORD PRESIDENTIAL LIBRARY

George and Barbara Bush take a last walk around the south grounds, near the moving truck transporting their possessions home to Texas. On the last day of his presidency, following his defeat in 1992.

it, which she did not. On the verge of collapse, Jackie was faced with the family rooms dominated by "Mamie pink," and later compared the place to the Lubianka, the Russian prison. Indeed, after Bess Truman took Mamie on her tour in 1952, the outgoing First Lady warned the staff that they would be seeing "a lot of pink." On her 1992 tour, Hillary Clinton noted the many television sets through the family quarters of the Bushes, and determined to have just one—so as not to have her family life dominated by constant breaking news and world crisis. Incoming tenants can't seem to help noting what they'll change. During the first such tour, hosted by Edith Roosevelt on March 2, 1909, Nellie Taft whispered loudly enough for Edith to hear, "I would have put that table over there."

In the nineteenth century, there were farewell balls and private dinners hosted by the outgoing family for the incoming. Van Buren warmly invited William Henry Harrison—the man who defeated him—for dinner in the mansion, saying that the two happiest days of his life in the White House were his "entrance" and "surrender of it." The Polks turned down the invitation of John and Julia Tyler to her grand ball of a thousand candles and ninety-six bottles of champagne, and even the offer to take early occupancy. When Julia's sister Margaret

Outgoing President William Howard Taft (left) leaves the White House with his successor, president-elect Woodrow Wilson, on right. Taft would come back to the house for a full lunch before finally leaving. He returned many times as a guest some eight years later when he had been appointed Chief Justice of the Supreme Court.

Jacqueline Kennedy and her son in their last hour in the White House, posing with some household staff members in the emptied West Sitting Hall.

A rare gathering of an incumbent First Lady and her predecessors. Left to right, Nancy Reagan, Lady Bird Johnson, Hillary Clinton, Rosalynn Carter, Betty Ford, and Barbara Bush. Jacqueline Onassis, ill at the time, died a week after this picture was taken. 1994. THE WHITE HOUSE

heard that Mrs. Polk would not use the federal appropriation to refurbish the family rooms, she pronounced her "monstrously small." Tyler further indulged Julia's ego by remarking, "Imagine, the idea of her being able to follow you!"

That the Grants' private dinner for the incoming Hayeses had a large guest list masked a political purpose. With the election in dispute—there was concern about having no president for twenty-four hours—Grant's term officially ended on a Sunday, but the official swearing-in ceremony was not scheduled until Monday. On Saturday night, Grant had Hayes spirited into the Red Room for a few moments with the chief justice. As guests promenaded into dinner with Julia Grant and Lucy Hayes, who were escorted by their eldest sons, Hayes was sworn into the presidency with Grant watching; it was the first time a president took the oath before his inaugural date, and in the mansion.

By 1893, the dinner had become a private meal involving the outgoing and incoming families—in this case, Harrison and his daughter Mary, and Grover and Frances Cleveland. So disastrous was the 1909 dinner hosted by the Roosevelts for the Tafts the night before the

Edith Roosevelt, in white, returns for her only visit back to the White House, joining incumbents Lou and Herbert Hoover.
LIBRARY OF CONGRESS

inaugural that it ended the tradition. Edith Roosevelt was crying the whole night, and daughter Alice so resented being replaced that she buried a voodoo doll in the lawn to curse the new family. The discord was exacerbated by the negative publicity focused on Edith's request to Taft that she be permitted to purchase and take a favorite antique sofa belonging to the White House.

Political tensions inevitably manipulate the human emotions of the families. As president-elect, Mexican War hero Zachary Taylor, who felt President Polk hadn't given him much credit during the war, refused to make the expected courtesy call. Polk then ordered his cabinet not to acknowledge Taylor. Not until a senator made peace between the factions did the Polks invite Taylor for dinner and his first walk through his new home. Resentful of the radical changes to social life that came with the Lincoln election and in anticipation of civil war, Buchanan's niece Harriet compared the new president to an awkward doorman and called his wife "western, loud and unrefined." When Franklin and Eleanor Roosevelt with their son and daughter-in-law, James and Betsey, came to call on the Hoovers on March 3, 1933, in the midst of a banking crisis, the president was delayed for a half-hour. FDR told him, "Mr. President, I know how busy you must be, so I suggest that it would be all right if you don't make the customary return call on me at the hotel." At this, Hoover snapped to the man who defeated him, "Mr. Roosevelt, when you have been in Washington as long as I have been, you will learn that the President of the United States calls on nobody." Although some presidents-elect would telephone or confer with their predecessor just before the inaugural, the Hoover-FDR confrontation put an end to the requisite social call.

As furniture and clothing, portraits and photographs, high chairs and armchairs, and the hundreds of books, papers, and other items are crated and sent ahead to the outgoing family's residence, the departure day arrives. In earlier years, the transition could be dismal. The Fillmores got themselves out of the mansion in time to relinquish it for Pierce on Inauguration Day. They moved into a hotel until all of their possessions were ready for ship-

Lady Bird Johnson holds a reunion of those who once lived in the mansion. In the front row, presidential granddaughters Julia Grant, with cane, and Marthena Harrison, beside her. 1966.
LYNDON BAINES JOHNSON LIBRARY

ping. An unexpected Inauguration Day storm scared the staff, who quit early, leaving the packed Fillmore crates mixed with the incoming Pierce boxes. The delay proved portentous. At the inaugural, Abigail Fillmore caught pneumonia in the storm. She never left her Willard Hotel suite and died there twenty-six days after moving out of the mansion.

Others were humiliated in their leaving. John Quincy Adams, mustering what graciousness he could for his hated successor, Andrew Jackson, sent him a note on suggested moving and household arrangements. Jackson ignored it and let it be known that Adams was not welcome at the inaugural. Adams simply walked out of the mansion and up a hill two miles to the retirement house he had bought. The day before his inaugural, Grant announced that he wouldn't ride with his predecessor, Andrew Johnson, to the ceremony. Eliza Johnson had already moved out of the mansion into the local home of a family friend, and her son and daughter Frank and Mary were already back in Tennessee, getting the house ready for the family's arrival. That morning, daughter Martha departed after making sure the mansion was cleaned for the Grants. Alone, Johnson worked in his office while Grant was being inaugurated. At noon, when he was technically no longer the chief executive, he bid farewell to the gathered staff on the North Portico, got into his carriage, and left without notice.

Vacating the White House was somewhat easier on earlier families, none of whom were rushed out at a specific day or time. Some left days before the inaugural, staying with local friends or at hotels, giving the new family extra time to move in. Several families remained in town for days or weeks because of poor traveling conditions or the desire to begin retirement more slowly. Others stayed in the White House beyond the end of a presidency for health or logistical reasons.

Hours after James Madison had taken the duties off his shoulders, Jefferson was so delighted with his freedom that he attended the Inaugural Ball, asking around how to behave because he hadn't been to a dance in some forty years. Earlier that day he and his grandson rode horseback up to the Capitol for Madison's inaugural. After the ceremony, the two presidents received guests together in the mansion. Tall, exuberant, Jefferson easily overshadowed the new president. That evening, Jefferson slept one more night in the White House—at the invitation of the new president, Madison, who remained in his private home. Andrew Jackson took *two weeks* to move out of the home that was no longer his and relinquish it to Van Buren.

On each transitional inaugural since 1921, the outgoing family has waited with other officials in the vestibule or a room for the new family to arrive. Together all the principals leave for the ceremony—but only the incoming family returns to the mansion. The very last moments a family has in the house before the new tenants arrive encompass a gamut of emotions. The Eisenhowers asked that the entire household staff line up in the hall of the state floor to be thanked personally by Ike and Mamie. The Coolidges gave out little gifts to the

One White House bride to another: Tricia Nixon talks to Alice Roosevelt Longworth.

NIXON PRESIDENTIAL MATERIALS

Jacqueline Kennedy Onassis, during a fund-raising dinner for the Kennedy Library in Washington, D.C., attended by the president and Mrs. Reagan. 1985.

RONALD REAGAN PRESIDENTIAL LIBRARY

staff. Frances Cleveland burst into tears, sobbing as she departed the house she had entered as a twenty-one-year-old bride and was leaving as a thirty-one-year-old mother of three. Bess Truman tried to calm her husband's rage at his angry successor Eisenhower's refusal to come into the house for coffee. Ronald Reagan spent his last hour in his office, feeding the squirrels that always came for acorns at the doors, while Nancy was nervously rechecking her bureau drawers to be certain she had not left anything. Her secretary finally assured her that if "you leave something behind, they'll send it to you. They have your address."

Others held tight to the last moments of glory. The Hayeses stayed with the Garfields through Inauguration Day and reviewed the parade with them, the children of both families having become so close that they had played together on the South Lawn in the snow a few days earlier. Arthur not only reviewed Cleveland's parade with the new president but left his side on the reviewing stand and went back into the home that was no longer his, ready for *his* lunch. He even stuck around for Cleveland's Inaugural Ball and formally received guests there, promenading about.

Julia Grant continued postponing the moment she would have to vacate by hosting an impromptu post–inaugural ceremony luncheon in the White House, then leisurely strolling through the rooms one last time. While Helen Taft breezily walked out of the house and down the driveway, her mother, Nellie, skipped the Wilson inaugural and lingered in the mansion, writing her last letters on White House stationery. The chief usher finally had to try to coax her out, lifting her spirits by reminding her that the Clevelands had once returned to the mansion after having been evicted. Meanwhile, her husband, gleeful former president Taft returned to the mansion after Wilson had been sworn in, joining him in a hearty luncheon there. "I'm glad to be going," Taft told Wilson. "This is the lonesomest place in the world."

Families Who Left the White House Suddenly

The William Henry Harrison family, death of the president, 1841

The Zachary Taylor family, death of the president, 1850

The Abraham Lincoln family, assassination of the president in second term, 1865

The James Garfield family, assassination of the president, 1881

The William McKinley family, assassination of the president in second term, 1901

The Warren Harding family, death of the president, 1923

The Franklin D. Roosevelt family, death of the president in fourth term, 1945

The John F. Kennedy family, assassination of the president, 1963

The Richard Nixon family, resignation of the president in second term, 1974

Before they left the city, both the outgoing Eisenhowers and the Johnsons were honored by friends at luncheons. However, leaving directly from the Capitol grounds at the conclusion of the inaugural ceremonies of those succeeding them, the Fords, Carters, Reagans, and Bushes helicoptered to Andrews Air Force Base and flew home. The only child among this group, Amy Carter, burst into tears on the stairs into the jet as she looked back on the tarmac and saw school friends.

Nine families left in tragedy—eight deaths, one resignation. It is uncertain how long the large William Henry Harrison clan stayed in the mansion after his death. Just four days after to christen the Website of the National First Ladies Library, while Laura Bush—another daughter-in-law—looked on, in her capacity as a governor's spouse.

Many times, political position is what brings former residents back. As Kennedy's commerce undersecretary, Franklin Roosevelt Jr. was frequently in the mansion to attend meetings and to socialize. In his capacity as a lawyer, railroad chairman, ambassador, and secretary of war, Robert Lincoln was a familiar face in the house, from Grant to Harding. Sometimes, having had residency in the White House has political influence with a current resident. After the Civil War, Mary Donelson, Jackson's great-niece who was born in the mansion, worked rather anonymously as a government clerk in Washington. When President Grant learned her identity she became a frequent

Presidents Who Served Two Full Terms

George Washington
Thomas Jefferson
James Madison
James Monroe
Andrew Jackson
Ulysses Grant
Grover Cleveland (non-consecutive)
Woodrow Wilson
Franklin Roosevelt
Dwight Eisenhower
Ronald Reagan

White House guest; when he discovered that she was a multi-linguist, he named her translator of foreign languages at the postal department.

Being born in the White House was so rarified an event that when Grant's granddaughter Julia Cantacuzene was invited back there by President McKinley, he insisted on escorting her arm-in-arm to the room where she first entered the world. She kept coming back. A half-century later, she joined children of both Roosevelts, Taft, Wilson, Coolidge, and grandchildren of Harrison and Hoover for a large First Families reunion hosted by Mamie Eisenhower. When Lady Bird Johnson repeated the custom, Mrs. Cantacuzene was there again, at ninety-two years.

Present at both reunions, of course, was Alice Roosevelt Longworth. A guest at dinners, dances, lectures, concerts, balls, lawn parties, and every other imaginable form of entertainment under every president from Taft to Ford, from 1909 to 1976, she obviously relished coming home. Longworth was perhaps the most frequently invited guest to the White House in its two-hundred-year history. "If the Communists take over the White House tomorrow," said a friend of hers in 1974, "Mrs. L would be one of the first people invited for dinner. And Mrs. L would be the first person to accept the invitation." Alice herself admitted that by 1970 she had had approximately "2.7 dinners a year in the White House—no matter *who* is President." Upon further reflection she added, "Nobody likes to leave."

Members of All the White House Families

It is impossible to enter the White House and not be touched by the lives of those who have come before.
—*First Lady Hillary Clinton*

The following list represents those family members who either had residency in the White House for the entire term of an administration, came for lengthy stays (as was often the case in the early nineteenth century), or were frequently visiting the White House but did not necessarily stay there (more commonly the case in the later twentieth century) and were closely associated with their relative's presidency. It is as inclusive a list as possible *but not exhaustive.* The core family residents who lived in the mansion nearly continuously, or from their birth or marriage, or until their death or marriage, and considered the White House their primary residence are marked with an asterisk (*). Unless otherwise identified, each member is listed in relation to the president.

John Adams, March 4, 1797–March 4, 1801
*John Adams
*Abigail Smith Adams, wife
*Thomas Adams, son
*Suzannah Adams, granddaughter (daughter of Charles Adams)
*William "Billy" Shaw, nephew of Abigail Adams
    (son of Elizabeth Smith Shaw)
*Louisa Smith, niece of Abigail Adams (daughter of William Smith)

Thomas Jefferson, March 4, 1801–March 4, 1809

*Thomas Jefferson, widower
Maria "Polly" Jefferson Eppes, daughter
John Wayles "Jack" Eppes, son-in-law
Francis Eppes, grandson
Martha "Patsy" Jefferson Randolph, daughter
Thomas Mann Randolph, son-in-law
Anne Randolph, granddaughter
Thomas Jefferson "Jeff" Randolph, grandson
Ellen Randolph, granddaughter
Cornelia Randolph, granddaughter
Virginia Randolph, granddaughter
Mary Randolph, granddaughter
James Madison Randolph, grandson, born in the White House

James Madison, March 4, 1809–March 4, 1817

*James Madison
*Dolley Payne Todd Madison, wife
Payne Todd, Dolley Madison's son by her first marriage
Anna Payne Cutts, Dolley Madison's sister
Richard Cutts, Dolley Madison's brother-in-law
James Madison Cutts, nephew of Dolley Madison (son of Anna Payne Cutts)
Thomas Cutts, nephew of Dolley Madison (son of Anna Payne Cutts)
Walter Coles Cutts, nephew of Dolley Madison (son of Anna Payne Cutts)
Richard Dominicus Cutts, nephew of Dolley Madison (son of Anna Payne Cutts)
Dolley Payne Cutts, niece of Dolley Madison (daughter of Anna Payne Cutts)
Mary Estelle Cutts, niece of Dolley Madison (daughter of Anna Payne Cutts)
Lucy Payne Washington Todd, Dolley Madison's sister
Samuel Walter Washington, nephew of Dolley Madison (son of Lucy Payne Washington Todd)
William Temple Washington, nephew of Dolley Madison (son of Lucy Payne Washington Todd)
George Steptoe Washington, nephew of Dolley Madison (son of Lucy Payne Washington Todd)
John G. Jackson, Dolley Madison's brother-in-law (widower of her sister Mary Payne Jackson)
John C. Payne, Dolley Madison's brother
*Edward "Ned" Coles, Dolly Madison's maternal cousin (son of Dolley Madison's mother's cousin John Coles)
Sally Coles, Dolley Madison's maternal cousin (daughter of Dolley Madison's mother's cousin John Coles)
William C. Preston, Dolley Madison's maternal cousin (son of Dolley Madison's third cousin Sally Campbell)
probably James Madison Hite, nephew (son of James Madison's sister Nelly), or James, John, Alfred, William, or Robert Madison (sons of James Madison's brother William)

James Monroe, March 4, 1817–March 4, 1825

*James Monroe
*Elizabeth Kortright Monroe, wife
*Eliza Monroe Hay, daughter

*George Hay, son-in-law

*Hortensia Hay, granddaughter

Maria Monroe Gouverneur, daughter

Hester Gouverneur, sister of Elizabeth Monroe

Samuel L. Gouverneur, son-in-law and Elizabeth Monroe's nephew

James Gouverneur, grandson, born in the White House

Elizabeth Gouverneur, granddaughter

Samuel Gouverneur Jr., grandson

Joseph J. Monroe, brother and briefly private secretary of James Monroe

Elizabeth Glasscock Monroe, sister-in-law (wife of Joseph Monroe)

James Monroe II, nephew (son of Joseph Monroe)

John Quincy Adams, March 4, 1825–March 4, 1829

*John Quincy Adams

*Louisa Catherine Johnson Adams, wife

Charles Francis Adams, son

John Adams, son

George Washington Adams, son

*Mary Catherine Hellen Adams, niece of Louisa Adams (by her sister Nancy Hellen) and daughter-in-law (wife of John Adams)

*Mary Louisa "Looly" Adams, granddaughter (daughter of John Adams)

*Abigail Smith Adams, niece of John Quincy Adams (daughter of Charles Adams)

Johnson Hellen, nephew of Louisa Adams (by her sister Nancy Hellen)

Thomas Hellen, nephew of Louisa Adams (by her sister Nancy Hellen)

Andrew Jackson, March 4, 1829–March 4, 1837

*Andrew Jackson, widower

Andrew Jackson "Jack" Donelson, nephew of late Mrs. Andrew Jackson (by her brother Samuel Donelson)

Emily Donelson, wife and cousin of Andrew Donelson, niece of late Mrs. Andrew Jackson (by her brother John)

Andrew Jackson "AJ" Donelson, great-nephew, son of Jack and Emily Donelson

Mary Rachel "Mary" Donelson, great-niece, daughter of Jack and Emily Donelson, born in the White House

John Samuel Donelson, great-nephew, son of Jack and Emily Donelson, born in the White House

Rachel Donelson, great-niece, daughter of Jack and Emily Donelson, born in the White House

Andrew "Andy" Jackson Jr., adopted son, nephew of late Mrs. Andrew Jackson (son of Severn Donelson)

Sarah Yorke Jackson, wife of adopted son

Rachel Jackson, adoptive granddaughter

Andrew Jackson III, adoptive grandson

Thomas Jefferson Jackson, adoptive grandson

Ralph E. W. Earle, widowed husband of Jane Caffery, great-niece of late Mrs. Andrew Jackson (by her sister Mary)

Elizabeth Martin, great-niece of late Mrs. Andrew Jackson, relation uncertain

Andrew Jackson Hutchings, nephew of late Mrs. Andrew Jackson (by her sister Catherine)

Daniel Donelson, nephew of late Mrs. Andrew Jackson (by her brother Samuel Donelson)

Samuel Jackson Hays, nephew of late Mrs. Andrew Jackson (by her sister Jane Hays)

Mary Eastin, great-niece of late Mrs. Andrew Jackson (by her brother John's daughter Rachel Eastin)

Mary McLemore, great-niece of late Mrs. Andrew Jackson (by her brother John's daughter Elizabeth McLemore)

Mary Coffee, great-niece of late Mrs. Andrew Jackson (by her brother John's daughter Mary Coffee)

Martin Van Buren, March 4, 1837–March 4, 1841
*Martin Van Buren, widower
*John Van Buren, son
*Martin Van Buren Jr., son
*Smith Van Buren, son
*Abraham Van Buren, son
*Angelica Singleton Van Buren, daughter-in-law
*Rebecca Van Buren, granddaughter (daughter of Abraham Van Buren), born in the White House
 Marion Singleton, sister of Angelica Van Buren
 Richard Singleton, father of Angelica Van Buren
 Rebecca Coles Singleton, mother of Angelica Van Buren

William Henry Harrison, March 4, 1841–April 4, 1841
*William Henry Harrison
*Jane Irwin Harrison, daughter-in-law (wife of William Henry Harrison Jr.)
*James Harrison, grandson (son of William Henry Harrison Jr.)
*William Henry Harrison III, grandson (son of William Henry Harrison Jr.)
*Montgomery Pike Harrison, grandson (son of John Cleves Harrison, the president's son)
*Lucy Taylor, niece (daughter of Lucy Singleton, the president's sister)
*William H. H. Taylor, great-nephew (son of Lucy Taylor)
*Benjamin Harrison, nephew (son of Benjamin Harrison, the president's brother)
*Henry Harrison, great-nephew (son of Benjamin Harrison, the president's nephew)
*David O. Coupeland, nephew (son of Anne Harrison, the president's sister)
*probably Anna Harrison Taylor, daughter (also married to first cousin William H. H. Taylor)
*probably William H. H. Taylor Jr., grandson (son of Anna Taylor and William H. H. Taylor)
*probably Lucy or Anna Taylor, granddaughter (daughter of Anna Taylor and William H. H. Taylor)
*Jane Irwin Findlay, aunt and adoptive mother of Jane Harrison
*possibly two daughters of Jane Irwin Findlay

John Tyler, April 4, 1841–March 4, 1845
*John Tyler
*Letitia Christian Tyler, first wife
*John Tyler Jr., son
*Letitia "Letty" Tyler Semple, daughter
*Elizabeth "Lizzie" Tyler, daughter
*Alice Tyler, daughter
*Tazewell Tyler, son
*Robert Tyler, son

*Priscilla Cooper Tyler, daughter-in-law (wife of Robert Tyler)

*Mary Fairlee Tyler, granddaughter (daughter of Robert Tyler)

*Letitia Tyler, granddaughter (daughter of Robert Tyler), born in the White House

 Louisa Cooper, sister of president's daughter-in-law (Priscilla Cooper Tyler)

 Mary Tyler Jones, daughter

 Henry Lightfoot Jones, son-in-law

 John Tyler Jones, grandson

 Henry Jones Jr., grandson

 Robert Jones, grandson, born in the White House

*Julia Gardiner Tyler, second wife

 Margaret Gardiner, sister-in-law

 Julianna Gardiner, mother-in-law

 Alex Gardiner, brother-in-law

 David Gardiner Jr., brother-in-law

James Polk, March 4, 1845–March 4, 1849

*James Knox Polk

*Sarah Childress Polk, wife

*James Knox Walker, nephew of James Polk (son of Jane Maria Polk Walker, the president's sister)

*Augusta Walker, niece by marriage, wife of James Walker

*four children of James Walker, two born in the White House

*Samuel Walker, nephew (son of Jane Maria Polk Walker)

 Jane Walker Barnett, niece (daughter of Jane Maria Polk Walker)

 Isaac Barnett, husband of president's niece Jane Walker Barnett

 Joanna Rucker, niece of Sarah Polk (daughter of Susan Childress Rucker)

 Sarah Polk Rucker, niece of Sarah Polk (daughter of Susan Childress Rucker)

 Ophelia Clarissa Polk Hayes, sister of James Polk

*John B. Hayes, brother-in-law of James Polk and physician to president (husband of Ophelia Clarissa Polk Hayes)

 Virginia Hayes, niece of James Polk (daughter of Ophelia Clarissa Polk Hayes)

*Marshall Tate Polk, nephew of James Polk (son of Marshall Tate Polk Sr.)

 William Polk, brother of James Polk

 Belinda Dickens Polk, sister-in-law, wife of William Polk

Zachary Taylor, March 4, 1849–July 9, 1850

*Zachary Taylor

*Margaret "Peggy" Mackall Smith Taylor, wife

*Mary Elizabeth "Betty" Taylor Bliss, daughter

*William Wallace Smith Bliss, son-in-law

 Joseph P. Taylor, brother of Zachary Taylor

 Evelyn Taylor, sister-in-law, wife of Joseph Taylor

 Arabella "Belle" Taylor, niece (daughter of Joseph Taylor)

 Rebecca "Becky" Taylor, niece (daughter of Joseph Taylor)

 Ann Taylor Wood, daughter

Dr. Robert Wood, son-in-law
John Taylor Wood, grandson
Bob Wood, grandson
Blandina Wood, granddaughter
Sarah Wood, granddaughter
Richard Taylor, son
Joseph Smith, brother of Margaret Taylor
John Gibson Taylor Jr., nephew (son of president's late sister Elizabeth Taylor Taylor)
Elizabeth Lee Taylor, niece (daughter of president's late sister Elizabeth Taylor Taylor)

Millard Fillmore, July 9, 1850–March 4, 1853
*Millard Fillmore
*Abigail Powers Fillmore, wife
*Mary Abigail "Abbie" Fillmore, daughter
*Powers Fillmore, son
 Nathaniel Fillmore, father
 Calvin Fillmore, brother

Franklin Pierce, March 4, 1853–March 4, 1857
*Franklin Pierce
*Jane Means Appleton Pierce, wife
*Abigail "Abby" Kent Means, aunt of Jane Pierce (widow of Jane Pierce's maternal
    uncle Robert Means Jr.)
 Colonel Henry D. Pierce, brother
 Frank Pierce, nephew (son of Henry Pierce)
 Kirk Pierce, nephew (son of Henry Pierce)
 Mary Appleton Aiken, sister of Jane Pierce
 John Aiken, brother-in-law (husband of Mary Aiken)
 Mary Elizabeth Aiken, niece of Jane Pierce (by her sister Mary Appleton Aiken)
 Jane "Jenny" Aiken, niece of Jane Pierce (by her sister Mary Appleton Aiken)
 William Aiken, nephew of Jane Pierce (by her sister Mary Appleton Aiken)
 John Aiken Jr., nephew of Jane Pierce (by her sister Mary Appleton Aiken)
 Elizabeth Appleton Packard, sister of Jane Pierce
 Alpheus Packard, brother-in-law (husband of Elizabeth Packard)
 Charles Packard, nephew of Jane Pierce (by her sister Elizabeth Appleton Packard)
 Frances "Fanny" Packard, niece of Jane Pierce (by her sister Elizabeth Appleton Packard)
 Nancy Means Lawrence, maternal aunt of Jane Pierce
 Amos A. Lawrence, cousin of Jane Pierce
 William Lawrence, cousin of Jane Pierce
 Mary Means Mason, maternal aunt of Jane Pierce
 Jane Mason, cousin of Jane Pierce
 Robert Mason, cousin of Jane Pierce

James Buchanan, March 4, 1857–March 4, 1861
*James Buchanan, unmarried

*Harriet Rebecca Lane, niece (daughter of Jane Buchanan Lane, president's sister, deceased)
*Elliott Eskridge Lane, nephew (son of Jane Buchanan Lane)
 James Buchanan "Buck" Henry, nephew (son of Harriet Buchanan Henry)
 James Buchanan II, nephew (son of Edward Buchanan, president's brother)

Abraham Lincoln, March 4, 1861–April 14, 1865
*Abraham Lincoln
*Mary Todd Lincoln, wife
 Robert Todd Lincoln, son
*William "Willie" Lincoln, son
*Thomas "Tad" Lincoln, son
 Emilie Todd Helm, half-sister of Mary Lincoln
 Katherine Helm, niece of Mary Lincoln
 Benjamin Hardin Helm Jr., nephew of Mary Lincoln
 Elizabeth Todd Edwards, sister of Mary Lincoln
 Elizabeth Todd Grimsley, cousin of Mary Lincoln
 Margaret Todd Kellogg, half-sister of Mary Lincoln
 Charles H. Kellogg, half-brother-in-law of Mary
    Lincoln
 Franklin Pierce Kellogg, half-nephew of Mary Lincoln

The Lincolns, mass-manufactured engraving
LIBRARY OF CONGRESS

Andrew Johnson, April 14, 1865–March 4, 1869
*Andrew Johnson
*Eliza McCardle Johnson, wife
*Mary Johnson Stover, daughter
*Lillian "Lillie" Stover, granddaughter
*Sarah Stover, granddaughter
*Andrew Stover, grandson
*Martha Johnson Patterson, daughter
*David T. Patterson, son-in-law
*Mary Belle Patterson, granddaughter
*Andrew Johnson Patterson, grandson
*Robert Johnson, son
*Andrew "Frank" Johnson Jr., son

Ulysses S. Grant, March 4, 1869–March 4, 1877
*Ulysses S. Grant
*Julia Dent Grant, wife
 Ulysses S. "Buck" Grant Jr., son
*Jesse Grant, son
*Ellen "Nellie" Grant, daughter
 Frederick Grant, son
 Ida Honore Grant, wife of Frederick Grant
 Julia Grant, granddaughter (daughter of Frederick Grant)

Orvil Grant, brother

*Frederick Dent, father of Julia Grant

Fred Dent, brother of Julia Grant

Madgie Dent, niece of Julia Grant (daughter of Fred Dent)

Jack Dent, nephew of Julia Grant (son of Fred Dent)

Nellie Sharp, sister of Julia Grant

Emma Casey, sister of Julia Grant

John Dent, brother of Julia Grant

Baine Dent, nephew of Julia Grant (son of John Dent)

Rutherford B. Hayes, March 4, 1877–March 4, 1881

*Rutherford B. Hayes

*Lucy Webb Hayes, wife

Birchard "Birch" Hayes, son

Webb Hayes, son

Rutherford "Ruddy" Hayes, son

*Scott Hayes, son

*Fanny Hayes, daughter

Emily Platt Hastings, niece of Rutherford Hayes (daughter of Fanny Hayes Platt, the president's sister)

Russell Hastings, husband of Emily Platt Hastings

James A. Garfield, March 4, 1881–September 19, 1881

*James Garfield

*Lucretia Rudolph Garfield, wife

*Harry Garfield, son

*James Garfield, son

*Mollie Garfield, daughter

*Irvin Garfield, son

*Abram Garfield, son

Eliza Ballou Garfield, mother of James Garfield

Chester A. Arthur, September 19, 1881–March 4, 1885

*Chester Arthur, widower

*Ellen Herndon "Nell" Arthur, daughter

Alan Arthur, son

Mary Arthur "Molly" McElroy, sister

May McElroy, niece

Jessie McElroy, niece

Brodie Herndon, cousin of the late Mrs. Chester Arthur

The Hayeses, mass-manufactured engraving

HAYES PRESIDENTIAL LIBRARY

The Garfield children

SCHERMER COLLECTION

Malvina Arthur Haynesworth, sister
Henry J. Haynesworth, brother-in-law
William Arthur, brother
Alice Arthur, niece
Regina Arthur Caw, sister

Grover Cleveland, March 4, 1885–March 4, 1889, and March 4, 1893–March 4, 1897
*Grover Cleveland
*Frances Folsom Cleveland, wife
*Ruth Cleveland, daughter
*Esther Cleveland, daughter, born in the White House
*Marion Cleveland, daughter
 Rose Elizabeth "Libbie" Cleveland, sister
 Mary Allen Cleveland Hoyt, sister
 Emma Folsom Perrin, mother of Frances Cleveland
 Benjamin Folsom, cousin of Frances Cleveland
 William Cleveland, brother

Benjamin Harrison, March 4, 1889–March 4, 1893
*Benjamin Harrison
*Caroline Scott Harrison, wife
*Mary "Mamie" Harrison McKee, daughter
*J. Robert McKee, son-in-law
*Benjamin Harrison "Baby" McKee, grandson
*Mary McKee, granddaughter
 Russell Harrison, son
 Mary Angelina "Mae" Harrison, daughter-in-law
 Marthena Harrison, granddaughter
*John W. Scott, father of Caroline Harrison
 Elizabeth "Lizzie" Lord, sister of Caroline Harrison
*Mary "Mame" Lord Dimmick, niece of Caroline
    Harrision (daughter of Elizabeth Lord)

William McKinley, March 4, 1897–September 14, 1901
*William McKinley
*Ida Saxton McKinley, wife
 Pina Saxton Barber, sister of Ida McKinley
 John Barber, nephew of Ida McKinley (son of Pina
    Saxton Barber)
 Mary Barber, niece of Ida McKinley (daughter of Pina
    Saxton Barber)
 Maria Saxton, aunt of Ida McKinley
 Abner McKinley, brother

Chester Arthur reading to his daughter, newspaper sketch
Leslie's NEWSPAPER, 1885

The Clevelands
LAST APPEARED IN *Grover Cleveland*, 1910

Anna McKinley, sister-in-law (wife of Abner McKinley)

Mabel McKinley Baer, niece (daughter of Abner McKinley)

Grace McKinley, niece (daughter of James Rose McKinley, the president's brother)

James "Jim" McKinley, nephew (son of James Rose McKinley)

Sarah Duncan, niece (daughter of Sarah McKinley Duncan, the president's sister)

Nancy Allison McKinley, mother

Theodore Roosevelt, September 14, 1901– March 4, 1909

*Theodore Roosevelt

*Edith Carow Roosevelt, wife

*Alice Roosevelt Longworth, daughter

 Nicolas Longworth, son-in-law

*Theodore Roosevelt Jr., son

*Kermit Roosevelt, son

*Archibald "Archie" Roosevelt, son

*Ethel Roosevelt, daughter

*Quentin Roosevelt, son

 Anna Roosevelt Cowles, sister

 Corinne Roosevelt Robinson, sister

 Emily Carow, sister of Edith Roosevelt

 Eleanor Roosevelt, niece (daughter of Elliott Roosevelt)

William Howard Taft, March 4, 1909–March 4, 1913

*William Howard Taft

*Helen "Nellie" Herron Taft, wife

*Robert Taft, son

*Helen Taft, daughter

*Charles Taft, son

 Charles P. Taft, half-brother

 Anne Taft, sister-in-law (wife of Charles Taft)

 Henry Waters Taft, brother

 Julia Taft, sister-in-law (wife of Henry Taft)

 Horace Dutton Taft, brother

 Frances "Fanny" Taft Edwards, sister

 William Edwards, brother-in-law

 Delia Torrey, maternal aunt

Caroline Harrison, her father, daughter, and grandson.
CREDIT: BENJAMIN HARRISON HOME

William McKinley, his wife, and mother; 1896 campaign poster
LIBRARY OF CONGRESS

Jennie Anderson, sister of Nellie Taft
Maria Herron, sister of Nellie Taft
Eleanor Moore, sister of Nellie Taft

Woodrow Wilson, March 4, 1913–March 4, 1921
*Woodrow Wilson
*Ellen Axson Wilson, first wife
*Margaret Wilson, daughter
*Eleanor "Nell" Wilson McAdoo, daughter
*Jessie Wilson Sayre, daughter
 Francis B. Sayre, son-in-law
 Francis B. Sayre Jr., grandson, born in the White
    House
 Eleanor Sayre, granddaughter
 Woodrow Sayre, grandson
*Helen Woodrow Bones, cousin
 Mary Randolph Smith, cousin
 Lucy Marshall Smith, cousin
 Florence Hoyt, cousin
 Joseph Wilson, brother
 Alice Wilson, niece (daughter of Joseph Wilson)
 Annie Wilson Howe, sister
 Annie Josephson Howe, niece (daughter of Annie
    Wilson Howe)
 John Wilson, cousin of Woodrow Wilson
 Stockton Axson, brother of Ellen Wilson
*Edith Bolling Galt Wilson, second wife
 Sally Bolling, mother of Edith Wilson
 Bertha Bolling, sister of Edith Wilson
 Lucy Maury, niece of Edith Wilson
    (daughter of Annie Lee Bolling Maury)
 Randolph Bolling, brother of Edith Wilson

Warren G. Harding, March 4, 1921–August 2, 1923
*Warren G. Harding
*Florence Kling DeWolfe Harding, wife
 Dr. George Tryon Harding, father
 Abigail "Daisy" Harding, sister
 Carolyn Harding Votaw, sister
 Heber Votaw, brother-in-law
 George Harding, brother
 Elsie Harding, sister-in-law
 George Harding Jr., nephew
 Warren Harding II, nephew

*Taft, his brothers and aunt, Nellie Taft and her sisters, and
their children gathered for silver wedding anniversary, 1911.*
Library of Congress

The Wilsons in Princeton
Library of Congress

Clifford Kling, brother of Florence Harding

Hazel Kling Longshore, niece of Florence Harding (daughter of Clifford Kling)

Esther Neely DeWolfe [Metzger], remarried widow of Florence Harding's son by her first marriage

Calvin Coolidge, August 2, 1923–March 4, 1929

*Calvin Coolidge

*Grace Goodhue Coolidge, wife

*John Coolidge, son

*Calvin Coolidge Jr., son

 John Coolidge Sr., father

 Lemira Goodhue, mother of Grace Coolidge

 Marion Pollard, second cousin of Calvin Coolidge
    (daughter of Calvin Coolidge's first cousin, Frank Pollard)

Herbert Hoover, March 4, 1929–March 4, 1933

*Herbert Hoover

*Lou Henry Hoover, wife

 Herbert Hoover Jr., son

*Margaret Hoover, daughter-in-law

*Margaret Ann "Peggy" Hoover, granddaughter

*Herbert "Peter" Hoover III, grandson

*Joan Leslie Hoover, granddaughter

*Allan Hoover, son

 May Hoover Leavitt, sister

 Theodore "Tad" Hoover, brother

 Mildred Hoover, sister-in-law (wife of Theodore Hoover)

 Jean Henry Large, sister of Lou Hoover

 Janet Large, niece of Lou Hoover

 Delano Large, nephew of Lou Hoover

 William Henry, uncle of Lou Hoover

Franklin D. Roosevelt, March 4, 1933–April 12, 1945

*Franklin D. Roosevelt

*Eleanor Roosevelt, wife

 Sara Delano Roosevelt, mother of Franklin D. Roosevelt

 Anna Roosevelt Dall Boettiger, daughter

 Eleanor "Sistie" Dall, granddaughter

 Curtis "Buzzie" Dall, grandson

 John Boettiger Jr., son-law (second husband of Anna Roosevelt Dall)

 John Roosevelt Boettiger, grandson (son of Anna and John Boettiger)

The Franklin Roosevelts on Sara Delano Roosevelt's eightieth birthday

THE FRANKLIN D. ROOSEVELT LIBRARY

James Roosevelt, son
Betsy Cushing Roosevelt, daughter-in-law (first wife of James Roosevelt)
Kate Roosevelt, granddaughter (daughter of James and Betsy Roosevelt)
Sara Roosevelt, granddaughter (daughter of James and Betsy Roosevelt)
Romelle Theresa Schneider Roosevelt, daughter-in-law (second wife of James Roosevelt)
Elliott Roosevelt, son
Betty Donner Roosevelt, daughter-in-law (first wife of Elliott Roosevelt)
William Donner Roosevelt, grandson (son of Elliott and Betty Roosevelt)
Ruth Googins Roosevelt, daughter-in-law (second wife of Elliott Roosevelt)
Ruth Roosevelt, granddaughter (daughter of Elliott and Ruth Roosevelt)
Elliott Roosevelt Jr., grandson (son of Elliott and Ruth Roosevelt)
David Boynton Roosevelt, grandson (son of Elliott and Ruth Roosevelt)
Faye Emerson Roosevelt, daughter-in-law (third wife of Elliott Roosevelt)
Franklin D. "Brud" Roosevelt Jr., son
Ethel DuPont Roosevelt, daughter-in-law
Franklin D. Roosevelt III, grandson (son of Franklin and Ethel Roosevelt)
Christopher Roosevelt, grandson (son of Franklin and Ethel Roosevelt)
John Roosevelt, son
Anne Clark Roosevelt, daughter-in-law (wife of John Roosevelt)
Haven Roosevelt, grandson (son of John and Anne Roosevelt)
Anne "Nina" Roosevelt, granddaughter (daughter of John Roosevelt)
Laura Delano, first cousin
Margaret "Daisy" Suckley, distant cousin
Hall Roosevelt, brother-in-law (brother of Eleanor Roosevelt)
Dorothy Kemp Roosevelt, sister-in-law of Eleanor Roosevelt (Hall Roosevelt's former wife)
Dora Delano Forbes, maternal aunt
Kassie Delano Collier, maternal aunt

Harry S. Truman, April 12, 1945–January 20, 1953
*Harry Truman
*Bess Truman, wife
*Margaret Truman, daughter
 Martha Ellen Truman, mother
 Mary Jane Truman, sister
*Madge Gates Wallace, mother-in-law
 Frank Wallace, brother-in-law
 Natalie Wallace, sister-in-law (wife of Frank Wallace)
 George Wallace, brother-in-law
 May Wallace, sister-in-law (wife of George Wallace)
 Fred Wallace, brother-in-law
 Christine Wallace, sister-in-law (wife of Fred Wallace)
 David Wallace, nephew (son of Fred Wallace)
 Marian Wallace, niece (daughter of Fred Wallace)
 Charlotte Margaret "Margo" Wallace, niece (daughter of Fred Wallace)

Dwight D. Eisenhower, January 20, 1953–
January 20, 1961
*Dwight D. Eisenhower
*Mamie Doud Eisenhower, wife
 John S. D. Eisenhower, son
 Barbara Eisenhower, daughter-in-law
 David Eisenhower, grandson
 Susan Eisenhower, granddaughter
 Barbara Anne "Anne" Eisenhower, grandaughter
 Mary Jean Eisenhower, granddaughter
 Milton Eisenhower, brother
 Milton "Buddy" Eisenhower, nephew (son of Milton
    Eisenhower)
 Ruth Eisenhower, niece (daughter of Milton
    Eisenhower)
 Edgar Eisenhower, brother
 Arthur Eisenhower, brother
 Earl Eisenhower, brother
*Elvira "Minnie" Doud, mother of Mamie Eisenhower
 Frances "Mike" Doud Gill Moore, sister of Mamie
    Eisenhower

The Kennedys on vacation, 1963.
THE JOHN F. KENNEDY LIBRARY

John F. Kennedy, January 20, 1961–November 22,
1963
*John F. Kennedy
*Jacqueline Lee Bouvier Kennedy, wife
*Caroline Bouvier Kennedy, daughter
*John F. Kennedy Jr., son
 Patrick Bouvier Kennedy, son
 Joseph P. Kennedy, father
 Rose Fitzgerald Kennedy, mother
 Robert F. Kennedy, brother
 Ethel Skakel Kennedy, sister-in-law (wife of Robert
    Kennedy)
 Edward M. Kennedy, brother
 Joan Bennett Kennedy, sister-in-law (wife of Edward
    Kennedy)
 Eunice Kennedy Shriver, sister
 Sargent Shriver, brother-in-law
 Jean Kennedy Smith, sister
 Stephen Smith, brother-in-law
 Patricia Kennedy Lawford, sister
 Peter Lawford, brother-in-law
 Janet Norton Lee Bouvier Auchincloss, mother of
    Jacqueline Kennedy

The Johnsons, including the president's brother Sam, at far right.
1967.

LYNDON BAINES JOHNSON PRESIDENTIAL LIBRARY

Hugh D. Auchincloss, stepfather to Jacqueline Kennedy

Lee Bouvier Radziwill, sister of Jacqueline Kennedy

Stanislaus "Stash" Radziwill, brother-in-law of Jacqueline Kennedy

James "Jamie" Auchincloss, half-brother of Jacqueline Kennedy

Janet Jennings Auchincloss, half-sister of Jacqueline Kennedy

Hugh D. "Yusha" Auchincloss Jr., stepbrother of Jacqueline Kennedy

Lyndon B. Johnson, November 22, 1963–January 20, 1969

*Lyndon Baines Johnson

*Claudia Alta "Lady Bird" Taylor Johnson, wife

*Lynda Bird Johnson Robb, daughter

 Charles S. Robb, son-in-law

 Lucinda Desha Robb, granddaughter

*Luci Baines Johnson Nugent, daughter

 Patrick Nugent, son-in-law

 Patrick Lyndon "Lyn" Nugent, grandson

 Sam Houston Johnson, brother of Lyndon Johnson

Richard M. Nixon, January 20, 1969–August 9, 1974

*Richard M. Nixon

*Thelma Catherine "Pat" Ryan Nixon, wife

*Patricia "Tricia" Nixon Cox, daughter

 Edward Finch Cox, son-in-law

 Julie Nixon Eisenhower, daughter

 David Eisenhower, son-in-law

 Ed Nixon, brother

 Gay Nixon, sister-in-law

 Amelia Nixon, niece

 Elizabeth Nixon, niece

 Tom Ryan, brother of Pat Nixon

 Bill Ryan, brother of Pat Nixon

Gerald R. Ford, August 9, 1974–January 20, 1977

*Gerald Rudolph Ford

*Elizabeth Ann "Betty" Bloomer Warren Ford, wife

 Michael Ford, son

 Gayle Brumbaugh Ford, daughter-in-law (wife of Michael Ford)

The Fords, 1976.

Gerald R. Ford Presidential Library

The Nixons on vacation, 1973.

Nixon Presidential Materials, National Archives

*Jack Ford, son
*Steve Ford, son
*Susan Ford, daughter
 Thomas Ford, brother
 Janet Ford, sister-in-law

James Earl Carter, January 20, 1977–January 20, 1981

*James Earl Carter Jr.
*Eleanor Rosalynn Smith Carter, wife
 John "Jack" Carter, son
 Judy Langford Carter, daughter-in-law
 Jason James Carter, grandson (son of Jack and Judy
    Carter)
 Sarah Rose Mary Carter, granddaughter (daughter of
    Jack and Judy Carter)
*James Earl "Chip" Carter, son
*Caron Griffith Carter, daughter-in-law
*James Earl Carter IV, grandson (son of Chip and Caron Carter)
*Jeffrey Donnell Carter, son
*Annette Jene Davis Carter, daughter-in-law
*Amy Carter, daughter
 Lillian Carter, mother of Jimmy Carter
 Ruth Carter Stapleton, sister
 William Alton "Billy" Carter, brother
 Allie Smith, mother of Rosalynn Carter

The Carters, 1979.
JIMMY CARTER PRESIDENTIAL LIBRARY

Ronald Wilson Reagan, January 20, 1981–January 20, 1989

*Ronald Wilson Reagan
*Ann Frances "Nancy" [Robbins] Davis Reagan, wife
 Maureen Reagan, daughter of Ronald Reagan and his
    first wife, Jane Wyman
 Dennis Revell, son-in-law (husband of Maureen
    Reagan)
 Michael Reagan, son of Ronald Reagan and his first
    wife, Jane Wyman
 Colleen Sterns Reagan, daughter-in-law (wife of
    Michael Reagan)
 Cameron Reagan, grandson (son of Michael and
    Colleen Reagan)
 Ashley Marie Reagan, granddaughter (daughter of
    Michael and Colleen Reagan)
 Patti [Reagan] Davis, daughter
 Paul Grilley, son-in-law (husband of Patti Davis)

The Reagans, 1981.
RONALD REAGAN PRESIDENTIAL LIBRARY

Ronald "Ron" Prescott Reagan, son

Doria Palmieri Reagan, daughter-in-law (wife of Ron Reagan)

John Neil "Moon" Reagan, brother

Ruth Elizabeth "Bess" Hoffman Reagan, sister-in-law

Edith "Edie" Luckett Robbins Davis, mother-in-law

Loyal Davis, father-in-law

Richard Davis, brother-in-law (brother of Nancy Reagan)

Patricia Davis, sister-in-law (wife of Richard Davis)

Geoffrey Davis, nephew of Nancy Reagan

Anne Davis, niece of Nancy Reagan

The Bushes at the Republican National Convention, 1992.
GEORGE BUSH PRESIDENTIAL LIBRARY

George H. W. Bush, January 20, 1989–January 20, 1993

*George Herbert Walker Bush

*Barbara "Bar" Pierce Bush, wife

George Walker "W." Bush, son

Laura Welch Bush, daughter-in-law (wife of George W. Bush)

Barbara Bush, granddaughter (daughter of George W. Bush)

Jenna Bush, granddaughter (daughter of George W. Bush)

John Ellis "Jeb" Bush, son

Columba Garnica Bush, daughter-in-law (wife of Jeb Bush)

George Prescott "George P." Bush, grandson (son of Jeb Bush)

Noella Bush, granddaughter (daughter of Jeb Bush)

John Ellis "Jebby" Bush, grandson (son of Jeb Bush)

Neil Bush, son

Sharon Smith Bush, daughter-in-law (wife of Neil Bush)

Lauren Bush, granddaughter (daughter of Neil Bush)

Pierce Bush, grandson (son of Neil Bush)

Ashley Bush, granddaughter (daughter of Neil Bush)

Marvin Bush, son

Margaret Molster Bush, daughter-in-law

Marshall Bush, granddaughter (daughter of Marvin Bush)

Walker Bush, grandson (son of Marvin Bush)

Dorothy "Doro" Bush LeBlond Koch, daughter

Bill LeBlond, son-in-law (first husband of Doro Bush)

Sam LeBlond, grandson (son of Doro Bush)

Ellie LeBlond, granddaughter (daughter of Doro Bush)

Bobby Koch, son-in-law (second husband of Doro Bush)

Dorothy Bush, mother

Prescott "Pres" Bush, brother

Elizabeth Louise Bush, sister-in-law (wife of Prescott Bush)

Nancy Bush Ellis, sister

Jonathan Bush, brother
Jody Bush, sister-in-law (wife of Jonathan Bush)
William "Bucky" Bush, brother
Patty Bush, sister-in-law (wife of William Bush)

William Jefferson Clinton, January 20, 1993–January 20, 2001
*William Jefferson Clinton
*Hillary Rodham Clinton, wife
*Chelsea Victoria Clinton, daughter
 Virginia Cassidy Clinton Kelley, mother
 Richard "Dick" Kelley, stepfather
 Roger Clinton, half-brother
 Molly Clinton, sister-in-law (wife of Roger Clinton)
 Tyler Clinton, nephew (son of Roger Clinton)
 Hugh Rodham, father-in-law
 Dorothy Rodham, mother-in-law
 Hugh "Hughey" Rodham Jr., brother of Hillary Clinton
 Maria Rodham, sister-in-law of Hillary Clinton (wife of Hughey Rodham)
 Anthony "Tony" Rodham, brother of Hillary Clinton
 Nicole Boxer Rodham, sister-in-law (wife of Tony Rodham)
 Zachary Rodham, nephew (son of Tony and Nicole Rodham)

The Clintons at Camp David, Thanksgiving 1999
THE WHITE HOUSE

Bibliography

Secondary Sources

Adamic, Louis. *Dinner at the White House.* New York: Harper & Brothers, 1948.

Aikman, Lonnelle. *The Living White House.* Washington, D.C.: White House Historical Association, 1970.

Alexander, John. *Ghosts: Washington's Most Famous Stories.* Washington, D.C.: Washingtonian Books, 1975.

American Bicentennial Presidential Inaugural Committee. *200 Years of the American Presidency.* Washington, D.C.: Walsworth Publishing, 1989.

Ammon, Harry. *James Monroe: The Quest for National Identity.* New York: McGraw-Hill, 1971.

Anthony, Carl Sferrazza. *First Ladies: The Saga of the Presidents' Wives and Their Power, 1789–1990.* 2 vols. New York: Morrow, 1990–1991.

———. *As We Remember Her: Jacqueline Kennedy Onassis in the Words of Her Friends and Family.* New York: HarperCollins, 1997.

———. *Florence Harding: The First Lady, the Jazz Age, and the Death of America's Most Scandalous President.* New York: Morrow, 1998.

Anthony, Katharine. *Dolley Madison: Her Life and Times.* Garden City, N.Y.: Doubleday, 1949.

Arnette, Ethel Stephens. *Mrs. James Madison: The Incomparable Dolley.* Greensborough, N.C.: Piedmont Press, 1972.

Asbell, Bernard, ed. *Mother & Daughter: The Letters of Eleanor and Anna Roosevelt.* New York: Coward, McCann & Geoghegan, 1982.

Bailey, Thomas A. *Presidential Saints and Sinners.* New York: Free Press, 1981.

Baker, Jean H. *Mary Todd Lincoln.* New York: Norton, 1987.

Balch, William Ralston. *The Life of James Abram Garfield.* Philadelphia: McCurdy & Co., 1881.

Boas, Norman F. *Jane M. Pierce: The Pierce-Aiken Papers.* Stonington, Conn.: Seaport Autographs, 1983.

———. *Jane M. Pierce: The Pierce-Aiken Papers, Supplement.* Stonington, Conn.: Seaport Autographs, 1989.

Boettiger, John R. *A Love in Shadow: The Story of Anna Roosevelt and John Boettiger.* New York: Norton, 1978.

Booth, Edward Townsend. *Country Life in America as Lived by Ten Presidents of the United States.* New York: Knopf, 1947.

Brant, Irving. *The Fourth President: A Life of James Madison.* Indianapolis: Bobbs-Merrill, 1970.

Britton, Nan. *The President's Daughter.* New York: Elizabeth Ann Guild, 1927.

Brodie, Fawn. *Thomas Jefferson: An Intimate History.* New York: Norton, 1974.

Brogan, Hugh, and Charles Mosley. *American Presidential Families.* New York: Macmillan, 1993.

Brough, James. *Princess Alice: A Biography of Alice Roosevelt Longworth.* Boston: Little, Brown, 1975.

Brown, Dale. *American Cooking.* New York: Time-Life Books, 1968.

Bryant, Traphes. *Dog Days at the White House.* New York: Macmillan, 1975.

Bumgarner, John Reed. *Sarah Childress Polk.* Jefferson, N.C.: McFarland, 1997.

Bush, Barbara. *Millie's Book.* New York: William Morrow, 1990.

———. *Barbara Bush: A Memoir.* New York: Scribner's, 1994.

Cable, Mary. *The Avenue of the Presidents.* Boston: Houghton Mifflin, 1969.

Cannon, Poppy, and Patricia Brooks. *The Presidents' Cookbook.* New York: Funk & Wagnalls, 1968.

Cantacuzene, Julia Grant. *My Life Here and There.* New York: Scribner's, 1921.

Cardigan, J. H. *Ronald Reagan: A Remarkable Life.* Kansas City, Mo.: Andrews & McMeel, 1995.

Carpenter, Francis B. *The Inner Life of Abraham Lincoln: Six Months at the White House.* Boston: Houghton, Osgood, 1880.

Carpenter, Frank G. *Carp's Washington.* New York: McGraw-Hill, 1960.

Carter, Jimmy. *Keeping Faith.* New York: Bantam, 1982.

Carter, Rosalynn. *First Lady from Plains.* Boston: Houghton Mifflin, 1984.

Clark, Allen C. *Abraham Lincoln in the National Capital.* Washington, D.C.: F. W. Roberts Co., 1925.

Cleaves, Freeman. *Old Tippecanoe: William Henry Harrison and His Time.* New York: Scribner's, 1939.

Clinton, Hillary Rodham. *It Takes a Village and Other Lessons Children Teach Us.* New York: Simon & Schuster, 1996.

Coleman, Elizabeth. *Priscilla Cooper Tyler and the American Scene.* Birmingham, Ala.: University of Alabama Press, 1955.

Collins, Herbert R. *Presidents on Wheels.* New York: Bonanza Books, 1971.

Committee for the Fiftieth American Presidential Inauguration. *A New Beginning: Ronald Reagan: The First Four Years.* Charlottesville, Va.: Thomasson, Grant & Howell, 1985.

————. *We the People: An American Celebration.* Charlottesville, Va.: Thomasson, Grant & Howell, 1985.

Crawford, Mary Caroline. *Romantic Days in the Early Republic.* Boston: Little, Brown, 1912.

Crook, William H. *Memories of the White House.* Boston: Little, Brown, 1911.

Cruse, Katherine. *An Amiable Woman: Rachel Jackson.* Nashville, Tenn.: The Ladies' Hermitage Association, 1994.

David, Lester, and Irene David. *Ike and Mamie.* New York: Putnam, 1981.

Davis, Patti [Reagan]. *The Way I See It.* New York: Putnam, 1992.

DeGregorio, William A. *The Complete Book of U.S. Presidents.* New York: Barricade Books, 1993.

Eisenhower, Dwight D. *At Ease: Stories I Tell My Friends.* Garden City, N.Y.: Doubleday, 1967.

————. *In Review: Pictures I've Kept.* Garden City, N.Y.: Doubleday, 1969.

Eisenhower, John S. D. *Strictly Personal.* Garden City, N.Y.: Doubleday, 1974.

Eisenhower, Julie Nixon. *Pat Nixon: The Untold Story.* New York: Simon & Schuster, 1986.

Eisenhower, Susan. *Mrs. Ike: Memories and Reflections on the Life of Mamie Eisenhower.* New York: Farrar, Straus and Giroux, 1996.

Evans, W. A. *Mrs. Abaraham Lincoln: A Study of Her Personality and Her Influence on Lincoln.* New York: Knopf, 1932.

Feis, Ruth S.-B. *Mollie Garfield in the White House.* Chicago: Rand McNally, 1963.

Felsenthal, Carol. *Alice Roosevelt Longworth.* New York: Putnam, 1988.

Fischer, Margaret Jane. *Calvin Coolidge Jr.* Rutland, Vt.: Academy Books, 1981.

Ford, Betty. *The Times of My Life.* New York: Harper & Row, 1987.

Ford, Gerald. *A Time to Heal.* New York: Harper & Row, 1979.

Fuess, Claude. *Calvin Coolidge: The Man from Vermont.* Boston: Little, Brown, 1940.

Fuller, Edmund, and David Green. *God in the White House.* New York: Crown, 1968.

Furman, Bess. *Washington By-line.* New York: Knopf, 1949.

————. *White House Profile.* Indianapolis: Bobbs-Merrill, 1951.

Gardner, Gerald. *Miss Caroline: The Little Girl in the Big White House.* New York: Golden Books, 1963.

Garland, Hamlin. *Ulysses S. Grant: His Life and Character.* New York: Doubleday, 1898.

Geer, Emily Apt. *First Lady: The Life of Lucy Webb Hayes.* Kent, Ohio: Kent State University Press, 1984.

Gilder, Richard Watson. *Grover Cleveland: A Record of Friendship.* New York: Century, 1910.

Gordon-Reed, Annette. *Thomas Jefferson and Sally Hemings.* Charlottesville: University Press of Virginia, 1997.

Gould, Lewis, ed. *American First Ladies.* New York: Garland Publishing, 1996.

Grant, Jesse. *In the Days of My Father, General Grant.* New York: Harper & Brothers, 1925.

Grant, Julia. *The Personal Memoirs of Julia Dent Grant,* ed. John Y. Simon. New York: Putnam, 1975.

Green, Constance. *The Church on Lafayette Square: 1850–1970.* Washington, D.C.: Potomac Books, 1970.

Greene, J. R. *Images of America: Calvin Coolidge's Plymouth, Vermont.* Dover, N.H.: Arcadia Publishing, 1997.

Haber, Joyce. *Caroline's Doll Book.* New York: Putnam, 1962.

Hagedorn, Hermann. *The Roosevelt Family of Sagamore Hill.* New York: Macmillan, 1954.

Haller, Henry, and Virginia Aronson. *The White House Family Cookbook.* New York: Random House, 1987.

Hamilton, Holman. *Zachary Taylor: Soldier in the White House.* Indianapolis: Bobbs-Merrill, 1951.

Hampton, Vernon. *Religious Background of the White House.* Boston: Christopher Publishing House, 1932.

Harding, Warren G. II, and J. Mark Stewart. *Mere Mortals: The Lives and Health Histories of American Presidents.* Worthington, Ohio: Renaissance Publications, 1992.

Harwood, Richard, and Haynes Johnson. *Lyndon.* New York: Praeger Publishers, 1973.

Hecht, Marie B. *John Quincy Adams.* New York: Macmillan, 1972.

Heckler-Feltz, Cheryl. *Heart and Soul of the Nation: How the Spirituality of Our First Ladies Changed America.* Garden City, N.Y.: Doubleday, 1997.

Hillman, William. *Mr. President: The First Publication from the Personal Diaries, Private Letters, Papers and Revealing Interviews of Harry S. Truman.* New York: Farrar, Straus & Young, 1952.

Holzer, Hans. *The Ghosts That Walk in Washington.* New York: Ballantine Books, 1971.

Hoover, Irwin. *Forty-Two Years in the White House.* Boston: Houghton Mifflin, 1934.

Hunt-Jones, Conover. *Dolley and the "Great Little Madison."* Washington, D.C.: AIA Foundation, 1977.

Hurd, Charles. *Washington Cavalcade.* New York: Dutton, 1948.

————. *The White House Story.* New York: Hawthorn Books, 1966.

James, Marquis. *The Life of Andrew Jackson.* New York: Bobbs-Merrill, 1938.

Jensen, Amy LaFollette. *The White House and Its Thirty-Five Families.* New York: McGraw-Hill, 1970.

Johnson, Haynes. *The Working White House.* New York: Praeger Publishers, 1975.

Johnson, Lady Bird. *A White House Diary.* New York: Holt, Rinehart, 1970.

Johnson, Lyndon. *The Vantage Point: Perspectives of the Presidency, 1963–1969.* New York: Holt, Rinehart, 1971.

Johnson, Sam Houston. *My Brother Lyndon.* New York: Cowles Book Co., 1969.

Jones, Olga. *Churches of the Presidents in Washington.* New York: Exposition Press, 1954.

Kane, Joseph Nathan. *Facts about the Presidents.* New York: H. W. Wilson, 1993.

Kellerman, Barbara. *All the President's Kin.* New York: Free Press, 1981.

Kelley, Virginia. *Leading with My Heart.* New York: Simon & Schuster, 1994.

Kelly, Niall. *Presidential Pets.* New York: Abbeville Press, 1992.

Kennedy, Rose Fitzgerald. *Times to Remember.* Garden City, N.Y.: Doubleday, 1974.

Kennon, Donald R., and Richard Striner. *Washington Past and Present: A Guide to the Nation's Capital.* Washington, D.C.: United States Capital Historical Society, 1983.

Kimball, Marie. *Thomas Jefferson's Cookbook.* Charlottesville: University Press of Virginia, 1976.

Kirk, Elise. *Music at the White House.* Urbana: University of Illinois Press, 1986.

Kittler, Glenn D. *Hail to the Chief: The Inauguration Days of Our Presidents.* New York: Chilton Book Co., 1965.

Klapthor, Margaret. *The First Ladies' Cookbook.* New York: Parents Magazine Press, 1969.

Klein, Philip Shriver. *President James Buchanan.* University Park: Pennsylvania State University Press, 1962.

————. *James Buchanan: Bachelor Father and Family Man.* Lancaster, Pa.: James Buchanan Foundation, 1991.

Kohlsaat, H. H. *From McKinley to Harding.* New York: Scribner's, 1923.

Koleman, Elizabeth Tyler. *Priscilla Cooper Tyler and the American Scene.* Birmingham: University of Alabama Press, 1955.

Lambert, Darwin. *Herbert Hoover's Hideaway.* Luray, Va.: Shenandoah Natural History Association, 1971.

Langhorne, Elizabeth. *Monticello: A Family Story.* New York: Workman Publishing, 1989.

Langston-Harrison, Lee. *A Presidential Legacy.* Fredericksburg, Va.: James Monroe Museum, 1997.

Lash, Joseph P. *Eleanor and Franklin.* New York: Norton, 1971.

Lawson, Dan. *Young People in the White House.* New York: Abelard-Schuman, 1970.

Leech, Margaret. *In the Days of McKinley.* New York: Harper & Row, 1959.

———, and Harry J. Brown. *The Garfield Orbit.* New York: Harper & Row, 1978.

Leish, Kenneth W., ed. *The American Heritage History of the Presidency.* New York: American Heritage, 1968.

———. *The American Heritage Pictorial History of the Presidents of the United States.* 2 vols. New York: American Heritage, 1968.

Levin, Phyllis Lee. *Abigail Adams: A Biography.* New York: St. Martin's Press, 1987.

Lindrop, Edmond, and Joseph Jares. *White House Sportsman.* New York: Houghton Mifflin, 1964.

Longworth, Alice Roosevelt. *Crowded Hours.* New York: Scribner's, 1935.

Lorant, Stefan. *The Glorious Burden.* New York: Harper & Row, 1969.

———. *Lincoln: A Picture Story of His Life.* New York: Norton, 1969.

Looker, Earle. *The White House Gang.* New York: Fleming H. Revell, 1929.

Lyons, Eugene. *Herbert Hoover.* Garden City, N.Y.: Doubleday, 1964.

MacMahon, Edward B., and Leonard Curry. *Medical Cover-Ups in the White House.* Washington, D.C.: Farragut Publishing, 1987.

Manchester, William. *Portrait of a President.* Boston: Little, Brown, 1962.

Manners, William. *TR and Will.* New York: Harcourt Brace Jovanovich, 1969.

Martin, Asa. *After the White House.* State College, Pa.: Penns Valley Publisher, 1951.

McAdoo, Eleanor Wilson. *The Woodrow Wilsons.* New York: Macmillan, 1937.

———. *The Priceless Gift: The Love Letters of Woodrow Wilson and Ellen Axson Wilson.* New York: McGraw-Hill, 1962.

McElroy, Richard L. *James A. Garfield: His Life and Times.* Canton, Ohio: Daring Books, 1986.

———. *William McKinley and Our America.* Canton, Ohio: Stark County Historical Society, 1996.

McElroy, Robert. *Grover Cleveland: The Man and the Statesman.* 2 vols. New York: Harper & Brothers, 1923.

McEwan, Barbara. *White House Landscapes: Horticultural Achievements of American Presidents.* New York: Walker, 1992.

McFeely, William S. *Grant: A Biography.* New York: Norton, 1982.

McKinley, Silas Bent, and Silas Bent. *Old Rough and Ready.* New York: Vanguard Press, 1946.

Mead, William, and Paul Dickson. *Baseball: The President's Game.* New York: Walker, 1997.

Means, Marianne. *The Woman in the White House.* New York: Random House, 1963.

Miller, Merle. *Plain Speaking: An Oral Biography of Harry S. Truman.* New York: Putnam, 1973.

———. *Lyndon: An Oral Biography.* New York: Putnam, 1980.

Moore, Virginia. *The Madisons: A Biography.* New York: McGraw-Hill, 1979.

Morgan, H. Wayne. *William McKinley and His America.* Syracuse, N.Y.: Syracuse University Press, 1963.

Nagel, Paul C. *Descent from Glory: Four Generations of the John Adams Family.* New York: Oxford University Press, 1983.

———. *Adams Women.* New York: Oxford University Press, 1987.

———. *John Quincy Adams: A Public Life, a Private Life.* New York: Knopf, 1997.

Neal, Steve. *The Eisenhowers.* Garden City, N.Y.: Doubleday, 1978.

Nevins, Allan. *Grover Cleveland: A Study in Courage.* New York: Dodd, Mead, 1938.

Nevins, Allan, ed. *Polk: The Diary of a President, 1845–1849.* New York: Longmans, Green & Co., 1929.

Nichols, Roy. *Franklin Pierce.* Philadelphia: University of Pennsylvania Press, 1958.

1965 Presidential Inaugural Committee. *Threshold of Tomorrow: The Great Society.* Washington, D.C.: 1965 PIC, 1965.

1969 Presidential Inaugural Committee. *The Inaugural Story.* New York: American Heritage Publishing, 1969.

1973 Presidential Inaugural Committee. *The Inaugural Book.* Washington, D.C.: 1973 PIC, 1973.

1977 Presidential Inaugural Committee. *A New Spirit, a New Commitment, a New America.* New York: Bantam Books, 1977.

1981 Presidential Inaugural Committee. *A Great New Beginning.* Glenn Dale, Md.: Merkle Press, 1981.

Nivven, John. *Martin Van Buren.* New York: Oxford University Press, 1983.

The Nixon 1968 Yearbook. Washington, D.C.: Nixon/Agnew Committee, 1968.

Nixon, Richard. *Memoirs.* New York: Grosset & Dunlap, 1978.

————. *In the Arena.* New York: Simon & Schuster, 1990.

Norton, Howard. *Rosalynn: A Portrait.* Plainfield, N.J.: Logos International, 1977.

Oudes, Bruce. *From the President: Richard Nixon's Secret Files.* New York: Harper & Row, 1989.

Packard, Jerrold. *American Monarchy: A Social Guide to the Presidency.* New York: Delacorte Press, 1983.

Parks, Lillian Rogers. *My Thirty Years Backstairs at the White House.* New York: Fleeting Publishing, 1961.

Parrish, T. Michael. *Richard Taylor: Soldier Prince of Dixie.* Chapel Hill: University of North Carolina Press, 1992.

Pearce, Lorraine, ed. *The White House: An Historic Guide.* Washington, D.C.: White House Historical Association, 1962.

Pendel, Thomas F. *Thirty-Six Years in the White House.* Washington, D.C.: Neal Publishing, 1902.

Perling, J. J. *Presidents' Sons.* New York: Odyssey Press, 1947.

Post, Robert C. *Every Four Years: The American Presidency.* Washington, D.C.: Smithsonian Institution, 1984.

Pringle, Henry F. *The Life and Times of William Howard Taft.* 2 vols. Hamden, Conn.: Archon Books, 1964.

Pryor, Helen B. *Lou Henry Hoover: Gallant First Lady.* New York: Dodd, Mead, 1969.

Quaife, Milo Milton, ed. *The Diary of James K. Polk During His Presidency, 1845 to 1849.* Chicago: A. C. McClurg & Co., 1910.

Randall, Ruth Painter. *Mary Lincoln.* Boston: Little, Brown, 1953.

Randolph, Sarah N. *The Domestic Life of Thomas Jefferson.* New York: Harper, 1871.

Reagan, Maureen. *First Father, First Daughter.* Boston: Little, Brown, 1989.

Reagan, Michael. *On the Outside Looking In.* New York: Zebra Books, 1987.

Reagan, Nancy. *My Turn.* New York: Random House, 1989.

Reagan, Ronald. *An American Life.* New York: Simon & Schuster, 1990.

Reeves, Thomas C. *Gentleman Boss: The Life of Chester Alan Arthur.* New York: Knopf, 1975.

Renehan, Edward J. *The Lion's Pride: Theodore Roosevelt in Peace and War.* New York: Oxford University Press, 1998.

Rigdon, William. *White House Sailor.* New York: Doubleday, 1962.

Robbins, Jhan. *Bess & Harry: An American Love Story.* New York: Putnam, 1980.

Roman, Alexander A. *JFK Coloring Book.* New York: Kanrom, 1962.

Roosevelt, Eleanor. *This I Remember.* New York: Harper & Brothers, 1949.

Roosevelt, Elliott, and James Brough. *An Untold Story: The Roosevelts of Hyde Park.* New York: Putnam, 1973.

————. *A Rendezvous with Destiny: The Roosevelts of the White House.* New York: Putnam, 1975.

————. *Mother R.: Eleanor Roosevelt's Untold Story.* New York: Putnam, 1977.

Roosevelt, James, and Sidney Shalette. *Affectionately, FDR: A Son's Story of a Man.* New York: Harcourt, Brace, Jovanovich, 1959.

Rosenbaum, Alvin. *A White House Christmas.* Washington, D.C.: Preservation Press, 1992.

Ross, Ishbel. *The General's Wife.* New York: Dodd, Mead, 1959.

————. *Grace Coolidge and Her Era.* New York: Dodd, Mead, 1962.

————. *The Tafts: An American Family.* Cleveland: World Publishing, 1964.

————. *Power with Grace: The Life Story of Mrs. Woodrow Wilson.* New York: Putnam, 1975.

Rowan, Roy, and Brooke Janis. *First Dogs.* New York: Workman Publishing, 1997.

Rysavy, Francois. *White House Menus and Recipes.* New York: Putnam, 1957.

Sadler, Christine. *Children in the White House.* New York: Putnam, 1967.

Schlesinger, Arthur M. Jr. *A Thousand Days: John F. Kennedy in the White House.* New York: Houghton Mifflin, 1965.

Seager, Robert. *And Tyler Too: A Biography of John and Julia Gardiner Tyler.* New York: McGraw-Hill, 1963.

Seale, William. *The President's House: A History.* 2 vols. Washington, D.C.: The White House Historical Association, 1986.

————. *The White House: The History of an American Idea.* Washington, D.C.: American Institute of Architects Press, 1992.

Shachtman, Tom. *Edith and Woodrow: A Presidential Romance.* New York: Putnam, 1981.

Shaw, John. *Crete and James: Personal Letters of Lucretia and James Garfield.* East Lansing: Michigan State University Press, 1994.

Shaw, Maud. *White House Nanny.* New York: New American Library, 1965.

Shepard, Jack. *The Adams Chronicles: Four Generations of Greatness.* Boston: Little, Brown, 1976.

————. *Cannibals of the Heart: A Personal Biography of Louisa Catherine and John Quincy Adams.* New York: McGraw-Hill, 1980.

Sievers, Harry J. *Benjamin Harrison.* Vol. 3, Hoosier President. Indianapolis: Bobbs-Merrill, 1968.

Singleton, Esther. *The Story of the White House.* 2 vols. New York: McClure Co., 1907.

Smith, Marie. *The President's Lady: An Intimate Biography of Mrs. Lyndon B. Johnson.* New York: Random House, 1964.

Smith, Marie, and Louise Durbin. *White House Brides.* Washington, D.C.: Acropolis Books, 1966.

Smith, Merriman. *Meet Mister Eisenhower.* New York: Harper & Brothers, 1955.

Smith, Gene. *When the Cheering Stopped: The Last Years of Woodrow Wilson.* New York: Morrow, 1964.

Smith, Page. *John Adams,* vol. 2. Garden City, N.Y.: Doubleday, 1962.

Smith, Richard Norton. *An Uncommon Man: The Triumph of Herbert Hoover.* New York: Simon & Schuster, 1984.

Somerville, Molly. *Eleanor Roosevelt As I Knew Her.* McLean, Va.: EPM Publications, 1996.

Sorensen, Theodore. *Kennedy.* New York: Harper & Row, 1965.

Spillman, Jane Shadel. *White House Glassware.* Washington, D.C.: White House Historical Association, 1989.

Starling, Edmund. *Starling of the White House.* Chicago: People's Book Club, 1936.

Stephanopoulos, George. *All Too Human.* Boston: Little, Brown, 1999.

Stoughton, Cecil, and Chester V. Cliffton. *The Memories: J.F.K. 1961–1963.* New York: Norton, 1973.

Sullivan, George. *Presidents at Play.* New York: Walker, 1995.

Sweetser, Kate Dickinson. *Famous Girls of the White House.* New York: Thomas Y. Crowell, 1930.

Taft, Helen Herron. *Recollections of Full Years.* New York: Dodd, Mead, 1917.

Taylor, Tim. *The Book of Presidents.* New York: Arno Press, 1972.

Teague, Michael. *Mrs. L: Conversations with Alice Roosevelt Longworth.* Garden City, N.Y.: Doubleday, 1981.

Teichmann, Howard. *Alice: The Life and Times of Alice Roosevelt Longworth.* Englewood Cliffs, N.J.: Prentice-Hall, 1979.

terHorst, J. F., and Ralph Albertazzie. *The Flying White House.* New York: Coward McCann, 1979.

Thayer, Mary Van Rensselaer. *Jacqueline Kennedy: The White House Years.* Boston: Little, Brown, 1967.

Thomas, Lately. *The First President Johnson.* New York: Morrow, 1968.

Thomson, David. *A Pictorial Biography: H.S.T.* New York: Grosset & Dunlap, 1973.

Townsend, G. W. *Memorial Life of William McKinley: Our Martyred President.* Washington, D.C.: D. Z. Howell, 1901.

Tribble, Edwin, ed. *A President in Love: The Courtship Letters of Woodrow Wilson and Edith Bolling Galt.* Boston: Houghton Mifflin, 1981.

Truman, Margaret. *Souvenir.* New York: McGraw-Hill, 1956.

———. *Harry S. Truman.* New York: Morrow, 1973.

———. *Bess W. Truman.* New York: Macmillan, 1986.

Truman, *Harry S. Mr. Citizen.* New York: Popular Library, 1953.

———. *Memoirs.* 2 vols. Garden City, N.Y.: Doubleday, 1955, 1956.

Tugwell, Rexford Guy. *Grover Cleveland.* New York: Macmillan, 1968.

Tully, Grace. *F.D.R., My Boss.* New York: Scribner's, 1949.

Turner, Justin G., and Linda Levitt Turner. *Mary Todd Lincoln: Her Life and Letters.* New York: Knopf, 1972.

Verdon, Rene. *The White House Chef Cookbook.* Garden City, N.Y.: Doubleday, 1967.

Vernon, Laura. *Harry Truman Slept Here.* Independence, Mo.: Posy Publications, 1987.

Ward, Geoffrey, ed. *Closest Companion: The Unknown Story of the Intimate Friendship Between Franklin Roosevelt and Margaret Suckley.* Boston: Houghton Mifflin, 1995.

West, J. B. *Upstairs at the White House.* New York: Coward, McCann & Geoghegan, 1973.

White, William Allen. *A Puritan in Babylon: The Story of Calvin Coolidge.* New York: Macmillan, 1938.

Willets, Gilson. *Inside History of the White House.* New York: The Christian Herald, 1908.

Williams, Charles Richard. *The Life of Rutherford Birchard Hayes.* Vol. 2. Columbus: Ohio State Archaeological and Historical Society, 1928.

Williams, Frank B., Jr. *Tennessee's Presidents.* Knoxville: University of Tennessee Press, 1981.

Wilson, Edith Bolling. *My Memoir.* Indianapolis: Bobbs-Merrill, 1938.

Withers, Bob. *The President Travels by Train.* Lynchburg, Va.: TLC Publishing, 1996.

Withey, Lynne. *Dearest Friend: A Life of Abigail Adams.* New York: Free Press, 1981.

Wooton, James E. *Elizabeth Kortright Monroe.* Charlottesville, Va.: Ash Lawn–Highland, 1987.

Manuscript Collections

Calvin Coolidge Memorial Foundation, Plymouth Notch, Vt.: "Calvin Coolidge to the American People," Dec. 25, 1927.

George Bush Presidential Library: Camp David Exhibit, Audio Loop Transcription.

Gerald R. Ford Presidential Library: Gerald Ford memos in preparation for *A Time to Heal;* "Advice to a young man going off on his own"; and "Definition of a Successful Marriage."

Library of Congress, Martin Van Buren Papers: Angelica Van Buren letterpress book.

Martin Luther King Memorial Library, Washingtonian Collection: clippings on presidents' wives and children.

New Hampshire Historical Society: Franklin Pierce to Jane Pierce, Concord, N.H., "Tuesday morning," n.d. [circa Feb. 1853].

New York Public Library, Manuscript and Archives Division: Emmet Collection, H. Cushing to Margaret Bowers, Jan. 29, 1801; Feb. 9, 1801.

Richard Nixon Presidential Library: Jacqueline Kennedy Onassis to Richard and Pat Nixon, Feb. 4, 1971; John F. Kennedy Jr. to Richard and Pat Nixon, Feb. 4, 1971; and Rose Fitzgerald Kennedy to Pat Nixon, n.d. [circa Feb. 1971].

University of Southern California, Doheny Library: Hamlin Garland Papers, Grant family.

White House Curator's Office: "Remarks of Mrs. Lyndon B. Johnson, Miss Lynda Bird Johnson, Charles Taft, Mrs. Barbara Eisenhower, Mrs. Van Seagraves [Sistie Dall], and Mrs. Margaret Truman Daniel, at the Congressional Reception, the Queen's Room," Mar. 2, 1967; James Robert McKee to Mr. Beatty, Jan. 28, 1941.

B i b l i o g r a p h y

Selected Newspaper Articles and Periodicals

Albany (N.Y.) Post, "Mrs. McElroy: The Little Woman from Albany," May 11, 1884.

Architectural Digest, "Architectural Digest Visits: President and Mrs. Ronald Reagan at the White House," Dec. 1981.

Associated Press stories, "Clinton Dines with Juror, Family Member," Jan. 10, 1999; "Summer Break a Hallowed Tradition," by Lawrence Knutson, Aug. 16, 1999; "Rodham Brothers Asked to Scrap Deal," Sept. 17, 1999; "Blair House Has a Long History," Dec. 15, 1999; "Clintons Attend Midnight Mass," by Rebecca Sinderbrand, Dec. 27, 1999.

Baltimore Sun, "Estate Over $1,000,000, Many Bequests in Mrs. Harriet Lane Johnston's Will," and "Her Will Is Discussed, Mrs. Johnston's Testament and Codicils Fill Many Pages," July 10, 1903.

Chocolatier, "White House Desserts," by Dede Wilson, June 1998.

Christian Science Monitor, "Touch of Mrs. Hoover Is Seen in Homeyness of White House," by Mary Hornaday, Oct. 17, 1932.

Cigar Aficionado, "Our Presidents and Cigars," by Carl Sferrazza Anthony, Autumn 1993.

Cleveland Plain Dealer, "A First Lady Due to Ride High Again [Harriet Lane]," by Albert C. Andrew, Jan. 11, 1983.

Cleveland Plain Dealer Magazine, "From the Diary of Eliza Garfield: A Mother's Inauguration Story," by Grace Goulder, Jan. 25, 1965.

Cosmopolitan, "Grand Person! My Mother," by Anna Roosevelt Dall, July 1934.

Creators Syndicate, "Talking It Over," column on the Marine Band by Hillary Rodham Clinton, July 8, 1998.

Daughters of the American Revolution Magazine, "A Shopping Tour with the First Lady of the Land," by Florence Seville Berryman, Aug. 1925.

Eastern Review/FYI, "The Other White Houses," by Carl Sferrazza Anthony, July 1984.

Frank Leslie's Weekly, "The Official Ladies at Washington [Mrs. Stover and Mrs. Patterson]," June 2, 1866.

Gerald R. Ford Foundation Newsletter, Winter 1998.

Good Housekeeping, "The Real Calvin Coolidge," ed. with comment by Grace Coolidge (3 parts), Feb.–Apr. 1935.

Harper's Weekly, "The Last Presidential Drawing Room," May 8, 1858.

Image, "Photographing the American Presidency," by Robert A. Mayer, Sept. 1984.

Irish America Magazine, "Presidents and First Ladies of Irish Ancestry," by Carl Sferrazza Anthony, July/Aug. 1994.

Kansas City Star, "Hail to the Irish," by Carl Sferrazza Anthony, March 17, 1987.

Liberty, "Behind the Scenes at the White House," Jan. 10, 1925; "What Mrs. Coolidge Does with Her Days," Feb. 23, 1925; "Behind the Scenes at the White House [pt. 2]," May 23, 1925. All by Winifred Mallon.

Life, "Memorable Night at the White House: The President's State Dinner for Margaret and Lord Snowden," Dec. 3, 1965; "Special Issue: The Presidency," July 5, 1968; "The Nixon Era Begins" and "Inside the White House," Nov. 15, 1968; "Nixon Warms Up for Europe on Key Biscayne: Winter White House," Feb. 21, 1969; "Tricia Nixon's Romance with Ed Cox," Jan. 22, 1971; "White House Bride," June 18, 1971; "She's at Ease in the White House—and Means to Stay: Pat Nixon," Aug. 25, 1972.

Literary Digest, "Mrs. Edith Galt Bolling," Oct. 16, 1915.

London Morning Post, "America's First Lady," May 7, 1929.

Mentor, "The Spoiled Son of Dolley Madison," by Mary Phelps, July 1929.

Miller Center Report, "A Writer in the Reagan White House: Miller Center Forum with Edmund Morris on September 24, 1990," Fall 1999.

National Geographic, "Inside the White House," Jan. 1961; "The Living White House," Nov. 1966. Both by Lonnelle Aikman.

National Magazine, "The Mistress of the White House," by George F. Richards, Apr. 1922.

National Republic, "First Ladies of the Land," by William B. Duff, July 1927.

National Spectator, "A Perfect Woman, Nobly Planned," by Winifred Mallon, Jan. 23, 1926.

New York Graphic, "An Interview with Mrs. Jesse Grant at Jersey City," Sept. 16, 1879.

New York Post, "First Brother Roger Helps Repay His Bill," by Adam Buckman, Dec. 28, 1998.

New York Times, "Rarely Seen Portrait of Mrs. Lincoln," Feb. 12, 1929; "Mr. Lincoln and Tad," July 13, 1934; "White House Food Can't Be Beat," by Carl Sferrazza Anthony, Jan. 13, 1993; "A Gift to My Father," by Patti Davis [Reagan], Dec. 27, 1998; "Here Comes the Son," by Maureen Dowd, Oct. 6, 1999; "She's Not the First Lady to Escape the White House," by John Broder, Nov. 28, 1999.

Newsweek, "My Father's Legacy," by Caroline Kennedy, June 1, 1992.

Once a Week, "The Funeral of Mrs. Harrison at Washington," Nov. 12, 1892.

Parade, "Welcome: Let's Celebrate Together the 200th Anniversary of the White House," by Hillary Rodham Clinton, July 4, 1999.

People, "Hillary and Chelsea: Grace Under Fire," by Susan Schindehette, Feb. 15, 1999.

Philip Morris Magazine, "An Executive Privilege," Summer 1986.

Reuters, "Clinton, Still in Counseling, Moved by Forgiveness," by Randall Mikkelsen, Sept. 29, 1999.

Saturday Evening Post, "Inside the White House: An Intimate Portrait of Our New First Lady," by Nan Robertson, Feb. 8, 1964.

Tobacco Observer, "Dolley's Delight: The First First Lady to Bring Tobacco into the White House," Oct. 1984.

Traces of Indiana and Midwestern History, "Anna Symmes Harrison: First Lady of the West," Fall 1990.

Washington Daily News, "Ike and Mamie Can Be Proud [Barbara Eisenhower]," Jan. 8, 1955.

Washington Herald, "Mrs. Hoover Liked Athletics as Girl," Mar. 14, 1929; "Spring Lures First Lady to Bridle Paths," Apr. 2, 1930; "Wife's Death Mourned by Woodrow Wilson," by Ray Stannard Baker, Jan. 24, 1932; "Mrs. McAdoo's 'The Wilsons' Casts New Light," by Jean Eliot, Nov. 11, 1935.

Washington News: "Mrs. Coolidge Goes Shopping," by Toussaint Dubois, Feb. 12, 1927; "Mrs. Hoover Shops Carefully and Buys at Many Stores in Washington," by Martha Strayer, Aug. 2, 1929; "First Lady and Son Take New Year's Day Canter," Jan. 2, 1939.

Washington Post serialization of "My Life in the White House," by Grace Coolidge: Jan. 12, Jan. 19, Jan. 25, Feb. 2, Feb. 9, Feb. 23, Mar. 2, Mar. 9, 1930.

Washington Post: "The White House: Baby Ruth and Her Predecessors," Feb. 5, 1897; "Smiles and Sorrow: Dolley Madison's Life Clouded by Scapegrace Son," Jan. 26, 1900; "White House of Old: Mrs. Semple Recalls," July 6, 1902; "Harriet Lane Johnston," July 5, 1903; "What Happened When I Was a Guest at the White House," by Kate Forbes, Dec. 25, 1921; "What Goes On Around the White House Fireside," by Kate Forbes, Jan. 1, 1922; "The Real Mrs. Harding," by Kate Forbes, Jan. 22, 1922; "Mrs. Coolidge Will Find Ready at Hand Every Convenience for Privacy and Comfort," by Sallie Pickett, Aug. 12, 1923; "Mrs. Hoover," June 15, 1928; "President and Wife Seek Escape from Formalities," Apr. 5, 1929; "Dean's Memory of Pranks in White House [Helen Taft Manning]," July 25, 1930; "Wife of President Camper Extraordinary," by Corinne Reid Frazier, Oct. 2, 1932; Oct. 1, 1936, "Debutantes Who Made Their Bows in Seasons Past: Mrs. Manning, the former Miss Helen Taft," by Vylla Poe Wilson; "Washington Scene [Grover Cleveland duck hunting]," by the Poe sisters, Mar. 21, 1937; "Mrs. Truman Guards Her Guards," by Drew Pearson, Nov. 4, 1951; Apr. 5, 1953, "First Grandmother Dotes on White House Invaders," by Evelyn Hayes and Anita Holmes; Jan. 28, 1956, "Eastland Scored for Slap at Ike's Grandchildren," by

Edward Folliard; "Mrs. Woodrow Wilson Leads a Quiet Life—But Does It Briskly," by Christine Sadler, May 22, 1960; "Prince's 1860 White House Visit," by Francis deSales Ryan, Nov. 3, 1960; "Sarah Polk," by C. S. Coe, Jan. 17, 1961; "Eliza Johnson," by C. S. Coe, Jan. 18, 1961; "First Ladies: Day of Destiny," by Carl Sferrazza Anthony, Jan. 20, 1985; June 16, 1985, "Like Father, Like First Lady," by Carl Sferrazza Anthony; "Dog-Paddle Diplomacy: First Families in the Swim," by C. S. Anthony, Aug. 18, 1985; "Hosts of Christmas Past," by C. S. Anthony, Dec. 25, 1985; Feb. 16, 1986, "Birthday Bafflement," by Carl Sferrazza Anthony; "The Presidential Progeny," by C. S. Anthony, May 14, 1986; "Executive Ardor: Of Presidents & Passions," Feb. 8, 1987; "A Month of Bum Days: No Wonder There's Flight in August," by C. S. Anthony, Aug. 27, 1989; "The Chief Laborers, on the Case: The Presidents and First Ladies Setting Their Own Schedules," by C. S. Anthony, Sept. 3, 1990; "Fifty Ways to Leave the White House," by C. S. Anthony, Nov. 4, 1992; "Handing Over the White House Keys: Friends and Foes, First Ladies' First Peek at the White House," by Carl Sferrazza Anthony; Dec. 19, 1992, "Presidents Set a Fast Pace," by Abigail Trafford [Health section], Feb. 9, 1999; "The Life of George W. Bush," by Lois Romano and George Lardner Jr., series July 25–July 30, 1999.

Washington Star: "Rose Elizabeth: The ex-First Lady," June 29, 1886; "Two Brilliant Women: Harriet Lane and Rebecca Black Hornsby," Feb. 16, 1889; "Harriet L. Johnston: Former Mistess of the White House Is Dead," July 4, 1903; "Mrs. Wilson Dies at White House," Aug. 7, 1914; "Sons of White House Are Also the Nation's," July 13, 1924; "Ideal First Lady Is Mrs. Coolidge," by Sallie Pickett, Nov. 5, 1924; "Wife Respects Coolidge's Taste When Selecting Her Wardrobe," by Robert Small, Apr. 11, 1925; "An Anniversary at the White House," by William A. Millen, Oct. 5, 1927; "Hoover Is Happy in Family Life," by Rex Collier, June 17, 1928; "Julia Gardiner, the 24-Year-Old Belle . . . ," by J. F. Glass, Oct. 22, 1928; "Edith Carow Roosevelt," by J. P. Glass, Nov. 24, 1928; "Mrs. Hoover Breaks Precedent by Driving Out on Her Own," by J. Russell Young, Apr. 4, 1929; "Mrs. Hoover Gives White House Atmosphere of West Coast," Sept. 21, 1929; "A Poem," by Grace Coolidge, Sept. 23, 1929; "Amusing Capital Social Life [Van Buren]," by Thomas R. Henry, Jan. 4, 1931; "First Lady Swamped by Mail Offering Books on Old D.C.," Aug. 3, 1931; "Mrs. Hoover Tries Out Her Voice on Sound Films," Nov. 5, 1931; "Wives of the Candidates," by Florence Davies, May 15, 1932; "An Honor Guard Calls at White House [Cleveland daughters]," by Alice C. Gardiner, June 23, 1946; July 16, 1954, "Eisenhower Grandchildren Frolic at the White House"; July 29, 1955, "The Young Eisenhowers Will Be Here After '56," by Isabelle Shelton; "Willie: Lincoln's Joy and Sorrow," by Kay Rinfrette, Apr. 12, 1959; "White House Aides All Tall, Terrific [Charles Robb]," by Frances Lewine, Sept. 17, 1967.

Washington Times [original]: "Last of the Antebellum Social Leaders: Mrs. Letitia Tyler Semple," May 7, 1903; "From Pocahontas to White House Mistress," Oct. 16, 1915.

Washington Times-Herald, "An Exclusive Interview with Robert Taft," by Nanette Kutner, Mar. 23, 1952.

Websites

Abraham Lincoln Research Site: www.members.aol.com/RVSNorton/Lincoln2.html

American Presidency: selected resources, an informal reference guide; www.interlink-cafe.com/uspresidents

Camp David: home.earthlink.net/~vpnelson/CDHistory

Chester Alan Arthur's ancestral home in Ireland: www.antrim.net/cullybackey

Dolley Payne Madison Project: www.moderntimes.vcdh.virginia.edu/madison/index.html

eBay listed an original anti–Ulysses Grant poem, "Grant's Mess-Age," n.d. #197235961

The National First Ladies' Library: www.firstladies.org

The Nixon Family Homepage: www.swiftsite.com/nixonfamily

Bibliography

POTUS [Presidents of the United States]: the Internet Public Library, www.ipl.org/ref/POTUS

Presidents on July 4, created by James Heintze: www.gurukul.american.edu/heintze/FourthPres.htm

Religious Beliefs of Our Presidents, by Franklin Steiner: www.infidels.org/library/historical/franklin_steiner/presidents.html

Ulysses S. Grant Homepage, created by Candace Scott: www.mscomm/~ulysses

Ulysses S. Grant Network, created by Marie Kelsey: www.saints.css.edu/mkelsey/gppg.html

White House, family life in White House, etc.: www.whitehouse.gov

Acknowledgments

I would like to thank the following for their volunteer time in helping me in the last difficult weeks of this project: Richard Sullivan, Anna McCollister, Nancy Hacskaylo, Raul Escuza, Bruce Johnson, Keith Kreeger, and Ellen McDougall. My editor, Lisa Drew, assistant editor Jake Klisivitch, production editor Edith Baltazar, copy editor Judy Eda, as well as my agent at ICM, Lisa Bankoff, and her assistant Patrick Price, all displayed patience and the sort of enthusiasm that helps carry a project to completion.

Three individuals whom I have known for some time and have always deeply cherished for their wisdom, passion for history, and generosity must be especially thanked. From the beginning, Betty Monkman, curator of the White House, and Craig Schermer of the National First Ladies Library were of invaluable aid as guides and sources. Ms. Monkman took her own personal time to review an early draft on the use of the family rooms. Mr. Schermer was a beacon of institutional knowledge on photography of the First Families.

Matthew Gilmore, reference librarian at the Washingtonian Division of the Martin Luther King Memorial Library in Washington, D.C., went far beyond my expectations in photocopying, earmarking, and generously providing information. He is a terrific source at a rare national treasure of a place that needs assistance before a rich record of Washington history deteriorates and is lost to the nation forever. Americans with a love of the history of their nation's capital can join Friends of the Washingtonian Division through the King Library.

Obtaining and tracking down all the images for this book was quite difficult and, in the end, an effort which required a hand above and beyond the normal call of duty. Without the generous and extra efforts of the following people, the illustrations for the book would not have come into place as they did:

Maureen Dilg at the National Geographic Society; Harmony Haskins at the White House Historical Association; Heather Egan at the National Portrait Gallery; Kristen L. Kertsos and Ann M. Brose at the National Museum of American Art; Sally Pierce and Hina Hirayama at the Boston Athenaeum; Jennifer Tolpa and Jennifer Smith at the Massachusetts Historical Society; Lydia Dufour at the Frick Art Reference Library; Bruce Scherer at the Historical Society of Pennsylvania; Sherman Howe, photographer, and Peter Fox Smith, owner of a private Clara Sipprell collection; Kelly Cobble and Caroline Keineth at the Adams National Historic Site; Whitney Epswich and Lesley Fore at Monticello/The Thomas Jefferson Foundation; James Kelly at the Virginia Historical Society; David Voelkel at the James Monroe

Museum; Anthony Guzzi at the Hermitage; Stephen Cox at the Tennessee State Museum; Jennifer Caps at the Benjamin Harrison Home; Susan Sutton at the Indiana Historical Society; Mr. and Mrs. Harrison Tyler at Sherwood Forest; Tom Price at the James K. Polk Home; Sally Stassi and John McGill at the Historic New Orleans Collection; Mary Bell and Linda Kennedy at the Buffalo and Erie County Historical Society; Janice Madhu at George Eastman House; Sheila Rohrer at the James Buchanan Foundation for the Preservation of Wheatland; Cindy Van Horne at the Lincoln Museum; Elaine Clarke at the Andrew Johnson National Historic Site; Gil Gonzales at the Hayes Presidential Center; Elizabeth B. McCahill, who shared the rich White House history of her family, the McElroys and the Arthurs; Cyndy Bittinger, director, Calvin Coolidge Memorial Foundation; Scott Nollen at the Herbert Hoover Presidential Library; Mark Renovich at the Franklin Delano Roosevelt Presidential Library; Pauline Testerman at the Harry S. Truman Presidential Library; Kathy Struss at the Dwight D. Eisenhower Presidential Library; James Hill at the John F. Kennedy Presidential Library; Phillip Scott at the Lyndon Baines Johnson Presidential Library; Karen King and Joanne Bromley at King Visual, who processed the Nixon family pictures at the National Archives; Nancy Mirshah at the Gerald R. Ford Presidential Library; David Stanhope at the Jimmy Carter Presidential Library; Steve Branch at the Ronald Reagan Presidential Library; Mary Finch at the George Bush Presidential Library; and Missy Kincaid and Jennifer Smith in the First Lady's Office at the White House.

Thanks also to the numerous members of First Families, some now gone, who shared their friendship or acquaintance or memories or an anecdote of their experiences, through the years of my research: Harrison and Paynie Tyler, Marion Cleveland Amen, Francis Cleveland, Jack Cadman, Alice Roosevelt Longworth, Ethel Roosevelt Derby, Archie Roosevelt Jr., Charles Taft, Mr. and Mrs. Fitz Woodrow, Louisa Kling, Dr. George Harding, John Coolidge, Lydia Coolidge Sayles, Peggy Hoover Brigham, James Roosevelt, Elliott Roosevelt, Eleanor Roosevelt Dall Seagraves, Barbara Eisenhower Foltz, Anne Eisenhower, Susan Eisenhower, David Eisenhower, Mary Jean Eisenhower, John Kennedy, Jacqueline Kennedy Onassis, Senator Edward M. Kennedy, Eunice Kennedy Shriver, Kathleen Kennedy Townsend, Lee Radziwill, Janet Auchincloss, Yusha Auchincloss, Jamie Auchincloss, Lady Bird Johnson, Lynda Johnson Robb, Luci Johnson Nugent Turpin, Richard M. Nixon, Pat Nixon, Julie Nixon Eisenhower, Ed Nixon, Gerald R. Ford, Betty Ford, Jack Ford, Susan Ford, Jimmy Carter, Rosalynn Carter, Nancy Reagan, George Bush, Barbara Bush, Doro Bush Koch, President Bill Clinton, Hillary Rodham Clinton, Dorothy Rodham, Hugh Rodham Jr., and Tony Rodham.

Index

Page numbers in *italics* refers to illustrations.

Tyler Clinton walks down
State Floor Hallway
THE WHITE HOUSE